New frontiers in cognitive aging

New frontiers in cognitive aging

Edited by

Roger A. Dixon
University of Alberta
Canada

Lars Bäckman
Karolinska Institute
Sweden

and

Lars-Göran Nilsson
Stockholm University
Sweden

OXFORD
UNIVERSITY PRESS

OXFORD

UNIVERSITY PRESS

Great Clarendon Street, Oxford OX2 6DP

Oxford University Press is a department of the University of Oxford.
It furthers the University's objective of excellence in research, scholarship,
and education by publishing worldwide in

Oxford New York

Auckland Bangkok Buenos Aires Cape Town Chennai
Dar es Salaam Delhi Hong Kong Istanbul Karachi Kolkata
Kuala Lumpur Madrid Melbourne Mexico City Mumbai Nairobi
São Paulo Shanghai Taipei Tokyo Toronto

Oxford is a registered trade mark of Oxford University Press
in the UK and in certain other countries

Published in the United States
by Oxford University Press Inc., New York

A catalogue record for this title is available from the British Library
ISBN 0 19 852569 9 (Hbk)

10 9 8 7 6 5 4 3 2 1

Typeset by Newgen Imaging Systems (P) Ltd., Chennai, India
Printed in Great Britain
on acid-free paper by
Biddles Ltd., King's Lynn

Contents

Contributors

Lars Bäckman
Aging Research Centre
Karolinska Institute
Stockholm
Sweden

Daniel B. Berch
Child Development and Behavior
Branch
National Institute of Child Health
and Human Development
Bethesda
MD, USA

Roberto Cabeza
Center for Cognitive Neuroscience
Duke University
Durham
NC, USA

Helen Christensen
Centre for Mental Health Research
The Australian National University
Canberra
Australia

Roger A. Dixon
Department of Psychology
University of Alberta
Edmonton
Canada

Laura Fratiglioni
Aging Research Centre
Karolinska Institute
Stockholm
Sweden

Paolo Ghisletta
Center for Interdisciplinary
Gerontology
University of Geneva
Geneva
Switzerland

Peter Graf
Department of Psychology
University of British Columbia
Vancouver
Canada

Agneta Herlitz
Aging Research Centre
Karolinska Institute
Stockholm
Sweden

Christopher Hertzog
School of Psychology
Georgia Institute of Technology
Atlanta
GA, USA

David F. Hultsch
Centre on Aging
University of Victoria
Victoria
Canada

Leah L. Light
Psychology Department
Pitzer College
Claremont
CA, USA

Ulman Lindenberger
Max Planck Institute for Human
Development
Berlin
Germany

Stuart W.S. MacDonald
Aging Research Centre
Karolinska Institute
Stockholm
Sweden

Andrew Mackinnon
Biostatistics & Psychometrics Unit
Mental Health Research Institute
Victoria
Australia

Meredith Minear
Department of Psychology
The University of Michigan
Ann Arbor
MI, USA

Lars-Göran Nilsson
Department of Psychology
Stockholm University
Stockholm
Sweden

Lars Nyberg
Department of Psychology
Umeå University
Umeå
Sweden

Denise Park
The Beckman Institute
The University of Illinois at
Urbana-Champaign
Urbana
IL, USA

Nancy L. Pedersen
Department of Medical
Epidemiology and Biostatistics
Karolinska Institute
Stockholm
Sweden

Naftali Raz
Institute of Gerontology
Wayne State University
Detroit
MI, USA

Brent J. Small
School of Aging Studies
University of South Florida
Tampa
FL, USA

Paul Verhaeghen
Department of Psychology
Syracuse University
Syracuse
NY, USA

Molly V. Wagster
Neuroscience and Neuropsychology
of Aging Program
National Institute on Aging
Bethesda
MD, USA

Åke Wahlin
Aging Research Centre
Karolinska Institute
Stockholm
Sweden

Julie E. Yonker
University of Cincinnati
Department of Psychiatry
Cincinnati
OH, USA

Part 1

Frontiers in cognitive aging

Chapter 1

Don't fence us in: Probing the frontiers of cognitive aging

Roger A. Dixon

Lars-Göran Nilsson

> I want to ride to the ridge where the west commences
> And gaze at the moon until I lose my senses
> I can't look at hobbles and I can't stand fences
> Don't fence me in.
> Cole Porter

Cole Porter's song, 'Don't Fence Me In', was a huge hit for American singer Bing Crosby (and the Andrews Sisters) during the Second World War. In fact, it spent about eight weeks atop the Billboard charts in 1944–1945. Later versions became veritable anthems of the postwar spirit of optimism and exploration. In retrospect, the song seems to be both an ode to the thrilling opportunities available in the wide-open frontiers of the Americas and a metaphor for even broader, if not universal, movements. The song captured an emerging zeitgeist with its provocative claim for new territory and boundless perimeters ('give me land, lots of land under starry skies above') and its buoyant notion that simple tools can enable lofty goals ('On my cayuse, let me wander over yonder till I see the mountains rise'). The world in the mid-twentieth century was beginning to open up and the jaws of cultural, geographic, and informational divides were yawning ever more broadly. Seemingly miraculous plans for probing the outer reaches of space – even targeting a visit to the moon by the end of the 1960s – were being hatched. Overall, the sentiment of the song represents a process of loosening borders and boundaries that was soon to be accelerated in the information-saturated Internet age. That it embodies an international – and perhaps even timeless – sentiment is reflected in the fact that 'Don't fence me in' is not only the title of the famous and oft-recorded song, but also of many published articles and at least two movies. The latter include the classic 1945 Roy Rogers/Dale

Evans cowboy movie, but also the 1998 film by director Nandini Sikand, which follows her mother's lifetime of pushing the boundaries of twentieth century circumstances for women in India. Why is this expression (and this sentiment) incorporated as part of the title for our introductory chapter to this volume?

We originally adopted the 'new frontier' motif for a small international conference we recently hosted in Whistler, Canada. Whereas excellent handbooks of biological aging, psychological aging, cognitive aging, and cognitive neuroscience have been published, the rapidly developing research directions emanating from the intersections of these topics – and the promising future they portend – had not previously been represented or collected into one room (or one volume). Leaders of these new directions in cognitive aging are succeeding in charting new and important territory, in part by transcending conventional boundaries (read: fences) circumscribing traditional research domains and methods. We illustrate this claim with the common case of memory. As the century advanced, it was becoming increasingly apparent that the study of memory and aging was no longer uniquely (or perhaps even principally) the province of experimental cognitive psychology. To be sure, much has been learned about memory and aging from decades of fine experimental work – and this perspective remains justifiably proud of its contributions and its avid exploration of important research. Nevertheless, to understand the broadest range of memory phenomena in aging, it is necessary to explore newly emerging frontiers of identifiable precursors and influences from the neighboring fields of cognitive neuroscience, medical health, behavioral genetics, biological factors, and research methods. In essence, we contend that to understand the *aging* of memory, it is helpful to learn more about the *aging neuroscience* of memory, the *aging health context* of memory, the *genetics* of memory, the *biological/physiological substrate* of memory, and new methodological techniques for measuring *aging-related changes* in memory and for representing multiple *aging-related influences* on memory. In addition, rather than viewing these aspects of the context as separate and non-interactive influences, one may imagine that a defined subset of them may operate to form the critical epidemiological context of targeted phenomena in cognitive aging.

With funding from the Swedish Foundation for International Cooperation in Research and Higher Education (STINT), we decided that it was timely to focus on a particularly promising new frontier in cognition and aging. Accordingly, we employed the 'new frontiers' theme for both the Whistler conference and for this book and subsequently adopted the 'don't fence us in' theme for this chapter. The latter, especially, is offered with an admitted touch of whimsy, but with a conviction that it vivifies the central tenet of this book.

Specifically, our goal is to present and integrate under one cover three new frontiers in the field of cognitive aging, frontiers that have been opened for exploration in part by transcending traditional disciplinary boundaries. In the book, as in the conference, these frontiers are reviewed not by a single scholar, but by three independent leading contributors to the field. Moreover, each of these authors was charged with focusing not only on the pre-eminent issues of the present, but on the likely cutting edge directions for important advances in the future. In addition, for each of these sections, a fourth major contributor has been asked to draw integrative conclusions about the status and future of these novel research directions. This was the synergistic format of the Whistler conference, and we have recreated it in this book.

Therefore, this book, unlike any others in the field of cognitive aging, is more about new frontiers than it is about past research and accomplishments. It is about stretching the boundaries of scholarship in cognition and aging by transcending selected conceptual and methodological fences. To be sure, the book is not about scholarly anarchy or ahistoricism, competitive or cross-paradigm nitpicking, or aimless wandering through a dusty haze of new fangled concepts and methods. In contrast, the book is about promoting problem-driven and theory-guided research, and following a hard-nosed but open-minded approach beyond the edges of conventionality. This inventive and serious perspective permeated the Whistler conference, and we are pleased that it is also reflected in the chapters of this volume. Accordingly, in intrinsically multifarious fields like cognitive aging, many of the new research ideas and directions presented in this volume are integrative, multidisciplinary, and innovative. We expect them to be attractive – if not provocative – to a wide range of readers.

Thus is the story of how we came to develop this book and this theme. In this first chapter we pursue two remaining goals. First, we provide a brief overview of our perspective on cognitive aging – and how this perspective underlies our identification of the new frontiers in the field. In brief, especially for the purposes of this book, we sponsor an integrative perspective on cognitive aging, with a pluralism of perspectives, theories, methods, and disciplines represented. Second, we summarize and integrate the outline of the book, including the sections, authors, and their chapters.

Cognitive aging: A pluralistic and epidemiological agenda

Especially for the purposes of this book – in which new frontiers of a rapidly growing field are explored – our view of cognitive aging is a broad and commodious one, accommodating multiple perspectives, theories, methods, and approaches. The pluralistic approach has an epidemiological twist. Cognitive changes in aging – ranging from normal to differential to neurodegenerative – are viewed as preceded (if not 'caused') by a wide range of influences and contexts. At the individual level, a unique combination of precursors may be responsible for cognitive outcomes. At the group or population levels, patterns of influence are identifiable across cohorts of cognitively aging adults. We turn now to a brief review of key terms, common to the chapters in this book.

Briefly, *cognition* itself refers not to a single or even preferred process, but to a collection of behaviors and performances in labs and everyday life that, whatever their present context, emanate from activities occurring in the brain, with observable manifestations or performances. Whether one is measuring constructs such as neurocognitive resources or episodic/semantic memory or intelligence, the crucial assumption in this field is that performance in such arenas changes across adulthood. The goal is to produce inferences pertaining to how (description) and why (explanation) these changes occur. Accordingly, *aging* is the term that implies change across adulthood – change that may be conventionally indexed by chronological or biological/functional age, but which is, at base, indicative of continued vitality across time through late life. Notably, by this definition, aging is neutral with respect to direction or inevitability of change; that is, it does not necessarily imply decline, degeneration, or impending death. Although not tantamount to 'disease', aging-related phenomena are under the 'causative' control of numerous precursors and contexts (from the biological to the sociocultural). Unsurprisingly, therefore, *cognitive aging* refers substantively to the fact that cognitive functions change in theoretically or practically relevant ways across adulthood. Although it carries no implication about direction of cognitive change, growing bodies of research in numerous cognitive functions have clearly shown robust (but not always universal) decline patterns (Craik and Salthouse, 2000; Dixon, 2003). In this book, the term *cognitive aging* also refers to the scientific field that investigates these phenomena.

Regarding research methods, we deliberately set an equally pluralistic context for this book. Naturally, it is crucial to select and employ methods that match the problem in human aging (Hertzog and Dixon, 1996). For some cognitive aging problems, these methods will be relatively simple extensions of procedures perfected in cognitive psychology laboratories over decades of research. The 'aging' aspect, in many such cases, will be included via a 'cross-sectional' research design, typically comparing younger with older adults. For other cognitive aging problems, more complex designs will be mandatory, including those that require longitudinal (multiple-occasion) data with multiple variables (multivariate time-structured statistical techniques). Required for still other cognitive aging problems are advanced statistical techniques for representing latent variables, data collected in multiple sites or with interdisciplinary teams, multi-modal representations of the epidemiological context of normal and neurodegenerative cognitive aging, and advanced technological procedures for observing brain activity and changes in older adults. No single cross-section of theories or methods has a monopoly on new frontiers of cognitive aging research. This book reflects this dictum both in its organization and its substantive coverage. Indeed, an entire section is devoted to the theoretical (and methodological) implications of these new developments in cognitive aging research.

In a sense, the field of cognitive aging is itself a recent frontier of the human sciences, long reflecting integrative influences from cognitive psychology and lifespan psychology. Notably, the phenomena of cognition and aging have been of interest to observers for more than a century, but as a science with substantial theoretical momentum it has a somewhat briefer history. Since the earliest days of psychology, scholars have expressed interest in how and why cognition or intelligence changes across adulthood and under what circumstances its course might be altered or improved (Dixon, Kramer, and Baltes, 1985). Long apparent is the understanding that changes occurring in the protracted period of adulthood – at typically more than 50 years it is the longest phase of the lifespan – would involve information about a variety of interacting influences and contexts (Baltes, Staudinger, and Lindenberger, 1997). Indeed, Stern and Carstensen (2000), in a report from the U.S. National Research Council, urged greater attention to broader contexts of cognitive aging such as health conditions, biological factors, and neurological changes. Changes that occur over long periods of time under the influences of multiple factors may require large-scale – perhaps even epidemiological – studies. Recently, Baltes and Smith (1997) urged the position that large-scale studies are appropriate to extensive and multidimensional problems such as human aging: if aging-related phenomena occur through many facets and processes of human-related phenomena then understanding can be promoted through theory-guided but ambitious and comprehensive research. In the case of cognitive aging, it may be useful under some circumstances to open the disciplinary fences surrounding smaller research pastures, and pursue the problem into neighboring frontiers. Consider the following:

◆ Cognitive performance and changes in late life must be at least in part occasioned by underlying neurological integrity, conditions, or changes. This connection, and pursuit of these implications, constitute one of the key new frontiers in cognitive aging today.

♦ Cognitive performance and changes in late life may be especially influenced by health conditions (e.g., cardiovascular health), health events (e.g., cerebrovascular disturbances), biological vitality (e.g., hormonal and physiological/sensory status), and genetic influences (e.g., presence of markers related to normal cognitive decline and that associated with neurodegenerative diseases). This connection, and pursuit of these implications, constitute one of the key new frontiers in cognitive aging today.

♦ Cognitive performance and changes in late life that are a function of such conditions and influences may produce profiles and be associated with predictors that, in concert, challenge simpler models and theories of cognitive aging: New theoretical developments in cognitive aging constitute one of the new frontiers of the field today.

Uniquely poised to tackle such problems are relatively large-scale studies of human aging. The Swedish STINT funding for the Whistler conference was, in fact, designed to promote comparative and collaborative research and training between two such studies, the Swedish Betula Project (BP; Lars-Göran Nilsson, Director) and the Canadian Victoria Longitudinal Study (VLS; Roger A. Dixon, Director). The BP is based in Umeå, Sweden, and features a three-wave prospective longitudinal design (of initially 35–80 year olds), with a fourth wave scheduled for 2003. It uses a broad-based battery to examine such issues as memory and aging, preclinical markers of dementia, and risk factors for dementia. Research has been published widely (Han and Nilsson, 1997; Nilsson *et al.*, 1997; Nyberg *et al.*, 2003; Wahlin, Bäckman, Hultdin *et al.*, in press) and a detailed summary is available on the BP website (www.apsy.umu.se/memory/ Betula.html). The VLS is based in Edmonton, Canada (with an ongoing laboratory in Victoria, Canada). It features multiple staggered samples (of initially 55–85 year olds) and both short- and long-term data (up to six waves for one sample) on cognitive, health, and biological functioning in normal and cognitively impaired aging. Research examples are available (Dixon and de Frias, in press; Hertzog, Dixon, Hultsch *et al.*, in press; Hultsch, Hertzog, Dixon *et al.*, 1998; MacDonald, Dixon, Cohen *et al.*, in press) and project details may be viewed on the VLS website (www.ualberta.ca/~vlslab).

Although these projects are indeed relatively large-scale, they nevertheless fall short of encyclopedic content, theoretical comprehensiveness, epidemiological exhaustiveness, and methodological perfection. Indeed, we gratefully acknowledge that the STINT funding has benefited both projects immensely, especially the opportunities to share complementary areas of expertise and to conduct live information exchanges in forums such as the Whistler conference. The editors – together with the staffs of the BP and VLS – were pleased to sponsor the uniquely rewarding Whistler conference and to organize the publication of this book.

Plan of the book

The scientific field of cognitive aging has its roots in both cognitive and lifespan developmental sciences, and is increasingly blended with influences from other neighboring disciplines. In recent years, researchers have pushed the boundaries of inquiry and knowledge about cognitive aging in an array of novel directions and at a pace that has dazzled theoreticians and practitioners alike. Specifically, they have thrust themselves into – and borrowed from – the research agendas of such neighboring disciplines as neurosciences, pharmacology, psychiatry, health, genetics, and epidemiology. In doing so, they have explored the linkages between such neighboring concerns of aging as (a) neurological phenomena and changes in cognitive performance, (b) health, physiological, and biomedical functioning and changes in cognitive performance, (c) genetic endowment and environmental influences and changes in cognitive performance, (d) normal changes in cognitive performance and those associated with neurodegenerative diseases, and (e) changes in cognitive performance with other changes in cognitive performance. To be sure, abundantly interesting, methodologically clean, and theoretically relevant cognitive aging research can be done without attention to such integrative concerns. In fact, excellent and informative cognitive aging research is conducted with methods and questions still linked principally to the neighboring fields of cognitive or lifespan psychology (Blanchard-Fields and Hess, 1996; Craik and Salthouse, 2000).

A veritable explosion of information has occurred in the literature regarding the contexts of (and influences on) cognitive aging. In fact, it would be possible to sympathize with a befuddled (hypothetical) cowboy who, on his trusty cayuse, had simply intended to explore one unfamiliar yonder peak, not the whole mountain range with which it was indivisibly integrated! For this book, we selected salient themes, novel and especially promising frontiers of cognitive aging. We recruited key players in each theme, and invited them to present their latest thoughts in a set of coordinated chapters. Our rendition of new frontiers in cognitive aging is certainly not definitive or exclusive – nor does it represent the last frontiers leaders in the field will encounter. We claim only that they are eminently important directions of new research in this booming field.

Three new sets of frontiers are covered sequentially, constituting the three middle sections of the book. Each frontier theme benefits from at least three independent chapter authors and at least one independent commentator. All contributors are prominent and prolific researchers in the field. These three sections are 'book-ended' by the present introductory chapter (Chapter 1) and by a closing commentary (Chapter 17) by U.S. National Institutes of Health representatives Daniel B. Berch and Molly V. Wagster. Excluding the introductory and closing chapters, 15 chapters are distributed amongst the middle three principal sections.

Part 2, *New Theoretical Orientations in Cognitive Aging*, addresses the question: How does research from the new frontiers of cognitive aging affect our theoretical understanding of the field? The section features new developments in theoretical (and associated methodological) issues in cognitive aging. Given that so much new integrative work has been published – and that the boundaries of the empirical field have been stretched so far – what are the implications for our theoretical understanding of the basic phenomena?

Setting the stage for this discussion is the overview in Chapter 2, *Cognitive Aging: New Directions for Old Theories*, by Denise Park (University of Illinois) and Meredith Minear (University of Michigan). The authors cleverly integrate key elements of the current state of knowledge in theoretical, behavioral, cultural, health, and neurobiological aspects of cognitive changes with aging. Subsequently weighing how broadly applicable (universal) are current cognitive aging theories, they identify the pre-eminent challenges for future theoretical advances in the field.

In Chapter 3 Christopher Hertzog (Georgia Tech) concentrates his efforts on a theoretically relevant methodological issue nipping at the heels of all developmental research: viz., to what extent do theories of cognitive aging based on cross-sectional (age comparative) research validly reflect actual changes with age (as indicated from longitudinal research)? Using new multivariate data from the VLS, Hertzog compares theoretically derived expectations based on cross-sectional comparisons to those actually observed in longitudinal change patterns. Provocative implications for cognitive aging theories – and how they are generated and supported – are highlighted in the chapter.

For the last half of the twentieth century, developmental methodologists have been interested in changes that occur in individual levels of performance, group mean levels of performance, and variability in individual and group performances. In focusing on the under-discussed variability aspect of cognitive performance in late life, David Hultsch and Stuart MacDonald (University of Victoria) review the work and relevance of consistency/inconsistency, and tackle several theoretical implications in Chapter 4. For example, they answer the question: What if variability in individual performance is a superior indicator of later trajectories of normal and neurodegenerative cognitive changes in late life?

Finally, the commentary chapter, Chapter 5, in this section is written by Leah Light (Pitzer College), who has regularly offered insightful comments on theoretical issues in cognitive aging (Light, 1991). Light identifies crucial common threads in the three chapters and adeptly links them to the larger picture in cognitive aging, with both theoretical and methodological implications. With these chapters, then, the momentum of the book is established. The next stop is in the booming frontier of neuroscience and cognitive aging.

Part 3, *New Directions in the Cognitive Neuroscience of Aging* presents the latest advances in the burgeoning field in which cognitive neuroscience is integrated with cognitive aging.

Chapter 6, by Naftali Raz (Wayne State University), reviews the fast-paced literature in which structural changes in the aging brain are identified and linked to cognitive performance changes in the aging adult. The advent and distribution of neuroimaging technology has provided researchers with increasingly precise knowledge about underlying neurological substrates of cognition and, in particular, the aging-indicative characteristics (e.g., volume, white matter) of the normally and neurodegeneratively aging brain. Raz, an internationally recognized leader in *in vivo* studies of the aging brain, identifies challenging but attainable new directions for future research.

Chapter 7 picks up on one of the challenges identified by Raz, in that it presents the perspective of Lars Nyberg (Umeå University) and Lars Bäckman (Karolinska Institute) on how brain imaging has elucidated the study of memory functioning and changes with aging. Imaging techniques such as positron emission tomography (PET) and functional magnetic resonance imaging (fMRI) are reviewed in the context of uncovering anatomical and functional correlates of memory. The authors identify important future directions of research, including expanding research on issues of neurotransmission and changes in brain activity.

The next chapter in this section addresses the timely issue of transitions from normal aging to preclinical (or cognitive impairment) to clinically diagnosed neurodegenerative diseases (such as Alzheimer's disease [AD]). Chapter 8 authors Lars Bäckman, Brent J. Small (University of South Florida) and Laura Fratiglioni (Karolinska Institute) focus on the thriving and pivotal topic of identifying accurate early markers of preclinical AD. As might be expected from research in both normal cognitive aging and cognitive neuroscience, the authors identify specific aspects of memory and other cognitive functions as primary targets for predictive purposes.

The enlightening commentary for this section is presented in Chapter 9 by Roberto Cabeza (Duke University). Cabeza provides a narrative linking the rationale for a cognitive neuroscience of aging with the empirical literature (to date) and the new directions for both theories and methods of the future. The promising future of the cognitive neuroscience of aging is sketched in scholarly but readable and practical terms.

Introduction to the fourth section. As noted above, Stern and Carstensen (2000) recently identified both the brain and health as important 'contexts' of cognitive aging. In the present section we explore the roles that health and related systems play in late-life cognitive changes. Accordingly, Part 4 of the book is entitled *Frontiers of Biological and Health Effects in Cognitive Aging.* Because of the diversity and abundance of new research in this area, we recruited five authors to explore the new frontiers of genetic, sensory, physiological, hormonal, and health influences on cognitive aging. In addition, two commentators offer unique perspectives on why and how (and whether!) such systems should be targeted for more research.

Chapter 10, written by Ulman Lindenberger (Saarland University) and Paolo Ghisletta (University of Geneva), provides a fluid transition from the previous two sections to the present one. The authors present critical comments and suggestions for modeling longitudinal changes in dynamic and interactive systems of biology – health and cognition relationships in late life. In a series of research examples from the Berlin Aging Study, the authors present new ways of examining such contemporary issues as sensory-cognition relationships and late-life differentiation/dedifferentiation of cognitive patterns in time-structured data.

Uniquely suited to this theme, Chapter 11 by Helen Christensen (Australian National University) and Andrew Mackinnon (Monash University) present an overview of the compelling theoretical issues and their own research pertaining to sensory, physiological, genetic, and health influences on cognitive aging. Approaching the topic from the perspective of differentiating between alternative theoretical representations (e.g., 'common' cause vs multiple causes), the authors present both new data and future directions for examining possible precursors of cognitive aging phenomena.

The content of Chapter 12 is adroitly summarized by the title: *New Frontiers in Genetic Influences on Cognitive Aging.* Chapter author Nancy L. Pedersen (Karolinska Institute) provides a welcome and enlightening overview of the study of genetic influences on all manner of behavioral phenotypes (including intelligence and cognition), using research from the Swedish Adoption Twin Study of Aging as a source for illustrations. Subsequently, she identifies future directions that include developments in methodological techniques (linking with those noted in the previous two chapters), additional topics such as mortality and variability, and the specific study of genes and cognitive aging.

In recent years, with advancing technology and theory, researchers have increasingly explored such select biological influences as steroid hormones on cognitive performance at various points in the lifespan. The authors of Chapter 13, Agneta Herlitz (Karolinska Institute) and Julie E. Yonker (Stockholm University), analyze the rationale for this trend, but focus on the usefulness of studying the influence of steroidal hormones in explaining sex differences in mature cognitive performance. The chapter benefits from careful discussions of testosterone and cognition, estrogen and cognition, and the provocative new work on the potential role of estrogen in predicting and treating Alzheimer's disease.

Åke Wahlin (Karolinska Institute) is a leader in the new frontier of research on health, disease, and cognitive aging. In Chapter 14 he reviews the key issues and methods for studying this multifarious and vital direction of research. An underlying theme is that, especially for older adults, it is imperative to account for selected health conditions, if the goal is to develop generalizable theories of cognitive aging. His argument, in many respects, is parallel to that offered by other observers in this book: just as cognition cannot occur without the context of the brain, aging does not occur without the context of health. Accordingly, Wahlin identifies new definitional and methodological directions for cognitive aging researchers to consider.

The first commentary for this section is by Peter Graf (University of British Columbia). Although acknowledging the indispensable contributions of biological and health factors on cognitive aging, in Chapter 15 Graf urges caution in pushing deeper into the analyses of their potential influences. In particular, he identifies several preliminary steps that new researchers and trainees in this field may wish to consider. However complex our theories and methods are, Graf notes, it is important to ensure that research details are not overlooked.

The second commentary chapter, by Paul Verhaeghen (Syracuse University), poses a series of three fundamental questions about cognitive aging, linking them to the directions of research established in the chapters of this section of the book. Verhaeghen identifies and articulates a set of underlying questions – and then integrates them with both the past (influential positions and achievements) and the future (new knowledge based on contemporary theories, methods, and technology) of the field. This commentary, too, provides a novel and thoughtful contribution to the ongoing discussion of new frontiers in cognitive aging.

As noted above, the book closes with a discussion by Daniel Berch and Molly Wagster on the support and activities of the U.S. National Institutes of Health (and, in particular, the National Institute on Aging, NIA) for cutting-edge research in cognitive aging. Berch and Wagster emphasize that, far from being simply a passive funding agency, the NIA actively provides a program through which new initiatives may be vetted, new frontiers may be explored, new collaborations may be initiated (and funded). It may not be coincidental that, among the NIA's agenda of new directions for research initiatives in cognitive aging, are those now profiled in this book.

Summary and Acknowledgments

For the purposes of this volume, we identified three new frontiers in the field of cognitive aging. Internationally visible leaders in each of these fields contributed chapters summarizing their perspectives on three new directions. The resulting volume is unique in its future perspective (without losing sight of the present) on three broad themes of cognitive aging. The next decade will inform us about how prescient we have all been. However, at minimum, it is a good bet that the fences of cognitive aging will continue to be breached, the new territories we have identified will continue to be explored, and that further surprising and influential major contributions are in the offing.

We are grateful to host of individuals, institutions, and agencies: without their coordinated advice and support, the outstanding Whistler conference and this subsequent book would not have been possible. First, all of the authors of these chapters accepted a challenging role – not only reviewing the past but anticipating the key elements of the future of their research areas in cognitive aging. Without exception, they met this challenge, and the concept of this book and the book itself benefits from their remarkable efforts. Second, without funding for the conference – and for several preceding planning meetings – this book would not have reached fruition. We are pleased to acknowledge the foresight and continuing support of STINT. Third, our own research projects – the Victoria Longitudinal Study and the Betula Project – are supported by several agencies, including (for the VLS) the National Institute on Aging and (for the BP) the Bank of Sweden Tercentenary Foundation and the Swedish Research Council. The continued funding by these agencies while we completed work on this book is appreciated. Finally, several staff members of the VLS provided essential support during the Whistler conference and the preparation of this book: we thank, especially, Michelle Audet, Anna-Lisa Cohen, Meghan Evans, and Jill Jenkins.

References

Baltes, P.B., and Smith, J. (1997). A systemic-wholisic view of psychological functioning in very old age: Introduction to a collection of articles from the Berlin Aging Study. *Psychology and Aging,* **12,** 395–409.

Baltes, P.B., Staudinger, U.M., and Lindenberger, U. (1997). Lifespan psychology: Theory and application to intellectual functioning. *Annual Review of Psychology,* **50,** 471–507.

Blanchard-Fields, F., and Hess, T.M. (eds) (1996). *Perspectives on cognitive change in adulthood and aging.* New York: McGraw-Hill.

Craik, F.I.M., and Salthouse, T.A. (eds) (2000). *The handbook of aging and cognition* (2nd ed.). Mahwah, NJ: Erlbaum.

Dixon, R.A. (2003). Themes in the aging of intelligence: Robust decline with intriguing possibilities. In R.J. Sternberg, J. Lautrey, and T.I. Lubart (eds), *Models of intelligence: International perspectives* (pp. 151–167). Washington, DC: American Psychological Association.

Dixon, R.A., and de Frias, C.M. (in press). The Victoria Longitudinal Study: From characterizing cognitive aging to illustrating changes in memory compensation. *Aging, Neuropsychology, and Cognition.*

Dixon, R.A., Kramer, D.A., and Baltes, P.B. (1985). Intelligence: A lifespan developmental perspective. In B.B. Wolman (ed.), *Handbook of intelligence: Theories, measurements, and applications* (pp. 301–350). New York: Wiley.

Han, B., and Nilsson, L.-G. (1997). A prospective cohort longitudinal research on memory, health, and aging: Introduction of the Betula project in Sweden. *Psychological Science,* 20, 272–273.

Hertzog, C., and Dixon, R.A. (1996). Methodological issues in research on cognition and aging. In F. Blanchard-Fields and T.M. Hess (eds), *Perspectives on cognitive change in adulthood and aging* (pp. 66–121). New York: McGraw-Hill.

Hertzog, C., Dixon, R.A., Hultsch, D.F., and MacDonald, S.W.S. (in press). Latent change models of adult cognition: Do changes in processing speed and working memory determine changes in episodic memory? *Psychology and Aging.*

Hultsch, D.F., Hertzog, C., Dixon, R.A., and Small, B.J. (1998). *Memory change in the aged.* Cambridge, UK: Cambridge University Press.

Light, L.L. (1991). Memory and aging: Four hypotheses in search of data. *Annual Review of Psychology,* 42, 333–376.

MacDonald, S.W.S., Dixon, R.A., Cohen, A-L., and Hazlitt, J.E. (in press). Biological markers predict 12-year cognitive change in older adults. *Gerontology.*

Nilsson, L-G., Bäckman, L., Erngrund, K., Nyberg, L., Adolfsson, R., Bucht, G., Karlsson, S., Widing, M., and Winblad, B. (1997). The Betula prospective cohort study: Memory, health, and aging. *Aging, Neuropsychology, and Cognition,* 1, 1–32.

Nyberg, L., Maitland, S.B., Rönnlund, M., Bäckman, L., Dixon, R.A., Wahlin, Å., and Nilsson, L-G. (2003). Selective adult age differences in an age-invariant multifactor model of declarative memory. *Psychology and Aging,* 18, 149–160.

Stern, P.C., and Carstensen, L.L. (eds). (2000). *The aging mind: Opportunities in cognitive research.* Washington, DC: National Academy Press.

Wahlin, Å., Bäckman, L., Hultdin, J., Adolfsson, R., and Nilsson, L-G. (2002). Reference values of serum levels of vitamin B12 and folic acid in a population-based sample of adults between 35 and 80 years of age. *Journal of Public Health Nutrition,* 5, 505–511.

Part 2

New theoretical orientations in cognitive aging

Chapter 2

Cognitive aging: New directions for old theories

Denise Park and Meredith Minear

What happens to our minds as we age? The obvious answer to this question is that different things happen to different people. But given the pervasiveness of the belief that as we age, we become less cognitively adept, the question as to whether there are universal trajectories of cognitive aging is an interesting one. In the present chapter, we will describe our state of knowledge with respect to what happens to our cognitive systems with age, including theoretical, behavioral, and neurobiological perspectives, as well as new directions and questions that have resulted from an integration of the three. After these discussions of basic systems, we will consider how the context and culture in which one ages can affect cognitive aging and assess the universality of cognitive aging theories. We will follow with a brief discussion of how theories of aging can be used as a model for understanding the mechanisms underlying cognitive symptoms associated with medical disorders, and close with a consideration of challenges for cognitive aging researchers for the future.

An overview of cognitive aging

Until quite recently, most of what we knew about the aging mind was based on behavioral findings. At the broadest level, a huge corpus of literature exists that suggests that cognitive performance does indeed deteriorate with age, but there are also domains that remain largely intact. More specifically, with age, the speed at which we perform mental operations decreases (Salthouse, 1996); the amount of working memory capacity available declines (Craik, Morris and Gick, 1990; Salthouse and Babcock, 1991; Park, Smith, Lautenschlager et al., 1996); and long-term memory functions less effectively (Kausler, 1991; Park, Smith, Lautenschlager et al., 1996). In addition, there is evidence that with age, it is more difficult to ignore irrelevant information or thoughts, and to inhibit dominant responses (Hasher and Zacks, 1988;

Lustig, Hasher and Tonev, 2001). Moreover, memories tend to become 'decontextualized'. That is, older adults remember items, facts or news relatively well, but are disproportionately impaired relative to young in remembering the context in which the information was presented (McIntyre and Craik, 1987; Henkel, Johnson, and De Leonardis, 1998; Frieske and Park, 1999). Despite all of these declines, there is also good evidence that knowledge about the world, vocabulary and semantic knowledge, remains largely intact, or may even grow with age (Park, Smith, Lautenschlager *et al.*, 1996). Additionally, implicit memory and recognition of complex pictures show little or no age-related decline (Light and La Voie, 1993; Park and Shaw, 1992; Park, Puglisi, and Smith, 1986).

A considerable amount of energy has been devoted to determining whether there is a single unitary mechanism that accounts for cognitive aging. Salthouse (1996) has argued that cognitive slowing, which is a decrease in the rate at which mental operations occur, is fundamental in explaining age-related declines on all other cognitive tasks. An alternative view has been proposed by Lindenberger and Baltes (1994) and Baltes and Lindenberger (1997). They measured basic visual and auditory function in samples of adults ranging from age 25 to 105, and provided surprising evidence that sensory function was fundamental in mediating age-related declines on a broad array of cognitive tasks, and was more basic than speed. They argue that it is not decreased sensory function, per se, that causes poor performance, but rather that sensory function is an indicator of overall neurological health. Recent work has clearly ruled out a peripheral explanation, as middle-aged adults who experienced simulated visual and auditory declines much like those of older adults, did not perform like older adults (Lindenberger, Scherer, and Baltes, 2001).

Another view is that decreased working memory capacity causes decreased cognitive performance with age (Craik and Byrd, 1982). Working memory can be thought of as the total amount of mental energy available to an individual to manage information in consciousness – that is to store, retrieve, process and manipulate information. Alphabetizing a list of six words that one had just heard would be a task high in working memory demands, as one would have to simultaneously hold the items in consciousness, reorder them, remember the order, and report it back. There is no question that with age, performance on working memory tasks decreases (Park, Smith, Lautenschlager *et al.*, 1996), but the question is why capacity appears to shrink with age.

Hasher and Zacks (1988) would argue that age-related decline in working memory does not represent a decrease in capacity, but rather argue that working memory becomes cluttered with irrelevant information due to decreased ability to control its contents. That is, information may enter working memory but not be effectively deleted. Thus, according to this view, if one received a series of word alphabetizing problems, an older adult might have trouble effectively deleting items from previous problems in working memory, and earlier items might interfere with later items (May, Hasher, and Kane 1999). From the inhibition perspective, it is this failure with age to control the access of irrelevant information to working memory and then subsequently delete irrelevant information that makes working memory appear to shrink with age. The inhibition view suggests that controlled processing is less effective with age, resulting in a breakdown of cognitive operations.

We recently completed a large study where we attempted to understand the interrelationship among the constructs of sensory function, speed, and working memory in predicting the higher order cognitive process of long-term memory (Park, Lautenschlager, Hedden *et al.*, 2002). Additionally, we were interested in whether there were differences in the way visuospatial and verbal processes were organized in young and old adults. Shah and Miyake (1996) had argued that visuospatial and verbal working memory operated independently in young adults, suggesting that they were distinct, differentiated stores. Park, Lautenschlager, Hedden *et al.* (in press) hypothesized that if such highly differentiated, domain-specific visuospatial and verbal stores existed in younger adults that with age, they might become less specific or dedifferentiate into a single, general cognitive resource with age. The dedifferentiation would occur as a result of general decreases in neuronal integrity hypothesized to occur by single factor or common cause models of aging (Baltes and Lindenberger, 1997; Salthouse, 1996). We tested a lifespan sample of 345 adults from age 20 to 95 to our laboratory. Each individual completed a series of cognitive tasks for a total of eight hours over three visits. The results appear in Figure 2.1. As can be seen, the rate of decline in speed of processing, visuospatial and verbal working memory, and visuospatial and verbal long-term memory were the same, regardless of modality. Figure 2.1 also illustrates the continuous nature of aging. There are no sharp drops in performance on any of the measures in late adulthood. Rather, the decline appears to be continuous, beginning in the twenties, with roughly the same amount of decline occurring from decade to decade. At the same time that the processing-intensive measures are decreasing with age, measures of verbal ability remain stable and even show small increases.

To further investigate interrelationships among the constructs and to determine whether cognitive structures were organized similarly across the lifespan, structural equation models were developed for younger and older adults. The model displayed in Figure 2.2 for the whole sample, fit the separate data of younger and older as well as all subjects combined. This suggests that the organization of speed, working memory, and long-term memory does

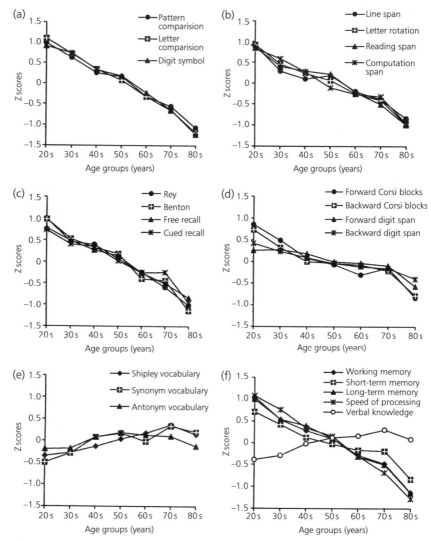

Fig. 2.1 Life span performance on: (a) speed of processing measures; (b) working memory measures (visuospatial and verbal); (c) long-term memory measures (visuospatial and verbal); (d) short-term memory measures (visuospatial and verbal); (e) knowledge-based verbal ability measures; and (f) a composite view of the above measures. Composite scores for each construct represent the z score of the average of all measures for that construct.

not change across the lifespan, so although function may decline with age, cognitive architecture does not dedifferentiate or deteriorate from specific to more general structures. Specifically, the model in Figure 2.2 indicates that differences in performance on the tasks that occur with increased age operate

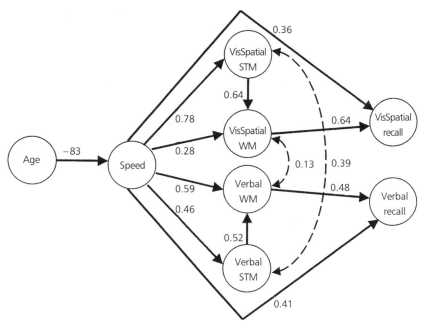

Fig. 2.2 Structural model of speed, working memory, and long-term memory. For each path in the model, the completely standarized path coefficient is presented. Dashed curved lines represent correlations among residuals. Speed = speed of processing; VisSpatial WM = visuospatial working memory; Verbal WM = verbal working memory; VisSpatial STM = visuospatial short-term memory; Verbal STM = verbal short-term memory; VisSpatial recall = visuospatial recall.

through the speed at which individuals process information. In this model, speed is the most basic construct and mediates variance (predicts function) in working memory. The working memory construct is differentiated for visuospatial and verbal working memory, but the bidirectional arrows between these two constructs suggests that they are highly interrelated and share much variance. Both speed and working memory together predict performance on visuospatial and verbal recall. Moreover, each type of working memory has a passive domain-specific short-term store (measured by digit span for verbal and a location span memory task, Corsi blocks, for visuospatial) that is related to working memory, but short-term memory does not predict any variance in long-term memory. The model presented is congruent with the executive function model proposed by Baddeley (1986) and with recent theorizing by Engle, Tuholski, Laughlin *et al.* (1999), suggesting that short-term memory is a part of working memory. Park, Lautenschlager, Hedden *et al.* (2002) also measured sensory function and attempted to model it, but unlike Baltes and Lindenberger (1997), they found no evidence that it was a more fundamental construct than speed in explaining age differences in performance. This was likely due to the large number of older adults that Baltes and Lindenberger (1997) had in extreme old age. Generally, this work suggests that speed is more basic than working memory, but that both speed and working memory operate together to predict performance on long-term memory tasks.

What do we know about poor inhibitory function and source memory as causes of diminished cognitive abilities with age? Certainly, disproportionate responsiveness to interfering events with age may be a cause of decreased efficiency in working memory. But the interference may occur either because older adults have difficulty inhibiting the irrelevant information, but also because they have source problems – that is, remembering which information was the primary target and which was interfering information (Jacoby, 1996; Jennings and Jacoby, 1993). There has been some debate as to whether older adults are more susceptible to interference in memory tasks. Jacoby, Debner and Hay (2001) reported evidence suggesting that older adults' recollection problems in a proactive interference paradigm were more related to an inability to discriminate target from interfering information than to difficulty inhibiting irrelevant information.

In a similar vein, Hedden and Park (2001a, 2002) were able to separate source and inhibitory deficit accounts as causes of retroactive interference in older adults. Hedden and Park (2001a) reported that when older adults studied a brief list of word pairs followed by a list of interfering pairs that they were required to read aloud, older adults were more negatively influenced by the interfering read material relative to control than young adults. This suggested greater susceptibility to interference. In a later series of studies, Hedden and Park (2002) reported two important findings. First, only older adults who were slower than the median, showed the interference effects. Second, the interference effects were due to older adults' difficulty in discriminating source from read items rather than to a failure to inhibit. When older adults were required to remember both sets of items and their list identity (so that no inhibition was required, but only source discrimination), there were disproportionate interference effects for the old regardless of the size of item sets. Another experiment indicated that when the subjects were required to simply make an inclusion/exclusion judgement from the two sets of items (e.g. disregard source), there were no interference effects for either age group. As Jacoby Debner and Hay (2001) note, it is important to separate source arguments from inhibition arguments when understanding interference effects, and any model of interference and cognitive aging will need to take into account both mechanisms.

A final theoretical point of great interest to cognitive aging researchers has been the notion that age-related deficits can be repaired by some type of environmental support (Craik and Byrd, 1982; Craik and Jennings, 1992). There is evidence that when tasks require less self-initiated processing, such as in recognition compared to recall, age differences in memory become smaller (Craik and McDowd, 1987). Similarly, when older adults can rely on pre-existing associations as cues that are based on semantic knowledge, age differences in recall become much smaller (Park, Smith, Morrell *et al.*, 1990; Smith, Park, Earles *et al.*, 1998).

What lies beneath? What does neuroimaging data reveal about cognitive aging?

In the past decade, cognitive aging researchers have had the opportunity to directly connect cognitive behavior to brain function through the use of neuroimaging techniques, primarily positron emission tomography (PET) and more recently, functional magnetic resonance imaging (fMRI). These techniques allow researchers to examine specific sites of neural activation while different cognitive tasks are being performed with excellent spatial and increasingly good temporal resolution. Neuroimaging has proven to be an extraordinarily powerful tool in revealing more about the aging brain than was previously known and the connection of theoretical frameworks and behavioral data with imaging results has led to some important new conceptualizations of how the aging mind functions. Below, we briefly connect the theories just described to appropriate imaging findings. For a detailed discussion of these issues, see reveiws by Cabeza (2001), Grady and Craik (2000) and Park, Polk, Mikels *et al.* (2001).

The finding of decreased speed of processing with age (Salthouse, 1996) can conceivably be explained by cellular and structural changes in the brain. The frontal cortex shows a greater decrease in volume across the lifespan than do the mediotemporal lobes, but both areas show some age-related shrinkage and play important roles in cognitive function. Interestingly, occipital (visual) cortex remains unchanged in volume well into late adulthood (Raz, 2000). Additionally, there are decreases in white matter volume due to demyelination of neurons, (Kemper, 1994), which could result in slowing of information processing, although direct connections between demyelination and speed have not been established. Finally, dopamine receptors, hypothesized to play an important role in cognition, decrease in quantity with age (Seeman, Bzowej, Guan *et al.*, 1987; Volkow, Wang, Fowler *et al.*, 1996). Adding credence to the notion that decreased dopamine receptors can account for slowing, are the striking findings of Backman, Ginovart, and Dixon (2000) and Volkow, Gur, Wang *et al.* (1998) who have demonstrated very substantial correlations between speed and dopamine receptor binding. More detailed discussion of these issues can be found in this volume in Chapter 6 by Raz and Chapter 8 by Backman.

The Lindenberger and Baltes (1994) hypothesis that sensory function is the single-mechanism mediator of age-related decline in higher-order cognitive functions cannot be so readily explained by the existing neurobiological data, as sensory cortex show no volumetric decrease with age. There is, however, evidence that the hemodynamic response is of lower amplitude in visual cortex with age (Buckner, Snyder, Raichle *et al.*, 2000; Ross, Yurgelun-Todd, and Renshaw, 1997). This diminished response may reflect overall decreased neural integrity with age, providing support for the 'common cause', single-mechanism view of age-related decline.

With respect to working memory, the imaging data largely confirm the organization of working memory presented in Figure 2.2. There is evidence from young adults for an active central executive residing bilaterally in the dorsolateral prefrontal cortex (represented by the shared variance associated with visuospatial and verbal working memory in Figure 2.2) (D'Esposito, Postle, Ballard *et al.*, 1999; Owen, 1997; Smith and Jonides, 1999), as well as passive, domain-specific visuospatial and verbal stores, residing in the right and left ventral lateral cortex, respectively (D'Esposito, Postle, Ballard *et al.*, 1999; Owen, 1997; Owen, Sterns, Look *et al.*, 1998). At first glance, decreased working memory function that occurs with age would appear to be simply explained by the volumetric decline in the frontal cortex that occurs with age (Raz, 2000), and decreased hemodynamic function. In fact, there is evidence that shrinkage does predict poor performance (Raz, 2000).

Functional imaging data, however, present a much more complex picture than that established by analysis of structural data. Reuter-Lorenz, Jonides, Smith *et al.* (2000) studied visuospatial and verbal working memory in young and old adults using PET. They reported well-defined activations in young adults in the right dorsolateral prefrontal cortex (DLPFC) for the visuospatial task and in left DLPFC for the verbal task. Older adults, however, did not show this pattern. They showed focal activations in both hemispheres (bilateral recruitment) in the DLPFC when performing the visuospatial and verbal tasks. The important question is why bilateral recruitment occurs. Is it a compensatory response where older adults recruit more neural tissue to perform to the maximum of their abilities, or is it a dysfunctional response related to a failure to suppress activation in the contralateral hemisphere? At this time, we simply do not know. Reuter-Lorenz, Marshuetz, Jonides *et al.* (2001) interpret the bilateral recruitment as compensatory, as they reported that such recruitment was correlated with fast performers in older adults. Also supporting a compensatory argument, Rypma and D'Esposito (2000) found a pattern of bilateral recruitment in a working memory task for old and young, but only when the load was high. However, in a study on long-term memory, Logan, Sanders, Snyder *et al.* (2002) reported a pattern of bilateral activation in old adults during encoding of words. They divided their sample into young–old and old–old adults, and found that only old–old adults showed evidence of bilateral recruitment ('nonselectivity' in their terms). This pattern of bilateral recruitment in only the oldest adults led the authors to suggest that this is a dysfunctional pattern that typifies a breakdown in selectivity of neural recruitment. This study of individual differences in recruitment patterns may be one of the most important new directions for understanding healthy cognitive aging, particularly since the conclusions diverge from the behavioral work on individual differences (Park, Smith, Lautenschlager *et al.*, 1996; Park, Lautenschlager, Hedden *et al.*, 2002) which provide little evidence for dedifferentiation in cognitive architecture with age.

There is also evidence that age-related decline in inhibitory mechanisms (Hasher and Zacks, 1988) has a neurobiological substrate. Nielson, Langenecker, and Garavan (in press) reported that in young adults, right prefrontal and parietal regions were activated while performing a letter inhibition task. Older adults showed more extensive activation than young in the same areas in the right prefrontal cortex and also showed a homologous activation in the left frontal area (bilateral recruitment). Smith, Geva, Jonides *et al.* (2001) presented evidence that older adults and poorly performing young adults recruited more frontal cortex than highly-performing young adults in a task-switching paradigm (which requires inhibition of earlier operations). In both studies, the authors interpret the additional activation to be compensatory.

The basis for source memory, the ability to bind a context to a target, has also been examined using neuroimaging. Mitchell, Johnson, Raye *et al.* (2000) found that when older adults had to remember both an item's identity and its location (binding of feature to target), older adults showed poorer memory but also less activation than young in the left anterior hippocampus as well as less activation in left prefrontal cortex. They suggest that these areas are important for binding and function less efficiently in older adults.

With respect to long-term memory, the pattern again is one of evidence for bilateral recruitment in older adults. Cabeza (in press, Chapter 9 present volume) provides detailed reviews of these issues. Younger adults tend to show left-lateralized activations at encoding and right-lateralized activations at retrieval (Backman, Andersson, Nordberg *et al.*, 1997), but older adults tend to show overall less activation at encoding (under-recruitment) but bilateral activations at retrieval (Cabeza, Grady, Nyberg *et al.*, 1997). Similar results have been reported by Backman, Almkvist, Andersson, Nordberg *et al.* (1997) and Madden, Turkington, Provenzale *et al.* (1999). Cabeza (in press) proposes the Hemispheric Asymmetry Reduction in Old Adults Model (HAROLD), arguing that brain activity tends to be less lateralized in old compared to young adults, under many different conditions. Again, Cabeza (in press) raises the question as to whether these bilateral activations are compensatory or reflect dysfunction. He argues that both functions can be integrated (see Chapter 9) within the HAROLD Model.

It is also noteworthy that there may be some genetic basis for recruitment patterns. Bookheimer, Strojwas, Cohen *et al.* (2000) reported that older adults with APOE-4 alleles (a risk-factor for Alzheimer's disease) showed more extensive recruitment of neural tissue, as well as stronger activations, than adults who were homozygous for the APOE-3 allele. The greater activations were primarily in the left anterior hippocampus, and were associated with memory decline two years hence.

One pervasive term in both the cognitive and neuroimaging literature is that of 'dedifferentiation'. The term is used in many contexts, but generally reflects decreased focus and specificity in either cognitive operations or neural activations. Given the centrality of this term, the controversy that surrounds the issue of functional versus dysfunctional activations, and the growing importance of individual differences in understanding the adaptive value or patterns of neural recruitment, it is important to develop precise terminology in describing 'dedifferentiated' recruitment patterns. Park, Glass, Minear *et al.* (2001) suggest that dedifferentiated neural recruitment may involve (a) bilateral recruitment of homologous areas; (b) additional recruitment of new areas (unique recruitment) and (c) substitution whereby older adults activate a site different from that used by young adults to perform a cognitive operation. In addition to dedifferentiated patterns, older adults may also show 'under-recruitment' of neural tissue, that is less activation in a site compared to young adults, or 'over-recruitment', more activation in sites compared to younger adults.

The notion that environmental support can ameliorate age differences in memory by altering processing demands as proposed by Craik and Byrd (1982) has been recently examined in the neuroimaging literature. In a seminal study, Logan, Sanders, Synder *et al.* (2002) contrasted neural activations during an intentional learning condition with activations during guided encoding. In the intentional learning condition, subjects were free to use a self-selected strategy to encode words, but in the guided or deep encoding condition, subjects evaluated whether a word was abstract or concrete, thus accessing its meaning. The results indicated that older adults showed under-recruitment (decreased activation) of left frontal cortex compared to young, as well as bilateral recruitment of this area in the intentional condition. In the deep processing condition, however, the age-related decrease in neural function was 'repaired', in the sense that left frontal activations were identical for old and young adults and age differences in subsequent memory also decreased. Moreover, both young–old and old–old adults showed increased activation in the left frontal area compared to the intentional condition. Thus, the insightful theorizing of Craik and Byrd (1982) with respect to environmental support nearly 20 years ago, has a neural analog.

The important new directions in basic theoretical work on cognitive aging involves not only establishing linkages between existing theories and neural organization, but also developing new theories based on the exciting findings suggestive of brain reorganization. The study of individual differences has a long and respected history in the cognitive aging literature. Integrating individual differences in brain activations and the cognitive trajectories such activations predict will prove to be a fertile ground for new inquiry. One notable attempt to unify cognitive aging theories with neuroscience has been proposed by Li, Lindenberger, and Frensch (2000). They have developed a neuro-computational model that relates dopaminergic deficiencies at the cellular level to less distinctive activation patterns in older adults, in response to stimulus inputs. The model is an important step in developing formal linkages among different levels of analysis of the aging mind.

Cognition in context

The work presented thus far has involved the measurement of cognitive and neural processes under highly constrained laboratory conditions. The laboratory approach allows researchers to measure cognitive function while minimizing the confounding variables introduced by the complexity and distraction present in the real world. Despite the potential confounds and methodological challenges more ecologically-valid research presents, it is important to understand how cognitive function might vary or change as a function of the cultural, social, or environmental conditions in which it occurs. We will consider how cultural context and context familiarity may mediate the relationship between aging and cognitive function.

Culture, aging, and cognition

There is evidence that higher-order cognitive processes such as judgement and decision-making are affected by culture. Nisbett and colleagues have focused on differences between East Asian and Western European cultures and argued that the American focus on individualism and the East Asian focus on interpersonal harmony and collectivism have resulted in differences in the way information is processed (Nisbett, 2002; Peng and Nisbett, 1999). East Asians attend to context when making judgements, whereas Western Europeans attend to the individual (Morris and Peng, 1994). East Asians process information holistically whereas Western Europeans require more effort to integrate features with target information (Masuda and Nisbett, 2001). Additionally, Westerners tend to focus more on hierarchical, categorical relationships, whereas East Asians process information in terms of relationships (Ji, Nisbett, and Zhang, 2002). How might aging interact with cultural differences in cognition? Park, Nisbett and Hedden (1999) propose that the amount of processing resource or working memory capacity that a task requires will affect the relationships among aging, culture, and cognition. They argue that when a cognitive task shows large cultural differences but is not resource intensive and relies primarily on world knowledge, there will be little interaction between culture and age. In contrast, when a task is culturally-biased but resource intensive and strategic, cultural differences should be larger in young adults than in older adults. This seemingly counter intuitive prediction occurs because neurobiological aging is a cross-cultural universal and acts to limit strategic flexibility and make the performance of the two cultures more similar in late adulthood on resource-demanding tasks.

Hedden, Park, Nisbett *et al.* (2002) investigated basic processes of speed and working memory in a Chinese and American sample of young and old adults. Their initial interest was in finding simple cognitive tasks that were not in any way biased by differences in processing tendencies between the two cultures. These tasks could then be used as measures of resource for equating samples cross-culturally in subsequent research. They reported that tasks that involved digits were culturally saturated, with young Asians showing better performance than young Americans, but with little difference between old Asians and old Americans. Tasks, however, that were primarily visuospatial in nature, showed age differences but cultural equivalence. Figure 2.3 illustrates these findings. A speed of processing task, Pattern comparison, that involved matching simple shapes showed no cultural differences, nor did the Corsi blocks task, a visuospatial measure of working memory. Hedden, Park, Nisbett *et al.* (2002) and Hedden and Park (2001b) suggest that digit-based measures showed differences across cultures due to linguistic differences between spoken Chinese (Mandarin or Putonghua) and English. Chinese syllables for digits are not as dense and have a measurably faster articulation rate and a lower processing load than English syllables (Cheung and Kemper, 1993, 1994). For example, 'eight' in English is 'ba' in Chinese.

In a later study, Park, Hedden, Jing *et al.* (2002) collected nine different measures of speed of processing and six of working memory. They developed

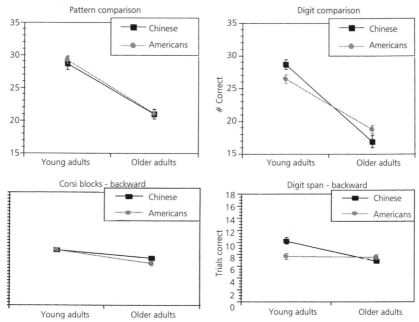

Fig. 2.3 Performance on a visuospatial and verbal measure of speed of processing by young and older Americans and Chinese. Top half: Cultural equivalence on the visuospatial measure (Pattern comparison) is shown in the left panel. Cultural differences in the numerically-based measure (Digit comparison) are depicted in the right panel. Bottom half: Performance on backward versions of working memory tasks by young and older Americans and Chinese. A visuospatial measure (Corsi blocks) shows cultural equivalence whereas the numerically-based measure, digit span, shows Chinese superiority in the young but not the old. Copyright © 2002 by the American Psychological Association. Reprinted (or Adapted) with permission.

structural models from the constructs and reported that as long as digit-based measures of working memory were excluded from the model, the structure of these basic constructs was the same for young Americans and Chinese and also for old Americans and Chinese. Thus, there is evidence that the aging mind is organized similarly across cultures at the level of basic cognitive mechanics. However, they also collected data from the Cattell Culture Fair Intelligence Test (Cattell, 1963). In this task, subjects must decide which abstract figure is the fourth in a series. The test requires analytic, feature-based processing, a strength of Americans (Nisbett, 2002; Peng and Nisbett, 1999). Consistent with this expectation, young and old Americans performed significantly better than their Chinese counterparts (suggesting that the Cattell Cultural-Fair Test was not exactly fair). However, when the speed and working memory constructs were used in the structural model to predict performance on the Cattell Culture Fair Test, these constructs accounted for 37 per cent of the variance for Americans, but 67 per cent of the variance in Chinese. Park, Hedden, Jing et al. (2002) argued that because the Cattell task was demonstrably harder for Chinese subjects, measures of cognitive resource better predicted performance on the task for Chinese compared to Americans. It is as if those Chinese individuals who were highest in speed and working memory were able to overcome the constraints of their culture and perform well on this task. Ongoing work in this domain is focused on understanding differences in binding features to target across age and culture as well as age and cultural differences in the use of category structure in remembering. We are also conducting work to determine if the cultures differ in neural recruitment patterns on tasks that appear to be biased towards one culture or the other. Understanding the role of culture in patterns of cognitive aging is an important new direction for researchers.

Aging and cognition in familiar contexts

All of the cognitive deficits described in the preceding pages might make one wonder how older adults manage the cognitive demands in their everyday work and personal lives. It is clear that older adults can perform very effectively, so it becomes important to understand a complex memory behavior in a real-world setting. Medication adherence is an interesting cognitive behavior to study because it involves working memory (integrating information across a number of medications to develop an adherence plan), long-term memory (remembering what the plan is), and prospective memory (remembering to implement the plan). Unless someone else is managing an individual's medications, medication adherence occurs in an everyday context across a huge range of settings (work, home, travel) and in the context of a variety of symptoms and goals (see Park and Jones, 1996; Park and Kidder, 1996; Park and Mayhorn, 1996 for reviews).

Park, Hertzog, Leventhal et al. (1999) studied medication adherence behaviors over a four-week period in adults aged 30–75 with rheumatoid arthritis. All subjects were taking a minimum of four medications and adherence was measured by having a pharmacist place each subject's medication in individual medication bottles with embedded microchips that recorded the date and the time the bottle was opened. This provided accurate but subtle monitoring of medication usage. In addition to measuring medication adherence, Park, Hertzog, Leventhal et al. (1999) also measured cognitive function on a wide range of tasks, as well as medication beliefs, depression, anxiety, health, and self-reported environmental demands (Martin and Park, 2002). The results from this study suggested the following. Despite showing age-related decline in cognitive function, older adults were the most adherent of any age group, a finding that has been reported previously (Park, Morrell, Frieske *et al.*, 1992; Morrell, Park, Kidder, *et al.*, 1997). Of particular interest in this study was the finding that the single best predictor of medication adherence was perceived environmental demands. People who reported leading chaotic, busy lives that were unpredictable (typically these were middle-aged adults) were the least adherent. This finding is notable for two reasons. First, this is a case where context (an orderly or chaotic environment) better predicted remembering than cognitive function did, including laboratory measures of speed of processing, working memory, and long-term memory. Second, this finding points to the importance of automatic processes in controlling everyday behaviors. Park (1999) argues that performing the same actions every day in the same context, results in environmental features serving as memory cues that automatically activate an appropriate behavior. Older adults who lead routine lives and take their medications with their orange juice, for example, every single morning at breakfast, will require little controlled or effortful processing to remember to perform the task. They will reach for the medications as soon as they drink the orange juice. In fact the biggest problem with a task that becomes routine is the difficulty one has in remembering whether one performed the task or not (Park and Kidder, 1996). Jacoby, Jennings, and Hay (1996) suggest that with age, familiarity or automatic processes remain intact, but that controlled or effortful processes decline. If controlled processes are decreasing with age, but automatic processes remain intact, an increasing proportion of behavior may be controlled by automatic processes and thus contextual cues.

To further understand the role of context in controlling memory behaviors of older adults, Chasteen, Park, and Schwarz (2001) utilized a framework proposed by Gollwitzer (1999) and Gollwitzer and Brandstetter (1997) Gollwitzer (1999) proposed that developing a detailed implementation plan for a future action results in an increased likelihood that the plan will be carried out relative to an intention rehearsal strategy or a deliberative strategy where detailed pros and cons of the action are considered. The implementation plan works because the environmental cues generated in the plan are available at the time the plan is to be implemented. These cues act to automatically increase the probability that the behavior will occur. Chasteen, Park, and Schwarz (2001) reported that older adults were nearly three times as likely to remember to write their name on the top of a page at the end of an experiment if they had prepared a detailed implementation plan compared to control conditions. In later work, Liu and Park (2002) reported that older adults were significantly more likely to profit from developing implementation intentions to remember to test their blood glucose over a three week period compared to young adults. Thus, these data suggest that context does indeed play an important role in driving the everyday behavior of older adults, with automatic processes as the mechanism underlying the facilitation. A complete theory of cognitive aging will need to integrate the role of automatic processes and context in explaining the differences between laboratory and everyday behaviors.

Cognitive aging as a model for cognitive disorders

Cognitive aging theories and mechanisms isolated by these theories may be useful for understanding memory complaints and memory disorders in populations other than the elderly. Fibromyalgia is a puzzling disorder that is characterized by chronic pain and fatigue (Wolfe, Smythe, Yunus et al., 1990). Patients afflicted with fibromyalgia frequently complain about poor cognitive function, but they are often dismissed by physicians as suffering from a psychiatric syndrome. There is evidence that fibromyalgia patients have disrupted hypothalamic–pituitary–adrenal function in a manner that is similar to that experienced by older adults (Crofford and Demitrack, 1996). For these reasons, we hypothesized that fibromyalgia patients might have cognitive functions typical of that of older adults (Park, Glass, Minear et al., 2001). We measured speed of processing, working memory, and free recall in a sample of fibromyalgia patients, age-matched controls and controls that were 20 years older than the fibromyalgia patients. The findings indicated that fibromyalgia patients performed like young adults on speed of processing tasks, but that they performed like older adults on measures of working memory and free recall. The findings suggest that fibromyalgia is characterized by decreased mental resources, as patients have suggested. The disorder does not, however, entirely mimic cognitive aging, as speed of processing is the hallmark deficit in older adults – a deficit not exhibited by the fibromyalgia patient. Park and collaborators are currently investigating the neurobiological underpinnings of cognitive function in fibromyalgia patients to determine if their neural recruitment patterns are more typical of young or older adults on working memory and long-term memory tasks. Theories and mechanisms of cognitive aging are relatively well-developed and understood and may provide fertile ground for understanding disorders and other conditions characterized by diminished cognitive function.

Summary

Cognitive aging has been heavily researched in the laboratory with impressive results. Researchers have isolated basic mechanisms that explain nearly all age-related variance on most laboratory tests of cognition. Less understood are the connections between basic mechanisms and the neurobiological substrates or neural activations associated with them. Additionally, we know that the demands of cognitive tasks may differ as a function of culture or familiar environments, but have not made much progress in specifying how these demands change and under what conditions. The relationship of basic mechanisms to everyday behaviors is not well understood, and it may be the case that basic mechanisms are most important in explaining cognitive behavior in older adults in highly novel environments (such as the laboratory). This suggests that a naturalistic study of cognitive aging in unfamiliar environments could be important in understanding cognitive aging. A study of cognitive performance in a natural macro-environment, such as when older adults move to a new and unfamiliar location, would be useful in understanding the relationship between cognitive function and novelty in the real world. The possibility that new environments may be cognitively stimulating and facilitate cognitive function, while at the same time demanding tremendous engagement of cognitive resources, is real. Biological research indicates that older rats show neuron growth when faced with new, stimulating environments (Greenough, McDonald, Parnisari et al., 1986). This is an important new frontier that needs investigation. Moreover, other data suggest that cognitive function in older adults may be improved by exercise (Kramer, Hahn, Cohen et al., 1999) and that even diets rich in certain antioxidants may be supportive of cognition (Joseph, Shukitt-Hale, Denisova et al., 1999). Data such as these, combined with data suggesting that simple instructions can change old brain activation patterns into youthful ones (Logan, Sanders, Snyder et al., 2002), suggest that interventions may be the new frontier in cognitive aging. Integrating existing research and theoretical frameworks with intervention strategies may help us understand what steps we can take across our lifespan to maintain healthy minds.

References

Backman, L., Ginovart, N., Dixon, R.A., Wahlin, T.R., Wahlin, A., Halldin, C., Farde, L. (2000). Age-related cognitive deficits mediated by changes in the striatal dopamine system. *American Journal of Psychiatry, 157,* 635–637.

Backman, L.A., Almkvist, O., Andersson, J., Nordberg, A. *et al.* (1997). Brain activation in young and older adults during implicit and explicit retrieval. *Journal of Cognitive Neuroscience,* **9,** 378–391.

Baddeley, A. (1986). *Working Memory.* Oxford, England: Clarendon Press.

Baltes, P.B., Lindenberger, U. (1997). Emergence of a powerful connection between sensory and cognitive functions across the adult life span: A new window to the study of cognitive aging? *Psychology and Aging,* **12,** 12–21.

Bookheimer, S.Y.S., M.H., Cohen, M.S., Saunders, A.M., Pericak-Vance, M.A., Mazziotta, J.C., Small, G.W. (2000). Patterns of brain activation in people at risk for Alzheimer's disease. *New England Journal of Medicine,* 343, 450–456.

Buckner, R.L., Snyder, A.L., Raichle, M.E., Morris, J.C. (2000). Functional brain imaging of young, nondemented, and demented older adults. *Journal of Cognitive Neuroscience,* 12 supplement, 24–34.

Cabeza, R., Grady, C.L., Nyberg, L., McIntosh, A.R., Tulving, E., Kapur, S., Jennings, J.M., Houle, S., Craik, F.I.M. (1997). Age-related differences in neural activity during memory encoding and retrieval: A positron emission tomography study. *Journal of Neuroscience,* 17, 391–400.

Cabeza, R. (2001). Functional neuroimaging and cognitive aging. In R. Cabeza, A. Kingstone, (eds), *Handbook of Functional Neuroimaging of Cognition* Cambridge, MA: MIT Press.

Cabeza, R. (In press). Hemispheric asymmetry reduction in older adults: The HAROLD model. *Psychology and Aging.*

Cattell, R.B., Cattell, A.K.S. (1963). *Test of 'g': Culture Fair Scale 3, Form A.* Champaign, IL: Institute for Personality Testing.

Chasteen, A.L., Park, D.C., Schwarz, N. (2001). Implementation interventions and facilitation of prospective memory. *Psychological Science,* 12, 457–461.

Cheung, H., Kemper, S. (1993). Recall and articulation of English and Chinese words by Chinese-English bilinguals. *Memory and Cognition,* 21, 666–670.

Cheung, H., Kemper, S. (1994). Recall and articulation of English and Chinese words under memory preload conditions. *Language and Speech,* 37, 147–161.

Craik, F.I.M., Byrd, M. (1982). Aging and cognitive deficits: The role of attentional resources. In F. I. M. Craik, S. Trehub (eds), *Aging and Cognitive Processes* (pp. 191–211). New York, NY: Plenum.

Craik, F.I.M., McDowd, J.M. (1987). Age differences in recall and recognition. *Journal of Experimental Psychology: Learning Memory and Cognition,* 13, 474–479.

Craik, F.I.M., Morris, R.G., Gick, M.L. (1990). Adult age differences in working memory. In G. Vallar (ed.), *Neuropsychological impairments of short-term memory* (pp. 247–267). New York, NY: Cambridge University Press.

Craik, F.I.M., Jennings, J.M. (1992). Human memory. In F. I. M. Craik (ed.), *The Handbook of Aging and Cognition* (pp. 51–110) Hillsdale, NJ: Lawrence Erlbaum.

Crofford, L.J., Demitrack, M.A. (1996). Evidence that the abnormalities of central neurohormonal systems are key to understanding fibromyalgia and chronic fatigue syndrome. *Rheumatic Disease Clinics of North America,* 22, 267–284.

D'Esposito, M., Postle, B.R., Ballard, D., Lease, J. (1999). Maintenance versus manipulation of information held in working memory: An event-related fMRI study. *Brain and Cognition,* 41, 66–86.

Engle, R.W., Tuholski, S.W., Laughlin, J.E., Conway, A.R.A. (1999). Working memory, short-term memory, and general fluid intelligence: A latent-variable approach. *Journal of Experimental Psychology General,* 128, 309–331.

Frieske, D.A., Park, D.C. (1999). Memory for news in young and old adults. *Psychology and Aging,* 14, 90–98.

Gollwitzer, P.M. (1999). Implementation intentions: Strong effects of simple plans. *American Psychologist,* 54, 493–503.

Gollwitzer, P.M., Brandstaetter, V. (1997). Implementation intentions and effective goal pursuit. *Journal of Personality and Social Psychology, 73*, 186–199.

Grady, C.L., Craik, F.I.M. (2000). Changes in memory processing with age. *Current Opinions in Neurobiology, 10*, 224–231.

Greenough, W.T., McDonald, J.W., Parnisari, R.M., Camel, J.E. (1986). Environmental conditions modulate degeneration and new dendrite growth in cerebellum of senescent rats. *Brain Research, 380*, 136–143.

Hasher, L., Zacks, R.T. (1988). Working memory, comprehension, and aging: A review and a new view. In G. H. Bower (ed.), *The Psychology of Learning and Motivation* (Vol. 22, pp. 193–225). San Diego, CA: Academic Press.

Hedden, T., Park, D.C. (2001a). Aging and interference in verbal working memory. *Psychology and Aging, 16*, 666–681.

Hedden, T., Park, D.C. (2001b). Culture, aging, and cognitive aspects of communication. In N. Charness, D. C. Park, B. Sabel, (eds), *Communication, Technology, and Aging: Opportunities and Challenges for the Future* (pp. 81–108). New York, NY: Springer.

Hedden, T., Park, D.C. (2002). *Aging and retroactive interference in working memory: The contributions of inhibition and source memory.* Unpublished manuscript.

Hedden, T., Park, D.C., Nisbett, R., Lijun, J., Jing, Q., Jiao, S. (2002). Cultural variation in verbal versus spatial neuropsychological function across the lifespan. *Neuropsychology, 16*, 65–73.

Henkel, L.A., Johnson, M.K., De Leonardis, D.M. (1998). Aging and source monitoring: Cognitive processes and neuropsychological correlates. *Journal of Experimental Psychology: General, 127*, 251–268.

Jacoby, L.L., Jennings, J.M., Hay, J.F. (1996). Dissociating automatic and consciously-controlled processes: Implications for diagnosis and rehabilitation of memory deficits. In D. J. Herrmann, C. L. McEvoy, C. Hertzog, P. Hertel, M.K. Johnson, (eds), *Basic and Applied Memory Research: Theory in Context* (Vol. 1, pp. 161–193). Hillsdale, NJ: Lawrence Erlbaum Associates.

Jacoby, L.L. (1999). Ironic effects of repetition: Measuring age-related differences in memory. *Journal of Experimental Psychology: Learning, Memory and Cognition, 25*, 3–22.

Jacoby, L.L., Debner, J.A., Hay, J.F. (2001). Proactive interference, accessibility bias, and process dissociations: Valid subject reports of memory. *Journal of Experimental Psychology: Learning, Memory, and Cognition: Special Issue, 27*(3) 686–700.

Jennings, J.M., Jacoby, L.L. (1993). Automatic versus intentional uses of memory: Aging, attention, and control. *Psychology and Aging, 8*, 283–293.

Ji, L., Nisbett, R.E., Zhang, Z. (2002). *Culture, Language and Categorization*: Queens University.

Joseph, J.A., Shukitt-Hale, B., Denisova, N.A., Bielinski, D., Martin, A., McEwen, J.J., Bickford, P.C. (1999). Reversals of age-related declines in neuronal signal transduction, cognitive, and motor behavioral deficits with blueberry, spinach, or strawberry dietary supplementation. *Journal of Neuroscience, 19*, 8114–8121.

Kausler, D.H. (1991). *Experimental Psychology, Cognition and Human Aging.* New York, NY: Springer-Verlag.

Kemper, T.L. (1994). Neuroanatomical and neuropathological changes during aging and in dementia. In M.L. Albert, E.J.E. Knoepfel (eds), *Clinical Neurology of Aging* (2nd ed., pp. 3–67). New York, NY: Oxford University Press.

Kramer, A.F., Hahn., S., Cohen, N.J., Banich, M.T., McAuley, E., Harrison, C.R., Chason, J., Vakil, E., Bardell, L., Boileau, R.A., Colcombe, A. (1999). Ageing, fitness and neurocognitive function. *Nature,* **400**, 418–419.

Li, S., Lindenberger, U., Frensch, P.A. (2000). Unifying cognitive aging: From neuromodulation to representation to cognition. *Neurocomputing: An International Journal, 32–33,* 879–890.

Light, L.L., La Voie, D. (1993). Direct and indirect measures of memory in old age. In P. Graf (ed.), *Implicit Memory: New Directions in Cognition, Development, and Neuropsychology* (pp. 207–230). Hillsdale, NJ: Lawrence Erlbaum Associates, Inc.

Lindenberger, U., Baltes P.B. (1994). Sensory functioning and intelligence in old age: A strong connection. *Psychology and Aging,* **9**, 339–355.

Lindenberger, U., Scherer, H., Baltes, P.B. (2001). The strong connection between sensory and cognitive performance in old age: Not due to sensory acuity reductions operating during cognitive assessment. *Psychology and Aging: Special Issue,* **16**, 196–205.

Liu, L., Park, D.C. (2002). *Implementation instructions improve blood glucose monitoring in older adults.* Paper presented at the Cognitive Aging Conference 2002, Atlanta, Georgia.

Logan, J.M., Sanders, A.L., Snyder, A.Z., Morris, J.C., Buckner, R.L. (2002). Under-recruitment and nonselective recruitment: Dissociable neural mechanisms associated with aging. *Neuron,* **33**, 827–840.

Lustig, C., Hasher, L., Tonev, S.T. (2001). Inhibitory control over the present and the past. *European Journal of Cognitive Psychology,* **13**, 107–122.

Madden, D.J., Turkington, T.G., Provenzale, J.M., Denny, L.L., Hawk, T.C., Gottlob, L.R., Coleman, R.E. (1999). Adult age differences in the functional neuroanatomy of verbal recognition memory. *Human Brain Mapping,* **7**, 115–135.

Martin, M., Park, D.C. (2002). *The Martin and Park Environmental Demands Questionnaire: Psychometric prospects of a brief instrument to measure environmental demands* (Unpublished Manuscript).

Masuda, T., Nisbett, R.E. (2001). *Change Blindness in Japanese and Americans:* University of Michigan.

May, C.P., Hasher, L., Kane, M.J. (1999). The role of interference in memory span. *Memory and Cognition,* **27**, 759–767.

McIntyre, J.S., Craik, F.I.M. (1987). Age differences in memory for item and source information. *Canadian Journal of Psychology: Special Issue: Aging and cognition,* **41**, 175–192.

Mitchell, K.J., Johnson, M.K., Raye, C.L., D'Esposito, M. (2000). fMRI evidence of age-related hippocampal dysfunction in feature binding in working memory. *Cognitive Brain Research,* **10**, 197–206.

Morrell, R.W., Park, D.C., Kidder, D.P., Martin, M. (1997). Adherence to antihypertensive medications across the life span. *Gerontologist,* **37**, 609–619.

Morris, M.W., Peng, K. (1994). Culture and cause: American and Chinese attributions for social and physical events. *Journal of Personality and Social Psychology,* **67**, 949–971.

Nielson, K.A., Langenecker, S.A., Garavan, H.P. (In press). Differences in the functional neuroanatomy of inhibitory control across the adult lifespan. *Psychology and Aging.*

Nisbett, R.E. (2002). *The Circle and the Line: The Geography of Thought:* The Free Press.

Owen, A.M. (1997). The functional organization of working memory processes within human lateral frontal cortex: The contribution of functional neuroimaging. *European Journal of Neuroscience,* **9**, 1329–1339.

Owen, A.M., Sterns, C.E., Look, R.B., Tracey, I., Rosen, B. (1998). Functional organization of spatial and nonspatial working memory processing within the human lateral frontal cortex. *Proceedings of the National Academy of Sciences USA*, **95**, 7721–7726.

Park, D.C., Smith, A.D., Morrell, R.W., Puglisi, J.T., Dudley, W.N. (1990). Effects of contextual integration on recall of pictures in older adults. *Journal of Gerontology: Psychological Sciences*, **45**, 52–58.

Park, D.C., Jones, T.R. (1996). Medication adherence and aging. In A.D. Fisk, W.A. Rogers, (eds), *Handbook of Human Factors and the Older Adult*. San Diego, CA: Academic Press.

Park, D.C., Kidder, D. (1996). Prospective memory and medication adherence. In M. Brandimonte, G. Einstein, M. McDaniel, (eds), *Prospective Memory: Theory and Applications* (pp. 369–390). Mahwah, NJ: Lawrence Erlbaum Associates.

Park, D.C., Mayhorn, C.B. (1996). Remembering to take medications: The importance of nonmemory variables. In D. Hermann, M. Johnson, C. McEvoy, C. Hertzog, P. Hertel, (eds), *Research on Practical Aspects of Memory* (Vol. 2, pp. 95–110). Mahwah, NJ: Lawrence Erlbaum Associates.

Park, D.C. (1999). Aging and the controlled and automatic processing of medical information and medical intentions, *Processing of Medical Information in Aging Patients: Cognitive and Human Factors Perspectives* (pp. 3–22). Mahwah, NJ: Lawrence Erlbaum Associates, Inc.

Park, D.C., Hertzog, C., Leventhal, H., Morrell, R.W., Leventhal, E., Birchmore, D., Martin, M., Bennett, J. (1999). Medication adherence in rheumatoid arthritis patients: Older is wiser. *Journal of American Geriatrics Society*, **47**, 172–183.

Park, D.C., Nisbett, R., Hedden, T. (1999). Aging, culture, and cognition. *Journal of Gerontology: Psychological Sciences*, **54B**, 75–84.

Park, D.C., Polk, T., Mikels, J., Taylor, S.F., Marshuetz, C. (2001). Cerebral aging: Integration of brain and behavioral models of cognitive function. *Dialogues in Clinical Neuroscience*, **3**, 151–165

Park, D.C., Glass, J., Minear, M, and Crofford, L. (2001). Cognitive function in fibromyalgia patients. *Arthritis and Rheumatism*, **44**, 2125–2133.

Park, D.C., Hedden, T., Jing, Q., Jiao, S., Lautenschlager, G., Nisbett, R. (2002). *The aging mind across cultures*. Unpublished manuscript.

Park, D.C., Lautenschlager, G., Hedden, T., Davidson, N., Smith, A.D., Smith, P. (2002). Models of visuospatial and verbal memory across the adult life span. *Psychology and Aging*, **17**, 299–320.

Park, D.C., Morrell, R.W., Frieske, D., Kincaid, D. (1992). Medication adherence behaviors in older adults: Effects of external cognitive supports. *Psychology and Aging*, **7**, 252–256.

Park, D.C., Puglisi, J.T., Smith, A.D. (1986). Memory for pictures: Does an age-related decline exist? *Psychology and Aging*, **1**, 11–17.

Park, D.C., Shaw, R.J. (1992). Effect of environmental support on implicit and explicit memory in younger and older adults. *Psychology and Aging*, **7**, 632–642.

Park, D.C., Smith, A.D., Lautenschlager, G., Earles, J.L., Frieske, D. Zwahr, M., Gaines, C.L. (1996). Mediators of long-term memory performance across the life span. *Psychology and Aging*, **11**, 621–637.

Peng, K., Nisbett, R.E. (1999). Culture, dialectics, and reasoning about contradiction. *American Psychologist*, **54**, 741–754.

Raz, N. (2000). Aging of the brain and its impact on cognitive performance: Integration of structural and functional findings. In F.I.M. Craik, T.A. Salthouse, (eds), *The Handbook of Aging and Cognition* (2nd. ed.). Mahwah, NJ, US: Lawrence Erlbaum Associates.

Reuter-Lorenz, P., Jonides, J., Smith, E.E., Hartley, A., Miller, A., Marshuetz, C., Koeppe, R. (2000). Age differences in the frontal laterlization of verbal and spatial working memory revealed by PET. *Journal of Cognitive Neuroscience, 12,* 174–187.

Reuter-Lorenz, P., Jonides, J., Smith, E.E., Hartley, A., Koeppe, R. (2001). Neurocognitive ageing of storage and executive processes. *European Journal of Cognitive Psychology. Special Issue, 13,* 257–278.

Ross, M.H., Yurgelun-Todd, D.A., Renshaw, P.F. (1997). Age-related reduction in functional MRI response to photic stimulation. *Neurology, 48,* 173–176.

Rympa, B., D'Esposito, M. (2000). Isolating the neural mechanisms of age-related changes in human working memory. *Nature Neuroscience, 3,* 509–151.

Salthouse, T.A., Babcock, R.L. (1991). Decomposing adult age differences in working memory. *Development Psychology, 27,* 763–776.

Salthouse, T.A. (1996). The processing-speed theory of adult age differences in cognition. *Psychological Review, 103,* 403–428.

Seeman, P., Bzowej, N.H., Guan, H.C., *et al.* (1987). Human brain dopamine receptors in children and aging adults. *Synapse, 1,* 399–404.

Shah, P., Miyake, A. (1996). The separability of working memory resources for spatial thinking and language processing: An individual differences approach. *Journal of Experimental Psychology General, 125,* 4–27.

Smith, A.D., Park, D.C., Earles, J.L.K., Shaw, R.J., Whiting, W.L. (1998). Age differences in context integration in memory. *Psychology and Aging, 13,* 21–28.

Smith, E.E., Jonides, J. (1999). Storage and executive processes in the frontal lobes. *Science, 283,* 1657–1661.

Smith, E.E., Geva, A., Jonides, J., Miller, A., Reuter-Lorenz, P.A., Koeppe, R.A. (2001). The neural basis of task-switching in working memory: Effects of performance and aging. *Proceedings of the National Academy of Science USA, 98,* 2095–2100.

Volkow, N.D., Wang, G.J., Fowler, J.S., Logan, J. (1996). Measuring age-related changes in dopamine D2 receptors with 11C-raclopride and 18F-N-methylspiroperidol. *Psychiatry Research, 67,* 11–16.

Volkow, N.D., Gur, R.C., Wang, G., Fowler, J.S., Moberg, P.J., Ding, Y., Hitzemann, R., Smith G., Logan, J. (1998). Association between decline in brain dopamine activity with age and cognitive and motor impairment in healthy individuals. *American Journal of Psychiatry, 155*(3), 344–349.

Wolfe, F., Smythe, H.A., Yunus, M.B., Bennett, R.M., Bombardier, C., Goldenberg, D.L., *et al.* (1990). The American College of Rheumatology 1990 criteria for the classification of fibromyalgia: report of the Multicenter Criteria Committee. *Arthritis and Rheumatology, 33,* 160–172.

Chapter 3

Does longitudinal evidence confirm theories of cognitive aging derived from cross-sectional data?

The sample case of processing resource accounts of episodic memory

Christopher Hertzog

The purpose of this chapter is to provide a brief summary of a line of research from the Victoria Longitudinal Study (VLS). From its inception, the VLS was designed to provide insight into a central question in research on aging and cognition. How should we think about changes in episodic memory in adulthood? Our perspective, and the empirical work it generates, is based on several major premises (see Hultsch, Hertzog, Dixon et al., 1998).

One set of premises involves the nature of memory development. First, we assume that there are both normative and non-normative influences on memory development in later life (Baltes, Staudinger, and Lindenberger, 2000). By normative influences, we refer to aspects of primary aging processes common to all individuals. Non-normative influences include a range of influences on memory that may be correlated with age (e.g., chronic diseases), but are not universally associated with aging. Second, we assume that there are individual differences in rates of normative episodic memory changes. Third, we adopt a contextual perspective, which suggests in part that age changes are manifested in contexts that include unique environmental influences, personal history and relevant experience, and personal construal of the task situation. Hence, performance on memory tasks will have multiple causes, with primary aging being only one of the influences on an older adult's task performance.

Another set of premises concerns how one should conceptualize and measure episodic memory. First, our work is predicated on the assumption that memory task performance is governed not just by the type of memory system required (episodic, semantic), but also by the confluence of cognitive processes utilized by the individual to encode and retrieve information. Some of these processes are fundamental and necessary (e.g., allocation of attention to the materials presented in the task), whereas others influence task performance but are optional and under the control of the participant (e.g., utilization of encoding strategies). Hence, individuals will differ in principle in the ways they approach a task, and these differences can be influenced by aging (e.g., via attempts to compensate for age-related decline in relevant cognitive processes).

Second, we adopt a processing-resource view of memory performance (Craik and Byrd, 1982), which states that individuals will vary in the effectiveness and efficiency of basic cognitive processes brought to bear in service of complex task performance (like episodic memory tasks). Salthouse (1991, 1996b) has articulated an especially influential version of processing resource approaches that emphasizes working memory, processing speed, and attention as basic primitives of the cognitive system, and our approach is broadly consistent with his perspective. However, we view resources in a more generic sense (see Zacks, Hasher, and Li, 2000), and do not limit, in principle, the set of relevant constructs to the three major classes articulated by Salthouse (1991). In particular, we embrace the possibility that the influence of such resource variables is indirect, being mediated through processes like encoding and retrieval strategies (Verhaeghen and Marcoen, 1994).

Third, we assume that memory involves the dynamic interplay of processing new information in the context of prior knowledge. Such relations are most obviously manifested in retention of information in narrative texts (Hultsch and Dixon, 1984; Radvansky, Zacks, and Hasher, 1996) or task-contents that rely heavily on expertise (Ericsson and Charness, 1994; Masunaga and Horn, 2001), but may be involved in simple list-learning tasks as well (Delaney, 1978; Kyllonen, Tirre, and Christal, 1991). Knowledge held in semantic memory guides encoding and retrieval processes and provides a basis for integrating new information into existing knowledge structures. One important implication of our view is that individual differences in knowledge and abilities should predict episodic memory performance, and that age-related changes in accessibility and efficiency of queried knowledge structures may be associated with age-related changes in memory (Zacks, Hasher, and Li, 2000).

A final set of relevant premises concerns measurement issues for study aging and episodic memory change. First, our approach assumes that psychological constructs, such as human cognitive abilities, are hypothetical entities, and that it is not possible in principle to measure a target ability construct without designing tasks that inevitably require multiple cognitive mechanisms. Some of the cognitive processes required for task performance are the targets of task design, some are by-products of requiring human judgement and discrimination. Thus, task design decisions inevitably and implicitly incorporate both targeted and irrelevant processes that determine individual differences in task performance (Hertzog, 1989). For example, decisions about how to measure working memory require theoretical assumptions about the interplay of storage and concurrent processing (Baddeley, 1986; Salthouse, 1990). However, contemporary dual-task measures of working memory (e.g., Salthouse and Babcock's (1991) Computation Span task) necessitate specific decisions about how to structure the dual-task requirements, pacing of stimuli, and selection of stimuli that may increase opportunities for unwanted influences such as limited speed of processing or vulnerability to proactive interference (May, Hasher, and Kane, 1999). These types of working memory measures may share relatively little variance in common with other working memory measures (Salthouse, 1991). Task selection can also result in a failure to measure critical target aspects of a construct. For example, some individuals choose to measure working memory with the Digit Span Backward task from the Wechsler Adult Intelligence Scale, despite research showing that it is most strongly associated with measures of short-term memory, and apparently de-emphasizes executive control processes thought to be critical to the construct of working memory (Engle, Tuholski, Laughlin *et al.*, 1999; Rogers, Hertzog, and Fisk, 2000). Using backward span measures to assess working memory can influence the extent to which an empirical study finds evidence of a relationship of working memory to episodic memory.

It is critical for progress in this field that one understands the constituent processes demanded by a task, and that one assesses whether measurement decisions have unintended consequences that skew research outcomes and theoretical inferences about those outcomes. Thus, the VLS utilizes a multivariate approach, in which one collects multiple measures of hypothetical constructs in an attempt to avoid bias due to task construction (Cook and Campbell, 1979; Nesselroade, 1977; Salthouse, 2000). This approach also utilizes statistical methods, principally structural equation modeling, that embody the multivariate approach as a set of models that can be used to identify sources of measurement specificity and limits on generalization due to selection of measures (Little, Lindenberger, and Nesselroade, 1999). We also assume that an analysis of processing requirements of tasks, including both ability tests and experimental tasks, is ultimately required before a full understanding of relationships between different measures are possible.

A second premise about measurement concerns the value of longitudinal data. We assume that measurement of age-related influences on episodic memory is best measured by assessing changes in predictor variables and episodic memory. Possible predictors of change will vary in level of causal influence, from the biological, for example changes in medial-temporal structures in the brain (Raz, 2000; this volume), to the cognitive (processing resources such as working memory) to the contextual – life style, experiential (Hultsch, Hertzog, Small *et al.*, 1999; Schooler, Mulatu, and Oates, 1999). We presume that age-related change in episodic memory is likely to have only a limited influence on individual differences in episodic memory performance, given a variety of influences on episodic memory that may not be implicated in developmental change. Hence, we gain a better understanding of age-related changes when we can show that variables predict individual differences in rates of episodic memory change in later life (see Hertzog, 1996; Hertzog and Dixon, 1996; Hultsch, Hertzog, Dixon *et al.*, 1998).

As such, the approach in the VLS is designed to integrate two different metatheoretical approaches to the study of aging and cognition (Dixon and Hertzog, 1996). Experimental cognitive psychologists interested in aging emphasize normative effects on psychological mechanisms relevant to memory, for example, age-related changes in encoding, storage, and retrieval mechanisms. Psychologists trained in a lifespan perspective and psychometric approaches emphasize individual differences in the course of adult development and the heterogeneity of phenotypic development and its underlying causes. The VLS is designed to combine both approaches. From experimental cognitive psychology we adopt theoretical approaches that delineate appropriate constructs (cognitive processes and mechanisms) that are affected by aging, as well as methods of measuring these constructs. From differential developmental psychology we adopt sampling designs, measurement approaches, and statistical methods that allow for and estimate individual differences in developmental trends, processes, and outcomes.

Processing resource accounts of aging and episodic memory

Studies of cognitive aging are often limited to descriptions of differences between older and younger adults in cognitive mechanisms as defined by experimental tasks (Hertzog, 1996). Tests of processing resource accounts of age differences represents an important exception in which cognitive mechanisms have been studied using methods from both experimental and differential psychology. The processing resource perspective stipulates that age changes in basic resources such as processing speed, working memory, and attention, account for age changes in episodic memory. In cross-sectional studies, developmental change is indirectly measured in terms of cross-sectional age differences in the constructs of interest. Hence, Salthouse (1996b, 2000) and others have argued that tests of resource accounts of cognitive aging require a partition of age-related variance in task performance. More specifically, the central idea is that age differences in complex task performance, like episodic memory tasks, will covary with age differences in resource variables, such as speed of processing. Hence, the hypothesis of reduced resources due to aging is evaluated by how much of the age-related variance in episodic memory is accounted for by basic mechanisms. This hypothesis has been routinely tested by means of multiple regression and structural regression models. Thus, this approach requires analysis of individual differences in cognition in the context of accounting for age-related variance in cognitive task performance.

Verhaeghen and Salthouse (1997) published a set of structural equation models that used data from multiple studies, many from Salthouse's laboratory (Salthouse, 1996a). Figure 3.1 shows a model from Verhaeghen and Salthouse (1997) that illustrates the processing resource account. Although these kinds of models have been increasingly used in gerontological research, a brief interpretation of the model is in order. The variables of interest (age, processing speed, etc.) are modeled as influencing one another through a series of nested regression equations. Figure 3.1 depicts the estimated regression coefficients as arrows from one variable to another. In structural modeling terminology, these coefficients are treated as *direct effects*. The numbers in

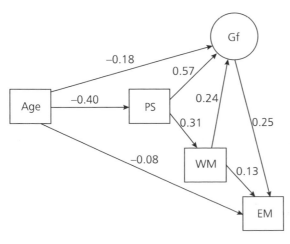

Fig. 3.1 Adapted from Verhaeghen and Salthouse (1997) processing resource model for adults over the age of 50. Abbreviations: PS: Perceptual speed; WM: Working memory; Gf: Fluid intelligence: EM: Episodic memory.

the diagram correspond to standardized regression coefficients, interpreted in the usual manner (SD unit changes in the predicted variable, given a 1 SD unit change in the predictor variable). If an arrow does not connect two variables, it is assumed that there is no effect of the corresponding variables on each other (regression coefficients of 0).

In Figure 3.1, chronological age has a strong direct effect on perceptual processing speed (-0.40), which in turn is posited to influence working memory and fluid intelligence. Chains of connections define *indirect effects*, in which the influence of one variable on another is mediated by an intervening variable. In Figure 3.1, perceptual speed mediates the effect of age on working memory (there is no direct effect of age on working memory); it also mediates some of the age effect on fluid intelligence. Working memory and fluid intelligence, in turn, influence episodic memory, and hence carry some of the effect of age to episodic memory as an indirect effect. Figure 3.1 does not directly depict indirect effects, although they are computable. It also does not directly depict the coefficient of determination (squared multiple correlation, analogous to R^2 in OLS regression), indicating how much variance in a variable is determined by the set of direct effects upon it. On occasion, I shall mention these statistics when they aid in interpretation of the structural regression models described in this chapter.[1]

A central finding of relevance for processing resource theory, as represented in the Verhaeghen and Salthouse (1997) model, is that there is relatively little age-related variance in working memory, fluid intelligence, and episodic memory that is statistically independent of age differences in perceptual speed. Note, specifically, that the direct effect of age on episodic memory in Figure 3.1 is only -0.08. Such findings have been frequently reported (Bors and Forrin, 1995; Bryan and Luszcz, 1996; Hertzog, 1989; Hultsch, Hertzog, and Dixon, 1990; Lindenberger, Mayr, and Kliegl, 1993; Park *et al.*, 1996, 2002; Salthouse, 1994, 1996a). This phenomenon has led to the hypothesis that age-related changes in the speed of information processing are a fundamental determinant of age changes in episodic memory (Salthouse, 1996b). There are other cross-sectional studies of this hypothesis in the literature that do not fully agree on the potency of processing speed as an explanatory mechanism for age differences in episodic memory (Graf and Uttl, 1995; Light, 1996; Zacks, Hasher, and Li, 2000). Nevertheless, virtually

---

[1] Unfortunately, space limitations preclude an extensive treatment of aspects of interpreting structural equation models. Readers with little familiarity with these techniques may want to consult additional reference materials (Bollen, 1979; Byrne, 1998; Hayduk, 1987).

all published studies show a reduction in age-related variance in episodic memory by measures of processing speed and working memory.[2]

To date, there has been little investigation of the extent to which attentional resources may serve as an explanation of age differences in episodic memory. However, given experimental evidence that deficits in attentional inhibition affect memory, as well as evidence that divided attention at encoding substantially affects learning of word lists (Anderson, Craik, and Naveh-Benjamin, 1998), one might expect that statistical control for attentional resources would account for much of the age-related variance in episodic memory as well. It may also be the case that age differences in sensory and perceptual function can also account for substantial proportions of age-related variance (Anstey, Luszcz, and Sanchez, 2001; Baltes and Lindenberger, 1997; Schneider and Pichora-Fuller, 2000). Nevertheless, I shall focus on the processing speed and working memory resource constructs for the remainder of this chapter, only because they are the resources most widely assessed in the literature, and the ones that are measured in the VLS.

As noted earlier, it may be the case that measurement decisions could have an impact on the extent to which statistical control for resource variables will reduce age-related variance in episodic memory. The VLS provides evidence that this is indeed the case. The VLS began in 1986 with a cross-sectional sample of 100 students and 484 adults, ages 55–85. I shall refer to this sample as Sample 1. The adult sample was then retested every three years to form a longitudinal panel. Originally, the VLS measurement battery included two measures of working memory – the Sentence Construction task and the N-Back task (see Hultsch, Hertzog, Dixon *et al.*, 1990, 1998). At the second testing in 1989, Salthouse's Computation Span and Listening Span measures were added to the battery.

The sentence construction task is similar to Daneman and Carpenter's (1980) Reading Span task, with an important difference. On each trial, individuals listen to multiple sentences in series and respond to comprehension questions after each sentence. They do so while attempting to hold the last word of each sentence in working memory. These words, in turn, form

---

[2] One important principle to keep in mind is that structural models estimate parameters under a set of assumptions about causal precedence. Rarely do the outcomes of models (parameter estimates, goodness-of-fit statistics) constitute a strong test of the causal assumptions reflected in the model. In particular, good fits of processing resource models to data do not confirm the validity of the assumptions about resources that generated the model (in this case, mediational hypotheses generated by processing resource theory). The models summarized in this review generally have good fit, but I shall not evaluate model fit as part of this chapter.

a sentence, and at the end of the series of sentences individuals are asked to report the sentence implied by the target words. The N-Back task measures running memory span; individuals listen to a series of digits and then respond to probes asking that they report the last digit, the preceding digit, the digit before that, etc. Given that these two measures did not correlate highly, our earlier work focused on the sentence comprehension task. However, as noted and critiqued by Salthouse (1991), this task allows individuals to use semantic processes to assist in maintenance of the target words through construction of the target sentence. As such it differs somewhat from the Salthouse Listening Span task, or Engle, Cantor, and Carullo's (1992) Operation Span task, in that those tasks do not provide an integrative context for target elements across trials in the span task.

One important finding from the VLS is that cross-sectional results regarding statistical control for speed and working memory differ according to which types of working memory measures are employed. Hultsch, Hertzog, Dixon *et al.* (1998) reported cross-sectional models using either sentence construction or the two Salthouse working memory measures, listening span and computation span, to index working memory. This analysis was only possible with the 308 adults with complete data that were measured in 1989, when all three working memory measures were administered.

Figure 3.2 shows a processing resource model using sentence construction as the measure of working memory. Most of the variables in Figure 3.2 are graphed as circles, representing latent rather than observed variables (age and education were treated as perfectly measured variables, and are hence depicted as squares). The circles reflect the fact that multiple indicators were available for each construct (see Hultsch, Hertzog, Dixon *et al.*, 1998, for details on the measurement model that defined these latent variables).[3] Age had a strong effect on Semantic speed, as measured by two complex semantic decision RT tasks (hence the positive regression coefficient; age was associated with longer response times). It also had a direct effect on working memory (sentence construction). Two latent variables represented the critical criterion – verbal episodic memory. The text recall latent variable was defined by gist recall on two narrative texts; the word recall latent variable was defined by the number of words recalled from categorized lists of nouns from taxonomic categories (e.g., fruits, furniture). Note that the direct effects of Semantic speed on text recall and word recall, were relatively small or nonexistent. Conversely, the direct effects of working memory

---

[3] When working memory was measured by the single indicator of sentence construction, Hultsch, Hertzog, Dixon *et al.* (1998) fixed residual error variances to correct for unreliability or random measurement error (Hayduk, 1987).

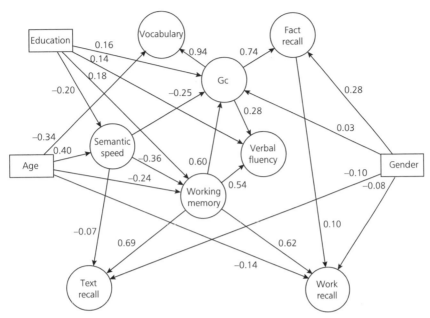

Fig. 3.2 VLS Model for Sample 1, Wave 2 data (Hultsch, Hertzog, Dixon *et al.*, 1998, Figure 8.3). Gc: Crystallized intelligence. Permission sought.

on the two recall factors were substantial (>0.6). Approximately 50 per cent of the variance in the two recall factors was determined by the regression equations, with working memory accounting for the bulk of the prediction. As in work by Salthouse and others, most of the effects of age on episodic memory was mediated by resources, but in this case the working memory variable was by far the most important resource predictor. Indeed, it was surprising that there were no effects of crystallized intelligence (Gc) on text recall independent of working memory (see Hultsch, Hertzog, Dixon *et al.*, 1998, for further discussion).

Figure 3.3 shows the corresponding model (from the same sample data) that used the two Salthouse measures to define a working memory latent variable. Although, similar, there are some important differences. The biggest difference is the dramatic reduction in the magnitude of prediction of recall by the working memory variable. On the other hand, the relationship of Semantic speed to working memory remained strong, and even increased slightly from the model with sentence construction. In the case of text recall, the direct effect of working memory dropped to 0.22, and direct effects from age and crystallized intelligence to text recall emerged in the new model. For word recall, the effects of age and fact recall increased somewhat. Finally, it was necessary to model a correlated residual component

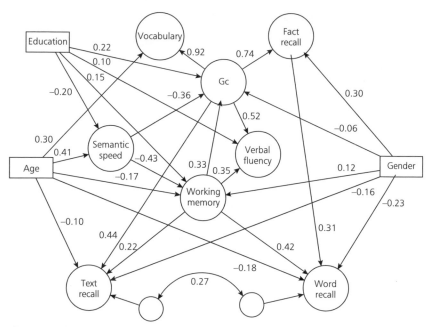

Fig. 3.3 VLS Model for Sample 1, Wave 2 data, using Listening span and Computation span to measure Working memory (Hultsch, Hertzog, Dixon *et al.*, 1998, Figure 8.5, permission sought.) Gc: Crystallized intelligence.

between the two recall measures, suggesting shared variance in episodic memory tasks not accounted for by the predictor variables. No such path was needed when sentence construction was used to measure working memory.

These differences in the two models are not a function of the fact that sentence construction lacks convergent validity with the Salthouse working memory measures. The sentence construction task correlated better than 0.5 with both Salthouse tasks, and a confirmatory factor model showed that sentence construction, listening span, and computation span all had significant loadings (0.6 or greater) on a working memory factor. However, the two Salthouse tasks correlated more highly with each other than with sentence construction. The difference in modeling outcomes was also not determined by differences in age-related patterns for the two types of working memory tasks. Figure 3.4 shows age curves for the working memory measures derived from an analysis that controls on possible cohort differences by estimating age, cohort, and time period parameters using all available data from the six-year longitudinal sequence from Sample 1 of the VLS (see Hultsch, Hertzog, Dixon *et al.*, 1998, for further details). Note that a composite variable from the

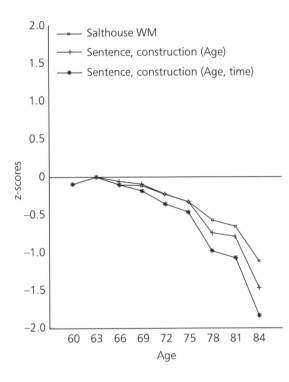

Fig. 3.4 Longitudinal age gradients from the VLS for Sentence construction and a composite measure of the Salthouse working memory tasks.
Note: Age 63 fixed to zero. Permission sought.

Salthouse measures and the sentence construction task showed similar (curvilinear) patterns of mean age-related changes beyond age 55.

These findings indicate a substantial impact of how one chooses to measure working memory on outcomes from the processing resource model. I shall return to this point later. However, the discrepancy between these findings and other studies may not merely be a function of the nature of the working memory measures. Another major difference between the VLS and other cross-sectional studies is in the use of complex semantic RT tasks to measure processing speed. Age-related changes in semantic processing speed may be smaller than nonsemantic processes (Hale and Myerson, 1996) and may be more determined by speed of access to semantic memory (Hunt, 1978) that may alter patterns of shared covariance among speed, working memory, and the verbal episodic memory measures employed in this study (see Salthouse, 1991). The pattern of results is not necessarily consistent with this view. The Semantic speed measures in the VLS also show robust age-related changes (Hultsch, Hertzog, Dixon *et al.*, 1998), as can be seen in the strong effect of chronological age on Semantic speed in Figures 3.2 and 3.3. Moreover, relations of Semantic speed to working memory increased when the Salthouse

measures were used (Figure 3.3). Ultimately the issue must be decided by measuring multiple aspects of processing speed, including the types of speed measures
favored by Salthouse (1996b). We did so in Sample 2 of the VLS (see below).

Longitudinal models of resource variables and episodic memory

The cross-sectional models of processing resources and memory performance
just described capture individual differences in age-related cognitive change
only in a *weak* sense. One's interpretive focus is, in effect, on partialled
chronological age curves for memory performance, controlling for age differences in resources (see Lindenberger and Pötter, 1998). Hence individual
differences in resource variables, in relationship to memory, are actually used
to infer whether average (possibly normative) age changes in memory (as in
Figure 3.4) are flattened out by statistical control for resources (Horn and
Hofer, 1992). Individual differences in rates of change are only one component contributing to cross-sectional variance on a given task (Hertzog, 1985;
Hertzog, Hultsch, Dixon *et al.*, 2002; Hofer and Sliwinski, 2001). Moreover,
individual differences in change, expressed as deviations around the average
age curve, cannot be analyzed. To the contrary, age-related change can only be
accounted for to the extent that they are captured by the aggregate regression
of cognitive tasks on chronological age (see Hertzog, Hultsch, Dixon *et al.*,
2002). The proportion of variance determined by average intraindividual
change and by individual differences in age-related change could well be over-
shadowed by stable correlations among cognitive variables (that could have
been observed at, say, age 20). Cross-sectional variation in a cognitive variable
will probably be least influenced by an individual's differential rate of change.
Finally, the cross-sectional models typically do not allow for age-related
changes in the relationships among variables (resource/episodic memory relations). The effects of aging may induce qualitative shifts in how cognitive tasks
are performed (e.g., compensation for resource decline) (Bäckman and
Dixon, 1992) that may cause variation in relationships between resource variables and episodic memory at different points in the adult lifespan. Cross-sectional studies rarely check for such shifts by stratifying into age subgroups
(but see Verhaeghen and Salthouse, 1997). For all these reasons, validation of
cross-sectional models through the use of parallel longitudinal models is
needed to assess the viability of processing resource theories.

To date, longitudinal data have not strongly supported the argument that
individual differences in speed of processing are an important cause of age
changes in episodic memory (Hultsch, Hertzog, Dixon *et al.*, 1998; Sliwinski

and Buschke, 1999), contrary to the processing speed theory (Salthouse, 1996b). The study by Sliwinski and Buschke (1999) used mixed-model approaches to determine whether covarying on change in speed of processing eliminated or reduced individual differences in episodic memory change. They used a copying speed test and the Digit Symbol Substitution test as measures of processing speed. Longitudinal changes in speed significantly predicted change in each of the other cognitive measures in their study, including tests from the Wechsler Memory Scale, Revised. However, significant longitudinal changes remained in the memory measures after controlling for changes in speed of processing. Whereas about 75 per cent of the cross-sectional age differences in a composite memory measure was mediated by processing speed, only about 10 per cent of the longitudinal change variance was mediated by changes in processing speed.

Models for the VLS data reported by Hultsch, Hertzog, Dixon *et al.* (1998) were even more striking in this regard, because they use latent variable models to examine relationships among change, correcting for measurement error. In this case latent variables of six-year change were constructed by implicit computation of a six-year latent difference score between Time 1 and Time 3 of the VLS (see McArdle and Nesselroade, 1994). This latent change model allowed initial level (Time 1) variables to intercorrelate freely; interest centered exclusively on modeling how change in one latent variable (in particular, a resource variable like Semantic speed or working memory) predicted change in other latent variables (in particular, text recall and word recall).

Figure 3.5 shows a processing resource model for the VLS Sample 1 data (see Hultsch, Hertzog, Dixon *et al.*, 1998 for additional discussion). Only the

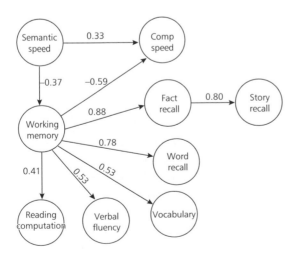

Fig. 3.5 Longitudinal processing resource model for VLS, Sample 1 (Hultsch, Hertzog, Dixon *et al.*, 1998; Figure 10.1). Permission sought.

Abbreviation:
Comp speed:
    Computational speed

relationships among the latent change variables are shown. The sentence construction task was used as the single measure of working memory, because it was available at the inception of the study (Time 1), whereas the Salthouse measures were not. As can be seen from this model, the critical determinant of longitudinal changes in episodic memory was longitudinal changes in working memory, as measured by sentence construction. Effects of change in Semantic speed on change in the memory variables were completely mediated by working memory. In this sense, the longitudinal model agreed with the cross-sectional model using sentence construction, but the effect was even more dramatic. It is also interesting to note that changes in the working memory latent variable were strongly associated with changes in world knowledge (fact recall). This latent variable was defined by two versions of a task requiring answers to world knowledge questions created by Nelson and Narens (1980). A surprising outcome from the longitudinal sample is that world knowledge performance declines in old age, and that individual differences in the amount of that decline covary strongly with declines in working memory and episodic memory. Those individuals who are experiencing decline in working memory and episodic memory are also experiencing declines in access to facts in semantic memory. Note that working memory had a 0.88 direct effect on fact recall that is modeled as mediating the effects of working memory on text recall. This outcome suggests that changes in semantic memory and episodic memory covary strongly in later adulthood, a finding that would not have been expected from standard theories of memory or human abilities, such as the fluid/crystallized theory of intelligence (Cattell, 1971; Horn, 1985). Those theories (see also Baltes, Standinger, and Lindenberger 2000) typically represent fluid intelligence and memory as declining, whereas crystallized intelligence does not. It is consistent with more recent trends in theorizing about age changes in working memory and episodic memory that emphasize susceptibility to interference and degraded access of retrieval processes to information held in memory (Light, 1996; Zacks, Hasher, and Li 2000).

Processing resource models from Sample 2 of the VLS

Although the VLS longitudinal data are not necessarily consistent with cross-sectional analyses (Verhaeghen and Salthouse, 1997), there can be multiple explanations for any discrepancies. The differences may not merely be due to better estimation of individual differences in developmental change. Like cross-sectional designs, longitudinal studies have their own set of methodological confounds, including practice effects, selective survival, and selection by time interactions (Schaie, 1977). Furthermore, the studies just reviewed did not use measures of processing speed and working memory favored by Salthouse (1991). In the case of the VLS, change in perceptual speed and working memory could only be assessed with complex semantic RT tasks and the Sentence Construction task, respectively.

Cross-sectional models

The second sample of the VLS began with an expanded measurement battery that included several psychometric tests measuring perceptual speed, the Salthouse computation span and listening span working memory tasks, and psychometric tests of inductive reasoning – along with the same measures of verbal episodic memory (word and text recall). Hertzog, Hultsch, Dixon *et al.* (2002) reported an analysis of the cross-sectional data of the 530 adults, ages 55–85, from Sample 2. Their structural equation models based on processing resource approaches were broadly consistent with results from Verhaeghen and Salthouse (1997).

Figure 3.6 shows one of the models (see Hertzog, Hultsch, Dixon *et al.*, 2002, for a full report). In this model, only the two Salthouse measures were used to define a working memory latent variable. Chronological age had a strong relationship to perceptual speed, which then mediated most of the age differences in other constructs, including working memory. There was evidence of a direct effect of age on fluid intelligence (inductive reasoning), independent of working memory, but relatively little evidence of direct effects of age on episodic memory, controlling for the effects mediated through perceptual speed, working memory, and fluid intelligence.

The issue of selection of measures was manifested again, both for working memory and for the speed measures. Substituting sentence construction for the Salthouse measures had similar results to those already reported. Working

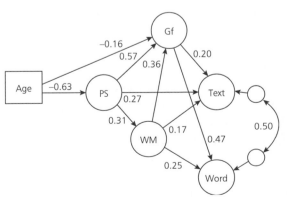

Fig. 3.6 Cross-sectional processing resource model for VLS, Sample 2, using Listening span and Computation span to measure Working memory (Hertzog, Hultsch, Dixon *et al.*, 2002, Figure 4). Abbreviations: PS: Perceptual speed; WM: Working memory; Gf: Fluid intelligence: EM: Episodic memory.

memory was the dominant predictor of episodic memory, above and beyond the perceptual speed factor. In addition, substituting an elementary choice RT task for the perceptual speed measures dramatically reduced the degree to which speed mediated age effects on working memory and fluid intelligence. The RT task had 2, 4, and 8 choice conditions, in which individuals pressed a button on the numeric keypad corresponding to a highlighted display analog shown on the computer screen. Such findings might corroborate Salthouse's (1996b) argument that tests of speed should be designed to be sufficiently complex to involve speed of cognitive processes rather than simple motor execution time or elementary perceptual matching. However, an alternative hypothesis is that psychometric tests of perceptual speed incorporate demands on working memory and attention that cause individual differences in test performance to be determined by factors other than the efficiency of cognitive processing per se. Piccinin and Rabbitt (1999) have suggested that coding tasks, like the Digit Symbol Substitution test, are inherently memory-demanding, and Lustig, Tonev, and Hasher (2000) reported data suggesting that the typical format of perceptual speed tests make them susceptible to failures to inhibit attention allocation to distracting elements. It seems likely that individual differences in tests designed to measure speed incorporate aspects of working memory and attention, so that partialling for speed may be slicing and dicing parts of baby to be thrown out with the bath water (see Hertzog and Bleckley, 2001).

Hertzog, Hultsch, Dixon *et al.* (2002) also noted that chronological age was more highly correlated with the perceptual speed factor (about 0.6) than with other cognitive factors in the VLS. This raises the possibility that the degree of mediation by perceptual speed could, in part, be an artifactual manifestation of its sensitivity to age effects (rather than due to its role as a mediating cognitive process). Indeed, an alternative model based on hierarchical factor logic (see Hertzog, Cooper, and Fisk, 1996; Rogers, Hertzog, and Fisk *et al.*, 2000; Salthouse and Czaja, 2000) fit the VLS measurement battery well without specifying a direct effect of speed on working memory or on episodic memory. Instead, fluid intelligence and semantic knowledge predicted episodic memory. Age had an independent relationship to a general speed factor, measured by RT tasks and perceptual speed tests, consistent with the robust age differences on such measures. Speed was also predicted by fluid intelligence, and there was little evidence of an independent relationship of speed to episodic memory, when effects from fluid intelligence and semantic knowledge to episodic memory were specified. This model leaves open the possibility that perceptual speed is found to be the covariate that most dramatically reduces chronological age effects on other variables because it is substantially correlated with fluid intelligence, and because it has the greatest correlation with chronological age (Roberts and Stankov, 1999). Salthouse and Czaja (2000) have also noted that a hierarchical model fits the data as well as the kind of mediated SEM shown in Figure 3.1, suggesting there are viable alternatives to the causal assumptions invoked by processing resource theories (Salthouse, 1996b).

Longitudinal models

We (Hertzog, Dixon, Hultsch *et al.*, 2003) recently completed a six-year longitudinal change model for data from Sample 2 of the VLS. These results confirm the potential impact of selection of measures on models assessing processing resource accounts of age changes in episodic memory. A latent change model was used to evaluate relationships of six-year changes in working memory and episodic memory. When sentence construction and Salthouse listening span were employed as measures of working memory, changes in working memory accounted for almost all of the change in episodic memory (consistent with Hultsch, Hertzog, Dixon *et al.*, 1998). However, when the Salthouse working memory tasks were used to define working memory, results differed.

Figure 3.7 shows the standardized structural regression model. In many respects, the model was consistent with previous models of cross-sectional

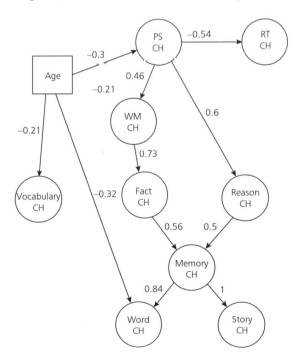

Fig. 3.7 Longitudinal processing resource model for VLS, Sample 2, using Listening span and Computation span to measure Working memory (from Hertzog *et al.*, 2003). Abbreviations: CH: Change; PS: Perceptual speed; WM: Working memory.

data. There were some important differences. Changes in story recall and word recall were so highly correlated we ended up modeling a higher-order episodic memory change factor to account for relationships of other factors to episodic memory change. Changes in perceptual speed predicted changes in both working memory and inductive reasoning (reason). Changes in fact recall and inductive reasoning were strong and roughly equivalent predictors of change in episodic memory. The latter effect was consistent with other cross-sectional models (compare Figure 3.1). However, the effect of fact recall change on episodic memory change was not. Note that this effect replicates, substantively, longitudinal results from Sample 1 of the VLS.

When the Salthouse working memory tasks are used to measure working memory, both speed and working memory predict memory change, but indirectly. The model represented changes in fact recall and inductive reasoning as mediating the effects of changes in working memory and perceptual speed on change in episodic memory. The standardized indirect effects of changes in perceptual speed and working memory on changes in episodic memory were 0.49 and 0.41, respectively.

An unexpected outcome was the weak relationship of change in working memory to change in induction. Some studies have suggested a strong relationship of working memory and fluid intelligence – Kyllonen and Christal (1990) once wondered whether fluid intelligence was little more than working memory (see also Engle, Tuholski, Laughlin *et al.*, 1999; Rogers, Hertzog, and Fisk, 2000). The longitudinal models shows that, to the contrary, working memory and fluid intelligence can be disassociated based upon divergent patterns of age-related changes after age 55.

Taken together, the models from the VLS using different measures of working memory confirm that selection of specific tasks can have surprisingly profound effects on parameter estimates in these kinds of structural equation models. In this sense, the multivariate measurement approach used in the VLS appears to be an important, perhaps even critical, feature of research designs addressing processing resource hypotheses. Given that cognition is a complex function of the interplay of multiple mechanisms, and that individual cognitive tests or tasks are inevitably a weighted mixture of multiple processing components, it is critical that we understand the variability in outcomes that can occur as a function of selecting some measures, and not others, to define our constructs. Standardization of tasks (Salthouse, Kausler, and Saults, 1988) can be important as a means of establishing comparisons between different studies. However, premature closure on a particular method for measuring a cognitive construct could promote an inference about relations between cognitive constructs that is specific to the mixture of processes in particular tasks rather than a general feature of construct relationships, per se.

Conclusions

The longitudinal and cross-sectional models described here have advanced our understanding of age-related changes in cognition. They can also serve as a basis for models using measured characteristics of individuals such as health status and life style to predict individual differences in cognitive change (see Hultsch, Hertzog, Small *et al.*, 1999). When used in concert with experimental studies that assist in our understanding of the cognitive processes that govern task performance, the kinds of methods described here can provide a powerful window into the nature of adult cognitive development. Indeed, we believe that optimal use of modeling approaches involves an integration of the types of models we report here with ongoing experimental studies that elucidate mechanisms and test alternative processing explanations of patterns observed in the longitudinal data.

The present series of studies have identified several important issues amenable to further experimental study. Two issues stand out. First, it appears that changes in accessibility of information in semantic memory is an important predictor of episodic memory change in late life. This inference is indirect, however, being based on the assumption that longitudinal declines in world knowledge measures reflect loss of access to information once held in semantic memory, and given evidence of increasing likelihood of tip-of-tongue states for older adults (Burke, MacKay, Worthley *et al.*, 1991; Cohen and Faulkner, 1986). The idea is that information once learned is retained but is possibly inaccessible. This claim is justified, given what is known about the nature of knowledge representation and maintenance (Bahrick, 2000; Cohen, 1993). Nevertheless, direct studies of temporary inaccessibility effects in semantic memory, in conjunction with tasks isolating retrieval failures in episodic tasks, could elucidate the phenomena and set the stage for correlational studies to determine whether declines in retrieval mechanisms required by both types of tasks explains the longitudinal change patterns (see Zacks, Hasher, and Li, 2000).

Second, the differences between the sentence construction task and the Salthouse working memory measures warrant further experimental investigation. It could be the case that sentence construction is a better measure of how semantic information is held in working memory in service of semantic elaboration during encoding. Although the requirement to form a sentence from the stored words can be viewed as a methodological limitation because of undue support based on verbal knowledge (Salthouse, 1991), it can also be viewed as a better analog of how working memory is used during normal text processing (for example), as in Kintsch's (1998) construction-integration model. One does not store random facts and maintain them in working memory during reading – to the contrary, one constructs rapid inferences about meaning and then integrates those inferences into a situation model. What is intriguing, then, is the possibility that this measure of working memory is more like the way in which working memory must be used during intentional encoding of verbal materials – even in list-learning tasks. New experiments are needed to address these rival accounts.

Author's note

Data reported in this paper are from the Victoria Longitudinal Study, a project currently funded by a grant (R01 AG08325) from the National Institute on Aging, one of the National Institutes of Health. Work summarized in this chapter involved collaboration with a number of members of the VLS research group, including especially Roger Dixon, David Hultsch, Stuart MacDonald and Brent Small.

References

Anstey, K. J., Luszcz, M. A., and Sanchez, L. (2001). A re-evaluation of the common factor theory of shared variance among age, sensory function, and cognitive function in older adults. *Journal of Gerontology: Psychological Sciences*, **56B**, P3–P11.

Anderson, N. D., Craik, F. I. M., and Naveh-Benjamin, M. (1998). The attentional demands of encoding and retrieval in younger and older adults: 1. Evidence from divided attention costs. *Psychology and Aging*, **13**, 405–423.

Bäckman, L., and Dixon, R. A. (1992). Psychological compensation: A theoretical framework. *Psychological Bulletin*, **112**, 259–283.

Baddeley, A. (1986). *Working Memory*. Oxford, England: Oxford University Press.

Bahrick, H. P. (2000). Long-term maintenance of knowledge. In E. Tulving and F. I. M. Craik (eds), *The Oxford Handbook of Memory* (pp. 347–362). Oxford, England: Oxford University Press.

Baltes, P. B., and Lindenberger, U. (1997). Emergence of a powerful connection between sensory and cognitive functions across the adult life span: A new window to the study of cognitive aging? *Psychology and Aging*, **12**, 12–21.

Baltes, P. B., Staudinger, U., and Lindenberger, U. (2000). Lifespan psychology: Theory and application to intellectual functioning. *Annual Review of Psychology*, **50**, 471–507.

Bollen, K. A. (1989). *Structural Equation Models with Latent Variables*. New York: Wiley.

Bors, D. A., and Forrin, B. (1995). Age, speed of information processing, recall, and fluid intelligence. *Intelligence*, **20**, 229–248.

Bryan, J., and Luszcz, M. A. (1996). Speed of information processing as a mediator between aging and free recall performance. *Psychology and Aging*, **11**, 3–9.

Burke, D. M., MacKay, D. G., Worthley, J. S., and Wade, E. (1991). On the tip of the tongue: What causes word finding failures in young and older adults? *Journal of Memory and Language*, **30**, 542–579.

Byrne, B. M. (1998). *Structural Equation Modeling with LISREL, PRELIS, and SIMPLIS: Basic concepts, applications, and programming.* Mahwah, NJ: Lawrence Erlbaum Associates.

Carroll, J. B. (1993). *Human Cognitive Abilities: A survey of factor-analytic studies.* New York: Cambridge University Press.

Cattell, R. B. (1971). *Abilities: Their structure, growth, and action.* New York: Houghton-Mifflin.

Cohen, G. (1989). *Memory in the Real World.* Hillsdale, NJ: Lawrence Erlbaum Associates.

Cohen G., and Faulkner, D. (1986). Memory for proper names: Age differences in retrieval. *British Journal of Developmental Psychology*, **4**, 187–197.

Cook, T. D., and Campbell, D. T. (1979). *Quasi-experimentation: Design and analysis issues for research in field settings.* Chicago, IL: Rand-McNally.

Craik, F. I. M., and Byrd, M. (1982). Aging and cognitive deficits: The role of attentional resources. In F. I. M. Craik and S. Trehub (eds), *Aging and Cognitive Processes* (pp. 191–211). New York: Plenum Press.

Daneman, M., and Carpenter, P. A. (1980). Individual differences in working memory and reading. *Journal of Verbal Learning and Verbal Behavior*, **19**, 450–466.

Delaney, H. D. (1978). Interaction of individual differences with visual and verbal elaboration instructions. *Journal of Educational Psychology*, **70**, 306–318.

Engle, R. W., Tuholski, S. W., Laughlin, J. E., and Conway, A. R. (1999). Working memory, short-term memory, and general fluid intelligence: A latent-variable approach. *Journal of Experimental Psychology: General*, **128**, 309–331.

Engle, R. W., Cantor, J., and Carullo, J. J. (1992). Individual differences in working memory and comprehension: A test of four hypotheses. *Journal of Experimental Psychology: Learning, Memory, and Cognition*, **18**, 972–992.

Ericsson, K. A., and Charness, N. (1994). Expert performance: Its structure and acquisition. *American Psychologist*, **49**, 725–747.

Graf, P., and Uttl, B. (1995). Component processes of memory: Changes across the adult lifespan. *Swiss Journal of Psychology*, **54**, 113–130.

Hale, S., and Myerson, J. (1996). Experimental evidence for differential slowing in the lexical and nonlexical domains. *Aging, Neuropsychology, and Cognition*, **3**, 154–165.

Hayduk, L. (1987). *Structural Equation Modeling with LISREL: Essentials and advances.* Baltimore: Johns Hopkins University Press.

Hertzog, C. (1985). An individual differences perspective: Implications for cognitive research in gerontology. *Research on Aging*, **7**, 7–45.

Hertzog, C. (1989). The influence of cognitive slowing on age differences in intelligence. *Developmental Psychology*, **25**, 636–651.

Hertzog, C. (1996). Research design in studies of aging and cognition. In J. E. Birren and K. W. Schaie (eds), *Handbook of the Psychology of Aging* (4th ed., pp. 24–37). New York: Academic Press.

Hertzog, C., and Bleckley, M. K. (2001). Age differences in the structure of intelligence: Influences of information processing speed. *Intelligence*, **29**, 191–217.

Hertzog., C., Cooper, B. P., and Fisk, A. D. (1996). Aging and individual differences in the development of skilled memory search performance. *Psychology and Aging,* 11, 497–520.

Hertzog, C., and Dixon, R. A. (1996). Methodological issues in research on cognition and aging. In F. Blanchard-Fields and T. Hess (eds), *Perspective on Cognitive Change in Adult Development and Aging* (pp. 66–121). New York: McGraw-Hill.

Hertzog, C., Dixon, R. A., Hultsch, D. F., and McDonald, S. W. S. (2003). Latent change models of adult cognition: Are changes in processing speed and working memory associated with changes in episodic memory? *Psychology and Aging,* 18.

Hertzog, C., Hultsch, D. F., Dixon, R. A., and Small, B. J. (2002). *Contrasting models for age differences in episodic memory: Is processing speed the key mediator?* Unpublished manuscript, Georgia Institute of Technology.

Hofer, S. M., and Sliwinski, M. (2001). Understanding ageing. *Gerontology,* 47, 341–352.

Horn, J. L. (1985). Remodeling old models of intelligence. In B. B. Wolman (ed.), *Handbook of Intelligence: Theories, measurements, and applications* (pp. 267–300). New York: Wiley.

Horn, J. L., and Hofer, S. M. (1992). Major abilities and development in the adult period. In R. J. Sternberg and C. A. Berg (eds), *Intellectual Development* (pp. 44–99). Cambridge, England: Cambridge University Press.

Hultsch, D. F., and Dixon, R. A. (1984). Memory for text materials in adulthood. In P. B. Baltes and O. G. Brim, Jr. (eds), *Life-span Development and Behavior* (Vol. 6, pp. 77–103). New York: Academic Press.

Hultsch, D. F., Hertzog, C., and Dixon, R. A. (1990). Ability correlates of memory performance in adulthood and aging. *Psychology and Aging,* 5, 356–368.

Hultsch, D. F., Hertzog, C., Dixon, R. A., and Small, B. J. (1998). *Memory Change in the Aged.* New York: Cambridge University Press.

Hultsch, D. F., Hertzog, C., Small, B. J., and Dixon, R. A. (1999). Use it or lose it? Engaged life style as a buffer of cognitive decline in aging. *Psychology and Aging,* 14, 245–263.

Hunt, E. (1978). Mechanics of verbal ability. *Psychological Review,* 85, 109–130.

Kintsch, W. (1998). *Comprehension: A paradigm for cognition.* Cambridge, England: Cambridge University Press.

Kyllonen, P. C., and Christal, R. E. (1990). Reasoning ability is (little more than) working memory capacity? *Intelligence,* 14, 389–433.

Kyllonen, P. C., Tirre, W. C., and Christal, R. E. (1991). Knowledge and processing speed as determinants of associative learning. *Journal of Experimental Psychlogy: General,* 120, 57–79.

Light, L. L. (1996). Memory and aging. In E. L. Bjork and R. A. Bjork (eds), *Memory* (pp. 332–490). San Diego, CA: Academic Press.

Lindenberger, U., Mayr, U., and Kliegl, R. (1993). Speed and intelligence in old age. *Psychology and Aging,* 8, 201–220.

Lindenberger, U., and Pötter, U. (1998). The complex nature of unique and shared effects in hierarchical linear regression: Implications for developmental psychology. *Psychological Methods,* 3, 218–230.

Little, T. D., Lindenberger, U., and Nesselroade, J. R. (1999). On selecting indicators for multivariate measurement and modeling with latent variables: When 'good' indicators are bad and 'bad' indicators are good. *Psychological Methods,* 4, 192–211.

Lustig, C., Tonev, S. T., and Hasher, L. (2000). *Visual distraction and processing speed I.* Paper presented at the Cognitive Aging Conference, Atlanta, GA.

Masunaga, H., and Horn, J. L. (2001). Expertise and age-related changes in components of intelligence. *Psychology and Aging,* **16**, 293–311.

May, C. P., Hasher, L., and Kane, M. (1999). The role of interference in memory span. *Memory and Cognition,* **27**, 759–767.

McArdle, J. J., and Nesselroade, J. R. (1994). Using multivariate data to structure developmental change. In S. H. Cohen and H. W. Reese (eds), *Life-span Developmental Psychology: Methodological contributions* (pp. 223–267). Mahwah, NJ: Lawrence Erlbaum Associates.

Nelson, T. O., and Narens, L. (1980). Norms of 300 general-information questions: Accuracy of recall, latency of recall, and feeling-of-knowing ratings. *Journal of Verbal Learning and Verbal Behavior,* **19**, 338–368.

Nesselroade, J. R. (1977). Issues in studying developmental change in adults from a multivariate perspective. In J. E. Birren and K. W. Schaie (eds), *Handbook of the Psychology of Aging* (2nd ed., pp. 59–87). New York: Academic Press.

Park, D. C., Smith, A. D., Lautenschlager, G., Earles, J. L., Frieske, D., Zwahr, M., and Gaines, C. (1996). Mediators of long-term memory performance across the life span. *Psychology and Aging,* **11**, 621–637.

Park, D. C., Lautenschlager, G., Hedden, T., Davidson, N., Smith, A. D., and Smith, P. K. (2002). Models of visuospatial and verbal memory across the adult lifespan. *Psychology and Aging,* **17**, 299–320.

Piccinin, A. M., and Rabbitt, P. M. A. (1999). Contribution of cognitive abilities to performance and improvement in a substitution coding task. *Psychology and Aging,* **14**, 539–551.

Radvansky, G. A., Zacks, R. T., and Hasher, L. (1996). Fact retrieval in younger and older adults: The role of mental models. *Psychology and Aging,* **11**, 258–271.

Raz, N. (2000). Aging of the brain and its impact on cognitive performance: Integration of structural and functional findings. In F. I. M. Craik and T. A. Salthouse (eds), *The Handbook of Aging and Cognition* (2nd ed., pp 1–90). Mahwah, NJ: Lawrence Erlbaum Associates.

Roberts, R. D., and Stankov, L. (1999). Individual differences in speed of mental processing and human cognitive abilities: Toward a taxonomic model. *Learning and Individual Differences,* **11**, 1–120.

Rogers, W. A., Hertzog, C., and Fisk, A. D. (2000). An individual differences analysis of ability and strategy influences: Age-related differences in associative learning. *Journal of Experimental Psychology: Learning, Memory, and Cognition,* **26**, 359–394.

Salthouse, T. A. (1990). Working memory as a processing resource in cognitive aging. *Developmental Review,* **10**, 101–124.

Salthouse, T. A. (1991). *Theoretical Perspectives on Cognitive Aging.* Hillsdale, NJ: Lawrence Erlbaum Associates.

Salthouse, T. A. (1996a). General and specific speed mediation of adult age differences in memory. *Journal of Gerontology: Psychological Sciences,* **51**, P30–P42.

Salthouse, T. A. (1996b). The processing-speed theory of adult age differences in cognition. *Psychological Review,* **103**, 403–428.

Salthouse, T. A. (2000). Methodological assumptions in cognitive aging research. In F. I. M. Craik and T. A. Salthouse (eds), *The Handbook of Aging and Cognition* (2nd ed., pp. 467–498). Mahwah, NJ: Lawrence Erlbaum Associates.

Salthouse, T. A., and Babcock, R. L. (1991). Decomposing adult age differences in working memory. *Developmental Psychology, 27*, 763–776.

Salthouse, T. A., and Czaja, S. J. (2000). Structural constraints on process explanations in cognitive aging. *Psychology and Aging, 15*, 44–55.

Salthouse, T. A., Kausler, D. H., and Saults, J. S. (1988). Investigation of student status, background variables, and the feasibility of standard tasks in cognitive aging research. *Psychology and Aging, 3*, 29–37.

Schaie, K. W. (1977). Quasi-experimental designs in the psychology of aging. In J. E. Birren and K. W. Schaie (eds), *Handbook of the Psychology of aging* (pp. 39–58). New York: Van Nostrand Reinhold.

Schaie, K. W. (1996). *Intellectual Development in Adulthood: The Seattle Longitudinal Study.* New York: Cambridge University Press.

Schneider, B. A., and Pichora-Fuller, M. K. (2000). Implication of perceptual deterioration for cognitive aging research. In F. I. M. Craik and T. A. Salthouse (eds), *The Handbook of Aging and Cognition* (2nd ed., pp 155–220). Mahwah, NJ: Lawrence Erlbaum Associates.

Schooler, C., Mulatu, M. S., and Oates, G. (1999). The continuing effects of substantively complex work on the intellectual functioning of older workers. *Psychology and Aging, 14*, 483–506.

Sliwinski, M., and Buschke, H. (1999). Cross-sectional and longitudinal relationships among age, cognition, and processing speed. *Psychology and Aging, 14*, 18–33.

Verhaeghen, P. and Marcoen, A. (1994). The production-deficiency hypothesis revisited: Adult age differences in strategy use as a function of processing resources. *Aging and Cognition, 1*, 323–338.

Verhaeghen, P., and Salthouse, T. A. (1997). Meta-analyses of age-cognition relations in adulthood: Estimates of linear and nonlinear age effects and structural models. *Psychological Bulletin, 122*, 231–249.

Zacks, R. T., Hasher, L., and Li, K. Z. H. (2000). Human memory. In F. I. M. Craik and T. A. Salthouse (eds), *The Handbook of Aging and Cognition* (2nd ed., pp 293–357). Mahwah, NJ: Lawrence Erlbaum Associates.

Chapter 4

Intraindividual variability in performance as a theoretical window onto cognitive aging

David F. Hultsch and Stuart W. S. MacDonald

Researchers examining cognitive functioning in adulthood have primarily been interested in age-related differences or changes in level of performance. Methodologically, this emphasis has translated into comparisons of average performance across different age groups using cross-sectional designs or examination of changes in average performance within persons across time using longitudinal designs. Research on average age-related differences and changes in cognition has been useful, but it has reflected certain assumptions about the nature of human development. Specifically, this emphasis is rooted in the assumption that either the behaviors of interest are stable over time or that the trajectory of change that does occur is similar for all persons. This assumption with respect to level of performance represents one instantiation of a more general stability perspective that has dominated developmental research (Gergen, 1977; Nesselroade and Featherman, 1997). By contrast, variability in performance, particularly variability within persons, has received relatively little attention. However, as noted by Nesselroade and Boker (1994), the concepts of stability and variability are logically dependent on one another – defining one demands consideration of the other. Our main purpose in this chapter is to argue that examination of lawful but transient sources of influence on performance can provide a useful window that will help to clarify our theoretical view of cognition in later life.

Defining and measuring variability

Before we consider substantive issues related to variability of cognitive performance and aging, it is important to address some basic issues of definition and measurement.

Types of variability

There are multiple classifications of types of stability and variability (Alwin, 1994; Cattell, 1957; Fiske and Rice, 1955; Nesselroade and Featherman, 1997), and sometimes the same label has been applied to different types (Christensen *et al.*, 1999; Shammi, Bosman, and Stuss, 1998). Our use of the term intraindividual variability is taken from Nesselroade (1991) who defines it as relatively short-term changes in behavior (states, moods, transient fluctuations in performance) that are more or less reversible and occur more rapidly than relatively enduring intraindividual changes typically construed as learning or development.

To place this type of variability in context, it is useful to consider it with reference to subsets of observations drawn from a generalized data box defined by persons, measures, and occasions as shown in Figure 4.1 (Cattell, 1966; Nesselroade and Ford, 1985). This data box can be used to define different types of variability by considering the minimum conditions necessary to observe them in relation to the three dimensions. First, one can consider differences between persons measured on a single task on a single occasion. Such variability between persons is typically referred to as interindividual differences, or *diversity* (Hale, Myerson, Smith, and Poon, 1988). Second, one can examine variability associated with measuring a single person once on multiple tasks. In this case, the variability is in the profile of relative performance across measures, sometimes referred to as intraindividual differences, or *dispersion* (Christensen *et al.*, 1999). The third type of variability is defined by the minimum condition of measuring a single person on a single task on multiple occasions. Variability in performance across occasions has been labeled intraindividual variability (Li, Aggen, Nesselroade, and Baltes, 2001), or *inconsistency* (Hultsch, MacDonald, Hunter, *et al.*, 2000). The latter two types of variability refer to variability within persons.[1] Consideration of the minimum conditions necessary to observe variability is useful for construct definition. However, in practice it is common to select subsets of observations across more than one dimension which results in the opportunity to observe more than one type of variability. For example, selection of a subset of observations including both persons and occasions (see Figure 4.1) can yield information on both diversity and inconsistency.

---

[1] Some investigators have used the term consistency to refer to fluctuations in a group's mean across multiple testing sessions and the term dispersion to refer to intraindividual variability across trials within a session (Shammi *et al.*, 1998). In our view, this terminology is confusing because of the differential focus on groups and individuals and because it suggests that variability across trials and sessions may represent different phenomena. We prefer to focus on definitions established by the logic of the data box as described above.

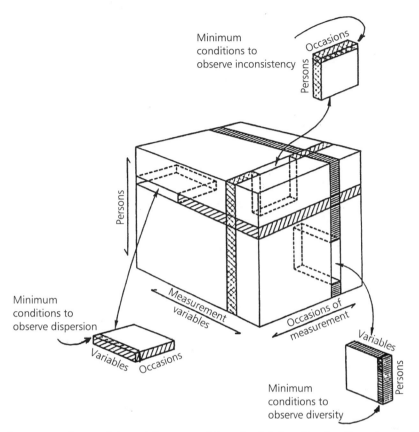

Fig. 4.1 Data box outlining minimum conditions for defining diversity, dispersion, and inconsistency in relation to persons, measures, and occasions. Adapted from Figure 3.4 from Nesselroade, J. R. (1990). Adult personality development: Issues in assessing constancy and change. In A. I. Rabin, R. A. Zucker, R. A. Emmons, and S. Franks (Eds.), *Studying Persons and Lives* (pp. 41–85). New York: Springer Publishing Company. Used by permission.

In the sections to follow, we will focus our attention primarily on intra-individual variability or inconsistency (using these terms interchangeably), although we will also touch on the issue of the potential relations among types of variability. It is important to note that although inconsistency is defined as short-term fluctuations in behavior, it can be observed across a relatively broad time range. Thus, inconsistency can be observed in the moment to moment fluctuations in response time observed across trials in a reaction time (RT) task. For example, Figure 4.2 shows substantial intraindividual variability across trials in word recognition latency for 13 mild dementia patients. Inconsistency may also be observed across longer intervals such as days or weeks. For example,

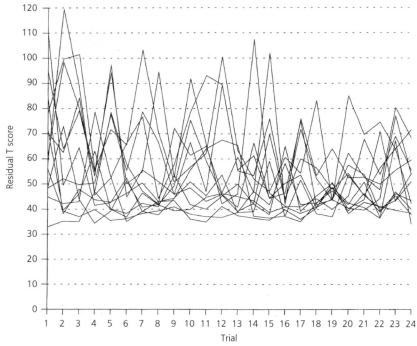

Fig. 4.2 Inconsistency in trial-to-trial word recognition latency for 13 patients diagnosed with mild dementia. From Figure 1, Hultsch, MacDonald, Hunter, Levy-Bencheton, and Strauss (2000). Copyright 2000 by the American Psychological Association. Adapted with permission.

Figure 4.3 shows fluctuations in performance for a 74-year-old woman who read and recalled narrative texts weekly for approximately 2 years. An interesting and still open question is whether inconsistency observed across different time frames is driven by the same mechanisms. Preliminary findings suggest that there is a positive relationship between inconsistency observed across trials within a session and inconsistency observed across longer intervals such as weeks (Hultsch *et al.*, 2000; Rabbitt, Osman, Moore *et al.*, 2001; West, Murphy, Armilio *et al.*, 2002).

Measuring inconsistency

There are multiple indices that may be computed as measures of inconsistency in performance (Slifkin and Newell, 1998). Perhaps the simplest of these is the intraindividual standard deviation (ISD). An ISD can be computed across tasks to examine dispersion or across time (trials or occasions) to examine inconsistency. However, computation of ISDs using raw-score responses

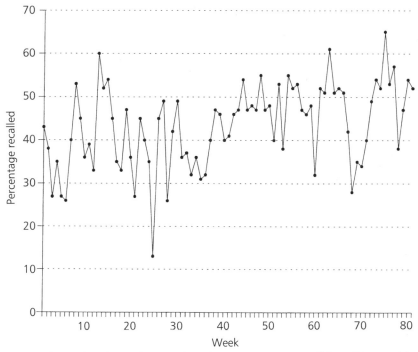

Fig. 4.3 Fluctuations in week-to-week performance on story recall for a 74-year-old woman. Reprinted from Figure 1 in Hertzog, C., Dixon, R. A., and Hultsch, D. F. (1992). Intraindividual change in text recall of the elderly. *Brain and Language*, **42**, 248–269, with permission from Elsevier.

(e g , reaction time latencies) is problematic. Group differences in average level of performance as well as systematic changes over time (across trials or occasions) associated with practice or different materials represent potential confounds for the analysis of intraindividual variability. For example, older adults may exhibit increased ISDs computed on raw RT scores simply as a function of their slower average response latencies (i.e., higher mean RTs are typically associated with higher standard deviations).

Performance inconsistency is defined as intraindividual variability that is unrelated to systematic between-subject effects as well as within-subject time-related effects. As such, its proper consideration requires controlling for potential confounds including mean group differences in speed, and time-related effects such as practice and learning to learn. In an attempt to address such confounds, some studies analyze the coefficient of variation (CV) as opposed to an ISD based on raw scores. The coefficient of variation expresses the standard deviation as a percentage of mean performance levels, and is typically used to permit variability comparisons across different variables or groups. In the context of performance inconsistency, CVs would be calculated as individual across-time standard deviations divided by individual across-time means, thus attempting to control for group and time-related effects by creating a measure of intraindividual variability relative to mean performance rather than separating systematic from unsystematic effects and analyzing only the latter. In contrast, a procedure proposed by Hultsch and colleagues (2000) statistically removes overall group and time-related influences from subjects' performance data prior to computing ISDs. Using a person by time data matrix, split-plot analysis of variance (ANOVA) is used to partial age group, gender, and occasions effects and all their interactions by regressing each dependent measure on these potential confounding variables. This approach to investigating inconsistency amounts to analyzing the residuals from a Groups by Occasions mixed-model ANOVA where all group and occasions effects and their interactions are partialed from subjects' scores prior to computing intraindividual standard deviations. If several performance tasks are included in a study, the resulting residual or *purified* scores are first converted to T-scores to permit comparisons across tasks in the same metric. Notably, it has been demonstrated that even though all systematic effects are partialed from the data using this technique (i.e., M = 50 and SD = 10 for all groups), substantial individual differences in intraindividual variability remain to be explained (Hultsch *et al.*, 2000; see Figure 4.2).

Other avenues for investigating intraindividual inconsistency can also be adopted. Whereas the procedure adopted by Hultsch *et al.* (2000) amounts to treating occasions as a fixed effect, a Hierarchical Linear Modeling (HLM) approach (Bryk and Raudenbush, 1992; Raudenbush, Bryk, Cheong *et al.*, 2002) would treat occasions as a random effect and permit partialing time-related variation at the individual rather than the global level. Such an approach has potential benefits: (a) if occasions truly is a random factor resulting in subjects being tested a different number of times and on different occasions, and (b) if one is reasonably confident that only lower-order time effects (e.g., linear, quadratic) are likely to be systematic. However, controlling for systematic effects using HLM can be equally problematic. If higher-order effects are suspected, or if a researcher is otherwise interested in removing all t-1 time effects and their interactions with grouping variables, then HLM cannot be used because fitting all of these systematic effects in order to partial them will produce a saturated HLM model having no residuals with which to calculate individual ISDs. In comparison, the mixed-model ANOVA approach permits partialing all polynomial effects and higher-order interactions while still yielding estimates of inconsistency.

Theoretical Rationales for a Focus on Inconsistency

Disciplines such as kinesiology (Latash, Scholz, Danion *et al.*, 2001) and economics (Stoll, 1999) have historically given significant attention to short-term fluctuations in various indicators. Psychologists have shown less interest in inconsistency in behavior, but suggestions that it is important are certainly not new. For more than three-quarters of a century, writers have periodically called on researchers to pay greater attention to intraindividual variability as a phenomenon that is central to understanding human behavior (Cattell, 1957; Fiske and Rice, 1955; Head, 1926; Woodrow, 1932). Despite these calls, examination of inconsistency in performance still represents a frontier of research relative to the more developed regions of average level of performance. However, within the current literature, several strands of theory and research point to the importance of exploring this frontier. In particular, writers in the areas of lifespan developmental psychology, neuropsychology–cognitive neuroscience, and mathematical–experimental psychology have argued that attention to both level and variability of performance is required to construct adequate theories of cognitive behavior.

Lifespan developmental psychology

Personality theorists have long distinguished between traits that are seen to be relatively stable and states that are viewed as relatively labile (Cattell and Scheier, 1961). Nesselroade has applied this dichotomy more broadly to lifespan development, distinguishing between intraindividual change and intraindividual variability (Nesselroade, 1991; Nesselroade and Featherman, 1997). The former refers to changes in behavior that are more or less enduring and occur relatively slowly, such as development, skill learning, and changes in traits, whereas the latter refers to what we have called inconsistency. This dichotomy is not precise and exhaustive but it carries some important implications (Dixon and Hertzog, 1996; Nesselroade and Boker, 1994).

First, any score conveying an individual's status on an attribute at any given time is composed of both relatively stable components and relatively changeable components (as well as error of measurement). At any one point in time, then, there is a hypothetical distribution of state values for an individual. As a result, some of the stable attributes of a person may reflect parameters of intraindividual variability distributions. Measuring a person once does not eliminate the influence of intraindividual variability on performance; it simply confounds it with more stable trait-like components. This suggests that more than one occasion of measurement may be required for an adequate assessment of competence, particularly in the case of constructs where the range of intraindividual variability is relatively large.

Second, intraindividual variability is separate from random or systematic errors of measurement. The assumption of most researchers operating within the dominant stability paradigm is that measurement operations reflect underlying traits accurately. Test–retest correlations are one key indicator of the reliability of measurement operations and any intraindividual variability is typically treated as error. However, low test–retest correlations may reflect poor reliability of the measures, substantial intraindividual variability of the attribute being measured, or both. Thus, intraindividual variability is associated with lawful but fluctuating endogenous (e.g., hormonal) or exogenous (e.g., environmental stressors) sources of influence. There is increasing evidence that attributes typically considered stable or trait-like, including cognitive abilities, show substantial intraindividual variability or state-like fluctuation (Hertzog, Dixon, and Hultsch, 1992; May, Hasher, and Stolzfus, 1993; Siegler, 1994).

Finally, this perspective suggests that consideration of both intraindividual change and intraindividual variability is necessary to construct a theory of developmental change. Lifespan theorists have emphasized that development at all points in the life course involves simultaneous gains and losses that reflect adaptive processes of selection, optimization, and compensation occurring within evolutionary and historical contexts (Baltes, Staudinger, and Lindenberger, 1999). Trajectories of change are seen to be multidimensional, multifunctional, differential, and dynamic rather than unidimensional, goal-directed, universal, and stable. One implication of this perspective is that the parameters of intraindividual variability distributions can change over time and these changes will influence the measurement of intraindividual change. For example, we propose the relationship between intraindividual variability and intraindividual change for many cognitive processes may be characterized by the pattern shown in Figure 4.4. That is, intraindividual variability is hypothesized to be greater both earlier and later in the lifespan, coinciding with periods of substantial intraindividual change.

Although the number of studies examining age differences in inconsistency is not large, those that are available appear to be consistent with the pattern proposed in Figure 4.4. Several studies have shown that inconsistency across trials on RT tasks increases with adult age (Anstey, 1999; Fozard, Vercruyssen, Reynolds *et al.*, 1994; Hultsch, MacDonald, and Dixon, 2002; Rabbitt, 2000; Salthouse, 1993; Shammi, 1998). For example, Hultsch and colleagues examined trial-to-trial performance on four RT tasks for younger adults and three groups of older adults ranging in age from 54 to 94 years. Greater inconsistency was observed for older compared with younger adults on all tasks, particularly for individuals over age 75. Importantly, these significant age differences were found even after statistical control of group differences in speed

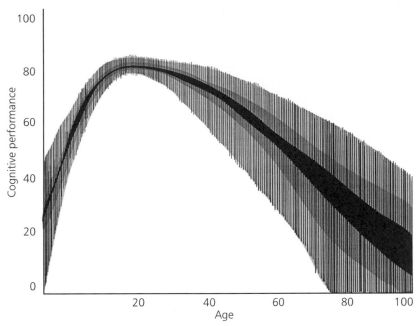

Fig. 4.4 Hypothetical confluence of lifespan trajectories for intraindividual variability and intraindividual change in cognitive performance.

of performance and practice. Significant age differences have also been observed across longer intervals. For example, Li *et al.* (2001) examined intraindividual variability for a set of memory and sensorimotor variables across 13 bi-weekly sessions in a sample of 24 older adults aged 64 to 86 years and reported that variability was positively correlated with age for most sensorimotor measures and one of the memory measures. Finally, consistent with Figure 4.4, Li (2001) has also reported data showing greater intraindividual variability in response time for younger compared with older children.

Thus, both theoretical arguments and empirical findings converge to suggest that a focus on intraindividual variability may be an important aspect of development. An essential feature of behavior is its labile, fluctuating, and dynamic quality – characteristics that will influence the assessment of attributes at any given point in time and their changing trajectories over time as a function of developmental principles (Nesselroade, 1991).

Neuropsychology and cognitive neuroscience

Neuropsychologists have commonly observed that patients with neurological disorders or injuries show not only impaired levels of performance but also abnormality in the consistency of their performance over time. For example, as early as 1926, Henry Head proposed that 'An inconsistent response is one of the most striking results produced by a lesion of the cerebral cortex.' From a clinical perspective, this observation suggests that one occasion of measurement may not provide an adequate assessment of cognitive competence (Dixon, Hertzog, Friesen *et al.*, 1993; Stuss, Pogue, Buckle, *et al.*, 1994). Intraindividual variability in performance may be particularly significant in the assessment of individuals whose disorders are mild or not easily definable (Gordon and Carson, 1990; Hultsch *et al.*, 2000; Stuss *et al.*, 1994). More recently, empirical research and theoretical conceptualizations have confirmed and expanded such early clinical observations.

There is an accumulating body of empirical work which shows that inconsistency in cognitive performance is prevalent in individuals with various types of neurological disturbance including epilepsy (Bruhn and Parsons, 1977), mental retardation (Wade, Newell, and Wallace, 1978), traumatic brain injury (TBI) (Stuss *et al.*, 1994), chronic fatigue syndrome (Fuentes, Hunter, Strauss *et al.*, 2001), and dementia (Hultsch *et al.*, 2000). For example, several studies have noted increased intraindividual variability in persons with TBI, at least for some tasks and at some points in the recovery process (Bleiberg, Garmoe, Halpern *et al.*, 1997; Collins and Long, 1996; Hetherington, Stuss, and Finlayson, 1996; Stuss *et al.*, 1994). In general, these studies have indicated that patients with TBI show greater inconsistency on RT tasks than normal controls, both within and across sessions. Some, but not all studies, have found that group differences are more pronounced for complex compared with simple tasks (Stuss *et al.*, 1994). There is also evidence to suggest that recovery of consistency of performance can be expected five or more years post injury in some cases (Hetherington *et al.*, 1996).

Increased intraindividual variability also appears to be characteristic of persons diagnosed with dementia (Gordon and Carson, 1990; Hultsch *et al.*, 2000; Knotek, Bayles, and Kaszniak, 1990). For example, Hultsch and colleagues observed greater intraindividual variability in individuals diagnosed with mild dementia than in neurologically intact adults, regardless of their health status. Patients with dementia showed approximately twice as much intraindividual variability as participants with arthritis or healthy adults. These data suggest that inconsistency may be a feature of neurological disturbances rather than somatic conditions such as pain, although a wider range of somatic conditions and accompanying levels of severity remain to be explored. Another open question is whether inconsistency is a generic feature of neurological disturbance or whether it is more prevalent in certain disorders. In a recent study, Murtha, Cismaru, Waechter *et al.* (2002) found greater inconsistency in performance for a group of frontal lobe dementia patients compared to individuals diagnosed with dementia of the Alzheimer's type, particularly for more demanding tasks. This suggests that measures of intraindividual variability may differentiate between different forms of brain damage.

The potential involvement of neurological mechanisms in producing age differences in intraindividual variability is also suggested by the relative consistency of individual differences in measures of inconsistency within and across cognitive tasks. For example, recent analyses have shown that

1   Individuals who show greater inconsistency across trials within a session also exhibit more inconsistency across testing sessions separated by longer intervals (e.g., weeks) (Fuentes *et al.*, 2001; Hultsch *et al.*, 2000; Rabbitt *et al.*, 2001);

2   Individuals who show greater inconsistency on one cognitive task also tend to show greater inconsistency on other tasks as well (Fuentes *et al.*, 2001; Hultsch *et al.*, 2000); and

3   There appear to be positive relationships among different measures of within-person variability.

For example, Hultsch *et al.* (2002) found individuals who showed more dispersion across four RT tasks (variability in profile across tasks) also showed greater inconsistency in performance across trials on all four tasks. Recent studies have also shown cross-domain linkages among measures of variability (Goldstein, Shapiro, LaRue *et al.*, 1999; Li *et al.*, 2001; Strauss, MacDonald, Hunter *et al.*, 2002). For example, Strauss and colleagues observed positive correlations between measures of inconsistency on physical and cognitive tasks; in general, greater variability in one domain was associated with greater variability in the other. Similarly, Li *et al.* (2001) showed that intraindividual variability in physical performance (walking tasks) across biweekly sessions correlated negatively with text and spatial memory performance. Thus, the magnitude of intraindividual variability appears to be somewhat characteristic of the individual – both across tasks and over time. This is what one would expect to find if such variability is substantially influenced by relatively stable endogenous mechanisms such as neurological dysfunction rather than relatively labile exogenous influences such as pain, fatigue, and stress.

More generally, greater intraindividual variability is associated with lower levels of general intelligence (Jensen, 1982; Rabbitt *et al.*, 2001) and poorer level of performance on cognitive tasks (Hultsch *et al.*, 2000, 2002; Li *et al.*, 2001; Rabbitt, 2000). For example, Rabbitt and colleagues (2001) measured both within session and across session inconsistency in older adults' reaction time on a letter identification task. They found that greater intraindividual variability was associated with poorer performance on the Culture Fair Intelligence Test for both trial-to-trial and week-to-week intervals. Similarly, Hultsch *et al.* (2002) found greater inconsistency in RT performance was associated with poorer level of performance on measures of perceptual speed, working memory, episodic memory, and crystallized abilities. Table 4.1 reports the correlations for the youngest (17–36 years) and oldest (75–94 years) age groups in this study, showing that significant relationships between intraindividual variability and level of performance appear to be more widespread for the older compared with the younger group. Importantly, several analyses have shown that measures of inconsistency and level of performance are unique predictors of cognitive performance (Fuentes *et al.*, 2001; Jensen, 1982; Li *et al.*, 2001; Hultsch *et al.*, 2000; 2002; Rabbitt, 2000). For example, Hultsch *et al.* (2002) used partial set correlation analysis to show that intraindividual variability in non-verbal RT latency uniquely accounted for between 11 and 20 per cent of the variance on other cognitive measures independent of mean-level RT performance. The fact that variability and level are unique predictors of cognitive performance points to the importance of considering both dimensions in constructing theories of cognitive functioning.

Table 4.1 Correlations of Intraindividual Standard Deviation (ISD) Across Trials on Four Reaction Time (RT) Tasks With Mean Performance on Other Cognitive Measures by Age Group

Age Group Cognitive Measure	RT-ISD (trials)			
	SRT	CRT	Lexical	Semantic
17–35 Years				
Perceptual speed	−.15	−.20*	−.41**	−.33**
Working memory	−.02	−.09	−.16	−.11
Episodic memory	−.14	−.15	−.31**	−.48**
Crystallized ability	−.11	−.04	−.13	−.14
75–94 Years				
Perceptual speed	−.35**	−.34**	−.42**	−.27**
Working memory	−.23**	−.15*	−.31**	−.28**
Episodic memory	−.21**	−.21**	−.29**	−.24**
Crystallized ability	−.24**	−.13	−.28**	−.28**

Note: SRT = simple reaction time; CRT = choice reaction time; Lexical = lexical decision reaction time; Semantic = semantic decision time.

*$p < .05$; **$p < .01$.

At the theoretical level, a number of writers have proposed that intraindividual variability at the behavioral level is an indicator of variability in central nervous system (CNS) functioning. For example, it has been suggested that inconsistency in response time performance on cognitive tasks could be caused by random errors or neural 'noise' in the transmission of signals in the CNS (Hendrickson, 1982). This view is consistent with hypotheses in the gerontological literature that age-related declines in cognitive performance are a function of increased information loss due to neural noise (Crossman and Szafran, 1956; Welford, 1965; Myerson, Hale, Wagstaff et al., 1990) or random breaks in neural networks (Cerella, 1990).

Li and Lindenberger (1999) have recently suggested that the signal-to-noise ratio of neural information processing may be regulated by the functioning of the catecholaminergic neurotransmitters such as epinephrine, norepinephrine, and dopamine. For example, age-related declines in dopamine are closely associated with poorer attention, memory, and motor performance (Arnsten, 1993; Bäckman et al., 2000). Experimental studies with animals also point to the role of modulation of the catecholaminergic system as a determinant of speed and variability of performance (MacRae, Spirduso, and Wilcox, 1988; Spirduso, Mayfield, Grant, et al., 1989). Finally, computational modeling has been used to show that simulating reduction of dopamine modulation of the signal-to-noise ratio in the aging brain leads to increased intra-network variability and age-related increases in both interindividual variability and intercorrelations between tasks (Li, Lindenberger, and Frensch, 2000).

These sorts of findings have led Lindenberger and his colleagues (e.g., Li and Lindenberger, Lindenberger, Li, and Brehmer, 2002) to theorize that greater intraindividual variability in older adults may be an agent as well as an outcome of ontogenetic change. That is, inconsistency in cognitive functioning at the neurological level may be responsible for age-related declines in level of performance as well as age-related increases in diversity (Morse, 1993) and dedifferentiation among cognitive abilities (Cunningham, 1980). This view also suggests that measures of intraindividual variability may be plausible behavioral indicators of aging induced deterioration of neurobiological mechanisms which compromise the integrity of the brain across a wide range of areas and functional circuitry. For example, it has been suggested that older brains may need to recruit additional resources to manage executive functions of otherwise relatively simple tasks (Cabeza, 2002; Dixon and Bäckman, 1999). Thus, even localized neural deficits may be expressed as a generalized impairment (Raz, 2000). Such changes have been hypothesized as the common cause for aging-associated losses in cognitive capacity and plasticity (Baltes and Lindenberger, 1997, Lindenberger and Baltes, 1994).

Mathematical and experimental psychology

Psychologists studying cognitive functioning have frequently examined RT as a primary dependent variable. Typically, latencies from multiple trials within a condition are collapsed into a measure of central tendency such as the mean or median RT. It has been suggested, however, that theoretically interesting and important aspects of response time data are not captured by measures of central tendency (Hockley, 1984; Ratcliff, 1978, 1979). For example, group (e.g. age) differences or experimental manipulations can result in a shift in mean RT either by increasing the skew of the distribution or by shifting the entire distribution.

Ratcliff (1979) and others have shown that it is possible to fit mathematical functions to RT distributions to quantify characteristics of the entire distribution rather than just its central tendency. Specifically, the convolution of a Gaussian and an exponential distribution, called the ex-Gaussian distribution, yields a good fit to empirical RT distributions under a wide variety of conditions (Heathcote, Popiel, and Mewhort, 1991; Hockley, 1984; Ratcliff, 1979). Fitting an ex-Gaussian distribution to an empirical RT distribution results in three parameter estimates: (a) μ, which reflects the mean of the Gaussian component of the distribution, (b) σ, which reflects the standard deviation of the Gaussian component, and (c) τ, which reflects the mean and standard deviation of the ex-Gaussian component. These parameter estimates can be used to determine whether increases in mean RT are the result of a shift in the distribution (changes in μ), an increase in the positive skew of the distribution (a change in τ), or both. A number of writers have argued that the various parameters of the ex-Gaussian distribution are differentially sensitive to different types of cognitive processing (Balota and Spieler, 1999; Hockley, 1984; Spieler, Balota, and Faust, 2000). Some have even suggested that separate cognitive processes are reflected in different parameters of the ex-Gaussian distribution (Hohle, 1965). Although researchers are unlikely to find a one-to-one mapping of cognitive processes to ex-Gaussian parameters, there is good reason to believe that select cognitive mechanisms or operations may differentially influence parameter estimates (Hockley, 1984; Spieler, Balota, and Faust, 1996). Indeed, a motivating factor for fitting an ex-Gaussian distribution to RT data is to characterize influences on RT distributions and to examine regularities in RT data that can inform theories of underlying cognitive processes (Spieler *et al.*, 2000).

Quantile–quantile plots (Q–Q plots) have also been used to examine characteristics of RT distributions. Of particular interest, Ratcliff, Spieler, and McKoon (2000) have recently demonstrated that Brinley plots (Brinley, 1965), widely used in cognitive aging research to examine slowing of response times for older relative to younger adults, are actually Q–Q plots. These plots chart corresponding quantile points from separate distributions and represent a useful means for studying shapes of RT distributions from separate groups. Ratcliff and colleagues (2000) have demonstrated that the slope of a Q–Q plot represents a ratio of standard deviations for one age group relative to another; a slope greater than 1 indicates more response-time variability for older adults. Thus, Q–Q plots can provide a rich source of evidence about age differences in variability.

Empirical examination of RT distributions using both mathematical functions and Q–Q plots reveal age differences in inconsistency across RT distributions. Studies fitting an ex-Gaussian distribution to empirical RT distributions have shown that age-related differences in intraindividual variability are due largely to increasing positive skew in the response distributions; that is, older adults' greater inconsistency is produced by an increasing number of very slow responses rather than a slowing of responses across the entire distribution (Spieler et al., 1996; West and Baylis, 1998; West et al., 2002). Similarly, using the Q–Q plot approach for examining inconsistency, Hultsch and colleagues (2002) plotted corresponding quantiles of mean-independent ISD scores for two separate age groups and calculated slopes to assess relative variability. For both verbal and non-verbal RT measures, observed slopes were greater than unity, indicating that the older group was more inconsistent than the younger group.

Notably, age differences in inconsistency appear to vary as a function of task demands. In particular, age differences appear to be exacerbated by tasks that place greater demands on executive processes (Hultsch et al., 2000; West et al., 2002), but ameliorated by tasks that are amenable to the implementation of compensatory processes based on world knowledge (Hultsch et al., 2002). Using Q–Q plots, Hultsch and colleagues (2002) demonstrated age group differences in the shape of ISD distributions, specifically in the upper-quantile tails. For simple process RT measures, distributions were more positively skewed with increasing age (i.e., the older age group had disproportionately more slow response trials in the tail of the distribution). In contrast, younger adults exhibited greater inconsistency on slower latency trials for semantic verification. Reduced variability for older adults on the verbal measures may reflect a compensatory mechanism based on superior verbal facility.

Examination of intraindividual variability and other characteristics of response distributions may also provide insight into the operation of different cognitive processes. Specifically, different cognitive mechanisms may exert differential influences on the shape and individual parameters of RT distributions. For example, varying task demands placed on specific cognitive processes may influence the shape of RT distributions. By fitting an ex-Gaussian function, group differences in parameter estimates can be examined for both the leading edge and tail components of the distribution. Of particular interest for the examination of inconsistency is whether group differences are observed across the entire distribution or differentially influence only select parameters.

Several studies have examined the shape of response time distributions as a means of identifying potential underlying cognitive mechanisms (Heathcote *et al.*, 1991; Hockley, 1984; Spieler *et al.*, 1996, 2000; West *et al.*, 2002). For example, Spieler and colleagues (1996) conducted an ex-Gaussian analysis to examine whether the magnitude of the Stroop interference effect was greater for older adults than for younger adults, specifically for the τ parameter (rightmost tail). Previous research suggests that the τ component of the ex-Gaussian distribution reflects a central processing component (Gordon and Carson, 1990). If true, the authors reasoned that decrements in inhibitory processing associated with poorer Stroop performance on incongruent trials should increase the τ due to the additional response time required. In contrast, Stroop conditions effecting a shift in the entire distribution will primarily reflect changes in μ. Results indicated that the magnitude of the Stroop interference effect was similar for younger and older adults for the μ parameter but was differentially magnified for older adults on trials that primarily contribute to estimates of the τ parameter. The observed difference in the τ parameter for incongruent Stroop trials is consistent with an age-related decrease in the efficiency of inhibitory processing. Similarly, West and colleagues (2002) examined whether age-related increases in performance variability were greater for task conditions requiring executive control processes compared with less demanding task conditions. An analysis of ex-Gaussian parameters revealed that, for the executive function task alone, increased variability for older adults was due to an increase in the positive skewing in the τ component of the RT distribution. The age-related increase in performance variability resulted from more slow response trials leading to a greater degree of positive skewing in the RT distribution, as opposed to a pervasive increase in variability. The authors concluded that lapses of intention were more frequent for older adults than for younger adults, with the increase in performance fluctuations for demanding task conditions reflecting an age-related waning of executive control processes (Bunce, Warr, and Cochrane, 1993).

Conclusions and Future Directions

Several preliminary conclusions are suggested by the modest amount of empirical research currently available:

1 Greater inconsistency in physical and cognitive performance is observed for older compared with younger adults;

2 Greater inconsistency is observed for individuals with neurological disorders compared with neurologically intact adults;

3 Inconsistency may be more prevalent in persons with some types of neurological damage compared with others;

4 The magnitude of inconsistency varies with the characteristics of tasks, particularly their executive demand and amenability to compensatory mechanisms;

5 There are consistent and stable individual differences in inconsistency across tasks and time intervals, respectively;

6 There are cross-domain links between inconsistency on cognitive tasks and both level and variability of physical performance;

7 Greater inconsistency is associated with poorer levels of performance on cognitive tasks and measures of intelligence; and

8 Individual differences in inconsistency are uniquely predictive of level of cognitive performance.

At a conceptual level, these findings argue that it is important to attend to both level and variability of performance. Each of these indices provides useful information that the other does not. Because a stability orientation tends to guide research, the current task is to supplement the dominant view by increasing attention to cycles, oscillations, and fluctuations in behavior and how these can contribute to the development of theories of cognitive aging. At the same time, it is important not to ascribe more significance to the concept of intraindividual variability than is warranted. For example, we do not wish to suggest that behavioral inconsistency represents some type of psychological 'primitive' that will account for all or most of the age-related variance in cognitive performance. Rather, we suggest that this phenomenon is an integral part of cognitive functioning that needs to be considered both in theory development and in clinical assessment.

It is clear that substantial work remains to be done both conceptually and empirically if the potential usefulness of the intraindividual variability construct is to be fulfilled. We highlight three broad research issues for future consideration, each of which contains multiple specific questions. First, extant work has shown that inconsistency is greater in older compared with younger adults and that greater inconsistency is associated with poorer level of performance. These conclusions hold true even when age differences in level of performance are carefully controlled. An implication of these cross-sectional results is that inconsistency of performance may be an indicator of cognitive decline. However, longitudinal data are required to address this question adequately, particularly because there is increasing evidence for dissociations between cross-sectional and longitudinal findings related to cognition and aging (Hultsch, Hertzog, Dixon and Small, 1998; Sliwinski and Buschke, 1999). Key questions are (a) whether inconsistency increases with age over time, and whether *changes* in inconsistency (increases) are associated with *changes* (declines) in cognitive functioning. Because inconsistency also appears to be associated with neurological disturbance, a related question is whether it is predictive of progression to a diagnosis of dementia. To the extent that this is the case, it is possible that measures of inconsistency may be more sensitive indicators of potential cognitive dysfunction than measures of level of performance. Such an early warning 'canary in the coal mine' would have obvious clinical benefit.

Second, the analysis of response time distributions is not adequately addressed by measures of central tendency alone. Recent findings suggest that characteristics of RT distributions, including performance inconsistency reflected as slow responses in the positively skewed tail, can facilitate an understanding of underlying cognitive processes. In particular, studies investigating inconsistency as an indicator of cognitive processing would benefit from using ex-Gaussian analyses to characterize the influence of different influences on RT distributions. Age effects on distribution parameters have been examined for only a few cognitive domains (e.g., working memory, attention, inhibition), each showing increased performance variability in the τ component as a function of differential response slowing for older adults. To build on these findings, it is critical to test whether cognitive processes from various domains, both fluid and crystallized, yield parameter estimates that vary as a function of age. Are increases in performance variability restricted to certain processes? Is inconsistency magnified as a function of task demands? Are age differences in parameter estimates universal or selective? Moreover, differences in parameter estimates should be compared for neurologically intact and impaired groups to determine whether performance inconsistency is further magnified as a function of pathological aging. Progressing from descriptive accounts of performance variability to the experimental manipulation of factors to observe their influence on the shape of RT distributions represents an important milestone for examining associations between performance inconsistency and cognitive process.

Finally, aging is associated with declines at both the behavioral level – processing speed, working memory – and at the neurobiological level – synaptic density, dopamine transmitter levels. Classic hypotheses in cognitive aging research have proposed links between these levels of functioning (Welford, 1965), but specifying the anatomical, metabolic, and neurochemical mechanisms involved and their proximal and distal behavioral consequences has been difficult. However, recent advances in neuroimaging and computational neuroscience provide new opportunities for integrating research. Li and her colleagues (Li and Lindenberger, 1999; Li *et al.*, 2000; Li, Lindenberger, and Sikström, 2001) have proposed a sequence of influence from aging-related declines in neuromodulation to increased neural noise and less distinctive cortical representations to aging-related deficits in cognitive performance. A key aspect of this proposed theoretical integration between the neurobiological and behavioral levels of analysis is that neurochemical mechanisms that increase the level of random variability may be central to cognitive aging. These sorts of links between the neurobiological and behavioral functioning can be profitably explored using both neuroimaging techniques and computational modeling. Animal studies could directly examine the effects of manipulation of neurotransmitters on intraindividual variability in performance. Finally, Li *et al.* (2001) note that attention should also be given to reciprocal influences from behavior to cognition to neural mechanisms via behavioral training and other experiences that result in skill maintenance or development.

We conclude with a quotation from Nesselroade and Featherman (1997) in response to their rhetorical question, 'What is the appropriate frame of reference against which to chart age-related changes?':

> Our conclusion is that they should be charted against a background of intraindividual variability rather than one of putative stability. Descriptively, how does the magnitude and other parameters of intraindividual variability change across the life span? From an explanatory perspective, what are the mechanisms by which intraindividual variability comes about and is modified over the life span? Phrasing developmental questions in these terms gives priority to variation and change. If stability is there it can still be identified as a special case. The converse is not true. Intraindividual variability is not a special case of stability. An overarching concern with stability should not be allowed to stifle further research on intraindividual variability in behavioral manifestations, the links of which to developmental phenomenon are beginning to be glimpsed – and that look exciting and important!
>
> (Nesselroade and Featherman, 1997: 205)

References

Alwin, D. F. (1994). Aging, personality, and social change: The stability of individual differences over the adult life span. In D. L. Featherman, R. M. Lerner, and M. Perlmutter (eds), *Life-span Development and Behavior* (Vol. 12, pp. 135–185). Hillsdale, NJ: Erlbaum.

Anstey, K. J. (1999). Sensorimotor and forced expiratory volume as correlates of speed, accuracy, and variability in reaction time performance in late adulthood. *Aging, Neuropsychology, and Cognition*, **6**, 84–95.

Arnsten, A. F. T. (1993). Catecholamine mechanisms in age-related cognitive decline. *Neurobiology of Aging*, **14**, 639–641.

Bäckman, L., Ginovart, N., Dixon, R. A., Wahlin, T-B. R., Wahlin, Å., Halldin, C., and Farde, L. (2000). Age-related cognitive deficits mediated by changes in the striatal dopamine system. *American Journal of Psychiatry*, **157**, 635–637.

Balota, D. A. and Spieler, D. H. (1999). Lexicality, frequency, and repetition effects: Beyond measures of central tendency. *Journal of Experimental Psychology: General*, **128**, 32–55.

Baltes, P. B. and Lindenberger, U. (1997). Emergence of a powerful connection between sensory and cognitive functions across the adult lifespan: A new window to the study of cognitive aging? *Psychology and Aging*, **12**, 12–21.

Baltes, P. B., Staudinger, U. M., and Lindenberger, U. (1999). Lifespan psychology: Theory and application to intellectual functioning. *Annual Review of Psychology*, **50**, 471–507.

Bleiberg, J., Garmoe, W. S., Halpern, E. L., Reeves, D. L., and Nadler, J. D. (1997). Consistency of within-day and across-day performance after mild brain injury. *Neuropsychiatry, Neuropsychology, and Behavioral Neurology*, **10**, 247–253.

Brinley, J. F. (1965). Cognitive sets, speed and accuracy of performance in the elderly. In A. T. Welford and J. E. Birren (eds), *Behavior, Aging and the Nervous System* (pp. 114–149). Springfield, IL: Thomas.

Bruhn, P. and Parsons, O. A. (1977). Reaction time variability in epileptic and brain damaged patients. *Cortex*, **13**, 373–384.

Bryk, A. S. and Raudenbush, S. W. (1992). *Hierarchical Linear Models: Applications and data analysis methods*. Newbury Park, CA: Sage Publications, Inc.

Bunce, D. J., Warr, P. B., and Cochrane, T. (1993). Blocks in choice responding as a function of age and physical fitness. *Psychology and Aging*, **8**, 26–33.

Cabeza, R. (2002). Hemispheric asymmetry reduction in older adults: The HAROLD model. *Psychology and Aging*, **17**, 85–100.

Cattell, R. B. (1957). *Personality and Motivation: Structure and measurement*. New York: World Book.

Cattell, R. B. (1966). The data box: Its ordering of total resources in terms of possible relational systems. In R. B. Cattell (ed.), *Handbook of Multivariate Experimental Psychology* (pp. 67–128). Chicago, IL: Rand McNally.

Cattell, R. B. and Scheier, I. H. (1961). *The Meaning and Measurement of Neuroticism and Anxiety*. New York: Ronald.

Cerella, J. (1990). Aging and information-processing rate. In J. E. Birren and K. W. Schaie (eds), *Handbook of the Psychology of Aging* (3rd ed., pp. 201–221). San Diego, CA: Academic Press.

Christensen, H., Mackinnon, A. J., Korten, A. E., Jorm, A. F., Henderson, A. S., and Jacomb, P. (1999). Dispersion in cognitive ability as a function of age: A longitudinal study of an elderly community sample. *Aging, Neuropsychology, and Cognition*, **6**, 214–228.

Collins, L. F. and Long, C. J. (1996). Visual reaction time and its relationship to neuropsychological test performance. *Archives of Clinical Neuropsychology*, **11**, 613–623.

Crossman, E. R. F. W. and Szafran, J. (1956). Changes with age in the speed of information intake and discrimination. *Experientia Supplementum*, **4**, 128–135.

Cunningham, W. R. (1980). Age comparative factor analysis of ability variables in adulthood and old age. *Intelligence, 4*, 133–149.

Dixon, R. A. and Bäckman, L. (1999). Principles of compensation in cognitive neurorehabilitation. In D. T. Stuss, G. Winocur, and I. H. Robertson (eds), *Cognitive Neurorehabilitation* (pp. 59–72). Cambridge: Cambridge University Press.

Dixon, R. A. and Hertzog, C. (1996). Theoretical issues in cognition and aging. In F. Blanchard-Fields and T. M. Hess (eds), *Perspectives on Cognitive Change in Adulthood and Aging* (pp. 25–65). New York: McGraw-Hill.

Dixon, R. A., Hertzog, C., Friesen, I. C., and Hultsch, D. F. (1993). Assessment of intraindividual change in text recall of elderly adults. In H. H. Brownell and Y. Joanette (eds), *Narrative Discourse in Neurologically Impaired and Normal Aging Adults* (pp. 77–101). San Diego, CA: Singular.

Fiske, D. W. and Rice, L. (1955). Intra-individual response variability. *Psychological Bulletin, 52*, 217–250.

Fozard, J. L., Vercruyssen, M., Reynolds, S. L., Hancock, P. A., and Quilter, R. E. (1994). Age differences and changes in reaction time: The Baltimore Longitudinal Study of Aging. *Journal of Gerontology: Psychological Sciences, 49*, P179–P189.

Fuentes, K., Hunter, M. A., Strauss, E., and Hultsch, D. F. (2001). Intraindividual variability in cognitive performance in persons with chronic fatigue syndrome. *The Clinical Neuropsychologist, 15*, 210–227.

Gergen, K. J. (1977). Stability, change, and chance in understanding human development. In N. Datan, and H. W. Reese (eds), *Life-span Developmental Psychology: Dialectical perspectives on experimental research* (pp. 135–158). New York: Academic Press.

Goldstein, I. B., Shapiro, D., LaRue, A., and Guthrie, D. (1999). Relationship between 24-hour ambulatory blood pressure and cognitive function in healthy elderly people. *Aging, Neuropsychology, and Cognition, 5*, 215–224.

Gordon, B. and Carson, K. (1990). The basis for choice reaction time slowing in Alzheimer's disease. *Brain and Cognition, 13*, 148–166.

Hale, S., Myerson, J., Smith, G. A., and Poon, L. W. (1988). Age, variability and speed: Between-subjects diversity. *Psychology and Aging, 3*, 407–410.

Head, H. (1926). *Aphasia and kindred disorders of speech*. Cambridge, UK: Cambridge University Press.

Heathcote, A., Popiel, S. J., and Mewhort, D. J. K. (1991). Analysis of response time distributions: An example using the Stroop task. *Psychological Bulletin, 109*, 340–347.

Hendrickson, A. E. (1982). The biological basis of intelligence Part I: Theory. In H. J. Eysenck (ed.), *A Model for Intelligence* (pp. 151–196). Berlin: Springer-Verlag.

Hertzog, C., Dixon, R. A., and Hultsch, D. F. (1992). Intraindividual change in text recall of the elderly. *Brain and Language, 42*, 248–269.

Hetherington, C. R., Stuss, D. T., and Finlayson, M. A. J. (1996). Reaction time and variability 5 and 10 years after traumatic brain injury. *Brain Injury, 10*, 473–486.

Hockley, W. E. (1984). Analysis of response time distributions in the study of cognitive processes. *Journal of Experimental Psychology: Learning, Memory, and Cognition, 10*, 598–615.

Hohle, R. H. (1965). Inferred components of reaction times as functions of foreperiod durations. *Journal of Experimental Psychology, 69*, 382–386.

Hultsch, D. F., Hertzog, C., Dixon, R. A., and Small, B. J. (1998). *Memory Change in the Aged.* New York: Cambridge University Press.

Hultsch, D. F., MacDonald, S. W. S., and Dixon, R. A. (2002). Variability in reaction time performance of younger and older adults. *Journal of Gerontology: Psychological Sciences,* **57b**, 101–115.

Hultsch, D. F., MacDonald, S. W. S., Hunter, M. A., Levy-Bencheton, J., and Strauss, E. (2000). Intraindividual variability in cognitive performance in older adults: Comparison of adults with mild dementia, adults with arthritis, and healthy adults. *Neuropsychology,* **14**, 588–598.

Jensen, A. R. (1982). Reaction time and psychometric g. In H. J. Eysenck (ed.), *A Model for Intelligence* (pp. 93–132). Berlin: Springer-Verlag.

Knotek, P. C., Bayles, K. A., and Kaszniak, A. W. (1990). Response consistency on a semantic memory task in persons with dementia of the Alzheimer type. *Brain and Language,* **38**, 465–475.

Latash, M. L., Scholz, J. F., Danion, F., and Schöner, G. (2001). Structure of motor variability in marginally redundant multifinger force production tasks. *Experimental Brain Research,* **141**, 153–165.

Li. S-C. (2001). *Evolving fields: A theoretical path from deficient neuromodulation to dedifferentiated cortical representations to cognitive aging deficits.* Paper presented at the 17th World Congress of Gerontology, Vancouver, British Columbia, Canada.

Li, S-C., Aggen, S. H., Nesselroade, J. R., and Baltes, P. B. (2001). Short-term fluctuations in elderly people's sensorimotor functioning predicts text and spatial memory performance: The MacArthur successful aging studies. *Gerontology,* **47**, 100–116.

Li, S-C. and Lindenberger, U. (1999). Cross-level unification: A computational exploration of the link between deterioration of neurotransmitter systems and dedifferentiation of cognitive abilities in old age. In L-G Nilsson and H. Markowitsch (eds), *Cognitive Neuroscience and Memory* (pp. 103–146). Toronto: Hogrefe and Huber.

Li, S-C., Lindenberger, U., and Frensch, P. A. (2000). Unifying cognitive aging: From neuromodulation to representation to cognition. *Neurocomputing,* **32–33**, 879–890.

Li, S-C., Lindenberger, U., and Sikström, S. (2001). Aging and cognition: from neuromodulation to representation. *Trends in Cognitive Science,* **5**, 479–486.

Lindenberger, U. and Baltes, P. B. (1994). Sensory functioning and intelligence in old age: A strong connection. *Psychology and Aging,* **9**, 339–355.

Lindenberger, U., Li, S-C., and Brehmer, Y. (2002). Variabilité dans le vieillissement comportemental: Résultat et agent des changements ontogénétiques. (Variability in behavioral aging: Outcome and agent of ontogenetic change). In J. Lautrey, B. Mazoyer, and P. van Geert (Eds.), *Invariants et variabilités dans le sciences cognitives.* Paris, France: Presses de la MSH.

MacRae, P. G., Spirduso, W. W., and Wilcox, R. E. (1988). Reaction time and nigrostriatal dopamine function. The effect of age and practice. *Brain Research,* **451**, 139–146.

May, C. P., Hasher, L., and Stoltzfus, E. R. (1993). Optimal time of day and the magnitude of age differences in memory. *Psychological Science,* **4**, 326–330.

Morse, C. K. (1993). Does variability increase with age? An archival study of cognitive measures. *Psychology and Aging,* **8**, 156–164.

Murtha, S., Cismaru, R., Waechter, R., and Chertkow, H. (2002). Increased variability accompanies frontal lobe damage in dementia. *Journal of the International Neuropsychology Society,* **8**, 360–372.

Myerson, J., Hale, S., Wagstaff, D., Poon, L. W., and Smith, G. A. (1990). The information-loss model: A mathematical theory of age-related cognitive slowing. *Psychological Review,* **97**, 475–487.

Nesselroade, J. R. (1990). Adult personality development: Issues in assessing constancy and change. In A. I. Rabin, R. A. Zucker, R. A., Emmons, and S. Franks (eds), *Studying Persons and Lives* (pp. 41–85). New York: Springer.

Nesselroade, J. R. (1991). The warp and woof of the developmental fabric. In R. Downs, L. Liben, and D. S. Palermo (eds), *Visions of Aesthetics, the Environment, and Development: The legacy of Joachim F. Wohwill* (pp. 213–240). Hillsdale, NJ: Earlbaum.

Nesselroade, J. R., and Boker, S. M. (1994). Assessing constancy and change. In T. F. Heatherton and J. L. Weinberger (eds), *Can Personality Change?* (pp. 121–147). Washington, DC: American Psychological Association.

Nesselroade, J. R., and Featherman, D. L. (1997). Establishing a reference frame against which to chart age-related changes. In M. A. Hardy (ed.), *Studying Aging and Social Change: Conceptual and methodological issues* (pp. 191–205). Newbury Park, CA: Sage.

Nesselroade, J. R. and Ford, D. H. (1985). P-technique comes of age: Multivariate, replicated, single-subject designs for research on older adults. *Research on Aging,* **7**, 46–80.

Rabbitt, P. M. A. (2000). Measurement indices, functional characteristics, and psychometric constructs in cognitive aging. In T. J. Perfect and E. A. Maylor (eds), *Models of Cognitive Aging* (pp. 160–187). New York: Oxford University Press.

Rabbitt, P. M. A., Osman, P., Moore, B., and Stollery, B. (2001). There are stable individual differences in performance variability, both from moment to moment and from day to day. *The Quarterly Journal of Experimental Psychology A,* **54**, 981–1003.

Ratcliff, R. (1978). A theory of memory retrieval. *Psychological Review,* **85**, 59–108.

Ratcliff, R. (1979). Group reaction time distributions and an analysis of distribution statistics. *Psychological Bulletin,* **86**, 446–461.

Ratcliff, R., Spieler, D., and McKoon, G. (2000). Explicitly modeling the effects of aging on response time. *Psychonomic Bulletin and Review,* **7**, 1–25.

Raudenbush, S. W., Bryk, A. S., Cheong, Y. F., and Congdon, R. (2002). *HLM 5: Hierarchical linear and nonlinear modeling* (2nd ed.). Lincolnwood, IL: Scientific Software International.

Raz, N., (2000). Aging of the brain and its impact on cognitive performance: Integration of structural and functional findings. In F.I.M. Craik and T. A. Salthouse (eds), *The Handbook of Aging and Cognition* (2nd ed., pp. 1–90). Mahwah, NJ: Erlbaum.

Salthouse, T. A. (1993). Attentional blocks are not responsible for age-related slowing. *Journal of Gerontology: Psychological Sciences,* **48**, P263–P270.

Shammi, P., Bosman, E., and Stuss, D. T. (1998). Aging and variability in performance. *Aging, Neuropsychology, and Cognition,* **5**, 1–13.

Siegler, R. S. (1994). Cognitive variability: A key to understanding cognitive development. *Current Directions in Psychological Science,* **3**, 1–5.

Slifkin, A. B. and Newell, K. M. (1998). Is variability in human performance a reflection of system noise? *Current Directions in Psychological Science,* **7**, 170–177.

Sliwinski, M. and Buschke, H. (1999). Cross-sectional and longitudinal relationships among age, cognition, and processing speed. *Psychology and Aging,* **14**, 18–33.

Spieler, D. H., Balota, D. A., and Faust, M. E. (1996). Stroop performance in healthy younger and older adults and in individuals with dementia of the Alzheimer's type. *Journal of Experimental Psychology: Human Perception and Performance,* **22**, 461–479.

Spieler, D. H., Balota, D. A., and Faust, M. E. (2000). Levels of selective attention revealed through analyses of response time distributions. *Journal of Experimental Psychology: Human Perception and Performance,* **26**, 506–526.

Spirduso, W. W., Mayfield, D., Grant, M., and Schaller, T. (1989). Effects of route of administration of ethanol on high-speed reaction time in young and old rats. *Psychopharmacology,* **97**, 413–417.

Stoll, H. R. (ed.). (1999). *Microstructure: The organization of trading and short-term price behavior* (vol. 1). Northampton MA: Elgar.

Strauss, E., MacDonald, S. W. S., Hunter, M. A., Moll, A., and Hultsch, D. F. (2002). Intraindividual variability in cognitive performance in three groups of adults: Cross-domain links to physical status and self-perceived affect and beliefs. *Journal of the International Neuropsychology Society,* **8**, 893–906.

Stuss, D. T., Pogue, J., Buckle, L., and Bondar, J. (1994). Characterization of stability of performance in patients with traumatic brain injury: Variability and consistency on reaction time tests. *Neuropsychology,* **8**, 316–324.

Wade, M. G., Newell, K. M., and Wallace, S. A. (1978). Decision time and movement time as a function of response complexity in retarded persons. *American Journal of Mental Deficiency,* **83**, 135–144.

Welford, A. T. (1965). Performance, biological mechanisms and age: A theoretical sketch. In A. T. Welford and J. E. Birren (eds), *Behavior, aging, and the nervous system* (pp. 3–20). Springfield, IL: Thomas.

West, R. and Baylis, G. C. (1998). Effects of increased response dominance and contextual disintegration on the Stroop interference effect in older adults. *Psychology and Aging,* **13**, 206–217.

West, R., Murphy, K. J., Armilio, M. L., Craik, F. I. M., and Stuss, D. T. (2003). Lapses of intention and performance variability reveal age-related increases in fluctuations of executive control. *Brain and Cognition,* **49**, 402–419.

Woodrow, H. (1932). Quotidian variability. *Psychological Review,* **39**, 245–256.

Chapter 5

Commentary: Measures, constructs, models, and inferences about aging

Leah L. Light

The three chapters in this section deal with very diverse topics. In Chapter 4 Hultsch and MacDonald present a strong argument for considering intra-individual differences in performance across tasks (dispersion) and intraindividual variability across occasions (inconsistency), in addition to mean level of performance, in characterizing groups and developing theoretical accounts of group differences and developmental trajectories. They review evidence that measures of intraindividual differences in variability tend to be stable over time and domains. These measures do a good job of differentiating patients with mild Alzheimer's disease from age-matched groups of healthy older adults and older adults who have arthritis (Hultsch, MacDonald, Hunter *et al.*, 2000). Measures of dispersion and inconsistency based on simple and complex RT measures also differentiate young and older groups, with greater inconsistency associated negatively with performance on perceptual speed, working memory, episodic memory, and crystallized abilities (Hultsch, MacDonald, and Dixon, 2002).

Hertzog describes a series of structural equation models to account for cross-sectional and longitudinal data on episodic memory (text and word list recall) in the Victoria Longitudinal Study (VLS) in Chapter 3. The take-home message is that choice of measures to index theoretical constructs makes a difference in the outcome of the modeling enterprise. Using some measures of working memory produces one set of outcomes, with working memory contributing more to age-related differences in episodic memory, but using others leads to different conclusions, with speed playing a greater role.

In Chapter 2 Park and Minear summarize a programme of research that includes a number of inter-related projects tied together within an expanded processing-resources framework. These include, but are not limited to, a large-scale structural equation model of the relationships among age, short-term memory, working memory, and episodic memory and studies of the structural relationships among age, working memory, and cognition in young and older Americans and Chinese.

My own research on direct and indirect measures of memory is quite different in both form and content from most of that described in these three chapters. Though it does deal with memory, my work involves experiments with relatively small numbers of participants, rather than large-scale studies with many observations on different variables. My lab does not produce structural equation models, though we have lately become quite enamored with curve-fitting, and we do not make strong inferences about causality, based on either cross-sectional or longitudinal data. Despite these differences, I believe that my own work and that represented by the chapters by Hultsch and MacDonald, Hertzog, and Park and Minear converge on two important points. The first is that conclusions about cognitive aging depend heavily on the ways in which we select our measures – how we operationalize constructs of interest matters. The second, illustrated especially in the Hertzog and Park and Minear chapters, is that conclusions drawn about relationships among constructs – the explanations that we give for age-related changes in cognition – are heavily dependent on assumptions that we make about the form that these explanations should take. In this chapter, I will first elaborate on these two points as they are exemplified in the three chapters under discussion. I will then describe some recent work from my own laboratory that makes similar points.

Choosing indicators of constructs

As investigators of cognitive aging, we are interested not only in performance per se, but also in what performance reveals about cognitive architecture and processes in particular domains. The variables that we choose to measure are indicators or markers of particular abilities and are often multiply determined, i.e., not process-pure. The challenge, then, is to choose either single indicators or multiple indicators of such latent constructs as working memory, perceptual speed, episodic memory, world knowledge, semantic memory, or – in my own work – familiarity and recollection, that capture the 'essence' of the construct of interest. Researchers generally choose measures that are easy to administer and that manifest convergent and divergent validity. Notions of convergent and divergent validity are, of course, embedded in particular theories that we hold about relationships among constructs. Little, Lindenberger, and Nesselroade (1999) observe that a high degree of internal consistency of measures used to index a single construct may prove useful, especially when there is strong theory to hone in on the processes tapped by the construct, but that in the absence of strong theory or a history of empirical findings, it might be better to sample broadly from possible measures.

When the focus is on testing very specific models, theory clearly motivates choice of measures. Thus, in modeling visuospatial and verbal memory across the adult life span, Park and her colleagues (Park, Lautenschlager, Hedden *et al.*, 2002) sought measures to tap constructs postulated by Baddeley's (1986) model of working memory, measures thought to index short-term rather than working memory in models developed by Engle, Tuholski, Laughlin *et al.* (1999), and to respect distinctions between verbal and visuospatial working and short-term memory identified in studies using functional neuroimaging.

Selection of constructs for the VLS was based on a comprehensive review of the literature on age-related changes in various aspects of memory and of predictors of memory change in old age, with many different aspects of memory being represented (e.g., word recall, text recall, semantic memory, implicit memory, working memory, and vocabulary) along with measures of speed and a variety of other potential predictors (Hultsch, Hertzog, Dixon *et al.*, 1998). Hertzog notes that the theoretical framework shaping the VLS is grounded in processing resource theory, but further assumes that strategies play a role in performance and that new information is processed in the context of prior knowledge. The approach, then, was somewhat eclectic and the motivation for choosing particular markers for each construct was not discussed in detail, though different markers for working memory and speed have been used at different timepoints.

The VLS is a longitudinal study and the needs of such studies are perhaps different from those of more narrowly focused investigations. In particular, use of a wide selection of constructs and markers of these constructs may be useful when multiple measurement occasions are envisioned, because the status of particular constructs may change over time as the result of the accumulation of empirical knowledge and also because of shifts in interest in constructs. For instance, using indirect measures of memory would not have been deemed important (or been considered at all) before the mid-1980s when research on this topic became popular.

Measures of working memory are not all fungible. Digit span forward was once considered to be a measure of short-term memory and to index mostly storage of information. Backward digit span, however, was taken to be a measure of working memory, because both storage and manipulation of information is needed to reverse the order of the digits during recall. More recently, though, backward digit span has been treated as another measure of short-term memory, rather than as a measure of working memory (e.g., Engle *et al.*, 1999) and other measures have gained greater currency (e.g., operation span, computation span, sentence span). One reason for the shift in classification of backward digit span is that the span measures, forward and backward, load on one factor and the other measures on a second. This might be thought somewhat unexpected, since backward span seems a priori to have both storage and manipulation requirements. Further, manipulations that reduce interference boost span measures in older adults (May, Hasher, and Kane, 1999) and alter relationships between prose memory and span (Lustig, May, and Hasher, 2001).

A similar situation has existed in the area of speed. According to general slowing theories, age-cognition relationships in cross-sectional data should be mediated by speed and in longitudinal studies change in cognition over time should be mediated by change in speed over the same period (e.g., Salthouse, 1996; Verhaeghen and Salthouse, 1997). The magnitude of the mediation of age-cognition relationships has varied from study to study, sparking considerable interest in the properties of measures that are optimal for testing the general slowing hypothesis. For instance, Salthouse (1996: 407) argues that

> the tasks used to assess processing speed should be relatively simple, such that most of the individual differences in performance are attributable to how quickly one can carry out the relevant operations rather than to variations in amount of knowledge or in other cognitive abilities. ...

and moreover that any speed measure

> should not merely represent input and output processes or sensory and motor processes, or else it may not reflect the duration of relevant cognitive operations.

Salthouse specifically cites lexical decision and reading speed measures as being likely to involve not only the speed with which elementary mental operations (unspecified) are carried out, but also general world knowledge and verbal ability. Presumably simple reaction time to the presence of a stimulus does not involve a sufficiency of elementary mental operations. However, some putatively simple measures of processing speed have proven more complex. Performance on the Digit Symbol Substitution Task appears to improve with practice as participants acquire digit-symbol associations (Piccinin and Rabbitt, 1999) and its power to mediate age–cognition relationships may arise because it is an index of general intelligence (Parkin and Java, 1999). Older adults' performance on simple letter comparison tasks is also more affected than that of young adults by the presence of distraction, so test format can influence the estimation of age–speed relationships (Hasher, Tonev, Lustig *et al.*, 2001). Moreover, it is not always easy to predict just which measures will be good mediators of age–cognition relationships – digit cancellation might be expected to work well given Salthouse's criteria, but does not always do so (Parkin and Java, 1999).

Analyses of the VLS data (Hertzog, this volume; Hertzog, Hultsch, Dixon *et al.*, 2002; Hultsch *et al.*, 1998) provide compelling examples of how selection of measures as markers for processing resource constructs can influence the nature of the conclusions drawn. In Sample 1 of the VLS, the working-memory measures used were the sentence construction task and the N-back task. The first of these is similar to the Daneman and Carpenter (1980) reading span task but the final words of the sentences within a set form a sentence that is reported when a recall cue is given. This task differs from other sentence span measures in that semantic processes can facilitate maintenance of the target words. The N-back task is a running memory span task that requires people to report the last digit, the last digit but one, or the last digit but two on a given trial. The speed measures for Sample 1 were two complex semantic tasks, one involving lexical decision and the other requiring a plausibility judgement for sentences, as well as reading time and comprehension time for passages (Hultsch *et al.*, 1998). Two measures from Salthouse and Babcock (1991) were added at the second measurement occasion for Sample 1. For listening span, people heard a sentence and answered a simple question about it, while retaining the final word of each sentence until recall of the set was requested. For computation span, a series of simple arithmetic problems was presented, with solution of each required, and the last digit of each problem to be retained for later recall.

Which measures were incorporated into structural equation models made a considerable difference. For instance, when semantic speed (indexed by lexical decision and plausibility judgement times) and working memory (indexed by sentence construction) were used in a mediational model to predict age differences in two episodic memory latent factors (word recall and text recall), it had little direct effect on the two episodic memory tasks, but the direct effect of working memory was substantial. Working memory accounted for the greater part of the variance in the two recall factors and there were no direct effects of crystallized intelligence (measured by vocabulary, verbal fluency, and fact recall). Age had a direct effect on word recall but not on text recall. However, when the two Salthouse and Babcock working-memory measures were substituted for sentence construction, the contribution of the working memory latent variable was reduced, and direct effects of age and crystallized intelligence emerged for text recall and age and fact recall relationships with word recall increased. The relationship between the speed construct and working memory was retained. Also, it was necessary to add a relationship between the residuals for the two episodic memory latent constructs. For a subsequent Sample 2, mediational models for age–episodic memory relationships were also tested in a cross-sectional analysis, using both the sentence construction and the two Salthouse working-memory measures and also varying whether perceptual speed measures favored by Salthouse or a choice–reaction time measure of speed was used (Hertzog *et al.*, 2002). One of the findings was that, again, choice of working-memory measures determined the contribution of the working memory latent construct. A second was that using choice-RT rather than perceptual speed reduced the extent of speed mediation of episodic memory. Results for longitudinal analyses from the Sample 1 and Sample 2 data, using different measures and combinations of measures, similarly led to differences in inferences about the nature of the relationships identified, not only for constructs representing processing resources, but for other constructs as well.

Work cited in Hultsch and MacDonald's chapter on variability illustrates a similar point. Young and older adults in the Hultsch *et al.* (2002) study showed within-person stability of variability across tasks and across trials within tasks and their measures of variability tended to correlate with each other, suggesting that variability within persons is a fairly stable trait-like characteristic. This was true across the entire sample and for each group individually, so we can be reasonably sure that there are no correlations of variability with age affecting the results here. However, not all measures of intraindividual variability proved equally effective as predictors of performance on perceptual speed, working memory, episodic memory, or crystallized abilities, each indexed in standard ways. For the purposes of this set of analyses, the latency measures were divided into those that were verbal (lexical decision and semantic decision) and those that were nonverbal (simple and complex reaction time). For all four cognitive composites, both mean task latency and intraindividual standard deviations predicted performance. However, only the nonverbal reaction time measures uniquely predicted performance. Thus, 'patterns of prediction differ as a function of type of RT measure and not as a function of cognitive domain assessed'.

Two straightforward conclusions can be drawn from this. First, had the VLS included only verbal or only non verbal measures of reaction times, Hultsch *et al.* (2002) might have concluded that intraindividual variability did or did not uniquely predict performance. Had verbal measures only been included, intraindividual variability might not have been a unique predictor of performance on various cognitive domains and the results might have looked like the typical results reported in the literature – mediation of age–performance relationships by mean speed. Had only nonverbal measures been included, the conclusion might have been that both means and intraindividual standard deviations predict performance on all four cognitive composites. This would have required an elaboration, but perhaps no fundamental changes in the view that speed is important in explaining cognitive aging. The issue of why only variability in the nonverbal measures contributed uniquely to variance in the cognitive composites remains somewhat puzzling. Hultsch *et al.* (2002) suggest that the verbal skill of older adults serves a compensatory function. Just why this should be the case is unclear (but see Burke, MacKay, and James, 2000, for a suggested mechanism) and it is further unclear why verbal variability should not prove to be a useful predictor within samples of young and older adults who vary in verbal ability.

What is also striking in the Hultsch *et al.* (2002) aging study is that only variability in response time measures was used as a predictor. In the dementia/arthritis/normal aging study (Hultsch *et al.*, 2000), accuracy variability proved not to differ across groups. It remains an interesting question as to why variability in accuracy measures doesn't do as good a job in differentiating groups. Hultsch *et al.* (2000) suggest that reaction time variability may index random errors in transmission signals in the brain that could translate into impaired performance. We might note again that it was only variability in the nonverbal measures of reaction time that uniquely predicted performance on other measures. When choice reaction time, however, was used as a marker for speed in the mediational analyses reported by Hertzog *et al.* (2002), speed was a less good mediator of age–episodic memory relationships than when this construct was indexed by other speed measures. This leads to the question of what would have happened had variability in other nonverbal speed measures or other simpler verbal speed measures (say word reading times) been assessed.

The structural models of working memory described by Park and Minear similarly exemplify issues having to do with selection of markers of latent constructs. Park, Lautenschlager, Hedden *et al.* (2002) examined the relationships among constructs for age, speed, short-term memory, working memory, and long-term verbal and visuospatial memory. The short-term measures selected for the verbal domain were forward and backward digit span. The measures of working memory that were used for the verbal domain were reading span and computation span from Salthouse and Babcock (1991). The speed measures were digit symbol, letter comparison, and pattern comparison. With these indicators, the results of structural equation modeling supported distinctions between domains for short-term memory, working memory, and long-term memory with each working memory having a separate short-term store associated with it, and strong associations between stores across domains for both short-term and working memory. Preliminary measurement models described in Park *et al.* (2002) indicated that the short-term memory measures could not be combined with those for working memory to yield single constructs within each domain. Speed was a strong mediator of age–recall measures, with age having no direct relationships with other latent constructs, and working memory also playing a role. Given the findings from Hertzog's models, we are inclined to ask whether other combinations of measures would have led to different conclusions about the mediational role of speed. In a related vein, though there is evidence for differential slowing in verbal and nonverbal domains (e.g., Hale, Myerson, Faust *et al.*, 1995; Laver and Burke, 1993), Park *et al.* (2002), like other investigators, used a general, rather than a domain-specific, slowing factor in their model. It is an open question as to how a model with domain-specific slowing factors might have fared. Interestingly, Hedden, Park, Nisbett *et al.*, (2002) used forward and backward digit span as indicators of working memory in a study comparing Chinese and Americans. If these are treated as indicators of short-term rather than working memory, the conclusions from this study might be better cast in terms of short-term memory.

To repeat, the take-home message is that selection of measures critically determines the conclusions to be drawn about resource mediation of age–cognition relationships. In some quarters, there have been calls for greater standardization of measures used as indicators of latent constructs across laboratories so that similarities and differences in findings can be evaluated against characteristics of the samples. This is a goal that is hard to argue with. Nonetheless, the results reported by both Hultsch and MacDonald and by Hertzog strongly suggest that diversity in measures across labs is also important. If we all use a given set of measures, we may be drawn to conclusions that would be different had we all selected some other set.

Models matter

The initial assumptions that we make about the structure of cognition have important consequences for the conclusions we draw about relationships among latent factors and about the role of age. This point is neatly demonstrated in the chapters by Hertzog and by Park and Minear. Both of these present models in which mediation of age differences by processing resources is tested. That is, in addition to any direct effects that age might have on word memory, text memory, or memory for visuospatial ability, age is also postulated to exert indirect influences through its effects on more general mechanisms involving speed and/or working memory. Such models have been used widely over at least the last 15 years as explanatory devices for age effects, especially with cross-sectional data (Salthouse, 1996; Verhaeghen and Salthouse, 1997).

There are several variants of these models (see e.g., Allen, Hall, Druley *et al.*, 2001; Salthouse and Czaja, 2000). For instance, in the single common factor or common cause model, age exerts its influence through a higher order latent factor onto which observable variables load. In independent factors models, independent age-related effects operate at the level of sets of variables (cognitive domains). In hierarchical models, age-related influences are hypothesized to operate only on a higher order factor, but there is also structure at lower levels (first order factors). In single common factor and hierarchical models, perceptual speed or working memory may be treated either as the common factor or as lower order factors, rather than having special status as mediators. Other accounts of the common factor include general intelligence (e.g., Hertzog *et al.*, 2002) with central nervous system integrity also proposed as the mechanism for the common factor (Lindenberger and Baltes, 1994). In hierarchical models, there may be more than one higher order factor. There may also be modeling of direct effects of age on lower order as well as higher order factors (see Allen *et al.*, 2001, Model 5).

Deciding among such models can be quite difficult. For instance, Allen *et al.* (2001) carried out Monte Carlo simulations for artifical data sets generated from models with known underlying structure. One of these data sets had four first-order latent factors organized into two higher order common factors. Both an independent factors model and a hierarchical model with a single higher order common factor provided good fits to the data, as measured by fit indices such as CFI and NNFI, and might have been accepted as good accounts of the simulated data, had it not been known that the underlying structure was in fact different! In addition, Allen *et al.* found that a model that incorporated direct effects of age on lower order factors as well as on a common factor did a better job on several data sets that had previously been analyzed with a simpler hierarchical model. Another wrinkle is that estimates of general (higher order) and specific (lower order) contributions of speed (or other factors) on age variance may be very sensitive to particular kinds of models. Hierarchical models may bias the solution towards a general factor over specific factors, whereas an alternative representation of the relationships among latent variables in nested factors models may avoid this problem (Schmiedek and Li, in press).

In modeling Sample 2 data from the VLS, Hertzog *et al.* (2002) found that common cause and hierarchical models provided as good a fit to their data as did mediational models. Interestingly, Gf (not speed) carried the age-related variance in episodic memory. Obviously, had only the simpler mediational model been tested, the conclusion would have been that this model was supported (though as noted above, the precise conclusions as to which variables were the strongest mediators would depend on the choice of measures for working memory and speed). In actuality, however, it was not possible to choose one of these models over the other on the basis of fit indices. Moreover, in a simulation using a synthetic data set based on a causal spuriousness (complete independence) model in which speed had no direct influence on other aspects of cognition, both mediational and common-factor models fit the data nicely. The latter did not capture residual correlations among cognitive latent variables, making it a poor candidate for further research, but it did provide a good fit to the data! So the moral of the story is that we can only draw conclusions about the goodness of fit of models that are actually tested, and model comparison ought to be the norm.

Work described in Park and Minear's chapter also emphasizes the critical role of starting theories. As discussed above, Park *et al.* (2002) test what may be deemed a hybrid model derived from Baddeley's (1986) model of working memory, from Engle *et al.*'s (1999) arguments in favor of distinct short-term and working memories, and from evidence in the experimental and neuroimaging literature that visuospatial and verbal working memories can be dissociated. Baddeley's model is arguably the most highly developed of the working memory models currently being investigated and it has led to the largest associated body of empirical work. Nonetheless, it is certainly not the only model of working memory in existence (see for instance, the ten models presented in Miyake and Shah, 1999). Although many models share common features (Kintsch, Healy, Hegarty *et al.*, 1999), they do not all agree on issues having to do with the control and regulation of working memory, the number of domain-specific codes or representational systems that are required, the precise role of working memory in complex cognition, the relationship between working memory and long-term memory, how capacity limits are best implemented (e.g., by production rules or activation in a connectionist network), or whether the concept of processing resources is useful.

The conclusions we draw depend on the models we test, but these models are not static. Not only do new models get formulated on a regular basis, but current models undergo changes to bring them into alignment with evolving empirical work. Thus, Baddeley (2000) has recently reconfigured his model. The original Baddeley (1986) model included a central executive and two slave systems, the visuospatial sketch pad and the articulatory loop. The 2000 version of this model includes these components but also adds an episodic buffer (to account for interactions between the slave systems and long-term memory). Distinctions between fluid systems (the central executive, visuospatial sketch pad, episodic buffer, and phonological loop) and crystallized systems (visual semantics, episodic LTM, and language) are also included.

Quite possibly, mediational models that include all of these components would lead to very different conclusions than models that exclude some, for example latent factors for the crystallized systems, as suggested by Hertzog *et al.* (2002). Moreover, there is considerable debate among workers in psycholinguistics as to whether it is necessary to postulate the existence of working memory at all to explain individual differences in syntactic processing (see the exchange by MacDonald and Christiansen, 2002, Just and Varma, 2002, and Caplan and Waters, 2002).

Extensions to dual-process models of memory and aging

Contemporary theories of memory often posit two processes, recollection and familiarity, that subserve recall and recognition (e.g., Atkinson and Juola, 1974; Jacoby, 1991; Mandler, 1980; see Yonelinas, 2002, for a review). Recollection, or in some models recall, is typically characterized as conscious or intentional, as attention demanding, and as having a slow recruitment rate, whereas familiarity is thought to be unconscious, to have relatively low attentional requirements, and to have a rapid rise time. In most two-process models, recollective processes involve conscious remembering of particular aspects of a prior episode, such as perceptual details, spatial or temporal information, the source of information, or thoughts and feelings that accompanied the episode. Evidence from many sources suggests that older adults have lower recollection than young adults, but that familiarity is relatively preserved (see Light, Prull, La Voie *et al.*, 2000, for a review). However, careful examination of the literature, as well as work from my laboratory, suggests that this conclusion is very much dependent on how we construe familiarity and what assumptions we make in modeling the data. To illustrate this point, I will consider two broad approaches to the study of familiarity and recollection in old age. These are the dissociation, or lack thereof, between direct and indirect memory tasks by aging and quantitative procedures for obtaining estimates of the contributions of recollection and familiarity to performance.

On direct measures of memory such as recall and recollection, people are asked to deliberately recall or recognize recently experienced materials. On indirect measures of memory deliberate recollection is not solicited by task instructions. Instead, the effects of prior experience are manifested by changes in accuracy or latency in tasks not generally thought of as requiring memory – such as reading words, naming pictures, classifying words, completing a word stem or a word fragment with the first word that comes to mind, or generating associates or exemplars of a category. Because deliberate recollection is not solicited in these tasks, it has been assumed that priming is supported largely by nonrecollective processes – i.e., familiarity mechanisms. Recognition has been assumed (but see below) to be less dependent on recollection than recall. If so, we would expect that age-related differences in performance should be greater for recall than for recognition and for recognition than for indirect measures. And indeed, La Voie and Light (1994) found this to be true in a meta-analysis. Mean weighted effect sizes were 0.97 for recall, 0.50 for recognition, and 0.30 for indirect measures of memory.

In a recent meta-analysis of indirect measures of memory, Light, Prull, La Voie *et al.* (2000), found a mean weighted effect size of 0.185, with a confidence interval from 0.133 to 0.237. This confidence interval does not include zero, suggesting a genuine age difference in these tasks, one that may be underestimated because priming tasks are not notoriously reliable measures. We were interested in whether it was possible to identify classes of tasks that would show age differences and classes of tasks that would not. We looked at three potential classificatory schemes, perceptual vs. conceptual priming, production vs. identification, and high vs. low competition. In doing these analyses we focused on a set of 79 effect sizes that came from studies of single-item priming. These analyses demonstrate persuasively that the magnitude of age differences in priming tasks depends on which tasks are used and that conlusions about the mechanisms contributing to age differences (and the presence or absence of these) depend on selection of measures, both tasks and dependent variables within tasks.

The perceptual priming tasks had a larger mean effect size (0.23) than the conceptual tasks (0.11). This might be thought to be a little surprising, given hypotheses that larger age effects should be found in tasks requiring semantic processing (see Burke and Light, 1981, for a review). It is also the conclusion that Jelicic (1995) and Rybash (1996) reached in reviews of the priming literature. Table 5.1 gives the task classification that we used. Three tasks were put an 'unknown' category: sentence completion, because at the time we did the meta-analysis no-one had done parametric studies needed to classify the task, semantic verification because the data from our lab and others suggested that such tasks share properties with both perceptual and conceptual tasks (i.e., are sensitive to semantic encoding manipulations, but not to division of attention, and may not respond to changes of format) and homophone spelling. We classed homophone spelling as *other* because we did not see any easy way to decide if it fitted the conventional criteria for either perceptual or conceptual tasks (e.g., Roediger and McDermott, 1993). It's pretty clear that the outcome and conclusion depends on which tasks are classified as perceptual and which are classed as conceptual. Jelicic (1995) treated homophone spelling and

Table 5.1 Perceptual and conceptual task classification

Perceptual	Conceptual
Anagram solution	Answering general knowledge questions
Inverted word reading	Exemplar generation
Lexical decision	Word association
Object decision	
Partial word identification	
Perceptual identification	
Picture fragment completion	
Picture naming	
Rhyme generation	
Turkish word naming	
Word fragment completion	
Word stem completion	
Word/nonword naming	

exemplar generation as conceptual. Homophone spelling had a large effect size, 0.754, and our results would have looked a little different had we classed it differently. Rybash (1996) included homophone spelling, word fragment completion, and word stem completion as conceptual. Most researchers have treated the last two as perceptual because they are allegedly insensitive to levels of processing effects at input and are sensitive to format changes at test, though Brown and Mitchell (1994) have argued that semantic processing boosts completion task performance. More generally, the classification of priming tasks as perceptual or conceptual has become more difficult as we have learned more about the characteristics of particular tasks (see, for example, the discussion of word-stem completion by Mitchell and Bruss (in press)).

Fleischman and Gabrieli (1998) classified priming tasks in terms of whether they require identification or generation. They argued that identification tasks require 'test phase identification of an item or verification of an attribute of an item as opposed to the production of an item'. The results of a meta-analysis based on this classification showed a sizable difference between identification and production tasks, with effect sizes of 0.25 for production and 0.09 for identification, the latter not being significantly different from zero. However, life is never simple. Table 5.2 shows the classification scheme that we used. Principled classification of tasks was not straightforward. For instance, naming pictures could be called an identification task for obvious reasons. On the other hand, a name has to be produced and it is unclear as to

Table 5.2 Production and identification task classification

Production	Identification
Anagram solution	Inverted word reading
Answering general knowledge questions	Lexical decision
Exemplar generation	Nonword naming
Homophone spelling	Object decision
Rhyme generation	Perceptual identification*
Sentence completion	Picture fragment completion
Word association	Picture naming
Word fragment completion	Semantic classification
Word stem completion	Turkish word naming
	Word naming

* Including perceptual identification under degraded conditions.

whether access to labels or phonology proceeds directly from the picture without access to meaning in the same way that word naming proceeds from the printed word. Fleischman and Gabrieli (1998) themselves were unclear as to what to do with word fragment completion. This requires production but may, especially if there is a single solution, 'depend relatively more than word-stem completion on identifying patterns of letters than on producing words'. As it happens, it doesn't much matter how it's classified since word fragment completion and word stem completion had similar effect sizes (0.34 and 0.28, respectively), but still it is disconcerting to have theoretical concepts be so difficult to apply when describing meaures. Also, some tasks such as item recognition don't fit neatly here – this task requires deciding whether a word was presented before and doesn't seem to be either identification or production by the definition above. There's also a confound – the production tasks all involve accuracy as the dependent variable, whereas the identification tasks involve both accuracies and latencies. For the 79 latency tasks in the analyses I'm talking about, the effect size was 0.041, with a CI from -0.086 to $+0.168$, so there is a problem here.

In my own lab, we have systematically compared an identification task, category exemplar verification, and a production task, category exemplar generation, using the same items and identical study conditions (Light, Prull, and Kennison, 2000). Neither task showed a reliable age difference, so under more tightly controlled conditions, even with the DV confound, there's no evidence that one of these tasks yields worse performance. We are also studying priming in a task that typically yields latency data, lexical decision, using a response signal paradigm. This gives us accuracy data to use in a priming analysis and lets us compare latency and accuracy data in the same paradigm.

A further distinction offered by Fleischman and Gabrieli (1998) is that between tasks involving high and low response competition. This distinction has a potential tie in with inhibition deficit theory (e.g., Hasher *et al.*, 2001), inasmuch as age differences might be expected to be more evident when there are competing responses. We classified tasks along this dimension and looked to see if the effect sizes were different, and indeed they were, with effect sizes of 0.25 and 0.09; only the former was significant. However, again, it's critical to examine the actual tasks that go into the analysis (see Table 5.3). For instance, we included picture naming in the high competition class because more than one response is possible for some pictures – these are said to be low in codability. Perceptual identification of briefly presented words was classed as low in competition, but words vary in whether their pronunciation is regular or irregular (*pint* vs. *hint*) and in the sizes of their neighborhoods. Indeed, for auditory word perception, the information comes in sequentially and the exact member of a cohort that is being spoken is not immediately apparent (Marslen-Wilson, 1987).

We have tried to get around some of these problems of task classification by studying production and identification within the same paradigm and by using manipulations that build in competition for some items. We've done this both with perceptual identification and with word fragment completion, with somewhat varying results. Light and Kennison (1996) replicated work of

Table 5.3 High and low response competition task classification

High	Low
Anagram solution	Lexical decision
Answering general knowledge questions	Nonword naming
Degraded word identification*	Object decision
Exemplar generation	Perceptual identification
Homophone spelling	Semantic verification
Picture fragment completion	Turkish word naming
Picture naming	Word fragment completion
Rhyme generation	Word naming
Sentence completion	
Word association	
Word stem completion	

* Either visual or auditory, and including inverted word reading.

Ratcliff, McKoon, and Verwoerd (1989) on word identification. The task required people to identify briefly presented words for which an orthographically similar competitor had or had not recently been presented. In neither a single stimulus version of this task nor a forced-choice version did we see reliable age effects. In word fragment completion, Light, Kennison, and Healy (2002) found evidence for greater priming in young adults on the typical single stimulus variant of the task, an unusual outcome in our experience (but see above), but no evidence for stronger effects of competition in older adults in terms of either intrusion errors in the single stimulus task or performance on the forced-choice test.

Jacoby (1991) has pointed out that neither direct nor indirect measures of memory are process-pure. Rather, both recollective and nonrecollective processes play a role in each. It is possible that the apparent age difference on some indirect measures of memory is due not to changes in nonrecollective processes in old age but to episodic contamination. Young adults have better recollection than older ones and may subvert efforts to study nonrecollective processes in indirect memory measures by invoking deliberate recollection. Moreover, we began with the assumption that 'familiarity' as measured by perceptual and conceptual priming was the same 'familiarity' that contributes to performance on recall and recognition, i.e., that there need be only one familiarity construct. This was the assumption that led us to compare effect sizes for priming tasks, recognition, and recall (La Voie and Light, 1994). This assumption, however, no longer seems altogether tenable because there is evidence from both experimental and neuropsychological studies for dissociations (e.g., Gabrieli, Fleischman, Keane *et al.*, 1995; Wagner, Gabrieli, and Verfaelli, 1997; see Yonelinas (2002) for a review). Because of the ambiguity inherent in the use of priming tasks, there is active interest in obtaining quantitative estimates of the contributions of recollection and familiarity in tasks that require deliberate recollection.

The Remember/Know (R/K) procedure introduced by Tulving (1985) and Gardiner (1988) assesses states of awareness that accompany positive recognition judgements. It does not estimate directly the hypothesized underlying processes of recollection and familiarity, but purportedly taps their products. After deciding whether a test item is old, participants judge whether they can also recollect elements of the original study experience (I thought about my new car when the word automobile was presented) or whether contextual details cannot be retrieved but the item feels sufficiently familiar to warrant a positive response. Researchers have often treated remember and know judgments as reflecting relatively pure measures of underlying processes of recollection and familiarity, respectively.

Light, Prull, La Voie *et al.* (2000) found 10 studies using the R/K procedure to compare young and older adults that had complete recognition data. A measure of recollection was computed taking R hits – R FAs – and a measure of K or familiarity by taking K hits – K FAs. For the unweighted means, the R estimate was higher for the young. For K, the old were on average a bit higher. Yonelinas and Jacoby (1995) have noted that the R/K procedure assumes that R and K judgements are mutually exclusive, whereas dual-process theories of memory typically assume that recollection and familiarity are independent. Assuming independence, R judgements can be used as an estimate of recollection. To get an estimate of F that works on the independence assumption, K is divided by 1-R. With this adjustment, we found that both recollection and familiarity estimates were lower for older adults. Of course, both R and K judgements require that an item be identified as old, and an old judgement must involve at least some minimal recollection of circumstances surrounding encoding, so perhaps the results of the R/K independence correction are not surprising. They are, however, quite different than conclusions based on raw R and K data. Yonelinas (2002) has recently hypothesized that familiarity estimates in this paradigm will not show age differences, unless there are ceiling effects for estimates of recollection. However, for the 12 studies in his corpus, the estimate of familiarity was numerically larger for the young in nine and there was one tie, so we stand by our conclusion that inferences about the constancy of familiarity across age depend on how familiarity is measured. Over and above this, we note that there is currently some lack of clarity as to the precise nature of familiarity as assessed in the R/K paradigm (e.g., Rajaram, 1998), making interpretation of any age-related change in familiarity as estimated in this procedure suspect.

The process dissociation procedure (Jacoby, 1991, 1999) uses tasks in which familiarity and recollection can be assumed to work in consort or to be in opposition. Simple algebra is used to obtain numerical estimates of recollection (R) and familiarity (F). This technique has been used with a number of different paradigms in cognitive aging studies and, generally speaking, the outcome has supported two-process theories (see reviews by Light, Prull, La Voie *et al.,* 2000, and Yonelinas, 2002). The process dissociation equations, however, assume that recollection and familiarity are independent, but other assumptions have been entertained (Joordens and Merikle, 1993) and some of these would lead to conclusions that familiarity is reduced in old age (see Light, Prull, La Voie *et al.,* 2000, for details and for additional concerns about interpreting age differences in estimated familiarity in some process dissociation paradigms).

For recognition, Yonelinas (1994, 1997) has proposed an alternative way of estimating R and F from receiver operating characteristics (ROCs) constructed from confidence ratings in item and in associative recognition. Healy and Light (2003) carried out a series of experiments in which young and older adults studied lists of word pairs and were tested for associative recognition. The test included intact (studied) pairs, rearranged pairs (two old items studied with different partners), and new (unstudied) pairs. Participants judged whether the two words in a given pair had been studied together, using a six-point rating scale (1 = sure new, 6 = sure old). Only 'old' responses to intact pairs are considered correct, with 'old' judgements of both new and rearranged pairs treated as false alarms. In judging previously studied pairs, both familiarity and recollection should work in the same direction. However, because items in rearranged pairs were both studied, the pair should be familiar, so that recollection is required to decide that the two words were not studied together. Recollection may involve retrieval of information that one member of a test pair was studied with the other (Ro, or recall to accept old pairs) or retrieval of information that one member of a test pair was studied with a different word (Rn, or recall to reject rearranged pairs). Recollection is not required for completely new pairs.

Item recognition is thought to involve primarily familiarity (as assessed by the signal detection measure d') whereas, under most test conditions, associ ative recognition is dominated by recollection (Rotello, Macmillan, and van Tassel, 2000; Yonelinas, 1994, 1997). The contributions of familiarity and recollection can be assessed by constructing receiver operating characteristics from confidence judgement data. ROC curves plot hit rates as a function of false alarm rates. With j confidence categories, j − 1 points can be generated. The first point is obtained from the strictest confidence judgement category (here 6). Old items given the rating of 6 are hits; new items given the rating of 6 are false alarms. The second and remaining points are obtained by cumulating across successive rating categories. We constructed ROCs for item recognition and for associative recognition for young and older adults. For associative recognition, p (old) for intact pairs is plotted against p (old) for rearranged pairs. To get an estimate of item recognition, we plotted p (old) for intact pairs against p (old) for new pairs.

According to signal detection models that hypothesize only a single continuous dimension (strength or familiarity) underlying recognition judgements, the ROC should be curvilinear when plotted in probability space and should intersect both 0,0 and 1,1. The upper-left panel in Figure 5.1 illustrates such an ROC for the case in which the variances of the old and new distributions of items are not assumed to be equal (the unequal variance signal detection

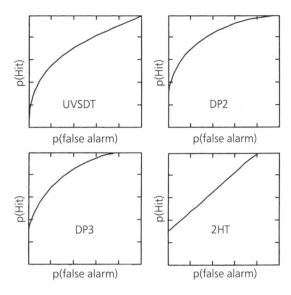

Fig. 5.1 Signal-detection models of recognition memory. UVSDT = unequal variance signal detection theory, DP2 = dual-process model with parameters d' and Ro, DP3 = dual-process model with parameters d', Ro, and Rn, 2HT = two high-threshold model with parameters Ro and Rn.

model). Models postulating only recollective processes (two high-threshold models, as shown in the lower right panel in Figure 5.1) predict ROCs that are linear in p-space, with lower-y intercepts greater than 0,0 (representing Ro), and upper-x intercepts less than 1,1 (representing Rn). A dual-process model with two parameters, one for familiarity (d') and one for Ro is shown in the top right panel of Figure 5.1, and a three parameter model incorporating familiarity, Ro, and Rn, is shown in the lower left panel.

We constructed ROC curves for item and associative recognition for each participant in three experiments and then fit each of the four models depicted in Figure 5.1 to the ROCs. Our associative ROCs were more curvilinear than expected by a pure recollection model (see Kelley and Wixted, 2001, for a similar outcome) and were generally best fit by the three-parameter dual-process model. In each experiment, we found age differences in Ro and Rn, the two recollection parameters in this model. If familiarity is appropriately indexed by d', as suggested by Yonelinas (1994, 1997), we would expect age constancy in d'. However, in all three experiments these estimates were greater for young adults, significantly so in two. For the item ROCs, the best fitting model was unequivocally the unequal variance signal detection model, which also has d' as an index of familiarity. In two of the experiments, the value of d' as estimated from this model was greater for young adults than for older adults. Although it was not the best fitting model, the dual-process model with two parameters, one for Ro and one for d', is arguably the most theoretically appropriate one for intact/new ROCs given that participants can use Ro for intact pairs. The dual-process model also provided a good fit to the item ROCs. When we compared parameter estimates across age for this model, d' estimates did not differ significantly across groups, but Ro did!

To summarize, we found clear evidence for age differences in two kinds of recollection in associative recognition, as well as some evidence for age differences in familiarity. For the item recognition ROCs, our inferences about age differences in familiarity depend on the choice of signal detection model. We should note, however, that Yonelinas (1994, 1997) makes particular assumptions about recollection and familiarity that are incorporated into the dual-process models we tested. These processes are assumed to be independent, and familiarity is assumed to be continuous, whereas both recollection parameters (Ro and Rn) are treated as all-or-none. If these assumptions (and others that we made in our particular application of Yonelinas' program) should prove incorrect, interpretation of our findings would of necessity change (cf. Kelley and Wixted, 2001; Malmberg, 2002).

Conclusion

The research described in the three chapters in this section as well as findings from my laboratory amply illustrate the interplay between measures, constructs, models, and inferences about cognitive aging. Models inform our selection of empirical findings for which explanations are sought, the choice of constructs to include in models, and the classes of dependent variables to be used. For instance, interest in indirect measures of memory increased as dissociations between direct and indirect measures of memory were identified (cf. Roediger and McDermott, 1993), and definitions of familiarity have evolved as our understanding of the processes involved in different memory paradigms has shifted. Park and Hertzog's chapters demonstrate the importance of theoretical framework in construct selection. Hultsch and MacDonald's emphasis on intraindividual variability is spurred by recent reaction time models that include entire distributions of responses (e.g., Ratcliff, Thapar, and McKoon, 2001; Spieler, Balota, and Faust, 1996) as well as by models that seek links between reaction time variability to brain integrity (Li, 2002). When putative markers of constructs fail to behave as expected, we look to theory for possible reasons and we, sometimes, revise our models. Thus, Hertzog discusses the role of semantic influences in the sentence construction task. Park models working memory and short-term memory as separate constructs. And in my laboratory, we seek accounts for why different indirect measures of memory lead to different conclusions about cognitive aging and try to evaluate alternative strategies for conceptualizing familiarity and recollection.

These ideas are not presented as revelations. Rather they describe the conditions of the research enterprise in which we are all engaged. We think that it is useful to be periodically reminded of the assumptions that underlie our activities. In doing so, we maintain receptivity to new measures, new constructs, new models, and perhaps new discoveries about the course of cognitive aging.

Author note

The support of National Institute on Aging Grant AG02452 during preparation of this chapter is gratefully acknowledged.

References

Allen, P. A., Hall, R. J., Druley, J. A., Smith, A. F., Sanders, R. E., and Murphy, M. D. (2001). How shared are age-related influences on cognitive and noncognitive variables? *Psychology and Aging,* **16**, 532–549.

Atkinson, R. C. and Juola, J. F. (1974). Search and decision processes in recognition memory. In D. H. Krantz, R. C. Atkinson, R. D. Luce, and P. Suppes (eds), *Contemporary Developments in Mathematical Psychology, Vol. 1: Learning, Memory and Thinking* (pp. 243–293). San Francisco, CA: W. H. Freeman.

Baddeley, A. (1986). *Working Memory.* New York: Oxford University Press.

Baddeley, A. D. (2000). The episodic buffer: A new component for working memory? *Trends in Cognitive Sciences,* **4**, 417–423.

Brown, A. S. and Mitchell, D. B. (1994). A reevaluation of semantic versus nonsemantic processing in implicit memory. *Memory & Cognition,* **22**, 522–541.

Burke, D. M. and Light, L. L. (1981). Memory and aging: The role of retrieval. *Psychological Bulletin,* **90**, 513–546.

Burke, D. M., MacKay, D. G., and James, L. E. (2000). Theoretical approaches to language and aging. In T. J. Perfect and E. A. Maylor (eds), *Models of Cognitive Aging* (pp. 204–237). Oxford: Oxford University Press.

Caplan, D. C. and Waters, G. (2002). Working memory and connectionist models of parsing: A reply to MacDonald and Christiansen (2002). *Psychological Review,* **109**, 66–74.

Daneman, M. and Carpenter, P. A. (1980). Individual differences in working memory and reading. *Journal of Verbal Learning and Verbal Behavior,* **19**, 450–466.

Engle, R. W., Tuholski, S. W., Laughlin, J. E., and Conway, A. R. A. (1999). Working memory, short-term memory, and general fluid intelligence: A latent-variable approach. *Journal of Experimental Psychology: General,* **128**, 309–331.

Fleischman, D. A. and Gabrieli, J. D. E. (1998). Repetition priming in normal aging and Alzheimer's Disease: A review of findings and theories. *Psychology and Aging,* **13**, 88–119.

Gabrieli, J. D. E., Fleischman, D. A., Keane, M. M., Reminger, S. L., and Morrell, F. (1995). Double dissociation between memory systems underlying explicit and implicit memory in the human brain. *Psychological Science,* **6**, 76–82.

Gardiner, J. M. (1988). Functional aspects of recollective experience. *Memory & Cognition,* **16**, 309–313.

Hale, S., Myerson, J., Faust, M., and Fristoe, N. (1995). Converging evidence for domain-specific slowing from multiple nonlexical tasks and multiple analytic methods: *Journal of Gerontology: Psychological Sciences*, **50B**, P202–P211.

Hasher, L., Tonev, S. T., Lustig, C., and Zacks, R. T. (2001). Inhibitory control, environmental support, and self-initiated processing in aging. In M. Naveh-Benjamin, M. Moscovitch, and H. L. Roediger, III (eds), *Perspectives on Human Memory and Cognitive Aging: Essays in honour of Fergus Craik* (pp. 286–297). New York: Psychology Press.

Healy, M. R. and Light, L. L. (2003). *Dual-Process Models of Associative Recognition in Young and Older Adults: Evidence from Receiver Operating Characteristics*. Manuscript submitted for publication.

Hedden, T., Park, D. C., Nisbett, R., Jing, Q., Jiao, S., and Ji, L-J. (2002). Cultural variation in verbal versus spatial neuropsychological function across the life span. *Neuropsychology*, **16**, 65–73.

Hertzog, C., Hultsch, D. F., Dixon, R. A., and Small, B. J. (2002). *Contrasting models for age differences in episodic memory: Is processing speed the key mediator?* Manuscript submitted for publication.

Hultsch, D. F., Hertzog, C., Dixon, R. A., and Small, B. J. (1998). *Memory Change in the Aged*. New York: Cambridge University Press.

Hultsch, D. F., MacDonald, S. W. S., and Dixon, R. A. (2002). Variability in reaction time performance of younger and older adults. *Journal of Gerontology: Psychological Sciences*, **57B**, P101–P115.

Hultsch, D. F., MacDonald, S. W. S., Hunter, M. A., Levy-Bencheton, J., and Strauss, E. (2000). Intraindividual variability in cognitive performance in older adults: Comparison of adults with mild dementia, adults with arthritis, and healthy adults. *Neuropsychology*, **14**, 588–598.

Jacoby, L. L. (1991). A process dissociation framework: Separating automatic from intentional uses of memory. *Journal of Memory and Language*, **30**, 513–541.

Jacoby, L. L. (1999). Ironic effects of repetition: Measuring age-related differences in memory. *Journal of Experimental Psychology: Learning, Memory, and Cognition*, **25**, 3–22.

Jelicic, M. (1995). Aging and performance on implicit memory tasks: A brief review. *International Journal of Neuroscience*, **82**, 155–161.

Joordens, S. and Merikle, P. M. (1993). Independence or redundancy? Two models of conscious and unconscious influences. *Journal of Experimental Psychology: General*, **122**, 462–467.

Just, M. A. and Varma, S. (2002). A hybrid architecture for working memory: Reply to MacDonald and Christiansen (2002). *Psychological Review*, **109**, 55–65.

Kelley, R. and Wixted, J. T. (2001). On the nature of associative information in recognition memory. *Journal of Experimental Psychology: Learning, Memory, and Cognition*, **27**, 701–722.

Kintsch, W., Healy, A. F., Hegarty, M., Pennington, B. F., and Salthouse, T. A. (1999). Models of working memory: Eight questions and some general issues. In A. Miyake and P. Shah (eds), *Models of Working Memory: Mechanisms of active maintenance and executive control* (pp. 412–441). New York: Cambridge University Press.

Laver, G. D. and Burke, D. M. (1993). Why do semantic priming effects increase in old age? *Psychology and Aging*, **8**, 34–43.

La Voie, D. J. and Light, L. L. (1994). Adult age differences in repetition priming: A meta-analysis. *Psychology and Aging*, **9**, 539–553.

Li, S.-C. (2002). Connecting the many levels and facets of cognitive aging. *Current Directions in Psychological Science*, **11**, 38–43.

Light, L. L. and Kennison, R. F. (1996). Guessing strategies, aging, and bias effects in perceptual identification. *Consciousness and Cognition*, **5**, 463–499.

Light, L. L., Kennison, R. F., and Healy, M. R. (2002). Bias effects in word fragment completion in young and older adults. *Memory & Cognition*, **30**, 1204–1218.

Light, L. L., Prull, M. W., and Kennison, R. F. (2000). Divided attention, aging, and priming in exemplar generation and category verification. *Memory & Cognition*, **28**, 856–872.

Light, L. L., Prull, M. W., La Voie, D. J., and Healy, M. R. (2000). Dual process theories of memory in old age. In T. J. Perfect and E. A. Maylor (eds), *Models of Cognitive Aging* (pp. 238–300). Oxford: Oxford University Press.

Lindenberger, U. and Baltes, P. B. (1994). Sensory functioning and intelligence in old age: A strong connection. *Psychology and Aging*, **9**, 339–355.

Little, T. D., Lindenberger, U., and Nesselroade, J. R. (1999). On selecting indicators for multivariate measurement and modeling with latent variables: When 'good' indicators are bad and 'bad' indicators are good. *Psychological Methods*, **4**, 192–211.

Lustig, C., May, C. P., and Hasher, L. (2001). Working memory span and the role of proactice interference. *Journal of Experimental Psychology: General*, **130**, 199–207.

MacDonald, M. C. and Christiansen, M. H. (2002). Reassessing working memory: Comment on Just and Carpenter (2002) and Waters and Caplan (1996). *Psychological Review*, **109**, 35–54.

Malmberg, K. J. (2002). On the form of ROCs constructed from confidence ratings. *Journal of Experimental Psychology: Learning, Memory, and Cognition*, **28**, 380–387.

Mandler, G. (1980). Recognizing: The judgment of previous occurrence. *Psychological Review*, **87**, 252–271.

Marslen-Wilson, W. D. (1987). Functional parallelism in spoken word-recognition. *Cognition*, **25**, 71–102.

May, C. P., Hasher, L., and Kane, M. J. (1999). The role of interference in memory span. *Memory & Cognition*, **27**, 759–767.

Mitchell, D. B. and Bruss, P. J. (in press). Age differences in implicit memory: Conceptual, perceptual, or methodological? *Psychology and Aging*.

Miyake, A. and Shah, P. (eds) (1999). *Models of Working Memory: Mechanisms of active maintenance and executive control*. New York: Cambridge University Press.

Park, D. C., Lautenschlager, G., Hedden, T., Davidson, N. S., Smith, A. D., and Smith, P. K. (2002). Models of visuospatial and verbal memory across the adult life span. *Psychology and Aging*, **17**, 299–320.

Parkin, A. J. and Java, R. I. (1999). Deterioration of frontal lobe function in normal aging: Influences of fluid intelligence versus perceptual speed. *Neuropsychology*, **13**, 539–545.

Piccinin, A. M. and Rabbitt, P. M. A. (1999). Contribution of cognitive abilities to performance and improvement on a substitution coding task. *Psychology and Aging*, **14**, 539–551.

Rajaram, S. (1998). The effects of conceptual salience and perceptual distinctiveness on conscious recollection. *Psychonomic Bulletin & Review*, **5**, 71–78.

Ratcliff, R., McKoon, G., and Verwoerd, M. (1989). A bias interpretation of facilitation in perceptual identification. *Journal of Experimental Psychology: Learning, Memory, and Cognition,* **15**, 378–387.

Ratcliff, R., Thapar, A., and McKoon, G. (2001). The effects of aging on reaction time in a signal detection task. *Psychology and Aging,* **16**, 323–341.

Roediger, H. L., III and McDermott, K. B. (1993). Implicit memory in normal human subjects. In F. Boller and J. Grafman (eds), *Handbook of neuropsychology* (Vol. 8, pp. 63–131). Amsterdam: Elsevier.

Rotello, C. M., Macmillan, N. A., and Van Tassel, G. (2000). Recall-to-reject in recognition: Evidence from ROC curves. *Journal of Memory and Language,* **43**, 67–88.

Rybash, J. M. (1996). Implicit memory and aging: A cognitive neuropsychological perspective. *Developmental Neuropsychology,* **12**, 127–179.

Salthouse, T. A. (1996). The processing-speed theory of adult age differences in cognition. *Psychological Review,* **103**, 403–428.

Salthouse, T. A. and Babcock, R. L. (1991). Decomposing adult age differences in working memory. *Developmental Psychology,* **27**, 765–776.

Salthouse, T. A. and Czaja, S. J. (2000). Structural constraints on process explanations in cognitive aging. *Psychology and Aging,* **15**, 44–55.

Schmiedek, F. and Li, S-C. (in press). Towards an alternative representation for disentangling general and specific effects of cognitive aging. *Psychology and Aging.*

Spieler, D. H., Balota, D. A., and Faust, M. E. (1996). Stroop performance in normal older adults and individuals with senile dementia of the Alzheimer's type. *Journal of Experimental Psychology: Human Perception and Performance,* **22**, 461–479.

Tulving, E. (1985). Memory and consciousness. *Canadian Psychology,* **26**, 1–12.

Verhaeghen, P. and Salthouse, T. A. (1997). Meta-analyses of age-cognition relations in adulthood: Estimates of linear and nonlinear age effects and structural models. *Psychological Bulletin,* **122**, 231–249.

Wagner, A. D., Gabrieli, J. D. E., and Verfaellie, M. (1997). Dissociations between familiarity processes in explicit recognition and implicit perceptual memory. *Journal of Experimental Psychology: Learning, Memory, and Cognition,* **23**, 305–323.

Yonelinas, A. P. (1994). Receiver-operating characteristics in recognition memory: Evidence for a dual-process model. *Journal of Experimental Psychology: Learning, Memory, and Cognition,* **20**, 1341–1354.

Yonelinas, A. P. (1997). Recognition memory ROCs for item and associative information: The contribution of recollection and familiarity. *Memory & Cognition,* **25**, 747–763.

Yonelinas, A. P. (2002). The nature of recollection and familiarity: A Review of 30 years of research. *Journal of Memory and Language,* **46**, 441–517.

Yonelinas, A. P. and Jacoby, L. L. (1995). The relation between remembering and knowing as bases for recognition: Effects of size congruency. *Journal of Memory and Language,* **34**, 622–643.

Part 3

New directions in the cognitive neuroscience of aging

Chapter 6

The aging brain: Structural changes and their implications for cognitive aging

Naftali Raz

When brains of healthy persons in their twenties and seventies are compared, nonspecific signs of aging such as loss of gross volume and expansion of the cavities filled with the cerebro-spinal fluid (CSF) may be readily apparent. Even when aging is not aggravated by disease, its impact on the brain can sometimes be discerned by the naked eye (Figure 6.1).

However, as striking as the overt differences between some young and old brains may be, in many instances, the appearance may be less than informative. In a population of healthy adults neuroanatomical distinctions do not define categorically separate groups but represent a continuous gradient of properties. Such a gradient is negatively slanted towards older ages, but nonetheless allows for a substantial overlap between the neuroanatomical features at the extremes

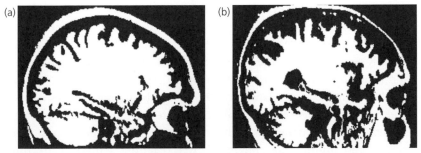

Fig. 6.1 An example of apparent differences in the brains of two asymptomatic healthy individuals. (a) – a 23-year-old woman (b) – a 77-year-old woman. Note enlargement of the temporal horns of the lateral ventricles and the Sylvian fissure; expanded sulci, especially in the prefrontal and superior parietal regions; and a shrunken hippocampus in the older brain.

of the age range. Thus, aging cannot be viewed as a lesion in the traditional neurological sense. The methods developed for examination of individual differences in other aspects of human physiology and behavior are appropriate for investigation of structural aging of the brain and the associations between brain and cognitive performance in normal aging.

Although after two decades of *in vivo* examination of gross brain morphology a complex pattern of age-related differences continues to emerge, some preliminary generalizations can be made. In this chapter, I will summarize volumetric studies of age-related differences in the human brain observed *in vivo* using magnetic resonance imaging (MRI), and will present several examples of their impact on cognitive performance in healthy adults. This account is an update, extension, and refinement of a previously published review (Raz, 2000), to which the reader is referred for a detailed description of the methods and approaches of MRI-based volumetry, as well as its relation to other methods of exploring the aging brain *in vivo*.

Differential aging of the brain

Although postmortem and *in vivo* studies reveal a moderate linear shrinkage of the brain in humans and other primates, more detailed examinations of regional volumes have demonstrated that not all brain structures are affected to the same extent. As far as the gross brain volume is concerned, most *in vivo* studies converge, regardless of methodological variations, onto the notion that the brain shrinks with age in a moderate linear fashion, and that age-related shrinkage of the brain is due primarily to reduction of the gray rather than white matter volume (Courchesne, Chisum, Townsend *et al.*, 2000; Good, Johnsrude, Ashburner *et al.*, 2001; Jernigan, Press, and Hesselink 1990; Jernigan, Archibald, Berhow *et al.*, 1991; Ohnishi, Matsuda, Tabira *et al.*, 2001, Passe, Rajagopalan, Tupler *et al.*, 1997; Raz, Gunning, Head *et al.*, 1997; Van Laere and Dirckx, 2001). Nonetheless, some reports indicate that white matter reduction is mainly responsible for the loss of cerebral volume during normal aging (Guttmann, Jolesz, Kikinis *et al.*, 1998; Jernigan, Archibald, Fenema-Notestine *et al.*, 2001; Salat, Kaye, and Janowsky, 1999). Notably, in some samples, a curvilinear relationship between age and white matter volume has been revealed. The implication is that the bulk of the white matter increases between late adolescence and middle age and then, after reaching a plateau, declines (Bartzokis, Beckson, Lu *et al.*, 2001; Courchesne *et al.*, 2000). It is, therefore, possible that samples tilted towards the older participants are more likely to show white matter shrinkage than those that were drawn from the younger end of the age range. Indeed, this is the case with the studies of significant decline of the white matter with age, especially the sample from the Oregon Healthy Brain Aging Study (Salat, Kaye, and Janowsky, 1999) in which the participants were older than 65 years of age, and a substantial number of octa- and nonagenarians were included. In contrast, all studies that showed gray matter shrinkage in the absence of white matter volume declines covered a broad age range, and included few if any participants who were older than 80.

Of course, the lack of volumetric differences does not imply that white matter somehow escapes the ill effects of senescence. Since the earliest days of magnetic resonance imaging (MRI), radiologists have reported limited areas of reduced signal intensity in the white matter of asymptomatic elderly patients (Bradley, Walluch, Brant-Zawadzki, Yadley, and Wycoff, 1984). In neuropathological sense, the WMH (see Figure 6.2 for an example) represent a final common outcome of many age-related processes and events (De Leeuw, De Groot, and Breteler, 2001). Reduction in cerebral perfusion in the vulnerable border zones (Brant-Zawadzki, 1987), and subclinical ischemia (Pantoni and Garcia, 1997) cause expansion of perivascular spaces (Ball, 1989). Gliosis (Chimowitz, Estes, Furlan, and Awad, 1992; Fazekas *et al.*, 1993), myelin pallor (Awad, Johnson, Spetzler, and Hodak, 1986; Fazekas *et al.*, 1993), and atrophy of the neuropil (Fazekas *et al.*, 1993) produce deep WMH. Breakdown of the subependymal ventricular lining (Leifer *et al.*, 1990; Scarpelli *et al.*, 1994) results in characteristic periventricular caps.

In a quantitative review of clinical and demographic risk factors associated with WMH we found that age, a history of transient ischemia attack/cerebrovascular accident (TIA/CVA), and, to a lesser extent, hypertension were robust predictors of WMH (Gunning-Dixon and Raz, submitted). Surprisingly, diabetes, alcohol use, smoking history, and elevated cholesterol

(a)　　　　　　　　　　　　　　　(b)

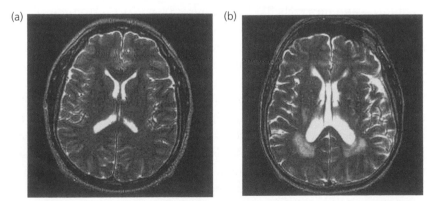

Fig. 6.2 White matter hyperintensities (WMH) in asymptomatic adults – a 24-year-old man (a) and a 79-year-old man (b). Note ventricular caps and punctate hyperintensities in the striatum in addition to mildly enlarged ventricles and sulci in the older brain (b).

were not significantly associated with WMH, although it is unknown whether these factors play a significant role when they reach a certain threshold of severity.

In my earlier attempt to summarize the findings on age-related differences in brain regions revealed by MRI-based volumetry (Raz, 2000), I did not take into account the differences in the age range samples in the reviewed studies. Below, I present a new summary of that literature with the addition of the studies published since the appearance of the previous account. The main change in this quantitative summary is that it is restricted to the studies in which the sample included participants who were younger than 30 and older than 60 years of age, thus excluding reports that dealt exclusively with older adults. The list of the studies is presented in Appendix 1 at the end of this chapter and their summary is depicted in the box plot in Figure 6.3. Pearson product moment correlation (r) was used as a common metric of effect size for comparison among the studies, and for the purpose of that comparison Spearman that was employed in one study (Jernigan et al., 2001) was treated as r as well.

From the quantitative analysis of the regional volumetry studies the prefrontal cortex emerges as the region that is more vulnerable to aging than the rest of the brain, with the median effect size of r = −0.58 (based on seven studies), indicating a relatively strong association between age and the regional volume in that brain location. The effect of this magnitude is classified as large (Cohen, 1988). Significant but more moderate age effects are observed in the striatum (median r = −0.47 for 12 studies of the caudate and r = −0.44 for 10 studies of the putamen), the temporal lobe or its separate gyri (r = −0.35, seven studies), the cerebellar vermis (median r = −0.37, 11 studies) and the cerebellar hemispheres (r = −0.33, 10 studies), the hippocampus (median r = −0.34, 18 studies), and the parahippocampal gyrus (median r = −0.27, eight studies). The prefrontal white matter also showed a moderate degree of age-related vulnerability (r = −0.36, five studies), whereas parietal white matter revealed a smaller age effect (r = −0.23, four studies), with a more substantial variability among the studies. The occipital, mainly primary visual, regions seem to be largely spared by senescence (median r = −0.19, five studies), and so is the thalamus (with all its distinct nuclei lumped into one region of interest), which shows a median r = −0.18 (four studies). Surprisingly, the anterior cingulate gyrus, which is implicated in many cognitive functions, motor control, arousal, and motivation (Allman, Hakeem, Erwin et al., 2001; Paus, 2001) appears spared (median r = −0.17, six studies). On the basis of only three available studies, the globus pallidus volume seems stable in normal aging (median r = −0.14, three studies), and no age differences were consistently observed in a lack of age-related shrinkage in the ventral pons area (median r = 0.05, six studies). Unfortunately, an insufficient number of volumetric studies examined specific regions of the posterior association cortices. Three available studies present

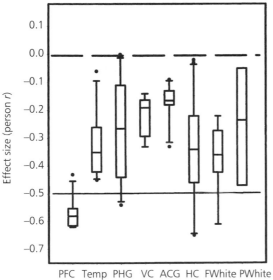

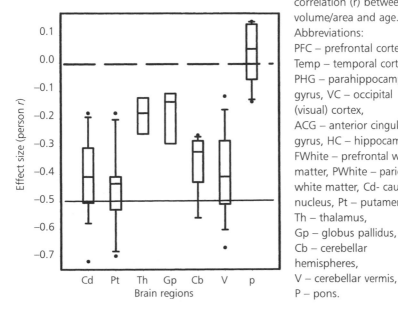

Fig. 6.3 Comparison of age effects on regional brain volumes across different studies. The effects are expressed as product moment correlation (r) between volume/area and age. Abbreviations: PFC – prefrontal cortex, Temp – temporal cortex, PHG – parahippocampal gyrus, VC – occipital (visual) cortex, ACG – anterior cingulate gyrus, HC – hippocampus, FWhite – prefrontal white matter, PWhite – parietal white matter, Cd- caudate nucleus, Pt – putamen, Th – thalamus, Gp – globus pallidus, Cb – cerebellar hemispheres, V – cerebellar vermis, P – pons.

discrepant accounts of parietal aging. In two samples, no age differences were observed in the inferior parietal lobule (IPL) volume, and a moderate age-related shrinkage has been noted in the postcentral gyrus and superior parietal cortex (Raz *et al.*, 1997; Raz *et al.*, submitted). Others revealed a significant age-related shrinkage of a broadly defined parietal gray and/or white matter (Ohnishi *et al.*, 2001; Resnick, Goldszal, Davatzikos *et al.*, 2000). The last study, however, sampled only healthy adults between ages 59 and 85, and thus is not directly comparable to our samples.

Recently we addressed the issue of the stability of the observed pattern of differential aging, by comparing the magnitude of the negative age-volume associations observed in two samples drawn from the same population (Raz *et al.*, 1997 and Raz *et al.*, in press). The comparison revealed that not only were the estimates of effect magnitude statistically equivalent across the two samples, their rank order was also closely reproduced, with the lateral prefrontal cortex showing the largest age-related difference, and the IPL and primary visual cortex revealing the smallest correlations with age. Notably, in both studies (Raz *et al.*, 1997 and Raz *et al.*, in press) the white matter volume exhibited mild (though statistically significant) age-related shrinkage only in the prefrontal region, whereas a zero effect was observed in the parietal area.

Unlike the number of studies of age effect on various cortical regions of interest, only a handful of studies have examined regional differences in WMH and other markers of white matter vulnerability. Both a comprehensive narrative review and a more recent meta-analysis concluded that vulnerability of the anterior regions to aging in that respect is also greater than that of the posterior parts of the brain (Pantoni and Garcia, 1997; Gunning and Raz, submitted). Age differences in white matter signal intensity suggests a more rapid deterioration of the frontal rather than posterior white matter (Jernigan *et al.*, 2001). A new neuroimaging approach, diffusion tensor imaging (DTI), allows assessment of the integrity and orientation of myelinated fibers (Peled, Gudbjartsson, Westin, Kikinis, and Jolesz, 1998). In several samples, DTI revealed that age-related increase in isotropy of diffusion is greater in the anterior rather than posterior regions (Nusbaum, Tang, Buchsbaum *et al.*, 2001; O'Sullivan, Jones, Summers *et al.*, 2001; Stebbins, Carillo, Medina *et al.*, 2001). In addition, the genu of the corpus callosum that connects prefrontal regions of the hemispheres was found to exhibit greater age-related deterioration than the splenium that bridges the two parietal lobes (Sullivan *et al.*, 2001).

In sum, the available cross-sectional evidence suggests that age-related differences are the most pronounced in the prefrontal (especially lateral) cortices, somewhat less substantial in the temporal cortices, the striatum, and the hippocampus, and rather mild in the primary visual cortex and the anterior cingulate gyrus.

One of the main limitations of the reviewed cross-sectional studies of the aging brain is that by their very nature, they cannot reveal age-related changes. On the other hand, longitudinal studies (Resnick *et al.*, 2000) reveal true changes in a selected sample of subjects who may be better off physically, and more motivated than the participants of cross-sectional studies. On the other hand, the participants of cross-sectional investigations may (and probably up to 20 per cent of them do) have a prodromal dementia, which is not yet clinically identifiable at the time of testing (Sliwinski and Buschke, 1999). Thus, for a more balanced picture of brain aging and more realistic estimates of the magnitude of age effects, Schaie (1992) has proposed the strategy of a cross-sequential study, in which participants are compared both to themselves longitudinally and to age-matched cohort cross-sectionally. Cross-sequential design has already produced interesting results in research on structural brain development (Giedd *et al.*, 1999). Its application to brain aging should also prove beneficial.

Regional volumetric correlates of cognitive aging

Although observing the aging brain has its own rewards, for the cognitive neuroscience of aging, the central question remains the one of the role played by regional brain differences in cognitive aging. Cognitive aging is, similarly to the aging of the brain, a differential process. In some individuals, negative effects of age on cognition are discernible on a basis of a simple observation of everyday activities. One does not have to be a scientist to notice that many older adults exhibit pronounced slowing of motor and mental activity, and report difficulties concentrating on more than one topic at a time, memorizing verbal and visual material, and acquiring new skills. On the other hand, the management of the individual's previously acquired fund of knowledge and the ability to express it using language is rarely diminished in all but exceptionally frail elders (Verhaeghen, 2003). As a rule, psychological tests and controlled cognitive experiments confirm these observations. Healthy older adults show significant slowing of the speed of information processing (Salthouse and Verhaeghen, 1996), deficits in division of attention (McDowd, and Shaw, 2000), and dual task performance (Salthouse, 1994), and less efficient acquisition of novel motor and cognitive tasks (Gutman, 1965; Vakil and Agmon-Ashkenazi, 1997) than their younger counterparts. At the same time, performance of older adults on various tests of expert skills that have been acquired through education and practice does not fall behind that of the young people, and in some instances even exceeds it (Krampe and Ericsson, 1996).

In examining this intricate pattern of differential aging, one cannot help noticing that even on the most difficult tasks, the age-related differences are not clear cut, and that there is a substantial overlap between cognitive indices of the young and the old. Cognitive aging does not lend itself to the categorical deficit metaphor. Rather it is better viewed as a pattern of multiple age-performance response surfaces, many of which are negatively inclined but all of which are continuous and monotonic. Because such age-task response functions are approximations of statistical ensembles of individual subjects, the question arises regarding the role of individual differences in shaping the trajectories of cognitive aging for a given task, skill or function. In the search for a better understanding of individual differences underlying age trends in cognition, it is only natural that we turn our attention to the brain. Noninvasive *in vivo* neuroimaging has made it possible to relate cognitive performance to the structural, electrical, and metabolic characteristics of the aging brain. Each of these associations among cognitive and neural characteristics of aging contributes to understanding of some aspects of cognitive aging, though none of them reveals the whole picture. Below, I present three examples of such associations observed in the studies of regional anatomical aspects of the brain and specific cognitive processes.

Age-related shrinkage of PFC and prefrontal WMH burden as independent mediators of age effects on an executive function

Age-related alterations of the brain anatomy (e.g., gray matter shrinkage and white matter hyperintensities) are associated with declines in cognitive performance. In a recent meta-analysis of studies that explored cognitive correlates of the WMH (Gunning-Dixon and Raz, 2000), we concluded that although the magnitude of the effects is moderate, increased burden of the WMH is linked to poorer performance on test of executive functions (median effect size r =0.30) and speed of information processing (median effect r = 0.22). We have also reported that age effects on one of the indices of executive functions, perseveration, are mediated by age-related shrinkage of the prefrontal cortex (Raz *et al.*, 1998). Because age-related differences in cortical volume and the severity of WMH are only weakly related, we tested the hypothesis that they might contribute independently to age-related cognitive declines (Gunning-Dixon and Raz, 2003). Specifically, we examined whether the effects of volume loss in the

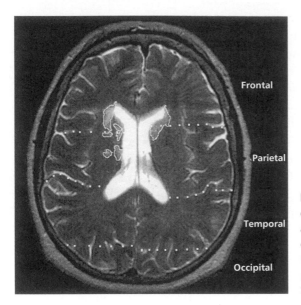

Fig. 6.4 An example of demarcation of regions and regional WMH traced on a T2-weighted axial MR image. Reprinted with permission Elsevier Scientific.

prefrontal cortex and the volume increase of the prefrontal WMH are associated with increase in perseverative error on the Wisconsin Card Sorting Test (WCST), a popular measure of executive functions.

The subjects of the study were 140 healthy highly educated volunteers (age 50–81 years) who showed no signs of dementia. They were administered a computerized version of the WCST and test of working memory (WM). The volume of the prefrontal cortex and the fusiform gyrus as well as the WMH volume were computed from the MRI scans (see examples in Figure 6.4).

The results of this study indicated that indeed, in healthy adults the volume of the prefrontal cortex and the volume of WMH in the prefrontal region are independently associated with age-related increases in perseverative behavior on the WCST. Neither reduced volume of the prefrontal cortex nor the frontal WMH volume was linked to age-associated declines in working memory.

Neuroanatomical correlates of age differences in skill acquisition

Motor skill (Pursuit Rotor)

In this study (Raz *et al.*, 2000), healthy volunteers (age 22–80) performed a pursuit rotor task. Performance, as measured by time on target (TOT), improved significantly across the blocks of trials. Although the short initial

TOT observed in all subjects became significantly longer with practice, older participants showed significantly lesser improvement and reached lower asymptotic levels than those of their younger counterparts. However, a clear difference between stage of learning was observed. There were no age differences in the rate of improvement during the initial stages of skill acquisition (first block). Age differences emerged and increased as the practice progressed. Whereas no cortical volumes were associated with performance, the age effects on the rate of improvement were differentially mediated by the volumes of the cerebellum and the putamen. Reduced volumes of the cerebellar hemispheres and the putamen in addition to lower working memory scores predicted shorter TOT at the initial acquisition stage. In contrast, at the later stage of skill acquisition, the reduction in putamen volume did not matter while the effects of the cerebellar volume and working memory remained.

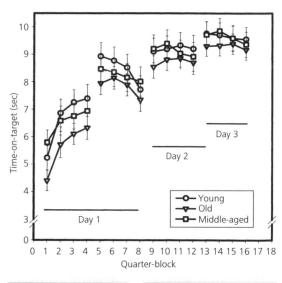

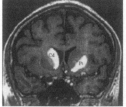

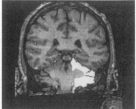

Fig. 6.5 Age-related differences in acquiring proficiency in a pursuit rotor task (upper panel) and the MRI tracing of the brain regions that mediate the age effects.

Caudate and putamen

Cerebellar cortex ROI

Cognitive skill acquisition (the Tower of Hanoi)

In a recent study of the links between age-related differences in regional brain volumes and acquisition of a cognitive skill we used Tower of Hanoi puzzle (ToH) as an example of a novel cognitive skill (Head *et al.*, 2002). We found that at the early stage of skill acquisition, ToH speed (time required per move) and efficiency (number of moves to complete the puzzle) were associated with age, prefrontal cortex volume, and working memory capacity. Notably, this pattern of anatomical – behavioral associations was similar to the one observed in the studies on WCST perseveration. No links with regional brain volumes and ToH performance were observed at the later stages of skill acquisition. As in the study of WCST perseveration, when hypertensive participants were excluded, the effect of prefrontal shrinkage on executive aspects of performance was no longer significant.

The latter is a noteworthy common thread that runs across the reviewed studies of the aging brain and cognition, i.e. attenuation and sometimes outright elimination of the effects of regional cerebral volumes on cognition after removal of hypertensive individuals from the sample. Except for carrying diagnosis of essential hypertension (reportedly controlled by the medication), those participants did not have any health problems that could have resulted in brain abnormalities. They did not have diabetes, cardiovascular disease or pulmonary disorders, nor had they ever undergone an open heart surgery, or kidney dialysis. Thus, the importance for factoring in the influence of even a well-controlled and relatively mild hypertension in studies of cognitive aging cannot be overestimated. In the general population, Waldstein (1995) reported a significant increase in impairment on neuropsychological tests that are loaded on executive functions, and in the population used in our studies, we found a similar effect (Raz, Rodrigue, and Acker, in press). In the latter study, age-, sex-, race-, and education-matched healthy middle-aged and older adults showed virtually no discrepancy in their scores on fluid intelligence and working memory tests, whereas a substantial (more than 20 percent) increase in perseveration was registered on the WCST. Thus, at least some of the age-related differences in cognition and in brain – cognition associations may be attributed to a mild and clinically unremarkable hypertension – something that the participants of the studies on cognitive aging and brain functions are rarely asked about.

One factor not taken into account in all of the reviewed studies is the generic variability. There is sufficient reason to suspect that asymptomatic carriers of homozygous ApoE 4/4 genotypes – a known genetic liability for Alzheimer-type dementia-exhibit mild but statistically significantly memory deficits (Bondi, Salmon, Monsch *et al.*, 1995; Reed, Carmelli, Swan *et al.*, 1994;

Kuller, Shemanski, Manolio *et al.*, 1998). Thus, identifying the carriers of that genotype may contribute to explaining additional variance in associations between neuroanatomy and cognition in normal elderly. However, low frequency of the 4/4 genotype makes genetic screening practical only in relatively large samples.

Summary and conclusions

Age-related differences in brain anatomy are regional and differential. The preponderance of the evidence indicated that prefrontal cortex is the region of the greatest age-related vulnerability. However, to date, almost all studies were conducted in a cross-sectional design, and a few longitudinal studies were limited in their duration and scope of the examined brain locations. Improvements in design, especially extension of neuroimaging methods to cross-sequential studies on substantial samples, will allow us to sort out true age-related changes from individual and cohort differences that stem from other sources. Improvement in brain *in vivo* measurements – DTI, advances in high field spectroscopy, higher resolution anatomic MRI, improvement in quantification of angiography – will bring refinement to assessment of the brain and will help to shed light on the mechanisms that underlie age-related changes in brain structure.

Age-related deficits in some cognitive functions (e.g., executive or motor skill) are mediated by shrinkage of their cortical substrates (e.g., prefrontal cortex or cerebellum) and deterioration of the white matter. However, only a relatively small proportion of variance in cognitive performance is accounted for by structural differences. Other factors to be considered are neurochemical and hormonal changes (e.g., glucose metabolism, cortisol release, altered dopamine kinetics), as well as changes in local blood flow. Genetic predisposition to age-related brain changes (increased reactivity to stress, familial hypertension, and ApoE 4/4 genotype) also need to be considered in studying the links between the aging brain and cognition. In general, closer attention needs to be paid to health risk factors such as hypertension (even in its mild and treatable forms), diabetes, cardiovascular insufficiency, and pulmonary problems. These disorders, even of the most benign and barely noticeable variety, may exert negative effects on age-related differences in cognitive performance, especially the executive dysfunctions.

References

Allman, J.M., Hakeem, A., Erwin, J.M., Nimchinsky, E., and Hof, P. (2001). The anterior cingulate cortex: The evolution of an interface between emotion and cognition. *Annals of New York Academy of Science*, **935**, 107–117.

Awad, I.A., Johnson, P.C., Spetzler, R.F., and Hodak, J.A. (1986). Incidental subcortical lesions identified on magnetic resonance imaging in the elderly. II. Postmortem pathological correlations. *Stroke,* 17, 1090–1097.

Bartzokis, G., Beckson, M., Lu, P.H., Nuechterlein, K.H., Edwards, N., and Mintz, J. (2001). Age-related changes in frontal and temporal volume in men: A Magnetic Resonance Imaging study. *Archives of General Psychiatry,* 58, 461–465.

Bondi, M.W., Salmon, D.P., Monsch, A.U., Galasko, D., Butters, N., Klauber, M.R., Thal, L.J., and Saitoh, T. (1995). Episodic memory changes are associated with the APOE-epsilon 4 allele in nondemented older adults. *Neurology,* 45, 2203–2206.

Bradley, W.G., Walluch, V., Brant-Zawadzki, M., Yadley, R.A., and Wycoff, R.R. (1984). Patchy, periventricular white matter lesions in the elderly: A common observation during NMR imaging. *Noninvasive Medical Imaging,* 1, 35–41.

Carmelli, D., Swan, G.E., Reed, T., Wolf, P.A., Miller, B.L., and DeCarli, C. (1999). Midlife cardiovascular risk factors and brain morphology in identical male twins. *Neurology,* 52, 1119–1124.

Chimowitz, M.I., Estes, M.L., Furlan, A.J., and Awad, I.A. (1992). Further observations on the pathology of subcortical lesions identified on magnetic resonance imaging. *Arch Neurol.,* 49 747–752.

Cohen, J. (1988). *Power Analysis in Behavioral Sciences.* Hillsdale, NJ: Lawrence Erlbaum.

Courchesne, E., Chisum, H.J., Townsend, J., Cowles, A., Covington, J., Egaas, B., Harwood, M., Hind, S., and Press, G.A. (2000). Normal brain development and aging: Quantitative analysis at in vivo MR imaging in healthy volunteers. *Radiology,* 216, 672–682.

De Leeuw, F.E., De Groot, J.C., and Breteler, M.M.B. (2001). White matter changes: Frequency and risk factors. In: L. Pantoni, D. Inzitari, A. Wallin, (eds) *The Matter of White Matter: Clinical and Pathophysiological Aspects of White Matter Disease Related to Cognitive Decline and Vascular Dementia,* (pp. 19–33). Utrecht, The Netherlands: Academic Pharmaceutical Productions.

Fazekas, F., Kleinert, R., Offenbacher, H., *et al.* (1993). Pathologic correlates of incidental MRI white matter signal hyperintensities. *Neurology,* 43, 1683–1689.

Giedd, J.N., Blumenthatl, Jeffries, N.O. *et al.* (1999). Brain development during childhood and adolescence: a longitudinal MRI study. *Nature Neuroscience,* 2, 861–863.

Good, C., Johnsrude, I.S., Ashburner, J., Henson, R.N.A., Friston, K.J., and Frackowiak, R.S. J. (2001). A voxel-based morphometric study of ageing in 465 normal adult human brains. *NeuroImage,* 14, 21–36.

Gunning-Dixon, F.M., Head, D.P., McQuain, J.M., Acker, J.D., and Raz, N. (1998). Differential aging of the human striatum: A prospective MR study. *American Journal of Neuroradiology,* 19, 1501–1507.

Gunning-Dixon, F.M., and Raz, N. (2000). The cognitive correlates of white matter abnormalities in normal aging: A quantitative review. *Neuropsychology,* 14, 224–232.

Gunning-Dixon, F.M., and Raz, N. (2003). Neuroanatomical correlates of selected executive functions in middle-aged and older adults: A prospective MRI study. *Neuropsychologia,* 41, 1929–1941.

Gunning-Dixon, F.M., and Raz, N. Demographic and clinical correlates of white matter abnormalities in normal aging: A quantitative review. Manuscript under review.

Gutman, G.M. (1965). The effects of age and extraversion on pursuit rotor reminiscence. *J. Gerontol.*, **20**, 346–350.

Guttmann, C.R., Jolesz, F.A., Kikinis, R., Killiany, R.J., Moss, M.B., Sandor, T., and Albert, M.S. (1998). White matter changes with normal aging. *Neurology,* **50**, 972–978.

Hartman, M., Bolton, E., and Sweeny, S.F. (2001). Working memory, the frontal lobes, and aging: Evidence from the Wisconsin Card Sorting Test. *Psychology and Aging,*

Head, D., Raz, N., Gunning-Dixon, F., Williamson, A., and Acker, J.D. (2002). Age-related shrinkage of the prefrontal cortex is associated with executive, but not procedural aspects of cognitive performance. *Psychology and Aging,* **17**, 72–84.

Jernigan, T.L., Press, G.A., and Hesselink, J.R. (1990). Methods for measuring brain morphological features on magnetic resonance images: Validation of and normal aging. *Archives of Neurology,* **47**, 27–32.

Jernigan, T.L., Archibald, S.L., Berhow, M.T., Sowell, E.R., Foster, D.S., and Hesselink, J.R. (1991). Cerebral structure on MRI, part I: Localization of age-related changes. *Biological Psychiatry,* **29**, 55–67.

Jernigan, T.L., Archibald, S.L., Fenema-Notestine, C., Gamst, A.C., Stout, J.C., Bonner, J., and Hesselink, J.R. (2001). Effects of age on tissues and regions of the cerebrum and cerebellum, *Neurobiology of Aging,* **22**, 581–594.

Krampe, R.T., and Ericsson, K.A. (1996). Maintaining excellence: deliberate practice and elite performance in young and older pianists. *Journal of Experimental Psychology: General,* **125**, 331–359.

Kuller, L.H., Shemanski, L., Manolio, T., Haan, M., Fried, L., Bryan, N., Burke, G.L., Tracy, R., and Bhadelia, R. (1998). Relationship between ApoE, MRI findings, and cognitive function in the Cardiovascular Health Study. *Stroke,* **29**, 388–398.

Leifer, D., Buonanno, F.S., and Richardson, E.P. (1990). Clinicopathologic correlations of cranial magnetic resonance imaging of periventricular white matter. *Neurology,* **40**, 911–918.

Luft, A.R., Skalej, M., Klockgether, T., and Voigt, K. (1997). Aging and gender do not affect cerebellar volume in humans. *AJNR Am J Neuroradiol,* **18**: 593–594.

McDowd, J.M., and Shaw, R.J. (2000). Attention and aging: A Functional perspective. In F. I. M. Craik and T. A. Salthouse (eds) *Handbook of Aging and Cognition – II.* Mahwah, NJ: Erlbaum.

Murphy, D.G., DeCarli, C., McIntosh, A.R., Daly, E., Mentis, M.J., Pietrini, P., Szczepanik, J., Schapiro, M.B., Grady, C.L., Horwitz, B., and Rapoport, S.I. (1996). Sex differences in human brain morphometry and metabolism: an *in vivo* quantitative magnetic resonance imaging and positron emission tomography study on the effect of aging. *Archives of General Psychiatry,* **53**, 585–594.

Ohnishi, T., Matsuda, H., Tabira, T., Asada, T., and Uno, M. (2001). Changes in brain morphology in Alzheimer disease and normal aging: Is Alzheimer disease an exaggerated aging process? *AJNR American Journal of Neuroradiology,* **22**, 1680–1685.

O'Sullivan, M., Jones, D.K., Summers, P.E., Morris, R.G., Williams, S.C., and Markus, H.S. (2001). Evidence for cortical 'disconnection' as a mechanism of age-related cognitive decline. *Neurology,* **57**, 632–638.

Pantoni, L., and Garcia, J.H. (1997). Pathogenesis of leukoaraiosis: a review. *Stroke,* **28**, 652–659.

Passe, T.J., Rajagopalan, P., Tupler, L.A., Byrum, C.E., MacFall, J.R., and Krishnan, K.R. (1997). Age and sex effects on brain morphology. *Progress in Neuropsychopharmacology and Biological Psychiatry,* **21**, 1231–1237.

Paus, T. (2001). Primate anterior cingulate cortex: where motor control, drive and cognition interface. *Nature Reviews: Neuroscience,* **2**, 417–424.

Peled, S., Gudbjartsson, H., Westin, C.F., Kikinis, R., and Jolesz, F.A. (1998). Magnetic resonance imaging shows orientation and asymmetry of white matter fiber tracts. *Brain Research,* **780**, 27–33.

Raz, N. (2000). Aging of the brain and its impact on cognitive performance: Integration of structural and functional findings. In: FIM Craik and TA Salthouse (eds) *Handbook of Aging and Cognition – II,* Mahwah, NJ: Erlbaum, 1–90.

Raz, N., Torres, I.J., Spencer, W.D., White, K., and Acker, J.D. (1992). Age-related regional differences in cerebellar vermis observed *in vivo. Archives of Neurology,* **49**, 412–416.

Raz, N., Torres, I.J., Spencer, W.D., and Acker, J.D. (1993). Pathoclysis in aging human cerebral cortex: Evidence from *in vivo* MRI morphometry. *Psychobiology,* **21**, 151–160.

Raz, N., Torres, I., and Acker, J.D. (1995). Age, gender, and hemispheric differences in human striatum: A Quantitative review and new data from *in vivo* MRI morphometry. *Neurobiology of Learning and Memory,* **63**, 133–142.

Raz, N., Gunning, F.M., Head, D., Dupuis, J.H., McQuain, J.D., Briggs, S.D., Loken, W.J., Thornton, A.E., and Acker, J.D. (1997). Selective aging of the human cerebral cortex observed in vivo: Differential vulnerability of the prefrontal gray matter. *Cerebral Cortex,* **7**, 268–282.

Raz, N., Dupuis, J.H., Briggs, S.D., McGavran, C., and Acker, J.D. (1998). Differential effects of age and sex on the cerebellar hemispheres and the vermis: A prospective MR study. *American Journal of Neuroradiology,* **19**, 65–71.

Raz, N., Dixon, F.M., Head, D.P., Dupuis, J.H., and Acker, J.D. (1998). Neuroanatomical correlates of cognitive aging: Evidence from structural MRI. *Neuropsychology,* **12**, 95–106.

Raz, N., Williamson, A., Gunning-Dixon, F., Head, D., and Acker, J.D. (2000). Neuroanatomical and cognitive correlates of adult age differences in acquisition of a perceptual-motor skill. *Microscopy Research and Technique, a special issue on Neuroimaging and Memory,* **51**, 85–93.

Raz, N., Gunning-Dixon, F., Head, D., Williamson, A., and Acker, J.D. (2001). Age and sex differences in the cerebellum and the ventral pons: A prospective MR study of healthy adults. *American Journal of Neuroradiology,* **22**, 1161–1167.

Raz, N., Rodrigue, K. M., and Acker, J. D. (in press). Hypertension and the brain: Vulnerability of the prefrontal regions and executive functions. *Behavioral Neuroscience,* **17**.

Reed, T., Carmelli, D., Swan, G.E., Breitner, J.C., Welsh, K.A., Jarvik, G.P., Deeb, S., and Auwerx, J. (1994). Lower cognitive performance in normal older adult male twins carrying the apolipoprotein E epsilon 4 allele. *Archives of Neurology,* **51**, 1189–1192.

Resnick, S.M., Goldszal, A.F., Davatzikos, C., Golski, S., Kraut, M.A., Metter, E.J., Bryan, R.N., and Zonderman, A.B. (2000). One-year age changes in MRI brain volumes in older adults. *Cerebral Cortex,* **10**, 464–472.

Salat, D.H., Ward, A., Kaye, J.A., and Janowsky, J.S. (1997). Sex differences in the corpus callosum with aging. *Neurobiology of Aging,* **18**, 191–197.

Salat, D.H., Kaye, J.A., Janowsky, and Jeri, S. (1999). Prefrontal gray and white matter volumes in healthy aging and alzheimer disease. *Archives of Neurology,* **56**, 338–344.

Salthouse, T.A. (1994). The aging of working memory. *Neuropsychology,* **8**, 535–543.

Scarpelli, M., Salvolini, U., Diamanti, L., Montironi, R., Chiaromoni, L., and Maricotti, M. (1994). MRI and pathological examination of post-mortem brains: The problem of white matter high signal areas. *Neuroradiology,* **36**, 393–398.

Strassburger, T.L., Lee, H.C., Daly, E.M., Szczepanik, J., Krasuski, J.S., Mentis, M.J., Salerno, J.A., DeCarli, C., Schapiro, M.B., and Alexander, G.E. (1997). Interactive effects of age and hypertension on volumes of brain structures. *Stroke,* **28**, 1410–1417.

Vakil, E., and Agmon-Ashkenazi, D. (1997). Baseline performance and learning rate of procedural and declarative memory tasks: younger versus older adults. *Journal of Gerontology: Psychological Sciences,* **52**, 229–234.

Valenzuela, M.J., Sachedev, P.S., Wen, W., Shnier, H., Brodaty, H., and Gillies, D. (2000). Dual voxel proton Magnetic Resonance Spectroscopy in the healthy elderly: Subcortical-frontal axonal N-acetylaspartate levels are correlated with fluid cognitive abilities independent of structural brain changes. *NeuroImage,* **12**, 747–756.

Van Laere, K.J. and Dierckx, R.A. (2001). Brain perfusion SPECT: age- and sex-related effects correlated with voxel-based morphometric findings in healthy adults. *Radiology,* **221**, 810–817.

Waldstein, S.R. (1995). Hypertension and neuropsychological functioning: a lifespan perspective. *Experimental Aging Research,* **21**, 321–352.

Appendix 1

Studies included in the effect size box plot (Figure 6.3) but not cited in the chapter

Blatter, D.D., Bigler, E.D., Gale, S.D., Johnson, S.C., Anderson, C.V., Burnett, B.M., Parker, N., Kurth, S., and Horn, S.D. (1995). Quantitative volumetric analysis of brain MR: Normative database spanning 5 decades of life. *American Journal of Neuroradiology,* **16**, 241–251.

Bigler, E.D., Blatter, D.D., Anderson, C.V., Johnson, S.C., Gale, S.D., Hopkins, R.O., and Bennet, B. (1997). Hippocampal volume in normal aging and traumatic brain injury. *American Journal of Neuroradiology,* **18**, 11–23.

Coffey, C.E., Wilkinson, W.E., Parashos, I.A., Soady, S.A.R., Sullivan, R.J., Patterson, L.J., Figiel, G.S., Webb, M.C., Spritzer, C.E., and Djang, W.T. (1992). Quantitative cerebral anatomy of the aging human brain: A cross-sectional study using magnetic resonance imaging. *Neurology,* **42**, 527–536.

Convit, A., de Leon, M.J., Hoptman, M.J., Tarshish, C., De Santi, S., and Rusinek, H. (1995). Age-related changes in brain: I. Magnetic Resonance Imaging measures of temporal lobe volumes in normal subjects. *Psychiatric Quarterly,* **66**, 343–355.

Convit, A., de Asis, J., de Leon, M.J., Tarshish, C., de Santi, S., Daisley, K., and Rusinek, H. (1998). The fusiform gyrus as the first neocortical site in AD? *Neurobiology of Aging,* **19** *(Suppl. 4S),* Abstract No. 1286.

Cowell, P., Turetsky, B.I., Gur, R.C., Grossman, R.I., Shtasel, D.L., and Gur, R.E. (1994). Sex differences in aging of the human frontal and temporal lobes. *Journal of Neuroscience,* **14**, 4748–4755.

DeCarli, C., Murphy, D.G.M., Tranh, M., Grady, C.L., Haxby, J.V., Gillette, J.A., Salerno, J.A., Gonzales-Aviles, A., Horwitz, B., Rapoport, S.I., and Schapiro, M.B. (1995). The effect of white matter hyperintensity volume on brain structure, cognitive performance, and cerebral metabolism of glucose in 51 healthy adults. *Neurology,* **45**, 2077–2084.

Escalona, P.R., McDonald, W.M., Doraiswamy, P.M., Boyko, O.B., Husain, M.M., Figiel, G.S., Laskowitz, D., Ellinwood, E.H., and Krishnan, K.R.R. (1991). In vivo stereological assessment of human cerebellar volume: Effects of gender and age. *American Journal of Neuroradiology,* **12**, 927–929.

Harris, G.J., Pearlson, G.D., Peyser, C.E., Aylward, E.H., Roberts, J., Barta, P.E., Chase, G.A., and Folstein, S.E. (1992). Putamen volume reduction on magnetic resonance imaging exceeds caudate changes in mild Huntington's disease. *Annals of Neurology,* **31**, 69–75.

Hayakawa, K., Konishi, Y., Matsuda, T., Kuriyama, M., Konishi, K., Yamashita, K., Okumura, R., and Hamanaka, D. (1989). Development and aging of the brain midline structures: Assessment with MRI imaging. *Radiology,* **172**, 171–177.

Hokama, H., Shenton, M.E., Nestor, P.G., Kikinis, R., Levitt, J.J., Metcalf, D., Wible, C.G., O'Donnell, B.F., Jolesz, F.A., and McCarley, R.W. (1995). Caudate, putamen, and globus pallidus volume in schizophrenia: A quantitative MRI study. *Psychiatry Research: Neuroimaging,* **61**, 209–229.

Insausti, R., Jouttonen, K., Soininen, H., Insausti, A.M., Partanen, K., Vainio, P., Laakso, M.P., and Pitkänen, A. (1998). MR volumetric analysis of the human entorhinal, perirhinal, and temporopolar cortices. *AJNR American Journal of Neuroradiology,* **19**, 659–671.

Krishnan, R.R., McDonald, W.M., Escalona, P.R., Doraiswamy, P.M., Na, C., Husain, M., Figiel, G.S., Boyko, O.B., Ellinwood, E.H., and Nemeroff, C.B. (1992). Magnetic resonance imaging of the caudate nuclei in depression: Preliminary observations. *Archives of General Psychiatry,* **49**, 553–557.

Laakso, M.P., Soininen, H., Partanen, K., Lehtovirta, M., Hallikainen, M., Hänninen, T., Helkala, E. L., Vainio, P., and Riekkinen, P.J. Sr (1998). MRI of the hippocampus in Alzheimer's disease: sensitivity, specificity, and analysis of the incorrectly classified subjects. *Neurobiology of Aging* **19**, 23–31.

Lim, K.O., Zipurski, R.B., Murphy, G.M., and Pfefferbaum, A. (1990). In vivo quantification of the limbic system using MRI: Effects of normal aging. *Psychiatry Research: Neuroimaging,* **35**, 15–26.

Luft, A., Skalej, M., Welte, D., Kolb, R., Bürk, K., Schultz, J., Klockgether, T., and Voigt, K. (1998). A new semi-automated three-dimensional technique allowing precise quantification of total and regional cerebellar volume using MRI. *Magnetic Resonance in Medicine,* **40**, 143–151.

Murphy, D.G.M., DeCarli, C.S., Williams, W., Rapoport, S.I., Schapiro, M.B., and Horwitz, B. (1992). Age-related differences in volumes of subcortical nuclei, brain matter, and cerebro-spinal fluid in healthy men as measured with Magnetic Resonance Imaging (MRI). *Archives of Neurology,* **49**, 839–845.

Murphy, D.G.M., DeCarli, C., McIntosh, A.R., Daly, E., Mentis, M.J., Pietrini, P., Szczepanik, J., Schapiro, M.B., Grady, C.L., Horwitz, B., and Rapoport, S.I., (1996). Age-related differences in volumes of subcortical nuclei, brain matter, and cerebro-spinal fluid in healthy men as measured with Magnetic Resonance Imaging (MRI). *Archives of General Psychiatry,* **53**, 585–594.

Raininko, R., Autti, T., Vanhanen, S.L., Ylikoski, A., Erkinjuntti, T., and Santavuori, P. (1994). The normal brain stem from infancy to old age. *Neuroradiology,* **36**, 364–368.

Rhyu, I.J., Cho, T.H., Le, N.J., Uhm, C.-S., Kim, H., and Suh, Y.-S. (1999). Magnetic resonance image-based cerebellar volumetry in healthy Korean adults. *Neuroscience Letters,* **270**, 149–152.

Schaefer, G.B., Thompson, J.N., Bodensteiner, J.B., Gingold, M., Wilson, M., and Wilson, D. (1991). Age-related changes in the relative growth of the posterior fossa. *Journal of Child Neurology,* **6**, 15–19.

Schulz, J.B., Skalej, M., Wedekind, D., Luft, A.R., Abele, M., Voigt, K., Dichgans, J., and Klockgether, T. (1999). MRI-based volumetry differentiates idiopathic Parkinson's syndrome from MSA and PSP. *Annals of Neurology,* **45**, 65–74.

Shah, S.A., Doraiswami, P.M., Husain, M.M., Figiel, G.S., Boyko, O.B., McDonald, W.M., Ellinwood, E.H., and Krishnan, K.R.R. (1991). Assessment of posterior fossa structures with midsagittal MRI: The effects of age. *Neurobiology of Aging,* **12**, 371–374.

Soininen, H.S., Partanen, K., Pitkänen, A., Vainio, P., Hänninen, T., Hallikainen, M., Koivisto, K., and Riekkinen, P.J. Sr (1994). Volumetric MRI analysis of the amygdala and the hippocampus in subjects with age-associated memory impairment: correlation to visual and verbal memory. *Neurology,* **44**, 1660–1668.

Sullivan, E.V., Marsh, L, Mathalon, D.H., Lim, K.O., and Pfefferbaum, A. (1995) Age-related decline in MRI volumes of temporal lobe gray matter but not hippocampus. *Neurobiology of Aging,* **16,** 591–606.

Sullivan, E.V., Deshmukh, A., Desmond, J.E., Lim, K.O., and Pfefferbaum, A. (2000). Cerebellar volume decline in normal aging, alcoholism, and Korsakoff's syndrome: relation to ataxia. *Neuropsychology,* **14,** 341–352.

Sullivan, M.P., de Toledo-Morrell, L. and Morrell, F. (1995). MRI detected cerebellar atrophy during aging. Presented at the 25th Annual Meeting of the Society for Neuroscience, November 1995, San Diego, CA., *Society for Neuroscience Abstracts,* **21,** 1708.

Tisserand, D.J., Visser, P.J., van Boxtel, M.P.J., and Jolles, J. (2000). The relation between global and limbic brain volumes on MRI and cognitive performance in healthy individuals across the age range. *Neurobiology of Aging,* **21,** 569–576.

Van Der Werf, Y.D., Tisserand, D.J., Visser, P.J., Hofman, P.A.M., Vuurman, E., Uylings, H.B.M., and Jolles, J. (2001). Thalamic volume predicts performance on tests of cognitive speed and decreases in healthy aging – A magnetic resonance imaging-based volumetric analysis. *Cognitive Brian Research,* **11,** 377–385.

Weis, S., Kimbacher, M., Wenger, E., and Neuhold, A. (1993). Morphometric analysis of the corpus callosum using MR: Correlation of measurements with aging in healthy individuals. *American Journal of Neuroradiology,* **14,** 637–645.

Chapter 7

Cognitive aging: A view from brain imaging

Lars Nyberg and Lars Bäckman

Introduction

The contributions in this volume, and numerous other journal articles and chapters, provide unequivocal evidence that cognitive functions decline across the adult lifespan. Importantly, though, some cognitive functions are more affected than others. For example, in recent work from the Betula project (Nilsson *et al.*, 1997), we contrasted episodic and semantic long-term memory (Nyberg *et al.*, 2003). It was found that episodic memory performance deteriorated gradually from middle age through young-old age to old-old age. By contrast, semantic memory performance increased from middle-age to young-old age, and the old-old participants performed at a level comparable to the middle aged (Figure 7.1a). Furthermore, within the domain of episodic memory, increasing age was associated with a greater reduction of performance on measures of recall compared to measures of recognition (Figure 7.1b). These results provide evidence that episodic long-term memory is more age-sensitive than semantic long-term memory, and that recall is more age-sensitive than recognition.

These age-related long-term memory changes can be related to patterns of data in working-memory tasks (Gick, Craik, and Morris, 1988). Working-memory tasks differ with regard to their demand on executive processing and it has been found that age differences are small when the executive demands are low, and substantial when such demands are high (see Morris, Gick and Craik, 1988). Many cognitive tasks require working memory functions to a smaller or greater extent, and it has been shown that working memory capacity accounts for a considerable portion of the variance in long-term memory tasks (Hultsch, Hertzog, and Dixon, 1990; Park *et al.*, 1996). Relatedly, the relationship between age and episodic memory has been found to be mediated by proficiency of executive functioning (Troyer, Graves, and Cullum, 1994).

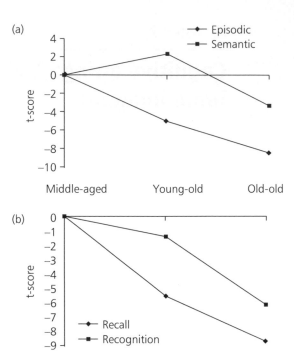

Fig. 7.1 Age differences in episodic and semantic memory. (a) Comparison of age-related changes in young-old and old-old age relative to middle aged adults for episodic and semantic memory. (b) Comparison of age-related changes in young-old and old-old age relative to middle aged adults for recall and recognition. Age differences are expressed as t-scores. Data adapted from Nyberg, Maitland *et al.* (2003).

Collectively, these and related findings indicate that age differences in cognitive performance are especially pronounced when the examined tasks put high demands on executive functions. Executive functioning is a broad concept, and it has been proposed that the traditional idea of a central executive as a unitary controller should be revised to accommodate multiple subsystems or subprocesses (Baddeley, 1996). There is no consensus about a taxonomy of executive processes as yet, but a tentative list has been proposed (Smith and Jonides, 1999; see also Hartley and Speer, 2000): attention and inhibition, task management, planning, monitoring, and coding of representations in working memory. Although it is almost certain that these different processes are mediated by at least partly non-overlapping neural systems, it is generally held that regions in the prefrontal cortex (PFC) are critical to executive functioning (Smith and Jonides, 1999).

If age differences in cognitive performance can be linked to executive functioning, and if executive functioning can be linked to the PFC, then old age should be associated with PFC dysfunction. Indeed, there is evidence that supports this assumption. Comparisons of PFC volume to that of temporal, parietal, or occipital regions indicate that PFC is differentially vulnerable to increased age (Raz, 1999, this volume; see also Fuster, 1989; Good *et al.*, 2001). In an application of PFC function theory to cognitive aging, West (1996) found support for the hypothesis that cognitive processes supported by the PFC are among the first to decline with increasing age. However, age differences are also observed on tasks traditionally considered to be 'non-frontal' (item recall and recognition), and West concluded: 'This age-related decline in item recall and recognition suggests that the frontal lobe hypothesis of aging provides a useful but incomplete neuropsychological model of cognitive aging' (West, 1996: 289).

Meta-analytic evidence that patients with circumscribed PFC damage are impaired on both recall and recognition tests (Wheeler, Stuss, and Tulving, 1995) indicates that reduced performance on tests of item recall and recognition in advanced age may in fact not be inconsistent with a frontal lobe account of cognitive aging. Moreover, during the last few years, a substantial number of functional brain imaging studies have been published that associate regions in the PFC with item recall and recognition (for a review, see Cabeza and Nyberg, 2000), and direct comparisons of younger and older adults have found reduced memory-related PFC activity in old age (for a review, see Cabeza, 2001). Below, we will summarize functional brain imaging studies of working memory and episodic memory in younger adults. Studies with positron emission tomography (PET) and functional magnetic resonance imaging (fMRI) are considered, with a special focus on PFC activations. We then review studies that have compared brain activity in younger and older adults during actual task performance. Following this, recent imaging research on dopaminergic neurotransmission as related to cognitive aging is discussed. Finally, some caveats and directions for future research are outlined.

Functional imaging studies of younger adults

Working memory

Much work in the working-memory domain has concerned the functional organization of PFC. According to one major theoretical framework, more dorsal PFC regions code for information about the spatial location of objects, whereas more ventral PFC regions code for information about object identity (Wilson *et al.*, 1993). Thus, this framework posits a *domain-specific* organization of PFC along the dorsal–ventral axis. A second major theoretical framework assumes a *process-specific* organization of PFC along the dorsal–ventral axis (Petrides, 1994). By this framework, more ventral PFC regions subserve simple maintenance and matching of information in working memory, whereas dorsal PFC regions mediate more complex processes that operate on the maintained information (manipulation of working-memory content).

The domain-specific view has received some support from imaging studies (Courtney *et al.*, 1996), but across studies the results are more in agreement with the position that dorsal PFC regions are recruited for tasks that require manipulation – regardless of whether the information is spatial in nature (i.e., the process-specific view, for a review, see Fletcher and Henson, 2001). This pattern of results has been interpreted to mean that dorsolateral PFC regions are activated when the demands on executive processes increase (Fletcher and Henson, 2001; Smith and Jonides, 1999). Increased executive demands are also associated with increased activity in medial PFC regions (anterior cingulate cortex). This pattern of PFC activation is illustrated in Figure 7.2, where results from two versions of a verbal *n-back* task are presented. As can be seen, the more demanding 2-back task is associated with pronounced medial and lateral PFC activation (2b). By contrast, the less demanding 1-back task is mainly associated with parietal activation (2a).

Taken together, brain-imaging studies of working memory have consistently found PFC activation. The degree of PFC activity, especially in more dorsal regions, tends to be modulated by the level of executive demands.

Episodic memory

In keeping with studies of working memory, brain-imaging studies of episodic memory have consistently shown activations in the PFC (for reviews, see Buckner and Wheeler, 2001; Cabeza and Nyberg, 2000; Fletcher

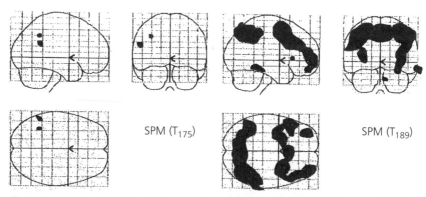

Fig. 7.2 Load-dependent working-memory related brain activity. (a) Increased brain activity during a 1-back working-memory task relative to a reading baseline task. (b) Increased brain activity during a 2-back working-memory task relative to a reading baseline task. Data from Nyberg, Forkstam *et al.* (2002).

and Henson, 2001). A significant feature of brain-imaging studies is that they have high analytical specificity. That is, it is possible to design brain-imaging studies to examine separate subprocesses of episodic memory. No doubt, the most fundamental distinction in this regard is that between encoding and retrieval, and many imaging studies have been directed at identifying the neural networks that are recruited during these stages of remembering. Some regions, mainly in posterior association cortices, are jointly activated during encoding and retrieval (Nyberg *et al.*, 2000; Wheeler *et al.*, 2000). However, there are also pronounced differences in encoding- and retrieval-related activity. As summarized below, these differences are especially salient within the PFC.

Regions in left PFC have consistently been activated during encoding, whereas regions in right PFC are strongly associated with tests of retrieval (both recognition and recall, see Cabeza and Nyberg, 2000). This asymmetrical involvement of left and right PFC during encoding and retrieval is captured by the HERA model (Tulving *et al.*, 1994; see also Nyberg, Cabeza, and Tulving, 1996), as illustrated in Figure 7.3. The asymmetry described by the HERA model is by no means absolute, and it is modulated by several factors including type of information (Kelley *et al.*, 1998) and task complexity (Nolde *et al.*, 1998). It should also be stressed that encoding as well as retrieval can be broken down into multiple subprocesses that are associated with specific sub-regions of the PFC (Buckner and Wheeler, 2001; Cabeza and Nyberg, 2000; Fletcher and Henson, 2001; Lepage *et al.*, 2000). Nevertheless, the HERA model is consistent with much imaging data, and it has recently received support from a study that used transcranial magnetic stimulation (TMS) to

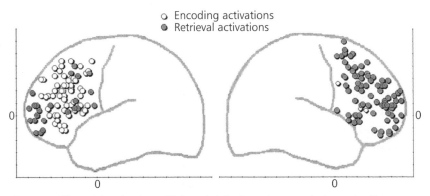

Fig. 7.3 Differential activation of left and right frontal cortex during episodic encoding and retrieval. Figure courtesy of Roberto Cabeza.

temporarily interfere with the functioning of left and right PFC (Rossi *et al.*, 2001). Consistent with the HERA model, it was found that the right dorsolateral PFC was critical for retrieval, whereas the left dorsolateral PFC was involved in encoding operations.

In summary, as is true with working memory, brain-imaging studies of episodic memory have consistently found PFC activation. Regions in left PFC are especially associated with encoding processes, whereas regions in right PFC are routinely recruited during retrieval.

Comparing functional brain activity in younger and older adults

In light of the consistent involvement of PFC regions in imaging studies of working and episodic memory in younger adults, and given the central role of PFC regions in models of cognitive aging (West, 1996), it is of critical interest to consider PFC activity in studies with elderly persons. Based on a recent review of imaging studies of younger and older adults, Cabeza (2001) concluded that age-related changes in PFC activity during memory processing are remarkably consistent, and appear much more regularly than age-related changes in temporal, parietal, occipital, or cerebellar regions. Next, we will consider the nature of these changes in more detail, with a special focus on reduced PFC activity for older relative to younger adults.

Working memory

Recent research on working memory has found increased activity in dorsolateral PFC for younger adults, along with a reduced activation in the same region for elderly adults. In one study (Rypma *et al.*, in press), a more demanding working memory task was contrasted to a less demanding task (memory load of 6 vs. 1 letters). In keeping with previous studies the more demanding task was associated with increased dorsolateral PFC activity, with a significant age-difference (young > old) in right dorsolateral PFC. In another study, event-related analysis of fMRI-data was used to separately examine neural activity associated with stimulus encoding, memory maintenance, and memory retrieval in working memory tasks (Rypma and D'Esposito, 2000). Specific focus was on activity in ventral and dorsal parts of the PFC, and the hypothesis was that age differences in activation would be found for dorsal but not ventral PFC regions. The results supported the hypothesis, and furthermore showed that these differences were limited to the retrieval stage.

Other patterns of age differences related to working memory have also been observed. These include age-related changes in non-frontal regions, such as the hippocampus (Mitchell *et al.*, 2000) and parietal cortex (Esposito *et al.*, 1999). Nonetheless, the most consistent finding across working memory studies is age differences in patterns of PFC activity (see Cabeza, 2001).

Episodic memory

Several studies that have contrasted brain activity associated with intentional encoding in younger and older adults have found reduced left PFC activity in old age (Anderson *et al.*, 2000; Cabeza *et al.*, 1997; Grady *et al.*, 1995; Stebbins *et al.*, in press). Left PFC activity during encoding has been found to be a good predictor of subsequent memory performance (Wagner *et al.*, 1998). Taken together, these findings indicate that the lower episodic memory performance of older compared to younger adults may, at least in part, reflect age-related deficits in episodic encoding.

Comparisons of retrieval-related activity in younger and older adults have shown lower activity in right PFC regions for the old (cf., Cabeza, 2001). This result has been demonstrated for a variety of tasks, including word-stem cued recall (Schacter *et al.*, 1996), word-pair cued recall (Anderson *et al.*, 2000; Cabeza *et al.*, 1997), and recognition (Cabeza *et al.*, 2000). These findings of altered retrieval-related PFC activity for older adults suggest that lowered episodic memory may not only be due to impaired encoding, but also reflect difficulties at the retrieval stage.

In sum, comparisons of brain activity associated with working memory and episodic memory in younger and older adults converge on reduced activity in task-relevant PFC regions for the elderly.

Studies of dopaminergic neurotransmission in younger and older adults

In this section, we review recent findings from brain imaging studies demonstrating a relationship between age-related losses in dopamine (DA) function and age-related cognitive changes. These findings have a direct bearing on the idea that changes in frontal lobe structure and function play an important role in cognitive aging.

DA function has traditionally been linked to motor performance (Freed and Yamamoto, 1985; McEntee, Mair, and Langlais, 1987). However, there is increasing evidence that DA is involved also in higher cognitive abilities such as memory and executive functions. This includes results from studies on patient populations with severe damage to the DA system, for example

Parkinson's disease and Huntington's disease (Brown and Marsden, 1988), lesion studies in monkeys (Goldman-Rakic, 1998), and pharmacological studies using DA agonists in young volunteers (Luciana, Collins, and Depue, 1998).

The majority of studies on DA function in relation to cognitive aging have been concerned with striatal rather than frontal DA function. Conceivably, this reflects the fact that more ligands for striatal DA markers are available in imaging research as compared to ligands for extrastriatal regions, because of the high dopaminergic innervention in the striatum. Importantly, however, there are abundant reciprocal connections between the striatum and the frontal cortex (Crosson, 1992; Graybiel, 2000). Therefore, the observed age-related losses in DA function may be seen as reflecting changes in the integrity of a frontostriatal network. Moreover, a few studies on age differences in extrastriatal DA function have been conducted; these studies appear to tell the same story as the related studies on striatal DA function.

There are morphological changes in the striatum with advancing age (see Eggers, Haug, and Fischer, 1984), but the corresponding changes in striatal DA function are even more pronounced. Post-mortem evidence indicates substantial age-related losses in both pre- and postsynaptic markers of the DA system (Fearnley and Lees, 1991; Roth and Joseph, 1994). Likewise, PET findings demonstrate marked age-related decreases in DA function for presynaptic markers such as utilization of L-DOPA (Martin, Palmer, Patlak *et al.*, 1989) and DA transporter (DAT) density (VanDyck *et al.*, 1995; Volkow, Ding, *et al.*, 1996), as well as for postsynaptic markers including D_1 (Suhara *et al.*, 1991; Wang *et al.*, 1998) and D_2 (Iyo and Yamasaki, 1993; Rinne *et al.*, 1993) receptor binding. A striking similarity in the post-mortem and imaging data on DA function and aging is the consistent and gradual nature of the negative relationship between adult age and DA. Across the relevant studies cited above, the average DA decline per decade is around 10 per cent. Further, the onset of decline appears to occur in early adulthood.

Given (a) the pronounced decline in DA function with advancing age, (b) the role of DA in cognitive functioning, and (c) the age-related changes observed in cognitive performance, researchers have set out to examine the relationship of age-related changes in DA function to age-related cognitive changes. Although only a handful of studies have addressed this issue, the pattern of findings is strikingly consistent, indicating a strong relationship among age, DA function, and cognitive performance.

Using PET, Wang and colleagues (1998) found a linear decrease of D_1 binding in both the caudate and the putamen from early to late adulthood. In addition, performance on a test of psychomotor speed was negatively related

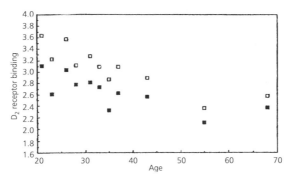

Fig. 7.4 Relationship between age and dopamine D_2 receptor density in the caudate ($r = 0.75$, $p < 0.01$) and the putamen ($r = 0.87$, $p < 0.001$). Adapted from L. Bäckman, N. Ginovart, R. A. Dixon, T.-B. Robins Wahlin, Å. Wahlin, C. Halldin, and L. Farde Age-related cognitive deficits mediated by changes in the striatal dopamine system, 2000, *American Journal of Psychiatry, 157*, p. 636. Copyright 2000 by the American Psychiatric Association.

to age and positively related to striatal D_1 binding. In two other PET studies, Volkow, Gur, *et al.* (1998) and Bäckman *et al.* (2000) demonstrated a similar decrease of striatal D_2 binding over the adult lifespan. Figure 7.4 shows the D_2 binding data in caudate and putamen across age from the Bäckman *et al.* study. As can be seen, the age-related reductions were characterized by an onset in the early twenties and a gradual trajectory across the age span examined. The latter studies also reported age-related deficits in tasks assessing executive functioning, motor speed, and perceptual speed (Volkow, Gur, *et al.*, 1998) and episodic memory and perceptual speed (Bäckman *et al.*, 2000). The most interesting feature of these studies was that D_2 binding was strongly related to motor and cognitive performance after controlling for age. Thus, these results indicate that age-related decreases in DA function are associated with decline in both motor and cognitive performance. In addition, the fact that the DA-performance relationships remained after age was partialed out suggests that DA activity may influence motor and cognitive functions irrespective of age.

In the three studies discussed above, postsynaptic markers of DA function were assessed. There are reasons to believe that concentrations of the DAT, a presynaptic marker of DA function, are more sensitive indicators of dopaminergic tone than postsynaptic receptor densities (Mozley *et al.*, 1999). The DAT is located on dopaminergic nerve terminals (Giros *et al.*, 1992) and serves as a main regulator of intrasynaptic DA levels (Jaber, Jones, Giros *et al.*, 1997). In a recent SPECT study, Mozley and colleagues (2001) found clear age-related reductions of the DAT in caudate and putamen along with age-related deficits in verbal episodic memory. Importantly, DAT availability in the striatum was strongly associated with memory performance in both young and older adults. Using PET, Erixon, Farde, Halldin *et al.* (2002) also found an age-related decrease of DAT density in caudate and putamen. In addition, age-related deficits were found in tests of episodic memory, perceptual speed, and word fluency, but not in tests of vocabulary and general knowledge. The key findings from this study were that the age-related cognitive deficits were completely mediated by DAT density, although DAT density contributed to the performance variation in memory, speed, and fluency over and above age. The latter finding was substantiated by the result that DAT density was also related to performance in the vocabulary and knowledge tests, for which no age-related differences were observed.

In summary, the available evidence suggests that pre- and postsynaptic markers of the DA system are extremely powerful mediators of the cognitive changes that occur across adulthood and old age, as well as strong general correlates of cognitive performance. With regard to the apparent similarity in patterns of data for pre- and postsynaptic DA markers, it may be noted that Volkow, Gur, Wang *et al.* (1998) demonstrated a sizable relationship between losses in DAT and D_2 receptors across adulthood. The DAT-D_2 association was independent of age, suggesting that common genetic or adaptive mechanisms may regulate the expression of DA receptors and transporters irrespective of age. Thus, change in pre- and postsynaptic DA function may be such an inter-dependent and generalized phenomenon in human aging (Morgan and Finch, 1998) that differential effects are unlikely to be observed. Further, it is of interest to note that several studies on DA and cognitive aging have used tasks that can be assumed to pose high executive demands and that have been associated with PFC regions in activation-imaging studies.

The present discussion of age-related changes in striatal DA function as a critical factor in cognitive aging can be related to a proposal by Rubin (1999). Rubin challenged the view that age-related cognitive changes reflect changes in the frontal cortex, and argued that proponents of the 'frontal view' have overlooked the potential role of age-related striatal changes in producing deficits in cognitive performance. Indeed, the age-related decrease of striatal volume is substantial and not very different from that of the frontal cortex (median age-volume correlation $= -0.57$ for frontal gray matter and -0.47 for the caudate; Raz, 1999). At the same time, frontostriatal connections are abundant (Crosson, 1992; Graybiel, 2000). In the context of cognitive aging, it has also been stressed that a declining nigrostriatal DA system would likely lead to impoverished inputs to the frontal lobes and thereby reduce the executive capacity of working memory (Prull, Gabrieli, and Bunge, 1999). Indeed, Volkow and colleagues (2000) demonstrated age-related decreases in both striatal D_2 binding and glucose metabolism in the frontal cortex and the cingulate. Most interestingly, there was a strong relationship between D_2 binding and frontal and cingulate metabolism that was independent of age. These findings underscore the functional interrelatedness between striatal and neocortical brain regions. Thus, the results from studies on the relation between aging, striatal DA function, and cognition may best be viewed as reflecting age-related alterations in the frontostriatal circuitry. Next, results from studies that have explicitly examined extrastriatal DA function in aging will be considered.

Although the empirical evidence is limited, there is research indicating that age-related losses in DA function may be as pronounced in extrastriatal regions as in the striatum. In an early PET study focusing on D_1 receptor binding, Suhara et al. (1991) found comparable rates of age-related loss in the striatum and the frontal cortex. A post-mortem investigation (de Keyser, de Backer, Vauquelin et al., 1990) also demonstrated an age-related decrease of frontal D_1 receptor densities. These findings were extended to the D_2 receptor subtype in two recent PET studies using a newly developed, highly selective ligand for extrastriatal D_2 binding (Inoue et al., 2001; Kaasinen et al., 2000). In these studies, substantial age-related losses in the amount of D_2 receptors were seen not only in the frontal cortex, but also in the temporal and parietal cortices as well as in the hippocampus and the thalamus. Thus, it appears that aging-related decrease of DA function occurs in a wide variety of brain regions as part of the normal aging process.

An interesting question regarding cognitive aging is whether DA losses in various brain regions are selectively related to age-related deficits in various cognitive domains. One possibility is that DA losses in a particular brain area (e.g., striatum) are more critical than DA losses in other areas (e.g., frontal cortex) for a certain domain of functioning (e.g., motor speed), although the opposite pattern may be seen for another cognitive domain (e.g., working memory). However, considering the integrated network of striatal and extrastriatal brain regions, and given that DA function appears to decline with age throughout the human brain, a more likely expectation is that selective effects will be difficult to observe.

A final point to note is that recent neurocomputational work (Li, Lindenberger, and Sikström, 2001) has successfully modeled age-related cognitive deficits as a function of deficient dopaminergic modulation. In brief, the idea is that loss of DA increases neural noise which, in turn, results in less distinctive representations in the brain. These less distinctive representations are hypothesized to be a key determinant of age-related cognitive deficits across a variety of domains (e.g., working memory, executive functions).

Some caveats

Converging evidence from activation and neurotransmission studies suggest that alterations of PFC functions can be related to cognitive deficits in old age. This is in good agreement with findings from neuropsychological studies (see West, 1996) and studies on age-related changes of brain structure (see Raz, 1999). At the same time, it must be noted that findings from several studies suggest a fairly complex relationship between PFC function and cognitive deficits in advanced age. These findings can be sorted into two categories: (i) findings suggesting that PFC regions *can* function as well in old as in young age, and (ii) findings that functions not typically linked to the PFC account for much age-related variance in cognitive performance. A further, and more general, concern is that a full understanding of the biological underpinnings of cognitive aging most surely requires consideration of additional brain regions and functions.

Intact PFC function in old age

One set of relevant findings comes from observations that although PFC activity may be decreased for elderly adults when a specific type of cognitive task is being performed, activity in the same general region can be *on par* with that of younger adults when a different task is performed. For example, as discussed above, left PFC activity has been found to be lower for older than younger adults during intentional encoding. Encoding of new information can also be *incidental*, and occur as a by-product of other types of processing. The typical example of such processing is some kind of semantic analysis of the information presented, such as deciding whether words refer to living or nonliving entities. In a recent fMRI-study, Logan *et al.* (2002) showed that activity in left dorsal and ventral PFC was higher for younger than older adults during intentional encoding, whereas activity in the same regions was of comparable magnitude during incidental encoding. Thus, the under-recruitment of PFC regions by older adults during intentional encoding was normalized during incidental encoding. As concluded by the authors, these findings indicate that, although not recruited, frontal resources are available to older adults during intentional encoding as well.

A second set of findings that is highly relevant to the understanding of PFC functioning in old age concerns *higher* regional activity for older than younger adults. As noted above, younger adults tend to preferentially activate right PFC regions during episodic retrieval and older adults have shown reduced right PFC activity during episodic retrieval compared to younger adults. Interestingly, though, several studies have found higher left PFC activity during episodic retrieval in older compared to younger adults (Bäckman *et al.*, 1997; Cabeza *et al.*, 1997). Similar findings have been observed in comparisons of healthy elderly adults with demented patients (demented patients > healthy elderly adults; Bäckman *et al.*, 1999), and in comparisons of people at high or low risk for developing dementia (high > low; Bookheimer *et al.*, 2000). Thus, young adults, normal old adults, and demented patients may be viewed as three instances on a continuum of bilateral PFC activation during episodic retrieval.

Figure 7.5 illustrates this continuum by comparing young and normal older adults (upper panel; Bäckman *et al.*, 1997) and normal older adults and demented patients (lower panel; Bäckman *et al.*, 1999) during word-stem cued recall. Note that a similar pattern of increased bilateral PFC activation in old age has been observed in working-memory tasks as a function of the nature of the materials (i.e., verbal vs. spatial; Reuter-Lorenz *et al.*, 2000). A compensation mechanism has been proposed to account for this pattern of results (see Cabeza, 2001). In brief, this view holds that recruitment of additional PFC regions is beneficial to performance and serves to compensate for cognitive deficits (see also Reuter-Lorenz *et al.*, 2000). Interestingly, there is also variability among younger adults such that bilateral PFC activation is more frequent for demanding episodic tasks (Nolde *et al.*, 1998). This suggests that when the individual's processing resources are heavily taxed (due to impairment or high increased task difficulty), both hemispheres may be recruited in tasks that normally engage only one hemisphere.

Taken together, the two sets of findings discussed above indicate that although older adults tend to show decreased PFC activity during cognitive performance, such under-recruitment can be reversed by adequate support and additional PFC regions can be recruited to support task performance. In turn, this indicates that although advanced age no doubt is associated with structural and functional changes of the PFC, regions of the PFC may have a greater potential in old age than what is typically assumed.

Age differences in processing speed

Perhaps the most robust finding in the cognitive aging literature is that the time with which many cognitive operations can be executed decreases with increasing age (see Salthouse, 1996). Age-related slowing has been documented in numerous tasks of varying complexity (Salthouse, 1985; Schaie, 1989). In addition, statistical control of simple measures of reaction time

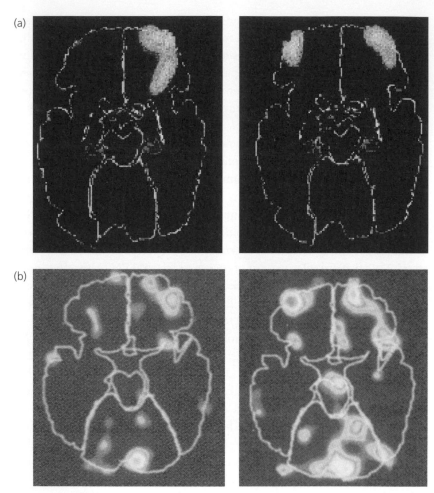

Fig. 7.5 Brain activity associated with episodic memory retrieval in young adults, old adults and demented patients. (a) Increased activity in right PFC for younger adults and in bilateral PFC for older adults during episodic memory retrieval. Adapted from Bäckman, L., Almkvist, O., Andersson, J., Nordberg, A., Reineck, R., Winblad, B., and Långström, B. (1997). Brain activation in young and older adults during implicit and explicit retrieval. *Journal of Cognitive Neuroscience, 9*, 378–391. Copyright 1997 by the MIT Press. (b) Increased activity in right PFC for older adults and in bilateral PFC for demented patients during episodic memory retrieval. Adapted from Bäckman, L., Andersson, J., Nyberg, L., Winblad, B., Nordberg, A., and Almkvist, O. (1999). Brain regions associated with episodic retrieval in normal aging and Alzheimer's disease. *Neurology, 52*, 1861–1870. Copyright 1999 by the American Academy of Neurology. (See Plates 1a and 1b.)

speed and perceptual speed has been found to eliminate or greatly attenuate the size of the age-related deficit in higher-order functions such as episodic memory (Salthouse, 1994) and working memory (Salthouse, 1992).

Findings that the performance of older adults is impaired on very basic tasks, and that such impairment is related to deficits on more high-level cognitive tasks, appear to stand in sharp contrast to the position that age differences are especially pronounced in tasks with high executive demands. At the same time, it should be noted that the possibility has been raised that age-related slowing reflects the need of older brains to recruit additional resources to manage the executive overhead of otherwise simple and largely automatic tasks (Raz, 1999). This possibility is supported by findings that well-learned sensorimotor skills such as walking are affected by increasing cognitive demands in old age (Lundin-Olsson, Nyberg, and Gustafson, 1997). Also, even in younger subjects, low-level tasks (e.g., identification of a specific letter) have been found to reliably activate PFC regions (D'Esposito *et al.*, 1998). Clearly, more work is needed to resolve this issue, but it seems as if findings of age differences in low-level tasks are not necessarily inconsistent with a frontal account of cognitive aging.

Additional neural correlates of cognitive aging

Few would probably disagree with the view that cognitive aging is multi-determined by numerous genetic, biological, and environmental factors (Bäckman, Small, and Wahlin, 2001). In this chapter, we have focused on age-related changes in the frontostriatal circuitry. However, cognitive functioning is inherently complex at the biological and behavioral levels alike. Thus, it is highly unlikely that age-related changes in the PFC and DA function would provide a complete account of the biological origins of cognitive aging. Rather, we are convinced that additional causative factors at different levels of analysis have to be considered. In the following, we briefly discuss two additional neural correlates of cognitive aging; (i) age-related changes in medial-temporal lobe structure and function, and (ii) age-related white-matter changes.

Converging evidence from studies on persons with focal brain lesions (Vargha-Khadem *et al.*, 1997), patients with Alzheimer's disease (Fox *et al.*, 1996), and imaging research with young adults (Nyberg *et al.*, 1996) indicates that the hippocampal complex plays a major role in the encoding, consolidation, and retrieval of episodic information. Interestingly, recent structural (Mungas *et al.*, 2001) and functional (Pihlajamaki *et al.*, 2000) imaging studies show substantial hippocampal involvement also in executive tasks (i.e., verbal fluency) typically associated with the left PFC (Cabeza and Nyberg, 2000).

Post-mortem research demonstrates age-related cell loss in the hippocampal formation among brains with no AD-related pathology (Simic, Kostovic, Winblad *et al.*, 1997; West, 1993). Even though the morphological evidence suggests that the effects of aging on hippocampal volume are not as pronounced and not as consistently observed as those on frontal volume, the bulk of research shows age-related hippocampal volume losses (Jernigan *et al.*, 1991; Raz, 1999). In addition, a relationship between the size of the hippocampus and episodic memory performance among normal old adults has been observed, both cross-sectionally (Golomb *et al.*, 1994) and longitudinally (Golomb *et al.*, 1996). Grady *et al.* (1995) reported reduced activity in the hippocampal complex during encoding of faces for older compared to young adults. Small and colleagues (1999) found that normal old adults with isolated episodic memory problems showed reduced activity in the hippocampus proper during encoding of faces. Note also that the age-related decrease in DA function appears to be as pronounced in the hippocampus as in the neocortex and the striatum (Kaasinen *et al.*, 2000). Collectively, these observations suggest that age-related changes in MTL structure and function contribute to age-related deficits in episodic memory, and perhaps also to age-related impairments in other cognitive tasks such as verbal fluency (Bäckman and Nilsson, 1996; Bryan and Luszcz, 2000).

Age-related changes in the white-matter of the brain, as determined from MRI studies, are well documented (Drayer, 1988; Kemper, 1994; Strassburger *et al.*, 1997). White-matter lesions result from loss of myelin that may have multiple origins, including arteriolar thickening and sclerosis (Grafton *et al.*, 1991), reduced cerebral perfusion (Drayer, 1988), and increased flow of cerebrospinal fluid (Sze *et al.*, 1986). White-matter lesions have been linked to deficits in numerous cognitive domains in which age-related deficits are typically observed. This includes motor and cognitive speed (Kail, 1998), episodic memory (Gupta *et al.*, 1988), visuospatial skill (Almkvist, Wahlund, Andersson-Lundman *et al.*, 1992), and executive functioning (Kertez, Polk, and Carr, 1990).

Although white-matter lesions may exert a rather general influence on cognitive functioning, the empirical evidence for a relationship between white-matter abnormalities and age-related cognitive deficits is mixed (O'Brien, Desmond, Ames *et al.*, 1997; Raz, Millman, and Sarpel, 1990; Raz *et al.*, 1993; Rao, Mittenberg, Benardin *et al.* 1989; Tupler, Coffey, Logue *et al.* 1992). As with many other biological alterations, this may reflect the fact that the degree of white-matter changes must reach a certain threshold before significant cognitive effects are observed (Boone *et al.*, 1992; DeCarli *et al.*, 1995). Another possibility is that the inconsistent findings reflect insensitivity in the methods traditionally used to assess white-matter lesions (i.e., structural

MRI). Using the recently developed diffusion tensor MRI technique, O'Sullivan and colleagues (2001) found age-related changes in several markers of white-matter tract integrity. Interestingly, changes were most pronounced in frontal regions, and strongly related to performance in a test of executive function (the Trail Making test). The findings were interpreted to mean that age-related loss of white-matter fibers results in cortical disconnection which may be particularly critical to executive functioning.

In the context of 'additional neural correlates of cognitive aging' it is indeed crucial to stress that aging may be associated with *disconnectivity*, that is deficient functional integration across a network of regions (Cabeza *et al.*, 1997; Esposito *et al.*, 1999). One candidate anatomical substrate for functional disconnection is disruption of white matter tracts (O'Sullivan *et al.*, 2001). Thus, although PFC regions seem to be key regions to consider in a biological account of cognitive aging, a full account likely has to consider additional gray-matter regions as well as the connecting white-matter tissue.

Future directions

The results discussed in this chapter suggest that age-related changes in cognitive performance can be related to age-related changes in the brain, notably the PFC. At present, this conclusion must be considered tentative because the number of imaging studies that have compared younger and older adults is still very limited. Additional studies are thus needed, and we conclude by briefly outlining some important questions to consider in future research.

One critical question concerns the relation between age-related declines in neuromodulation and age-related decreases in task-specific regional activity during actual cognitive performance. It is tempting to relate findings of deficient neurotransmission (dopaminergic as well as other) to decreased levels of task-related brain activity (as reflected by rCBF), such that impaired neurotransmitter function underlies decreased activity. Indeed, findings of a strong relationship between striatal D_2 binding and frontal and cingulate resting-state metabolism (Volkow *et al.*, 2000) provide support for a transmitter-activation relationship. However, this relationship may be quite complex and potentially moderated by cognitive activity.

For example, as noted, brain activity can be as high for older adults as for younger adults under supportive conditions for remembering (Logan *et al.*, 2002). If the lowered brain activity of old relative to young adults in less supported conditions is related to neurotransmitter deficiency, then the ability to increase activity by support suggests that the remaining transmitter activity is sufficient for older adults to enhance their brain activity as well as their cognitive performance. It would be of considerable interest if it could be shown that increased cognitive support is associated with increased release and binding of some neurotransmitter, such as dopamine in old age. Technically, it should be possible to conduct such a study; PET imaging of younger adults has revealed condition-specific fluxes of DA activity during performance of a video game (Koepp *et al.*, 1998). If the level of neurotransmitter activity can be affected by behavioral manipulations also in old age, this may open up for new possibilities in understanding the nature of gains from cognitive intervention in late adulthood (for an overview, see Hill, Bäckman, and Stigsdotter, 2000).

Moreover, older adults can have higher regional activity than younger adults during cognitive task performance, which has been related to compensatory behavioral strategies (Cabeza, 2001; Cabeza *et al.*, 1997). By this view, increased activity by the older person is associated with better cognitive performance. However, it has also been proposed that differential regional activity by older adults may reflect compensation for age-related declines in neuromodulation (Li *et al.*, 2001). By the latter view, then, *higher* levels of task-related regional activity are related to *impaired* neurotransmitter function. This further underscores the impression that the relation between results from neurotransmitter studies and activation studies is quite complex. One possibility is that optimal PFC function requires an optimal level of dopaminergic tone (cf., Esposito *et al.*, 1999). We are confident that future studies will shed light on these issues and thereby further our understanding of the biological basis of cognitive aging.

Acknowledgements

Preparation of this chapter was supported by grants from the Swedish Council for Research to Lars Nyberg and from the Swedish Council for Research to Lars Bäckman.

References

Almkvist, O., Wahlund, L.-O., Andersson-Lundman, G., Basun, H., and Bäckman, L. (1992). White-matter hyperintensity and neuropsychological functions in dementia and healthy aging. *Archives of Neurology,* **49,** 626–632.

Anderson, N. D., Iidaka, T., McIntosh, A. R., Kapur, S., Cabeza, R., and Craik, F. I. M. (2000). The effects of divided attention on encoding- and retrieval related brain activity: A PET study of younger and older adults. *Journal of Cognitive Neuroscience,* **12,** 775–792.

Bäckman, L., Almkvist, O., Andersson, J., Nordberg, A., Reineck, R., Winblad, B., and Långström, B. (1997). Brain activation in young and older adults during implicit and explicit retrieval. *Journal of Cognitive Neuroscience,* **9,** 378–391.

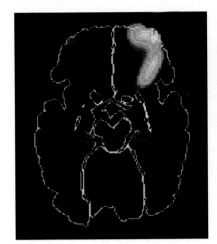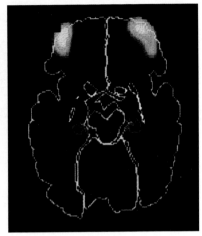

Plate 1A. Increased activity in right PFC for younger adults and in bilateral PFC for older adults during episodic memory retrieval. Adapted from Bäckman, L., Almkvist, O., Andersson, J., Nordberg, A., Reineck, R., Winblad, B., and Långström, B. (1997). Brain activation in young and older adults during implicit and explicit retrieval. *Journal of Cognitive Neuroscience, 9,* 378–391. Copyright 1997 by the MIT Press.

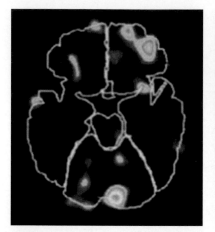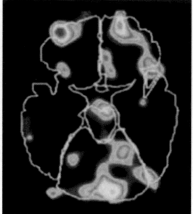

Plate 1B. Increased activity in right PFC for older adults and in bilateral PFC for demented patients during episodic memory retrieval. Adapted from Bäckman, L., Andersson, J., Nyberg, L., Winblad, B., Nordberg, A. and Almkvist, O. (1999). Brain regions associated with episodic retrieval in normal aging and Alzheimer's disease. *Neurology, 52,* 1861–1870. Copyright 1999 by the American Academy of Neurology.

Bäckman, L., Andersson, J., Nyberg, L., Winblad, B., Nordberg, A., and Almkvist, O. (1999). Brain regions associated with episodic retrieval in normal aging and Alzheimer's disease. *Neurology, 52*, 1861–1870.

Bäckman, L., Ginovart, N., Dixon, R. A., Robins Wahlin, T.-B., Wahlin, Å., Halldin, C., and Farde, L. (2000). Age-related cognitive deficits mediated by changes in the striatal dopamine system. *American Journal of Psychiatry, 157*, 635–637.

Bäckman, L., and Nilsson, L.-G. (1996). Semantic memory functioning across the adult life span. *European Psychologist, 1*, 27–33.

Bäckman, L., Small, B. J., and Wahlin, Å. (2001). Aging and memory: Cognitive and biological perspectives. In J. E. Birren and K. W. Schaie (eds), *Handbook of the psychology of aging* (5th ed., 349–377). San Diego, CA: Academic Press.

Baddeley, A. (1996). The fractionation of working memory. *Proceedings of the National Academy of Sciences, 93*, 13468–13472.

Bookheimer, S. Y., Strojwas, M. H., Cohen, M. S., Saunders, A. M., Pericak-Vance, M. A., Mazziotta, J. C., and Small, G. W. (2000). Patterns of brain activation in people at risk for Alzheimer's disease. *The New England Journal of Medicine, 343*, 450–456.

Boone, K. B., Miller, B. L., Lesser, I. M., Mehringer, M., Hill-Gutierrez, E., Goldberg, M. A., and Berman, N. G. (1992). Neuropsychological correlates of white-matter lesions in healthy elderly subjects: A threshold effect. *Archives of Neurology, 49*, 549–554.

Brown, R. G. and Marsden, C. D. (1988). Subcortical dementia: The neuropsychological evidence. *Neuroscience, 25*, 363–387.

Bryan, J. and Luszcz, M. A. (2000). Measures of fluency as predictors of incidental memory among older adults. *Psychology and Aging, 15*, 483–489.

Buckner, R. L. and Wheeler, M. E. (2001). The cognitive neuroscience of remembering. *Nature Reviews Neuroscience, 2*, 1–12.

Cabeza, R. (2001). Cognitive neuroscience of aging: Contributions of functional neuroimaging. *Scandinavian Journal of Psychology, 42*, 277–286.

Cabeza, R., Anderson, A. D., Mangels, J., Nyberg, L., and Houle, S. (2000). Age-related differences in neural activity during item and temporal-order memory retrieval: A positron emission tomography study. *Journal of Cognitive Neuroscience, 12*, 197–206.

Cabeza, R., Grady, C. L., Nyberg, L., McIntosh, A. R., Tulving, E., Kapur, S., Jennings, J. M., Houle, S., and Craik, F. I. M. (1997). Age-related differences in neural activity during memory encoding and retrieval: A positron emission tomography study. *Journal of Neuroscience, 17*, 391–400.

Cabeza, R., McIntosh, A. R., Tulving, E., Nyberg, L., and Grady, C. L. (1997). Age-related differences in effective neural connectivity during encoding and recall. *Neuroreport, 8*, 3479–3483.

Cabeza, R., and Nyberg, L. (2000). Imaging cognition II: An empirical review of 275 PET and fMRI studies. *Journal of Cognitive Neuroscience, 12*, 1–47.

Courtney, S. M., Ungerleider, L. G., Keil, K., and Haxby, J. V. (1996). Object and spatial visual working memory activate separate neural systems in human cortex. *Cerebral Cortex, 6*, 39–49.

Crosson, B. (1992). *Subcortical Functions in Language and Memory*. New York: Guilford.

D'Esposito, M. D., Ballard, D., Aguirre, G. K., and Zarahn, E. (1998). Human prefrontal cortex is not specific for working memory: A functional MRI study. *NeuroImage, 8*, 274–282.

DeCarli, C., Murphy, D. G. M., Tranh, M., Grady, C. L., Haxby, J. V., Gillette, J. A., Salerno, J. A., Gonzales-Aviles, A., Horwitz, B., Rapoport, S. I., and Schapiro, M. B. (1995). The effect of white-matter hyperintensity volume on brain structure, cognitive performance, and cerebral metabolism of glucose in 51 healthy adults. *Neurology*, **45**, 2077–2084.

De Keyser, J., De Backer, J. P., Vauquelin, G., and Ebinger, G. (1990). The effect of aging on the D1 dopamine receptors in human frontal cortex. *Brain Research, s*, 308–310.

Drayer, B. P. (1988). Imaging of the aging brain, 1: Normal findings. *Radiology*, **166**, 785–796.

Eggers, R., Haug, H., and Fischer, D. (1984). Preliminary report on macroscopic age changes in the human prosencephalon: A stereologic examination. *Journal für Hirnforshung*, **25**, 129–139.

Erixon, N., Farde, L., Halldin, C., Robins Wahlin, T.-R., and Bäckman, L. (2002). *Age-related reduction in striatal dopamine transporters and cognitive aging: A strong relationship*. Manuscript submitted for publication.

Esposito, G., Kirby, G. S., Van Horn, J. D., Ellmore, T. M., and Faith Berman, K. (1999). Context-dependent, neural system-specific neurophysiological concomitants of ageing: mapping PET correlates during cognitive activation. *Brain*, **122**, 963–979.

Fearnley, J. M., and Lees, A. J. (1991). Aging and Parkinson's disease: Substantia nigra regional selectivity. *Brain*, **114**, 2283–2301.

Fletcher, P. C., and Henson, R. N. A. (2001). Frontal lobes and human memory: Insights from functional neuroimaging. *Brain*, **124**, 849–881.

Fox, N. C., Warrington, E. K., Freeborough, P. A., Hartikainen, P., Kennedy, A. M., Stevens, J. S., and Rossor, M. N. (1996). Presymptomatic hippocampal atrophy in Alzheimer's disease. *Brain*, **119**, 2001–2007.

Freed, C. R., and Yamamoto, B. K. (1985). Regional brain dopamine metabolism: A marker for the speed, direction, and posture of moving animals. *Science*, **229**, 62–65.

Fuster, J. M. (1989). *The Prefrontal Cortex* (2nd ed). New York: Raven Press.

Gick, M. L., Craik, F. I. M., and Morris, R. G. (1988). Task complexity and age differences in working memory. *Memory and Cognition*, **16**, 353–361.

Giros, B., El Mestikawy, S., Godinot, N., Zheng, K. Q., Han, H., Yanfeng, T., and Caron, M. G. (1992). Cloning, pharmacological characterization, and chromosome assignment of the human dopamine transporter. *Molecular Pharmacology*, **3**, 383–390.

Goldman-Rakic, P. S. (1998). The cortical dopamine system: Role in memory and cognition. *Advances in Pharmacology*, **42**, 707–711.

Golomb, J., Kluger, A., de Leon, M. J., Ferris, S. H., Convit, A., Mittelman, M. S., Cohen, J., Rusnick, H., De Santi, S., and George, A. E. (1994). Hippocampal formation size in normal human aging: A correlate of delayed secondary memory performance. *Learning and Memory*, **1**, 45–54.

Golomb, J., Kluger, A., de Leon, M. J., Ferris, S. H., Mittelman, M. S., Cohen, J., and George, A. E. (1996). Hippocampal formation size predicts declining memory performance in normal human aging. *Neurology*, **47**, 810–813.

Good, C.D., Johnsrude, I. S., Ashburner, J., Henson, R. N. A., Friston, K. J., and Frackowiak, R. S. J. (2001). A voxel-based morphometric study of ageing in 465 normal adult brains. *NeuroImage*, **14**, 1–16.

Grady, C. L., McIntosh, A. R., Horwitz, B., Maisog, J. M., Ungerleider, L. G., Mentis, M. J., Pietrini, P., Schapiro, M. B., and Haxby, J. V. (1995). Age-related reductions in human recognition memory due to impaired encoding. *Science,* **269,** 218–221.

Grafton, S. T., Sumi, S. M., Stimac, G. K., Alvord, E. C., Shaw, C. M., and Nochlin, D. (1991). Comparison of post-mortem magnetic resonance imaging and neoropathologic findings in the cerebral white matter. *Archives of Neurology,* **48,** 293–298.

Graybiel, A. M. (2000). The basal ganglia and adaptive motor control. *Current Biology,* **10,** 509–511.

Gupta, S. R., Naheedy, M. H., Young, J. C., Ghobrial, M., Rubino, F. A., and Hindo, W. (1988). Periventricular white matter changes and dementia: Clinical, neuropsychological, radiological, and pathological correlation. *Archives of Neurology,* **45,** 637–641.

Hartley, A., and Speer, N. K. (2000). Locating and fractionating working memory using functional neuroimaging: Storage, maintenance, and executive functions. *Microscopy Research and Technique,* **51,** 45–53.

Hill, R. D., Bäckman, L., and Stigsdotter Neely, A. (eds) (2000). *Cognitive Rehabilitation in Old Age.* New York: Oxford University Press.

Hultsch, D. F., Hertzog, C., and Dixon, R. A. (1990). Ability correlates of memory performance in adulthood and aging. *Psychology and Aging,* **5,** 356–368.

Inoue, M., Suhara, T., Sudo, Y., Okubo, Y., Yasuno, F., Kishimoto, T., Yoshikawa, K., and Tanada, S. (2001). Age-related reduction of extrastriatal dopamine D_2 receptor measured by PET. *Life Sciences,* **69,** 1079–1084.

Iyo, M., and Yamasaki, T. (1993). The detection of age-related decrease of dopamine of D_1, D_2, and serotonin 5-HT$_2$ receptors in living human brain. *Progress in Neuropsychopharmacology and Biological Psychiatry,* **17,** 415–421.

Jaber, M., Jones, S., Giros, B., and Caron, M. G. (1997). The dopamine transporter: A crucial component regulating dopamine transmission. *Movement Disorders,* **12,** 629–633.

Jernigan, T. L., Archibald, S. L., Berhow, M. T., Sowell, E. R., Foster, D. S., and Hesselink, J. R. (1991). Cerebral structure on MRI: Part I. Localization of age-related changes. *Biological Psychiatry,* **29,** 55–67.

Kaasinen, V., Vilkman, H., Hietala, J., Nagren, K., Helenius, H., Olsson, H., Farde, L., and Rinne, J. O. (2000). Age-related D_2/D_3 receptor loss in extrastriatal regions of the human brain. *Neurobiology of Aging,* **21,** 683–688.

Kail, R. (1998). Speed of information processing in patients with multiple sclerosis. *Journal of Clinical and Experimental Neuropsychology,* **20,** 98–106.

Kelley, W. M., Miezin, F. M., McDermott, K. B. *et al.* (1998). Hemispheric specialization in human dorsal frontal cortex and medial temporal lobe for verbal and nonverbal memory encoding. *Neuron,* **20,** 927–936.

Kemper, T. L. (1994). Neuroanatomical and neuropathological changes during aging and in dementia. In M. L. Albert and E. J. E. Knoepfel (eds), *Clinical Neurology of Aging* (2nd ed., pp. 3–67). New York: Oxford University Press.

Kertesz, A., Polk, M., and Carr, T. (1990). Cognition and white matter changes on magnetic resonance imaging in dementia. *Archives of Neurology,* **47,** 387–391.

Koepp, M. J., Gunn, R. N., Lawrence, A. D. *et al.* (1998). Evidence for striatal dopamine release during a video game. *Nature,* **393,** 266–268.

Lepage, M., Ghaffar, O., Nyberg, L., and Tulving, E. (2000). Prefrontal cortex and episodic memory retrieval mode. *Proceedings of the National Academy of Sciences, USA,* **97**, 506–511.

Li, S.-C., Lindenberger, U., and Sikström, S. (2001). Aging cognition: From neuromodulation to representation to cognition. *Trends in Cognitive Sciences,* **5**, 479–486.

Logan, J. M., Sanders, A. L., Snyder, A. Z., Morris, J. C., and Buchner, R. L. (2002). Under-recruitment and non selective recruitment: Dissociable neural mechanisms associated with aging. *Neuron,* **33**, 827–840.

Luciana, M., Collins, P. F., and Depue, R. A. (1998). Opposing roles for dopamine and serotonin in the modulation of human spatial working memory functions. *Cerebral Cortex,* **8**, 218–226.

Lundin-Olsson, L., Nyberg, L., and Gustafson, Y. (1997). 'Stops walking when talking' as a predictor of falls in the elderly. *The Lancet,* **349**, 616.

Martin, W. R. W., Palmer, M. R., Patlak, C. S., and Caine, D. B. (1989). Nigrostriatal function in humans studied with positron emission tomography. *Annals of Neurology,* **26**, 535–542.

McEntee, W. J., Mair, R. G., and Langlais, P. J. (1987). Neurochemical specificity of learning: Dopamine and motor learning. *Yale Journal of Biology and Medicine,* **60**, 187–193.

Mitchell, K. J., Johnson, M. K., Raye, C. L., and D'Esposito, M. (2000). fMRI evidence of age-related hippocampal dysfunction in feature binding in working memory. *Brain Research Interactive – Cognitive Brain Research, 1.*

Morgan, D. G., and Finch, C. E. (1998). Dopaminergic changes in the basal ganglia: A generalized phenomenon of aging in mammals. *Annals of the New York Academy of Sciences,* **515**, 145–160.

Morris, R. G., Gick, M. L., and Craik, F. I. M. (1988). Processing resources and age differences in working memory. *Memory and Cognition,* **16**, 362–366.

Mozley, L. H., Gur, R. C., Mozley, P. D., and Gur, R. E. (2001). Striatal dopamine transporters and cognitive functioning in healthy men and women. *American Journal of Psychiatry,* **158**, 1492–1499.

Mozley, P. D., Acton, P. D., Barraclough, E. D., Plössl, K., Gur, R. C., Alavi, A., Mathur, A., Saffer, J., and Kung, H. F. (1999). Effects of age on dopamine transporters in healthy humans. *Journal of Nuclear Medicine,* **40**, 1812–1817.

Mungas, D., Jagust, W. J., Reed, B. R., Kramer, J. H., Weiner, M. W., Schuff, N., Norman, D., Mack, W. J., Willis, L., and Chui, H. C. (2001). MRI predictors of cognition in subcortical ischemic disease and Alzheimer's disease. *Neurology,* **57**, 2229–2235.

Nilsson, L.-G., Bäckman, L., Nyberg, L., Erngrund, K., Adolfsson, R., Bucht, G., Karlsson, S., Widing, M., and Winblad, B. (1997). The Betula prospective cohort study: Memory, health, and aging. *Aging, Neuropsychology, and Cognition,* **4**, 1–32.

Nolde, S. F., Johnson, M. K., and Raye, C. L. (1998). The role of prefrontal cortex during tests of episodic memory. *Trends in Cognitive Sciences,* **2**, 399–406.

Nyberg, L., Cabeza, R., and Tulving, E. (1996). PET studies of encoding and retrieval: The HERA model. *Psychonomic Bulletin and Review,* **3**, 134–147.

Nyberg, L., Maitland, S. B., Rönnlund, M., Bäckman, L., Dixon, R. A., Wahlin, Å., and Nilsson, L.-G. (2003). Selective adult age differences in an age-invariant multi-factor model of declarative memory. *Psychology and Aging,* **18**, 149–160.

Nyberg, L., Petersson K. M., Cabeza, R., Forkstam, C., and Ingvar, M. (2002). Brain imaging of human memory systems: Between-systems similarities and within-system differences. *Cognitive Brain Research*, **13**, 281–292.

Nyberg, L., Habib, R., McIntosh, A. R., and Tulving, E. (2000). Reactivation of encoding-related brain activity during memory retrieval. *Proceedings of the National Academy of Sciences, USA*, **97**, 11120–11124.

Nyberg, L., McIntosh, A. R., Houle, S., Nilsson, L.-G, and Tulving, E. (1996). Activation of medial temporal structures during episodic memory retrieval. *Nature*, **380**, 715–717.

O'Brien, J. T., Desmond, P., Ames, D., Schweitzer, I., and Tress, B. (1997). Magnetic resonance imaging correlates of memory impairment in the healthy elderly: Association with medial temporal lobe atrophy but not white-matter lesions. *International Journal of Geriatric Psychiatry*, **12**, 369–374.

Park, D. C., Smith, A. D., Lautenschlager, G., Earles, J. G., Frieske, D., Zwahr, M., and Gaines, C. L. (1996). Mediators of long-term memory performance across the life span. *Psychology and Aging*, **11**, 621–637.

Petrides, M. (1994). Frontal lobes and working memory: Evidence from investigations of the effects of cortical excisions in nonhuman primates. In F. Boller and J. Grafman (eds), *Handbook of Neuropsychology* (Vol. 9, pp. 59–82). Amsterdam: Elsevier.

Pihlajamaki, M., Tanila, H., Hanninen, T., Kononen, M., Laakso, M., Partanen, K., Soininen, H., and Aronen, H. J. (2000). Verbal fluency activates the left medial temporal lobe: A functional magnetic resonance imaging study. *Annals of Neurology*, **47**, 470–476.

Prull, M. W., Gabrieli, J. D. E., and Bunge, S. A. (1999). Age-related changes in memory: A cognitive neuroscience perspective. In F. I. M. Craik and T. A. Salthouse (eds), *The Handbook of Aging and Cognition* (Vol. 2, pp. 91–153). Mahwah, NJ: Erlbaum.

Rao, M. S., Mittenberg, W., Bernardin, L., Haughton, V., and Leo, G. J. (1989). Neuropsychological test findings in subjects with leukoaraiosis. *Archives of Neurology*, **46**, 40–44.

Raz, N., Millman, D., and Sarpel, G. (1990). Cerebral correlates of cognitive aging: Grey-white matter differentiation in the medial-temporal lobes and fluid vs. crystallized abilities. *Psychobiology*, **18**, 475–481.

Raz, N., Torres, I. J., Spencer, W. D., Baertschie, J. C., Millman, D., and Sarpel, G. (1993). Neuroanatomical correlates of age-sensitive and age-invariant cognitive abilities: An in vivo MRI investigation. *Intelligence*, **17**, 407–422.

Raz, N. (1999). Aging of the brain and its impact on cognitive performance: Integration of structural and functional findings. In F. I. M. Craik and T. A. Salthouse (eds), *The Handbook of Aging and Cognition* (Vol. 2, pp. 1–90). Mahwah, NJ: Erlbaum.

Reuter-Lorenz, P., Jonides, J., Smith, E. S., Hartley, A., Miller, A., Marshuetz, C., and Koeppe, R. A. (2000). Age differences in the frontal lateralization of verbal and spatial working memory revealed by PET. *Journal of Cognitive Neuroscience*, **12**, 174–187.

Rinne, J. O., Hietala, H., Ruotsalainen, U., Sälö, E., Laihinen, A., Någren, K., Lehikoinen, P., Oikonen, V., and Syvälahti, E. (1993). Decrease in human striatal dopamine D_2 receptor binding with age: A PET study with [^{11}C] raclopride. *Journal of Cerebral Blood Flow and Metabolism*, **13**, 310–314.

Rossi, S., Cappa, S. F., Babiloni, C., Pasqualetti, P., Miniussi, C., Caducci, F., Babiloni, F., and Rossini, P. M. (2001). Prefrontal cortex in long-term memory: an 'interference' approach using magnetic stimulation. *Nature Neuroscience*, **4**, 948–952.

Roth, G. S., and Joseph, J. A. (1994). Cellular and molecular mechanisms of impaired dopaminergic function during aging. *Annals of the New York Academy of Sciences,* **31,** 129–135.

Rubin, D. C. (1999). Frontal-striatal circuits in cognitive aging: Evidence for caudate involvement. *Aging, Neuropsychology, and Cognition,* **6,** 241–259.

Rypma, B., Prabhakaran, V., Desmond, J. D., and Gabrieli, J. D. E. (in press). Age differences in prefrontal cortical activity in working memory. *Psychology and Aging.*

Rypma, B., and D'Esposito, M. (2000). Isolating the neural mechanisms of age-related changes in human working memory. *Nature Neuroscience,* **3,** 509–515.

Salthouse, T. A. (1985). Speed of behavior and its implications for cognition. In J. E. Birren and T. A. Salthouse (eds), *Handbook of the Psychology of Aging* (2nd ed., pp. 400–426). New York: Van Nostrand Reinhold.

Salthouse, T. A. (1992). Influence of processing speed on adult age differences in working memory. *Acta Psychologia,* **79,** 155–170.

Salthouse, T. A. (1994). Aging associations: Influence of speed on adult age differences in associative learning. *Journal of Experimental Psychology: Learning, Memory, and Cognition,* **20,** 1486–1503.

Salthouse, T. A. (1996). The processing-speed theory of adult age differences in cognition. *Psychological Review,* **103,** 403–428.

Schacter, D. L., Savage, C. R., Alpert, N. M., Rauch, S. L., and Albert, M. S. (1996). The role of hippocampus and frontal cortex in age-related memory changes: A PET study. *Neuroreport,* **7,** 1165–1169.

Schaie, K. W. (1989). Perceptual speed in adulthood: Cross-sectional and longitudinal analyses. *Psychology and Aging,* **4,** 443–453.

Simic, G., Kostovic, I., Winblad, B., and Bogdanovic, N. (1997). Volume and number of neurons of the human hippocampal formation in normal aging and Alzheimer's disease. *Journal of Comparative Neurology,* **379,** 482–494.

Small, S. A., Perera, G. M., DeLaPaz, R., Mayeux, R., and Stern, Y. (1999). Differential regional dysfunction of the hippocampal formation among elderly with memory decline and Alzheimer's disease. *Annals of Neurology,* **45,** 466–472.

Smith, E. E., and Jonides, J. (1999). Storage and executive processes in the frontal lobes. *Science,* **283,** 1657–1661.

Strassburger, T. L., Lee, H. C., Daly, E. M., Szcepanik, J., Krasuski, J. S., Mentis, M. J., Salerno, J. A., DeCarli, C., Schapiro, M. B., and Alexander, G. E. (1997). Interactive effects of age and hypertension on volumes of brain structures. *Stroke,* **28,** 1410–1417.

Stebbins, G. T., Carrillo, M. C., Dorfman, J., Dirksen, C., Desmond, J., Turner, D. A., Bennett, D. A., Wilson, R. S., Glover, G., and Gabrieli, J. D. E. (in press). Aging effects on memory encoding in the frontal lobes. *Psychology and Aging.*

Suhara, T., Fukuda, H., Inoue, O., Itoh, T., Suzuki, K., Yamasaki, T., Tateno, Y. (1991). Age-related changes in human D_1 dopamine receptors measured by positron emission tomography. *Psychopharmacology,* **103,** 41–45.

Sze, G., DeArmond, S., Brant-Zawadski, M., Davis, R. L., Norman, D., and Newton, T. H. (1986). Foci of MRI signal (pseudo lesions) anterior to the frontal horns: Histologic correlations of a normal finding. *American Journal of Neuroradiology,* **7,** 381–387.

Troyer, A. K., Graves, R. E., and Cullum, C. M. (1994). Executive functioning as a mediator of the relationship between age and episodic memory in healthy aging. *Aging and Cognition,* **1,** 45–53.

Tulving, E., Kapur, S., Craik, F. I. M., Moscovitch, M., and Houle, S. (1994). Hemispheric encoding/retrieval asymmetry in episodic memory: Positron emission tomography findings. *Proceedings of the National Academy of Sciences, USA*, **91**, 2016–2020.

Tupler, L. A., Coffey, C. E., Logue, P. E., Djang, W. T., and Fagan, S. M. (1992). Neuropsychological importance of subcortical white matter hyperintensity. *Archives of Neurology*, **49**, 1248–1252.

VanDyck, C. H., Seibyl, J. P., Malison, R. T., Laruelle, M., Wallace, E., Zoghhbi, S. S., Zeaponce, Y., Baldwin, R. M., Charney, D. S., Hoffer, P. B., and Innis, R. B. (1995). Age-related decline in striatal dopamine transporter binding with iodine-123. CIT. *Journal of Nuclear Medicine*, **36**, 1175–1181.

Vargha-Khadem, F., Gadian, D. G., Watkins, K. E., Connellly, A., Van Paesschen, W., and Mishkin, M. (1977). Differential effects of early hippocampal lesions on episodic and semantic memory. *Science*, **277**, 376–380.

Volkow, N. D., Ding, Y.-S., Fowler, J. S., Wang, G.-J., Logan, J., Gatley, S. J., Hitzemann, R., Smith, G., Fields, F., Gur, R., and Wolf, A. P. (1996). Dopamine transporters decrease with age in healthy subjects. *Journal of Nuclear Medicine*, **37**, 554–558.

Volkow, N. D., Gur, R. C., Wang, G.-J., Fowler, J. S., Moberg, P. J., Ding, Y.-S., Hitzemann, R. R., Smith, G., and Logan, J. (1998). Association between decline in brain dopamine activity with age and cognitive and motor impairment in healthy individuals. *American Journal of Psychiatry*, **155**, 344–349.

Volkow, N. D., Logan, J., Fowler, J. S., Wang, G. J., Gur, R. C., Wong, C., Felder, C., Gatley, S. J., Ding, Y. S., Hitzemann, R., and Pappas, N. (2000). Association between age-related decline in brain dopamine activity and impairment in frontal and cingulate metabolism. *American Journal of Psychiatry*, **157**, 75–80.

Wagner, A. D., Schacter, D. L., Rotte, M. *et al.* (1998). Building memories: Remembering and forgetting as predicted by brain activity. *Science*, **281**, 1188–1191.

Wang, Y., Chan G. L. Y., Holden, J. E., Dobko, T., Mak, E., Schulzer, M., Huser, J. M., Snow, B. J., Ruth, T. J., Calne, D. B., and Stoessl, A. J. (1998). Age-dependent decline of dopamine D_1 receptors in human brain: A PET study. *Synapse*, **30**, 56–61.

West, M. J. (1993). Regionally specific loss of neurons in the aging human hippocampus. *Neurobiology of Aging*, **14**, 287–293.

West, R. L. (1996). An application of prefrontal cortex function theory to cognitive aging. *Psychological Bulletin*, **120**, 272–292.

Wheeler, M. A., Stuss, D. T., and Tulving, E. (1995). Frontal lobe damage produces episodic memory impairment. *Journal of the International Neuropsychological Society*, **1**, 525–536.

Wheeler, M. E., Petersen, S. E., and Buckner, R. L. (2000). Memory's echo: Vivid remembering reactivates sensory-specific cortex. *Proceedings of the National Academy of Sciences, USA*, **97**, 11125–11129.

Wilson, F. A., O'Scalaidhe, S. P., and Goldman-Rakic, P. S. (1993). Dissocation of object and spatial processing domains in primate prefrontal cortex. *Science*, **260**, 1955–1958.

Chapter 8

Cognitive deficits in preclinical Alzheimer's disease: Current knowledge and future directions

Lars Bäckman, Brent J. Small, and
Laura Fratiglioni

Because of their high frequency and dramatic course, dementing disorders such as Alzheimer's disease (AD) are associated with substantial societal and individual costs (Launer and Hofman, 2000). Thus, progress in understanding how the disease develops in order to prevent or delay its onset has become an urgent scientific and public health imperative (Fratiglioni, 2000; Post, 1999). The availability of drugs that may improve cognitive functioning in AD has directed research interest toward the early phases of the disease (for an overview, see Flicker, 1999). The possibility of a vaccine to reduce the deposition of amyloid in the brain of transgenic mice (Schenk *et al.*, 1999) has reinforced this interest. Ideally, future AD patients would be identified several years before diagnosis in order to stop the evolution of the disease before the appearance of clear clinical symptoms (Petersen *et al.*, 1999). By increasing our knowledge of the preclinical phase of the disease, highly predictive tools of incipient AD may be identified. The purpose of this chapter is to review the current state of knowledge regarding the preclinical phase of AD, focusing largely on cognitive markers of an impending dementia disease. Promising avenues for future research on the identification of persons at risk of developing AD are discussed.

Cognitive markers of preclinical Alzheimer's disease

Although it has been known since long that most cognitive functions (e.g., attention, memory, verbal ability, visuospatial skill) are severely compromised already in early clinical AD (for overviews, see Morris, 1996; Nebes, 1992), a more recent observation is that there is a preclinical phase of this disease during which cognitive deficits are detectable (Hodges, 1998). Evidence indicates preclinical deficits in AD for global indicators of cognitive functioning, such as the Mini-Mental State Examination or MMSE (Small, Viitanen, and Bäckman, 1997; Yoshitake *et al.*, 1995), as well as for specific measures of psychomotor functioning (Masur, Sliwinski, Lipton *et al.*, 1994), perceptual speed (Fabrigoule *et al.*, 1998), attention (Linn *et al.*, 1995), verbal ability (Jacobs *et al.*, 1995), reasoning (Fabrigoule *et al.*, 1996), and visuospatial skill (Small, Herlitz, Fratiglioni *et al.*, 1997). Indeed, Fabrigoule and colleagues (1998) showed that a general factor subsuming a wide variety of cognitive abilities was related to the risk of developing AD over a two-year interval.

The primacy of episodic memory

Despite the seemingly global nature of the cognitive impairment in preclinical AD, several studies indicate that the most pronounced deficit occurs within the domain of episodic memory (Howieson *et al.*, 1997; Linn *et al.*, 1995; Small, Herlitz Fratiglioni *et al.*, 1997; Tierney *et al.*, 1995). A common result in this research is that, although indicators of multiple cognitive abilities differentiate incident AD cases from controls when examined individually, multivariate analyses (e.g., logistic regressions) routinely reveal a dominance of episodic memory measures in the prediction models.

Episodic memory involves travelling backwards in time in order to recollect personally experienced events from the distant or recent past. This form of memory is based on conscious retrieval of information acquired in a particular place at a particular time, and is typically assessed by having subjects recall or recognize some information acquired in the experimental setting (Tulving, 1983). An interesting observation is that the episodic memory deficit in persons who will develop AD appears to be highly generalizable across different materials and testing conditions. Thus, preclinical episodic memory deficits have been observed for both verbal (Linn *et al.*, 1995; Tierney *et al.*, 1995) and nonverbal (Fuld, Maur, Blau *et al.*, 1990; Small, Herlitz Fratiglioni *et al.*, 1997) materials, as well as across different retrieval conditions, including free recall (Grober, Lipton, Hall *et al.*, 2000; Howieson *et al.*, 1997), cued recall (Bäckman and Small, 1998; Linn *et al.*, 1995), and recognition (Fuld *et al.*, 1990; Small, Herlitz Fratiglioni *et al.*, 1997).

In addition to their marked episodic memory impairment, patients with clinical AD show deficits in the ability to utilize supportive conditions to improve memory performance, such as directed instructions, organizational structure, or retrieval cues (Almkvist, Fratiglioni, Agüero-Torres *et al.*, 1999; Herlitz, Adolfsson, Bäckman *et al.*, 1991). These failures indicate a reduction of cognitive reserve capacity in clinical AD (Bäckman and Herlitz, 1996; Stern, 2001).

Bäckman and Small (1998) compared groups of incident AD cases and controls on four episodic memory tasks that varied systematically with regard to the degree of cognitive support provided: free recall of rapidly presented random words, free recall of slowly presented random words, free recall of organizable words, and cued recall of organizable words. These four tasks may be viewed as instances along a continuum of cognitive support, where more study time, organizability, and semantic retrieval cues are incrementally added to the memory task.

In Bäckman and Small (1998), subjects were tested both at baseline and at a three-year follow-up, the time at which the incident AD cases were diagnosed with dementia. The main results from this study are portrayed in Figure 8.1. As can be seen, although the normal old declined slightly across the three-year retest interval, they showed proficient utilization of all three forms of cognitive support at both times of measurement, with performance increasing

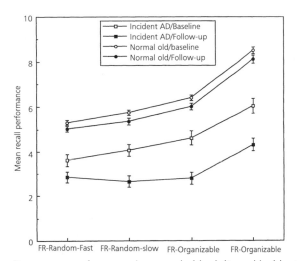

Fig. 8.1 Episodic memory performance in normal old adults and incident AD patients across level of cognitive support at baseline (three years before diagnosis) and follow-up (diagnosis). Bars represent standard errors around the means. Adapted from L. Bäckman and B. J. Small, 1998, Influences of cognitive support on episodic remembering: Tracing the process of loss from normal aging to Alzheimer's disease, *Psychology and Aging*, *13*, 267–276. Copyright 1998 by the American Psychological Association.

gradually with the addition of more study time, organizability, and retrieval cues. The incident AD cases showed a clear performance deficit at baseline, which was exacerbated at follow-up. The latter finding indicates that the time period just preceding the diagnosis of AD is characterized by a marked decline of episodic memory functioning. Most interestingly, although they were impaired at baseline assessment, the incident AD cases showed the same qualitative pattern as the controls, with performance gradually increasing across increasing levels of cognitive support. Finally, at the time of diagnosis, the incident AD cases failed to benefit from more study time and organizability in free recall; here, performance gains were observed only in the most supportive condition – when an organizational structure was combined with retrieval cues. The latter result was expected, as several studies have demonstrated that it may be necessary to provide support at both encoding and retrieval to show memory improvement in early clinical AD (for a review, see Bäckman and Herlitz, 1996).

These results suggest that the size of the preclinical episodic memory impairment in AD may not vary as a function of the level of cognitive support. Further, the fact that the incident AD cases showed a normal pattern of utilization of cognitive support although they performed worse than the controls at baseline indicates that losses in cognitive reserve capacity may occur somewhat later in the pathogenesis of AD than a general episodic memory impairment. This suggests an interesting difference regarding the nature of the episodic memory impairment in early clinical AD and preclinical AD: clear reductions in reserve capacity may be present only among clinically diagnosed patients, although both conditions are associated with deficits in episodic memory.

An interesting point to note is that a marked episodic memory impairment is observed also in numerous other more or less severe conditions, including schizophrenia, stroke, depression, vitamin deficiency, sleep deprivation, and alcohol intoxication (for an overview, see Bäckman, Small, and Wahlin, 2001). Evidence suggests that episodic memory evolved late phylogenetically and emerges late ontogenetically compared to other forms of memory and cognition (Tulving, 1999). Perhaps because of its advanced nature, a large distributed network is engaged during encoding and retrieval of episodic information, including the hippocampal formation, the prefrontal cortex, anterior cingulate, specific parietal regions, and the cerebellum (for an overview, see Cabeza and Nyberg, 2000). Thus, changes at any of the multiple sites in this widespread network are capable of disrupting performance. This may account for the fact that episodic memory deficits are legion in a variety of diverse conditions that alter normal brain functioning.

Although episodic memory draws on a widespread neural network, the critical importance of the hippocampal complex to successful episodic memory functioning is well established in both lesion (Vargha-Khadem *et al.*, 1997) and brain imaging (Nyberg, McIntosh, Houle *et al.*, 1996) research. This is an important observation with regard to the episodic memory impairment in preclinical AD, because evidence from histopathology (Braak and Braak, 1995), structural brain imaging (Laakso *et al.*, 1998), and functional brain imaging (Small *et al.*, 1999) indicates that the earliest brain changes in this disease occur in the hippocampus and neighboring regions. In a structural magnetic resonance imaging study, seven at-risk members of a familial AD pedigree were examined across a three-year interval (Fox *et al.*, 1996). For the three persons who were diagnosed with AD during the study, volumetric measurement of the hippocampus revealed atrophy before the appearance of clinical symptoms. Most interestingly, the hippocampal shrinkage observed occurred in parallel with decline in measures of episodic memory.

How does the preclinical phase in AD evolve?

Although the research reviewed hitherto has yielded important insights with regard to the cognitive transition from normal aging to dementia, some issues deserve further comment. One such issue concerns the length of time before the diagnosis of AD that cognitive deficits may be observed. The bulk of studies showing such deficits have used follow-up periods between two and four years, although similar deficits have been observed in studies using considerably longer follow-up intervals (Elias *et al.*, 2000; Yoshitake *et al.*, 1995). However, a problem with the latter studies is that the length of the follow-up period has varied across individuals. Combining persons with diverse follow-up periods may obscure the effects related to early cognitive deficits.

Of equal concern is that most studies demonstrating preclinical cognitive deficits in AD have included only one testing occasion prior to diagnosis. In some studies in which subjects have been assessed on multiple occasions, the focus has been on the single point in time at which preclinical deficits are first detectable rather than on the course of the preclinical phase. This research demonstrates that preclinical cognitive deficits in AD may be observed more than 10 years before diagnosis (Elias *et al.*, 2000; LaRue and Jarvik, 1987). However, these studies do not address the course of cognitive deficits before the diagnosis of AD. In a few studies, persons have been assessed cognitively both before and at the time of diagnosis. Consistently, patients in a preclinical phase of AD exhibit precipitous cognitive decline during the time period just preceding diagnosis (Fox *et al.*, 1998; Rubin *et al.*, 1998). These findings raise

the important question of whether those who will develop AD show disproportionate cognitive decline longer before diagnosis.

In a recent report, persons from a population-based study were assessed at
three occasions over six years, using tests of verbal free recall and recognition
(Bäckman, Small, and Fratiglioni, 2001). At the last occasion, some individuals
were diagnosed with AD, although the entire study sample was non-demented at
the first two times of measurement. The key finding was that the incident AD
cases did not deteriorate selectively from six to three years before diagnosis,
although they showed clear deficits in both free recall and recognition already at
the first time of assessment (see Figure 8.2). Thus, the degree of episodic memory
impairment remained unchanged over the two preclinical measurement points.

A similar pattern of findings was obtained in another study examining a
larger sample of subjects with a similar design (Small, Fratiglioni, Viitanen *et al.*,
2000). In this study, the MMSE was used to assess cognitive functioning. At both
preclinical occasions, the incident AD cases showed deficits on only one MMSE
subscale, namely the one assessing episodic memory (delayed recall; see
Figure 8.3). Again, however, the incident AD group did not exhibit selective
decline from the six- to the three-year interval, although they showed precipitous
decline across most cognitive domains assessed by the MMSE during the last
three years preceding diagnosis.

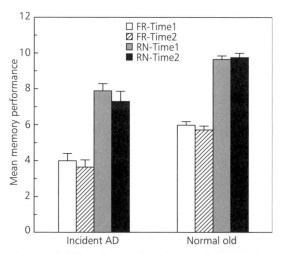

Fig. 8.2 Mean free recall (FR) and recognition (RN) performance for normal old
and incident AD persons six years (Time 1) and three years (Time 2) before the
diagnosis of dementia. Bars represent standard errors around the means. Adapted
from L. Bäckman, B. J. Small, and L. Fratiglioni, Stability of the preclinical
episodic memory deficit in Alzheimer's disease, *Brain*, 2001, *124*, 96–102.
Copyright 2001 by Oxford University Press.

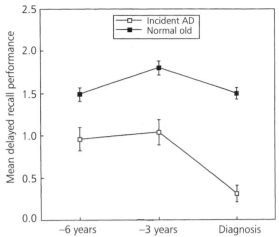

Fig. 8.3 Mean performance on the delayed recall item from the Mini-Mental State Examination in incident AD patients and normal old adults six years before diagnosis, three years before diagnosis, and at the time of diagnosis. Bars represent standard errors around the means. Adapted from B. J. Small, L. Fratiglioni, M. Viitanen, B. Winblad, and L. Bäckman, The course of cognitive impairment in preclinical Alzheimer's disease: Three- and six-year follow-up of a population-based sample, *Archives of Neurology*, 2000, *57*, 839–844. Copyright 2000 by the American Medical Association.

However, Chen and colleagues (2001) recently reported disproportionate cognitive decline, particularly in episodic memory and executive functions, among persons who would go on to develop AD between 3.5 and 1.5 years before diagnosis. Conceivably, the source of the discrepant outcomes in this study and those from our group is the time to diagnosis (1.5 years versus 3 years), for the likelihood of observing differential change in preclinical AD should increase as the distance to diagnosis decreases.

Thus, the results from this research suggest that the episodic memory deficit in preclinical AD is characterized by an early onset, which interestingly is followed by relative stability until a few years before a diagnosis may be rendered. Consistent with this pattern, Kaye and colleagues (1999) found that the rate of brain volume loss accelerates as AD progresses from the preclinical to the clinical stage.

When does the preclinical phase of AD begin?

Along with other research demonstrating cognitive deficits in those who will develop AD many years before diagnosis (Elias *et al.*, 2000; LaRue and Jarvik, 1987), these results beg the question of when the preclinical period of AD actually begins. This intriguing issue requires consideration of multiple sources of evidence. Snowdon and colleagues (1996) reported one of the most striking observations concerning the length of the preclinical period in AD. Using data from the Nun Study, these investigators showed that measures of linguistic skill (idea density and grammatical complexity) assessed when participants were in the early 20s were highly predictive of who would develop AD more than 50 years later. Relatedly, Whalley and colleagues (2000) found that lower scores on tests of mental ability in childhood were associated with an increased risk of having AD in late life. In a similar vein, histopathological data demonstrate that initial signs of the formation of neurofibrillary tangles (i.e., cytoskeletal changes) may emerge in the medial-temporal lobe in early adulthood (Braak, Braak, and Mandelkow, 1993). Other research has estimated that the neurofibrillary tangles and neuropil threads that are abundant in AD brains may develop over a time period as long as 50 years (Ohm, Müller, Braak *et al.*, 1995).

Given that these behavioral and biological data suggest that the process that eventually leads to clinical AD may cover a considerable period of the life span, it would appear paradoxical that accelerated cognitive decline in preclinical AD is not observed until the time period just before diagnosis. One possibility is that the neural changes resulting in clinical AD progress at a rather slow rate, and that accelerated cognitive decline may not be expected until various biological events (the accumulation of amyloid and neurofibrillary tangles, inflammation, oxidative stress, loss of synapses, death of neurons) have reached a certain threshold (Hardy and Allsop, 1991; Jobst *et al.*, 1994). This notion rests on the assumption that the brain is capable of counteracting these slowly occurring neural changes for a substantial period of time. Indeed, there is converging behavioral and biological evidence that the aging mind possesses compensatory capabilities.

Compensation in normal aging

Numerous investigations demonstrate that normal older adults have the ability to compensate for age-related memory deficits when task conditions at encoding and retrieval of information are supportive (Bäckman, Small, Wahlin *et al.*, 1999). Additional evidence for behavioral compensation in normal aging comes from studies demonstrating substantial gains following cognitive training focusing on both intelligence (Baltes, Dittmann-Kohli, and Kliegl, 1986) and memory (Verhaeghen, Marcoen, and Goosens, 1992). However, research indicates that the magnitude of improvement following the provision of cognitive support or after training is larger among those who are privileged with regard to various subject characteristics (education, social activity levels, verbal ability) than among their less fortunate counterparts (Bäckman *et al.*, 1999). This is an interesting observation in view of the brain reserve hypothesis of AD development (Katzman, 1993). This hypothesis assumes that favorable hereditary and environmental factors increase the brain reserve which, in turn, may postpone the clinical onset of dementia.

In addition, several studies show that the histopathological hallmarks of AD, senile plaques and neurofibrillary tangles, may be found among older adults whose cognitive functions are intact (Arriagada, Marzloff, and Hyman, 1992; Morris *et al.*, 1996) Schmitt and colleagues (2000) observed that a large proportion of a group of non-demented and well-educated older adults with high cognitive functioning not only had plaques and tangles, but actually met established neuropathological criteria for AD. Finally, recent brain imaging research provides evidence suggestive of functional brain compensation in old age during performance of both episodic memory (Bäckman *et al.*, 1997) and working memory (Reuter-Lorenz *et al.*, 2000) tasks. For both classes of tasks, the patterns of brain activation, particularly in the frontal cortex, are typically more bilateral in older than in young adults. These findings may reflect that older adults attempt to counteract neurocognitive deficits by recruiting both hemispheres in tasks for which young adults normally engage only one hemisphere (for an overview, see Cabeza, 2002).

At some point, however, which is likely to be multi-determined by different genetic and environmental factors, a threshold of alterations in the brain is reached beyond which cellular mechanisms of response may no longer be able to compensate. This may be the time point at which accelerated cognitive decline is observed leading to clinically diagnosed AD within a few years.

Additional markers of preclinical Alzheimer's disease

Although memory and other cognitive tests show reliable associations to future development of AD, the predictive accuracy of such tests is far from optimal. To be sure, it may not be realistic to expect non-overlapping distributions of cognitive performance scores years before diagnosis, given the large interindividual variability in preclinical AD cases (Fox *et al.*, 1996; Rubin *et al.*, 1998) as well among those who will remain non-demented (Bäckman *et al.*, 2001; Hultsch, Hertzog, Dixon *et al.*, 1998). This fact obviously hampers the utility of cognitive tests in identifying persons eligible for clinical trials and other applied purposes. However, evidence suggests that indicators of other domains of functioning may also serve as early harbingers of AD. This includes subjective memory complaints (Geerlings, Jonker, Bouter *et al.*,

1999) family reports of cognitive impairment (Daly *et al.*, 2000), and depressive symptoms (Berger, Fratiglioni, Forsell *et al.*, 1999). In addition, markers for genetic predisposition (presence of the apolipoprotein E-ε4 allele; Farrer *et al.*, 1997), CSF markers of amyloid deposition and neurofibrillary tangles (Klunk, 1998) as well as brain imaging measures of regional volumes (Fox *et al.*, 1996) and glucose metabolism (Silverman *et al.*, 2001) may contribute to the identification of persons at risk of developing AD.

The identification of specific risk factors which may act as precipitating factors may provide further help in differentiating between preclinical AD and non-progressive cognitive impairment. Possible precipitating factors include medical events such as unrecognized hypertension (Launer *et al.*, 2000), head trauma (Plassman *et al.*, 2000) and stroke (Snowdon *et al.*, 1997), as well as social factors such as isolation (Fratiglioni, Wang, Ericsson *et al.*, 2000).

The point is that although a variety of different factors may show relatively good predictive accuracy in identifying persons in a preclinical phase of AD, these markers are rarely used in the same prediction model. An important avenue for future research is to combine predictors from different behavioral and biological domains. Such a multidisciplinary approach may not only increase overall prediction accuracy; it also enables examining possible inter-active effects among various preclinical markers.

Even though including multiple preclinical markers may enhance predic-tion accuracy, a notable caveat is that the bulk of research on preclinical AD has been retrospective, in the sense that baseline measures in patients and control subjects have been examined after a diagnosis has been rendered. Given that treatment may be most effective if implemented before the clinical diagnosis can be made, we, of course, need to identify specific individuals at risk and then follow these persons prospectively.

Attempts to identify 'high-risk' individuals based on their cognitive performance indicate that a sizable proportion of these persons progress to dementia within a few years (Bowen *et al.*, 1997; Tierney *et al.*, 1996). However, a substantial number of persons in this category remain stable or even improve cognitively over a relatively long time period (Daly *et al.*, 2000; Helkala *et al.*, 1997). For example, Palmer, Wang, Bäckman *et al.* (2002) recently examined a group of non-demented older adults classified as mildly impaired based on their performance on a global cognitive test. They found that approximately one-third of the sample became demented, one-third died, and one-third remained stable or improved across a three-year time interval. Importantly, those who remained stable or improved had no increased risk of progressing to dementia three years later. Obviously, these figures call into question the utility of the single indicators of cognition in identifying persons eligible for interventions aiming at delaying disease progression.

However, data from a follow-up study (Palmer, Bäckman, Winblad *et al.*, 2003) show that among persons identified as impaired based on (a) subjective memory complaints, (b) low global cognitive performance, and (c) low performance on tasks assessing episodic memory and verbal fluency, the proportion converting to dementia within three years was around 95 per cent. These contrasting patterns of findings provide strong evidence for the importance of considering multiple markers in the identification of persons at risk for developing AD.

Conclusions

Although many cognitive domains are affected in preclinical AD, the largest and most robust impairment is seen for episodic memory. This pattern is consistent with evidence from histopathological and brain imaging studies that the medial-temporal lobe is affected in the preclinical phase of AD. The vital importance of this brain region for successful episodic memory functioning is well documented in both lesion and brain imaging research.

An intriguing recent observation is that the size of the memory impairment in preclinical AD appears to be quite stable up until the time period just preceding diagnosis, although cognitive deficits in these persons may be observed several decades before diagnosis. These phenomena may reflect the facts that those biological events that eventually lead to clinically diagnosed AD progress at a very slow rate, and that the aging brain can counteract these alterations until a certain threshold is reached beyond which compensatory processes no longer can withstand the accumulation of neural changes.

The identification of persons during the transition from normal aging to AD may be enhanced by combining objective cognitive markers with indicators of other factors, including subjective reports, biological markers, as well as precipitating factors. Importantly, provided that the level of cognitive impairment among those who will develop AD remains relatively stable for a long period until the dramatic decline seen in the last years before diagnosis, there is a large time window during which different types of intervention should be possible. This includes reducing the influence of precipitating factors, pharmacological treatment, as well as cognitive stimulation.

Finally, one might ask whether the term 'preclinical' routinely used to define the time period preceding the diagnosis of AD is somewhat of a misnomer. Perhaps this period should rather be referred to as 'prediagnostic,' given that several cognitive, clinical, and biological signs may be present many years, if not decades, before we are able to make a diagnosis of AD using current diagnostic criteria. Future research should delineate the changes occurring at different time intervals before the diagnosis of AD. By adopting a multidisciplinary approach in this endeavor, we may be able to better identify persons at risk and intervene in order to delay disease onset and, ultimately, to decrease the occurrence of AD in the general population.

Acknowledgments

Preparation of this article was supported by grants from the Swedish Council for Research in the Humanities and the Social Sciences to Lars Bäckman, and the Swedish Council for Social Research to Lars Bäckman and Laura Fratiglioni.

References

Almkvist, O., Fratiglioni, L, Agüero-Torres, H., Viitanen, M., and Bäckman, L. (1999). Cognitive support at episodic encoding and retrieval: Similar patterns of utilization in community-based samples of Alzheimer's disease and vascular dementia patients. *Journal of Clinical and Experimental Neuropsychology,* **21**, 816–830.

Arriagada, P. V., Marzloff, K., and Hyman, B. T. (1992). Alzheimer-type pathologic changes in nondemented elderly individuals match the pattern in Alzheimer's disease. *Neurology,* **42**, 1681–1688.

Bäckman, L., Almkvist, O., Andersson, J., Nordberg, A., Reineck, R., Winblad, B., and Långström, B. (1997). Brain activation in young and older adults during implicit and explicit retrieval. *Journal of Cognitive Neuroscience,* **9**, 378–391.

Bäckman, L. and Herlitz, A. (1996). Knowledge and memory in Alzheimer's disease: A relationship that exists. In R. G. Morris (ed.), *The Cognitive Neuropsychology of Alzheimer-type Dementia* (pp. 89–104). Oxford: Oxford University Press.

Bäckman, L. and Small, B. J. (1998). Influences of cognitive support on episodic remembering: Tracing the process of loss from normal aging to Alzheimer's disease. *Psychology and Aging,* **13**, 267–276.

Bäckman, L., Small, B. J., and Fratiglioni, L. (2001). Stability of the preclinical episodic memory deficit in Alzheimer's disease. *Brain,* **124**, 96–102.

Bäckman, L., Small, B. J., and Wahlin, Å. (2001). Aging and memory: Cognitive and biological perspectives. In J. E. Birren and K. W. Schaie (eds), *Handbook of the Psychology of Aging* (5th ed., pp. 349–377). San Diego: Academic Press.

Bäckman, L., Small, B. J., Wahlin, Å., and Larsson, M. (1999). Cognitive functioning in very old age. In F. I. M. Craik and T. A. Salthouse (eds), *Handbook of Aging and Cognition* (2nd ed., pp. 499–558). Mahwah, NJ: Erlbaum.

Baltes, P. B., Dittmann-Kohli, F., and Kliegl, R. (1986). Reserve capacity of the elderly in aging-sensitive tests of fluid intelligence: Replication and extension. *Psychology and Aging,* **1**, 172–177.

Berger, A.-K., Fratiglioni, L., Forsell, Y., and Bäckman, L. (1999). The occurrence of depressive symptoms in the preclinical phase of Alzheimer's disease: A population-based study. *Neurology,* **53**, 1998–2002.

Bowen, J., Trei, L., Kukull, W., McCormick, W., McCurry, S. M., and Larson, E. B. (1997). Progression to dementia in patients with isolated memory loss. *Lancet*, **349**, 763–765.

Braak, H. and Braak, E. (1995). Staging of Alzheimer's disease-related neurofibrillary tangles. *Neurobiology of Aging*, **16**, 271–284.

Braak, E., Braak, H., and Mandelkow, E. M. (1993). Cytoskeletal alterations demonstrated by the antibody AT8: Early signs for the formation of neurofibrillary tangles in man. *Society for Neuroscience Abstracts*, **19**, 228.

Cabeza R. (2002). Hemispheric asymmetry reduction in older adults: The HAROLD model. *Psychology and Aging*, **17**, 85–100.

Cabeza, R. and Nyberg, L. (2000). Imaging cognition II: An empirical review of 275 PET and fMRI studies. *Journal of Cognitive Neuroscience*, **12**, 1–47.

Chen, P., Ratcliff, G., Belle, S. H., Cauley, J. A., DeKosky, S. T., and Ganguli, M. (2001). Patterns of cognitive decline in pre-symptomatic Alzheimer's disease: A prospective community study. *Archives of General Psychiatry*, **58**, 853–858.

Daly, E., Zaitchik, D., Copeland, M., Schmahmann, J., Gunther, J., and Albert, M. (2000). Predicting conversion to Alzheimer disease using standardized clinical information. *Archives of Neurology*, **57**, 675–680.

Elias, M. F., Beiser, A., Wolf, P. A., Au, R., White, R. F., and D'Agostino, R. B. (2000). The preclinical phase of Alzheimer's disease: A 22-year prospective study of the Framingham cohort. *Archives of Neurology*, **57**, 808–813.

Fabrigoule, C., Lafont, S., Letenneur, L., Rouch, I., and Dartigues, J. F. (1996). WAIS similarities subtest performances as predictors of dementia in elderly community residents. *Brain and Cognition*, **30**, 323–326.

Fabrigoule, C., Rouch, I., Taberly, A., Letenneur, L., Commenges, D., Mazaux, J. M., Orgogozo, J. M., and Dartigues, J. F. (1998). Cognitive processes in preclinical phase of dementia. *Brain*, **121**, 135–141.

Farrer, L. A., Cupples, L. A., Haines, J. L., Hyman, B., Kukull, W. A., Mayeux, R., Myers, R. H., Pericak Vance, M. A., Risch, N., and vanDuijn, C. M. (1997). Effects of age, sex, and ethnicity on the association between apolipoprotein E genotype and Alzheimer disease. A meta-analysis. *Journal of the American Medical Association*, **278**, 1349–1356.

Flicker, L. (1999). Acetylcholinesterase inhibitors for Alzheimer's disease. *British Medical Journal*, **318**, 615–616.

Fox, N. C., Warrington, E. K., Freeborough, P. A., Hartikainen, P., Kennedy, A. M., Stevens, J. S., and Rossor, M. N. (1996). Presymptomatic hippocampal atrophy in Alzheimer's disease. *Brain*, **119**, 2001–2007.

Fox, N. C., Warrington, E. K., Sieffer, A. L., Agnew, S. K., and Rossor M. N. (1998). Presymptomatic cognitive deficits in individuals at risk of familial Alzheimer's disease: A longitudinal prospective study. *Brain*, **121**, 1631–1639.

Fratiglioni, L. (2000). Dementia: A public health emergency and a scientific challenge. In E. Maj and N. Sartorius (eds), *Dementia* (pp. 47–50). Chichester, UK: John Wiley.

Fratiglioni, L., Wang, H.-X., Ericsson, K., Maytan, M., and Winblad, B. (2000). Influence of social network on occurrence of dementia: A community-based longitudinal study. *Lancet*, **355**, 1315–1319.

Fuld, P. A., Masur, D. M., Blau, A. D., Crystal, H. A., and Aronson, M. K. (1990). Object-memory evaluation for prospective detection of dementia in normal functioning elderly. *Journal of Clinical and Experimental Neuropsychology*, **12**, 520–528.

Geerlings, M. I., Jonker, C., Bouter, L. M., Adèr, H. J., and Schmand, B. (1999). Association between memory complaints and incident Alzheimer's disease in elderly people with normal baseline cognition. *American Journal of Psychiatry,* **156**, 531–537.

Grober, E., Lipton, R. B., Hall, C., and Crystal, H. (2000). Memory impairment on free and cued selective reminding predicts dementia. *Neurology,* **54**, 827–832.

Hardy, J. and Allsop, D. (1991). Amyloid deposition as the central event in the etiology of Alzheimer's disease. *Trends in Pharmacological Sciences,* **12**, 383–388.

Helkala, E.-L., Koivisto, K., Hanninen, T., Vanhanen, M., Kuusisto, J., Mykkanen, L., Laakso, M., and Riekkinen, P. (1997). Stability of age-associated memory impairment during a population-based study. *Journal of the American Geriatrics Society,* **45**, 120–122.

Herlitz, A., Adolfsson, R., Bäckman, L., and Nilsson, L. G. (1991). Cue utilization following different forms of encoding in mildly, moderately, and severely demented patients with Alzheimer's disease. *Brain and Cognition,* **15**, 119–130.

Hodges, J. R. (1998). The amnestic prodrome of Alzheimer's disease. *Brain,* **121**, 1601–1602.

Howieson, D. B., Dame, A., Camicioli, R., Sexton, G., Payami, H., and Kaye, J. A. (1997). Cognitive markers preceding Alzheimer's dementia in the healthy oldest old. *Journal of the American Geriatrics Society,* **45**, 584–589.

Hultsch, D. F., Hertzog, C., Dixon, R. A., and Small, B. J. (1998). *Memory Change in the Aged.* Cambridge: Cambridge University Press.

Jacobs, D. M., Sano, M., Dooneief, G., Marder, K., Bell, K. L., and Stern, Y. (1995). Neuropsychological detection and characterization of preclinical Alzheimer's disease. *Neurology,* **45**, 317–324.

Jobst, K. A., Smith, A. D., Szatmari, M., Esiri, M. M., Jaskowski, A., Hindley, N., McDonald, M., and Molyneux, A. J. (1994). Rapidly progressing atrophy of medial temporal lobe in Alzheimer's disease. *Lancet,* **343**, 829–830.

Katzman, R. (1993). Education and the prevalence of dementia and Alzheimer's disease. *Neurology,* **43**, 13–20.

Kaye, J., Moore, M., Kerr, D., Quinn, J., Camicioli, R., Howieson, D., Payami, H., and Sexton, G. (1999). The rate of brain volume loss accelerates as Alzheimer's disease progresses from a presymptomatic phase to frank dementia. *Neurology,* **52**, 569–570.

Klunk, W. E. (1998). Biological markers of Alzheimer's disease. *Neurobiology of Aging,* **19**, 145–147.

Laakso, M. P., Soininen, H., Partanen, K., Lehtovirta, M., Hallikainen, M., Hanninen, T., Helkala, E. L., Vainio, P., and Riekkinen, P. J. (1998). MRI of the hippocampus in Alzheimer's disease: Sensitivity, specificity, and analysis of the incorrectly classified subjects. *Neurobiology of Aging,* **19**, 23–31.

Launer, L. J. and Hofman, A. (2000). Frequency and impact of neurologic diseases in the elderly of Europe: A collaborative study of the Neurologic Diseases in the Elderly Research Group. *Neurology,* **54**, 1–3.

Launer, L. J., Ross, G. W., Petrovitch, H., Masaki, K., Foley, D., White, L. R., and Havlik, R. J. (2000). Midlife blood pressure and dementia: The Honolulu-Asia aging study. *Neurobiology of Aging,* **21**, 49–55.

La Rue, A. and Jarvik, L. F. (1987). Cognitive function and prediction of dementia in old age. *International Journal of Aging and Human Development,* **25**, 75–89.

Linn, R. T., Wolf, P. A., Bachman, D. L., Knoefel, J. E., Cobb, J. L., Belanger, A. J., Kaplan, E. F., and D'Agostino, R. B. (1995). The 'preclinical phase' of probable Alzheimer's disease. *Archives of Neurology*, **52**, 485–490.

Masur, D. M., Sliwinski, M., Lipton, R. B., Blau, A. D., and Crystal, H. A. (1994). Neuropsychological prediction of dementia and the absence of dementia in healthy elderly persons. *Neurology*, **44**, 1427–1432.

Morris, J. C., Storandt, M., McKeel, D. W., Jr., Rubin, E. H., Price J. L., Grant, E. A., and Berg, L. (1996). Cerebral amyloid deposition and diffuse plaques in 'normal' aging: Evidence for presymptomatic and very mild Alzheimer's disease. *Neurology*, **46**, 707–719.

Morris, R. G. (ed.) (1996). *The Cognitive Neuropsychology of Alzheimer-type Dementia*. Oxford: Oxford University Press.

Nebes, R. D. (1992). Cognitive dysfunctions in Alzheimer's disease. In F. I. M. Craik and T. A. Salthouse (eds), *Handbook of Aging and Cognition* (pp. 373–446). Hillsdale, NJ: Erlbaum.

Nyberg, L., McIntosh, A. R., Houle, S., Nilsson, L.-G., and Tulving, E. (1996). Activation of medial temporal structures during episodic memory retrieval. *Nature*, **380**, 715–717.

Ohm, T., Müller, H., Braak, H., and Bohl, J. (1995). Close-meshed prevalence rates of different stages as a tool to uncover the rate of Alzheimer's disease-related neurofibrillary changes. *Neuroscience*, **64**, 209–217.

Palmer, K., Bäckman, L., Winblad, B., and Fratiglioni, L. (2003). Detection of dementia in the preclinical phase: High predictivity of a three-step procedure in the general population. *British Medical Journal*.

Palmer, K., Wang, H.-X., Bäckman, L., Winblad, B., and Fratiglioni, L. (2002). Differential evolution of cognitive impairment in non-demented older persons: Results from the Kungsholmen Project. *American Journal of Psychiatry*, **159**, xxx–xxx.

Petersen, R. C., Smith, G. E., Waring, S. C., Ivnik, R. J., Tangalos, E., and Kokmen. E. (1999). Mild cognitive impairment: Clinical characterization and outcome. *Archives of Neurology*, **56**, 303–308.

Plassman, B. L., Havlik, R. J., Steffens, D. C., Helms, M. J., Newman, T. N., Drosdick, D., Philips, C., Gau, B. A., Welsh-Bohmer, K. A., Burke, J. R., Guralnik, J. M., and Breitner, J. C. S. (2000). Documented head injury in early adulthood and risk of Alzheimer's disease and other dementias. *Neurology*, **55**, 1158–1166.

Post, S. G. (1999). Future scenarios for the prevention and delay of Alzheimer disease onset in high-risk groups. An ethical perspective. *American Journal of Preventive Medicine*, **16**, 105–110.

Reuter-Lorenz, P., Jonides, J., Smith, E. S., Hartley, A., Miller, A., Marshuetz, C., and Koeppe, R. A. (2000). Age differences in the frontal lateralization of verbal and spatial working memory revealed by PET. *Journal of Cognitive Neuroscience*, **12**, 174–187.

Rubin, E. H., Storandt, M., Miller, J. P., Kinscherf, D. A., Grant, E. A., Morris, J. C., and Berg, L. (1998). A prospective study of cognitive function and onset of dementia in cognitively healthy elders. *Archives of Neurology*, **55**, 395–401.

Schenk D., Barbour, R., Dunn, W., Gordon, G., Grajeda, H., Guido, T., Hu, K., Huang, J. P., Johnson-Wood, K., Khan, K., Kholodenko, D., Lee, M., Liao, Z. M., Lieberburg, I., Motter, R., Mutter, L., Soriano, F., Shopp, G., Vasquez, N., Vandevert, C., Walker, S., Wogulis, M., Yednock, T., Games, D., and Seubert. P. (1999). Immunization with amyloid-beta attenuates Alzheimer-disease-like pathology in the PDAPP mouse. *Nature,* **400**, 173–177.

Schmitt, F. A., Davis, D. G., Wekstein, D. R., Smith, C. D., Ashford, J. W., and Markesbery, W. R. (2000). 'Preclinical' AD revisited: Neuropathology of cognitively normal older adults. *Neurology,* **55**, 370–376.

Silverman, D. H. S., Small, G. W., Chang, C. Y., Lu, C. S., Kung de Aburto, M. A., Chen, W., Czernin, J., Rapoport, S. I., Pietrini, P., Alexander, G. E., Schapiro, M. B., Jagust, W. J., Hoffman, J. M., Welsh-Bohmer, K. A., Alavi, A., Clark, C. M., Salmon, E., de Leon, M. J., Mielke, R., Cummings, J. L., Kowell, A. P., Gambhir, S. S., Hoh, C. K., and Pkelps, M. E. (2001). Positron emission tomography in evaluation of dementia: Regional brain metabolism and long-term outcome. *Journal of the American Medical Association,* **286**, 2120–2127.

Small, B. J., Fratiglioni, L., Viitanen, M., Winblad, B., and Bäckman, L. (2000). The course of cognitive impairment in preclinical Alzheimer's disease: 3- and 6-year follow-up of a population-based sample. *Archives of Neurology,* **57**, 839–844.

Small, B. J., Herlitz, A., Fratiglioni, L., Almkvist, O., and Bäckman, L. (1997). Cognitive predictors of incident Alzheimer's disease: A prospective longitudinal study. *Neuropsychology,* **11**, 413–420.

Small, B. J., Viitanen, M., and Bäckman, L. (1997). Mini-Mental State Examination item scores as predictors of Alzheimer's disease: Incidence data from the Kungsholmen project, Stockholm. *Journal of Gerontology: Medical Sciences,* **52**, 299–304.

Small, S. A., Perara, G., DeLaPaz, R., Mayeux, R., and Stern, Y. (1999). Differential regional dysfunction of the hippocampal formation among elderly with memory decline and Alzheimer's disease. *Annals of Neurology,* **45**, 466–472.

Snowdon, D. A., Greiner, L. H., Mortimer, J. A., Riley, K. P., Greiner, P. A., and Markesbery, W. R. (1997). Brain infarction and the clinical expression of Alzheimer's disease: The Nun Study. *Journal of the American Medical Association,* **277**, 813–817.

Snowdon, D. A., Kemper, S. J., Mortimer, J. A., Greiner, L. H., Wekstein, D. R., and Markesbery, W. R. (1996). Linguistic ability in early life and cognitive function and Alzheimer's disease in late life. *Journal of the American Medical Association,* **275**, 528–532.

Stern, Y. (in press). What is cognitive reserve? Theory and research application of the reserve concept. *Journal of the International Neuropsychological Society.*

Tierney, M. C., Szalai, J. P., Snow, W. G., Fisher, R. H., Nores, A., Nadon, G., Dunn, E., and St. George-Hyslop, P. H. (1996). Prediction of probable Alzheimer's disease in memory-impaired patients: A prospective longitudinal study. *Neurology,* **46**, 661–665.

Tulving, E. (1983). *Elements of Episodic Memory.* Oxford: Oxford University Press,

Tulving, E. (1999). On the uniqueness of episodic memory. In L.-G. Nilsson and H. Markowitsch (eds), *Cognitive Neuroscience of Memory* (pp. 11–42). Göttingen: Hogrefe and Huber.

Vargha-Khadem, F., Gadian, D. G., Watkins, K. E., Connelly, A., Van Paesschen, W., and Mishkin, M. (1997). Differential effects of early hippocampal lesions on episodic and semantic memory. *Science,* **277**, 376–380.

Verhaeghen, P., Marcoen, A., and Goossens, L. (1992). Improving memory performance in the aged through mnemonic training: A meta-analytic study. *Psychology and Aging,* **7**, 242–251.

Whalley, L. J., Starr, J. M., Athawes, R., Hunter, D., Pattie, A., and Deary, I. J. (2000). Childhood mental ability and dementia. *Neurology,* 55, 1455–1459.

Yoshitake, T., Kiyohara, Y., Kato, I., Ohmura, T., Iwamoto, H., Nakayama, K., Ohmori, S., Nomiyama, K., Kawano, H., Ueda, K., Sueishi, K., Tsuneyosh, M., and Fujishima, M. (1995). Incidence and risk factors of vascular dementia and Alzheimer's disease in a defined elderly Japanese population: The Hisayama study. *Neurology,* 45, 1161–1168.

Chapter 9

Commentary: Neuroscience frontiers of cognitive aging: Approaches to cognitive neuroscience of aging

Roberto Cabeza

Nobody would seriously challenge the idea that age-related changes in cognition are in great part a consequence of age-related changes in the brain. Yet, although both types of phenomena have been thoroughly studied in isolation, the relationships between them are not well understood. On one hand, post-mortem studies, structural MRI, and resting PET studies have provided detailed information about the effects of aging on the anatomy and physiology of the brain, including grey and white matter atrophy, synaptic loss, receptor and metabolic changes, and so forth. These studies constitute the rich discipline of *neuroscience of aging*. On the other hand, behavioral studies have systematically described and analyzed the effects of aging on measures of memory, attention, executive functions, and so on. These behavioral studies comprise the fruitful discipline of *cognitive psychology of aging*. However, despite abundant evidence about cerebral aging and about cognitive aging, the link between these two domains is still missing. Fortunately, this situation is being rapidly resolved due to the birth of the new discipline of *cognitive neuroscience of aging*, which focuses on the relationships between age-related changes in the brain and age-related changes in cognition (for reviews see, Cabeza, 2001a, 2001b). The present chapter describes three methodological approaches of cognitive neuroscience of aging, and for each one, it underscores some interesting findings and notes some current issues.

To describe the methodological approaches to cognitive neuroscience of aging, it is useful to organize the critical variables in a simple model like the one in Figure 9.1. In this model, aging is assumed to affect both the brain and cognition. The distinction between brain and cognition is artificial but useful for conceptual purposes. The same can be said about the distinction between structure and processes in the brain and in cognition. Structures and processes

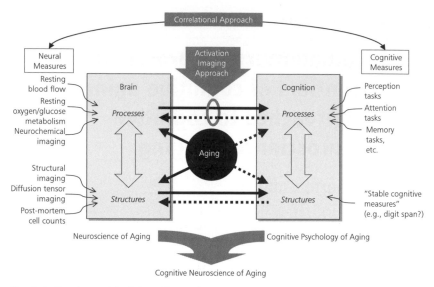

Fig. 9.1 Simple model of the effects of aging on the brain and on cognition, and the approaches to relate these effects.

interact with each other and differ only in degree: structures are more stable (e.g., neurons, memory stores); processes are more dynamic (blood flow, cognitive operations). The structures and processes of the brain can be assessed using *neural measures*, such as resting blood flow and structural MRI (see left side of Figure 9.1), whereas the structures and processes of cognition can be assessed using *cognitive measures*, such as perception and memory tasks (see right side of Figure 9.1).

Although any change in cognition implies a change in the brain, it is useful to differentiate between two types of age effects: neurogenic and psychogenic. *Neurogenic age effects* (solid arrows in Figure 9.1) occur when a change in the brain causes a change in cognition. For example, age-related atrophy of prefrontal gray matter may lead to decline in working memory function. In contrast, *psychogenic age effects* (dashed arrows in Figure 9.1) occur when a change in cognition causes a change in the brain. For instance, age-related disuse of cognitive strategies may lead to atrophy of certain brain regions. As illustrated by Figure 9.1, neurogenic effects may lead to psychogenic effects and vice versa. For instance, a decline in neural function may originate a compensatory change in cognitive strategies, which in turn may initiate a change in brain function.

As noted before, the goal of cognitive neuroscience of aging is to reveal the relationships between age-related changes in the brain (neuroscience of aging) and age-related changes in cognition (cognitive psychology of aging). There are three basic methodological approaches to achieve this goal. First, the *neuropsychological approach* compares cognitive changes in healthy aging and in patients with brain damage due to trauma, stroke, or degenerative disorders. Second, the *correlational approach* associates neural measures to cognitive measures that were independently obtained (see curved bidirectional arrow at the top of Figure 9.1). Finally, the *activation imaging approach* measures brain activity in young and older adults during cognitive performance (see arrow pointing to bidirectional links between brain and cognitive processes in Figure 9.1). The section below describes these three approaches, emphasizing some of the points made by Raz (Chapter 6), by Nyberg and Bäckman (Chapter 7), and by Bäckman *et al.* (Chapter 8), in their respective chapters in this book. The following section discusses the strengths and weaknesses of each approach.

Approaches to cognitive neuroscience of aging

Neuropsychological approach

The neuropsychology approach to cognitive neuroscience of aging involves comparing neurocognitive changes in healthy aging to those associated with brain damage (for a review, see Prull *et al.*, 2000). This approach is based on analogical reasoning: if patients with damage in specific brain regions display cognitive deficits that are qualitatively similar to the ones displayed by elderly adults, then age-related cognitive deficits may be related to alterations in these specific regions. In contrast, if damage of a certain brain area yields a kind of cognitive deficit that is uncommon in healthy aging, then it is unlikely that the area is a major contributor to age-related cognitive decline.

The patient populations that are most often compared to healthy elderly are frontal-lobe patients, Parkinson's Disease (PD) patients, medial temporal lobe (MTL) amnesics, and Alzheimer's Disease (AD) patients. Frontal-lobe patients show in augmented fashion many of the cognitive deficits displayed by healthy elderly, including difficulties with recall, context memory, working memory, and executive functions (for a review, see Moscovitch and Winocur, 1995). This pattern provides support to the idea that frontal dysfunction plays an important role in the cognitive deficits observed in healthy aging (for a review, see West, 1996). Likewise, PD patients also show cognitive deficits that resemble those of healthy aging (for a review, see Prull *et al.*, 2000), suggesting that dopamine deficits contribute to age-related cognitive decline. As described later, this idea has received strong support from receptor imaging studies. In contrast with frontal and PD patients, cognitive deficits in MTL amnesics tend to differ from those of healthy elderly. For example, whereas amnesics can show severe episodic memory deficits in both strategic and associative retrieval tasks (Haist *et al.*, 1992), healthy older adults are usually impaired in strategic tasks, such as context memory, but little in associative tasks, such as recognition (for a review, see Spencer and Raz, 1994). Thus, frontal damage and PD seem to provide better models for healthy aging than MTL amnesia, suggesting that frontal deficits and dopamine dysfunction may play a more important role in age-related cognitive decline than MTL dysfunction.

In contrast, memory deficits in AD patients have been strongly associated with MTL dysfunction, as reviewed in the chapter by Bäckman, Small, and Fratiglioni in this volume (Chapter 8). These authors note that cognitive deficits in AD are global but tend to be more pronounced in episodic memory. They relate this pattern to evidence that episodic memory is critically dependent on the hippocampal complex, which is the region showing the earliest brain changes in AD. However, episodic memory measures do not provide a simple tool for early diagnosis of AD. For example, Bäckman and collaborators (Bäckman *et al.*, 2000b; Small *et al.*, 2000) found that although preclinical AD individuals were impaired in episodic memory measures compared to healthy older adults, the size of these impairments remained quite stable until the period just preceding diagnosis. In their chapter, Bäckman *et al.* point out that this finding is paradoxical, given the wealth of evidence that the brain changes that lead to AD start several decades before the diagnosis. According to these authors, one possible explanation is that the brain can counteract slowly occurring neural changes until a certain threshold is reached. As discussed later, one way in which the aging brain may counteract neural changes is by recruiting both cerebral hemispheres for tasks that require basically one hemisphere in young adults (Cabeza, 2002).

One of the main questions of the neuropsychology approach is whether analogous patterns of cognitive decline in healthy older adults and in brain-damaged patients reflect not only similarities in the regions involved but also similarities in neural mechanisms. Obviously, the mechanism of frontal dysfunction is different in the case of healthy aging and in the case of frontal damage due to trauma or stroke. In the case of PD and AD, however, the boundary between healthy and pathological mechanisms is not always clear. In the case of AD, in particular, such a boundary may not exist. Actually, it is possible to think that there is a continuum from older adults without cognitive impairment to those with AD, with older adults with mild cognitive impairment (MCI) in the middle. As noted by Bäckman *et al.* in Chapter 8, the histopathological features of AD, senile plaques and neurofibrillary tangles, can be found among older adults with intact cognitive functions. A possible explanation is that different individuals vary in terms of 'brain reserve'

(Katzman, 1993), and that it is only when these reserves are exhausted that dramatic declines in cognitive performance are observed. At any rate, regardless of whether healthy aging and AD are seen as two different phenomena or as two stages of the same continuum, it is clear that comparing healthy older adults to brain-damaged patients can yield important insights concerning the neural correlates of cognitive aging.

Correlational approach

The correlational approach involves associating a neural measure, such as structural imaging measures (see left side of Figure 9.1), to a cognitive measure, such as memory performance (see right side of Figure 9.1). Instead of neural measures, some studies have employed behavioral tests assumed to be sensitive to the function of a certain brain region, such as the so-called 'frontal lobe tests' (e.g., Wisconsin Card Sorting Task—WCST). Since the relationship between these tests and the anatomical and functional integrity of the brain region of interest is uncertain, the usefulness of this type of studies has been limited. In contrast, studies using direct neural measures, such as *in vivo* structural, neurochemical, blood flow, and metabolism imaging, can provide a more direct link between cerebral and cognitive aging. Correlational studies using structural and neurochemical imaging were respectively reviewed in the chapters by Naftali Raz and by Nyberg and Bäckman.

As reviewed by Raz, the effects of aging on brain structure have been observed primarily as volume decreases and white matter deterioration. Age-related decreases in brain volume tend to be large in the prefrontal cortex (PFC), moderate in the striatum, MTL, and the cerebellum, and minimal in the visual cortex. Age-related reductions in the integrity of white matter can be observed as white matter hyperintensities (WMH) in MRI images, and these changes are also greater in anterior brain regions. Raz points out that age-related changes in brain structure are relevant to cognitive neuroscience of aging as long as they can be linked to age-related changes in cognitive performance. He reviews examples of studies linking age-related changes in brain structure to age-related changes in measures of executive functions, motor skill learning, and cognitive skill learning (Raz, 2000). In one study, PFC volume and prefrontal WMH volume were independently associated with age-related deficits in executive functions (Gunning-Dixon and Raz, submitted). In another study, cerebellar and putamen volumes were associated age-related deficits in motor skill learning (Raz *et al.*, 2000). Finally, in a third study, PFC volume was associated with age-related decreases in cognitive skill learning (Head *et al.*, in press). These studies are excellent examples of how correlational studies can link age-related deficits in cognitive performance to anatomical deterioration in specific brain regions. Current challenges in this domain include conducting longitudinal studies (Raz, 2002) and using new statistical techniques to analyze correlational data (McArdle *et al.*, submitted).

Age-related deficits in cognitive performance can be linked not only to deficits in brain anatomy but also to deficits in brain function. For example, there is now clear evidence that cognitive decline in older adults is in great part a consequence of deficits in dopamine (DA) function. As reviewed by Nyberg and Bäckman in the present volume, DA function declines during aging at a steady rate of about 10 per cent per decade, and this decline is significantly associated with age-related deficits in cognitive performance. Reliable correlations have been found for both presynaptic (DA transporter—DAT) and postsynaptic (D_1 and D_2 receptor binding) markers of DA function. For instance, the PET studies have associated age-related deficits in striatal D_2 binding to age-related deficits in executive function and speed (Volkow *et al.*, 1998), and episodic memory and speed (Bäckman *et al.*, 2000a). Importantly, in these studies the association between DA function and cognitive performance remained after controlling for age.

Activation imaging approach

Whereas the correlational approach relates cognitive and neural measures of aging that were independently obtained, the activation imaging approach assess the effects of aging on brain activity and cognitive performance in direct relation to each other. Activation imaging studies have investigated a variety of cognitive functions (for reviews, see Cabeza, 2001a, 2001b), and those in the working memory and episodic memory domain were reviewed by the chapter by Nyberg and Bäckman. In general, lower activity in older adults has been attributed to deficits in neurocognitive processing whereas greater activity in older adults has been attributed to compensation mechanisms.

The most consistent result of activation imaging studies is probably the finding that older adults tend to show a more bilateral pattern of PFC activation than young adults, a pattern known as Hemispheric Asymmetry Reduction in Older Adults or HAROLD model (Cabeza, 2002). Table 9.1 lists PET and fMRI studies consistent with this model various cognitive domains. In the case of episodic memory retrieval, in which PFC activity in young adults tends to be right lateralized, age-related asymmetry reductions involved an increase in left PFC activity. Conversely, in the case of episodic encoding/semantic retrieval, in which PFC activity in young adults tends to be left lateralized, age-related asymmetry reductions involved a decrease in left PFC activity or an increase in right PFC activity. Despite this variety of age effects, the basic outcome was always the same: PFC activity was less lateralized in older adults than in younger adults.

Table 9.1 PET/fMRI activity in left and right PFC in younger and older adults

Cognitive domain	Younger		Older	
Imaging technique: Materials/task (reference)	Left	Right	Left	Right
Episodic retrieval				
PET: Word pair cued-recall (Cabeza et al., 1997a)	−	++	+	+
PET: Word stem cued-recall (Bäckman et al., 1997)	−	+	+	+
PET: Word recognition (Madden et al., 1999)	−	+	++	++
PET: Face recognition (Grady et al., 2002)	−	++	+	+
Episodic encoding/Semantic retrieval				
fMRI: Word − incidental (Stebbins et al., 2002)	++	+	+	+
fMRI: Word − intentional (Logan et al., 2002)	++	+	+	+
fMRI: Word − incidental (Logan et al., 2002)	++	+	++	++
fMRI: Word − SME (Morcom et al., 2002)	++	+	++	++
Working memory				
PET: Letter DR (Reuter-Lorenz et al., 2000)	+	−	+	+
PET: Location DR (Reuter-Lorenz et al., 2000)	−	+	+	+
PET: Number N-Back: (Dixit et al., 2000)	+	+++	++	++
Perception				
PET: Face matching (Grady et al., 1994, Exp. 2)	−	+	++	++
PET: Face matching (Grady et al., 2000)	+	+++	++	++
Inhibitory control				
fMRI: No-go trials (Nielson et al., 2002)	−	+	+	+

Note: Plus signs indicate significant activity in the left or right PFC, and minus signs indicate nonsignificant activity. The number of pluses is an approximate index of the relative amount of activity in left and right PFC in each study, and it cannot be compared across studies. DR = delayed response task; SME = subsequent memory effect.

It has been suggested that bihemispheric involvement play a compensatory role in the aging brain (Cabeza et al., 1997a). This *compensation account* is consistent with evidence that bilateral activity in older adults is associated with enhanced cognitive performance (Reuter-Lorenz et al., 2000), and that the particular brain regions showing age-related increases in activation are likely to enhance performance in the task investigated (left PFC during episodic retrieval, Nolde et al., 1998). The compensation account is also consistent with evidence that recovery of function following unilateral brain damage is associated with the recruitment of the unaffected contralateral hemisphere (Cao et al., 1999; Silvestrini et al., 1998). However, there is also an alternative view of age-related asymmetry reductions: they may reflect age-related difficulty in engaging specialized neural mechanisms (Li and Lindenberger, 1999). This *dedifferentiation account* is consistent with evidence that correlations among different cognitive measures, and between cognitive and sensory measures, tend to increase with age (Baltes and Lindenberger, 1997). Randy Buckner recently suggested that if one assumes that in young

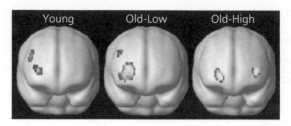

Fig. 9.2 During source memory, young and low-performing older adults showed right prefrontal activations, whereas high-performing older adults showed bilateral prefrontal activations. This evidence supports the compensation account of the HAROLD model. Reprinted with permission from Elsevier.

adults there is competition between the two hemispheres, an age-related decrease in lateralization could reflect an age-related reduction of interhemispheric transfer due to callosal deterioration (Buckner, 2002). Yet, the notion that in young adults the two hemispheres compete with each other has not received strong empirical support (Chiarello and Maxfield, 1996).

Recently, we tested compensation and dedifferentiation accounts of HAROLD using PET (Cabeza *et al.*, 2002). Before scanning, we selected from a larger sample of older adults a group that performed as well as the young group in a battery of memory tests (old-high group), and a group that performed significantly more poorly that the young group in the same battery (old-low group). The two groups of older adults and a group of young adults were then scanned in a source memory task, which was known from a previous study to be associated with right PFC activity in young adults. The compensation hypothesis predicted bilateral PFC activity in old-high participants, whereas the dedifferentiation hypothesis predicted bilateral PFC in old-low participants. As illustrated by Figure 9.2, the results supported the compensation hypothesis. Old-low participants showed some additional PFC activity in the same hemisphere as young adults but no reduction in lateralization, whereas old-high participants showed a bilateral activation pattern. We interpreted this finding as suggesting that old-low participants recruited similar PFC regions to young adults but used them inefficiently, whereas old-high participants compensated age-related memory decline by reorganizing the episodic retrieval network.

Strengths and weaknesses of each approach

Table 9.2 lists some of the strengths and weaknesses of the neuropsychological, correlational, and activation imaging approaches. These strengths and weaknesses are discussed in the next three subsections.

Table 9.2 Examples of the strengths and weaknesses of three methodological approaches to cognitive neuroscience of aging

	Strengths	Weaknesses
Neuropsychological approach	• Identifies age effects on brain regions that are necessary for cognitive performance • Clarifies the neural mechanisms of age-related neural decline	• Cannot easily identify compensatory changes in the aging brain • Inferences about neural mechanisms are based on obscure phenomena
Correlational approach	• Can employ neural measures close to the neural mechanisms underlying age-related cognitive changes • Correlations are likely to reflect neurogenic rather than psychogenic changes	• Neural measures are only indirectly related to age-related changes in cognitive performance • Cannot easily identify compensatory changes in the aging brain
Activation imaging approach	• Age-related changes in brain activity are directly related to age-related changes in cognitive performance • Can detect compensatory changes in the aging brain	• Brain activity measures are removed from the neural mechanisms underlying age-related cognitive changes • Age-related changes in brain activity may reflect neurogenic as well as psychogenic changes

Neuropsychological approach

The main strength of the neuropsychological approach to cognitive neuroscience of aging is that it identifies age effects on brain regions that are *necessary* for cognitive performance. For example, evidence that both older and PD patients are impaired in strategic retrieval tasks (for a review, see Prull *et al.*, 2000) suggests, first, that dopaminergic fronto-striatal loops are necessary for strategic memory performance, and second, that strategic memory decline in older adults is related to dopamine deficits. This brings us to a second strength of the neuropsychological approach: it clarifies the neural mechanisms for age-related neural decline. The neuropsychology approach suggest what neural mechanisms are likely (e.g., dopamine deficits), and what neural mechanisms are unlikely. For example, studies identifying differences between healthy and pathological aging (e.g., AD) can help discard hypotheses concerning neural mechanisms of cognitive decline in healthy aging.

The main weakness of the neuropsychological approach is that it cannot easily identify compensatory changes in the aging brain. When healthy older adults do not show a cognitive deficit typically observed in a certain form of brain pathology, this may be interpreted as suggesting that the neural mechanism of the pathology does not play an important role in healthy aging. Yet, it is also possible that the pathological mechanism is actually affecting normal elderly but they can compensate for it. For example, Bäckman and collaborator noted in their chapter that senile plaques and neurofibrillary tangles can be found among older adults with intact cognitive functions, and discussed that possibility that the effects of these pathological changes may be compensated by older adults for decades until a certain threshold is reached. Since the neuropsychological approach is based on behavioral performance, neural changes that decrease differences in performance are difficult to detect. In contrast, compensatory changes can be detected using activation imaging methods (see Figure 9.2).

Another weakness of the neuropsychological approach is that it tries to clarify an obscure phenomenon (neural mechanism of cognitive changes in healthy aging) by comparing it to another obscure phenomenon (neural mechanism of cognitive changes in brain damaged populations). For example, the fact that older adults (Spencer and Raz, 1994) and frontal lobe patients (Schacter, 1987; Stuss *et al.*, 1994) tend to be more impaired in context than in item memory suggests that age-related deficits in context memory are related to frontal dysfunction. Yet, the specific role of the frontal lobes in context memory is yet understood.

Correlational approach

The main strength of correlational studies is that they employ neural measures that are relatively close to the neural mechanisms underlying age-related cognitive changes, such as structural and neurochemical imaging measures. Of course, changes in brain volume and neurochemical function are still removed from the original molecular causes of neural aging. Yet, these measures can be obtained *in vivo* and correlated with behavioral measures, thereby allowing the establishment of critical links between neural and cognitive aging. Another strength of the correlational approach is that correlations are likely to reflect neurogenic rather than psychogenic changes. Even though correlations do not imply causation, if the atrophy of a certain brain region is correlated with poor performance in a certain cognitive task it is reasonable to assume that brain atrophy caused poor cognitive performance rather than the other way round.

The main weakness of the correlational approach is that neural measures are related to cognitive measures only indirectly. This is particularly true in the case of structural measures. As illustrated in Figure 9.1, age-related changes in brain structure are likely to affect cognitive processes only if they are associated with changes in brain processes. However, structural changes may not lead to functional changes until a certain threshold is reached. Correlational studies may employ functional measures, such as resting blood flow and metabolism measures, but resting measures are not directly associated with cognitive performance either. For example, older adults may show reduced resting blood flow in a certain region but recruit this region as much as young adults during a cognitive challenge. Conversely, a region may not show age-related blood flow differences during rest, but these differences may become apparent under the demands of cognitive tasks (for a discussion, see Anderson and Craik, 2000).

Related to this last point, another weakness of the correlational approach is one previously noted for the neuropsychological approach: they cannot easily detect compensatory changes in the aging brain. Since the effects of neural changes on behavior are modulated by compensatory changes, this limitation could partly explain inconsistencies in studies correlating structural and behavioral measures. For example, among studies that correlated the volume of MTL structures with episodic memory performance in older adults (for a review, see Raz, 2000), some studies found a moderate positive correlation (Golomb *et al.*, 1994), others found a lack of correlation (Raz *et al.*, 1998), and still others found negative correlations (Kohler *et al.*, 1998). A possible explanation of these mixed results is that MTL atrophy may be counteracted in different degrees by the recruitment of other brain regions. Since these compensatory changes are difficult or impossible to detect using structural or resting functional measures, correlational studies can only provide a partial picture of the complex series of neural events underlying age-related changes in cognitive performance.

Activation imaging approach

The strengths and weaknesses of the activation imaging approach tend to be a mirror image of the strengths and weaknesses of neuropsychological and correlational approaches. For example, whereas a weakness of the correlational approach is the relatively indirect relationship between neural and cognitive measures, an important strength of the activation imaging approach is that neural and cognitive measures are acquired simultaneously and in direct relation to each other. As illustrated in Figure 9.1, activation imaging measures the interaction between the brain and cognition (see arrow in the middle of Figure 9.1). Thus, age-related differences in the performance of a particular cognitive task (e.g., reduced context memory accuracy) can be directly linked to age-related changes in brain activity (e.g., reduced frontal activity) during the performance of that particular task.

Another advantage of activation imaging is the possibility of detecting compensatory changes in the aging brain, which is something difficult to do with neuropsychological and correlational approaches. Since activation imaging can identify brain regions involved in cognitive performance, including those recruited to support cognitive performance, this approach is ideally suited for investigating compensatory changes in the aging brain. As previously discussed, there is evidence that one form of compensation displayed by older adults involves a more bilateral pattern of PFC activity (Cabeza, 2002). It would have been difficult or impossible to detect this phenomenon using only neuropsychological or correlational approaches.

Conversely, some of the weaknesses of the activation imaging approach correspond to strengths of neuropsychological and correlational approaches. For example, whereas the neural measures employed by correlational approaches (e.g., structural and neurochemical imaging) are relatively close to the original neural mechanisms underlying age-related cognitive decline, activation imaging measures are farther apart from these mechanisms. Age-related differences in activation detected by PET and fMRI are the result of a complex series of neural events, and hence, linking these differences to specific neural mechanisms is a complicated task. In particular, since brain activity is the result of the interaction between the brain and cognitive processes, it is difficult to attribute age-related differences in activation to the function of a particular region. Actually, older adults may show weaker activity in a certain brain region during a particular cognitive task but greater activity in the same region during a different task (Cabeza *et al.*, 1997b). This fact precludes a simple one-to-one association between age-related changes in activity and the functional integrity of the brain regions involved.

Another disadvantage of the activation imaging approach is that age-related changes in brain activity may reflect neurogenic as well as psychogenic changes. This is the downside of measuring brain processes in direct relation to cognitive processes. In activation studies, the relation between brain and cognitive processes is so close that the direction of causal effect is unclear: do older adults perform differently because their brain activity is dissimilar, or is their brain activity dissimilar because they perform differently? In Figure 9.1, this 'chicken-and-egg' problem is illustrated by the oval that surrounds neurogenic and psychogenic arrows. Activation imaging does not measure the effect of the brain on cognition or the effect of cognition on the brain, but both simultaneously. Psychogenic effects of brain activity include differences in cognitive strategies and levels of performance (Cabeza, 2001b). Differences in cognitive strategies can be attenuated by using very simple tasks (McIntosh *et al.*, 1999) or by manipulating strategies (Logan *et al.*, 2002), and differences in performance can be reduced by matching (Cabeza *et al.*, 1997a) or manipulating (Cabeza *et al.*, 2000) performance levels. As discussed in the section below, another way of disambiguating age-related differences in activation is to relate these differences to structural and/or neurochemical imaging measures.

Summary and conclusions

In summary, the new discipline of cognitive neuroscience of aging tries to establish links between age-related changes in the brain and age-related changes in cognition using three main methodological approaches.

First, the neuropsychological approach compares cognitive changes in healthy aging and in patients with brain damage due to trauma, stroke, or degenerative disorders. This approach includes studies investigating similarities and differences between healthy aging and AD (reviewed Bäckman *et al.*, in this volume). The neuropsychological approach can identify age effects on regions necessary for performance and clarify the mechanisms of age-related neural decline, but it has difficulties identifying compensatory changes in the aging brain and is based on comparing aging to other unclear phenomena.

Second, the correlational approach associates cognitive measures to neural measures that were independently obtained. This approach includes studies correlating cognitive measures with structural imaging measures (reviewed by Raz, in this volume), as well as those correlating cognitive measures and dopamine imaging measures (reviewed by Nyberg and Bäckman, in this volume). The correlational approach employs neural measures that are close to the neural mechanisms underlying age-related cognitive changes and can isolate neurogenic effects, but the measures it investigates are only indirectly related to cognitive performance and relatively insensitive to compensatory changes.

Finally, the activation imaging approach measures brain activity in young and older adults during cognitive performance. This approach includes studies investigating age-related changes in brain activity during episodic memory and working memory performance (reviewed by Nyberg and Bäckman, in this volume). The activation imaging approach investigates neural measures that are directly related to cognitive performance and can detect compensatory changes in the aging brain, but the measures it employs are removed from basic neural mechanisms and are sensitive to both neurogenic and psychogenic effects.

It is clear that the three approaches to cognitive neuroscience of aging have complementary strengths and weaknesses. The neuropsychological approach can clarify the neural mechanisms of age-related neural decline but it cannot easily identify compensatory changes in the aging brain. The activation imaging approach can identify compensatory changes in the aging brain but has difficulties differentiating neurogenic and psychogenic effects. Etcetera. Thus, one way of addressing the limitations of available approaches it to combine them in a way in which the strengths of an approach counteract the weakness of another approach.

A powerful strategy is to combine neuropsychological and activation imaging approaches, and compare healthy older adults and brain-damaged patients using PET or fMRI (Bäckman *et al.*, 1999; Bookheimer *et al.*, 2000). The activation imaging approach can help with the identification of compensatory changes, and the neuropsychological approach can help with the interpretation of activation results. For example, in a PET study investigating episodic retrieval in healthy older adults and early AD patients (Bäckman *et al.*, 1999), AD patients failed to show a left hippocampal activation displayed by healthy older adults, but recruited fronto–parietal-cerebellar network typically associated with episodic retrieval, and displayed increases in PFC activity possibly associated with functional compensation. These results support the idea that the degree of MTL dysfunction is a critical difference between healthy and pathological aging, and the notion that compensatory changes in brain activity may partially counteract cognitive decline in AD patients.

Another powerful strategy is to integrate correlational and activation imaging approaches, and combine resting imaging measures with activation imaging measures. Combining structural and activation imaging is an important goal of cognitive neuroscience of aging, not only because volumetric measures should be used to adjust activation measures, but also because volumetric data could help disambiguate activation imaging data. For example, the issue about whether hemispheric asymmetry reductions in older adults reflect compensation or dedifferentiation could be investigated by correlating activity in the regions showing age-related increases with volumetric data. If decreased lateralization is correlated with decreased brain volume, then it is more likely to reflect dedifferentiation rather than compensation. Combining neurochemical imaging measures with activation imaging measures is another challenge for the future of cognitive neuroscience of aging. As mentioned before, age-related dopamine decline can account for a large portion of older adults' deficits in cognitive performance (Bäckman *et al.*, 2000a). A strong relationship has been demonstrated between age-related decreases in dopamine function and age-related decreases in frontal and cingulate metabolism (Volkow *et al.*, 2000), and it is quite likely that dopamine measures will be also strongly associated with activation imaging measures. One can envisage future studies in which age-related differences in brain activity are directly associated with age-related differences in brain anatomy and function, thereby linking activation findings to specific neural mechanisms.

Thus, cognitive neuroscience of aging is a new discipline with a very promising future. Its rapid growth during the last decade is likely to become even more intense as the three basic methodological approaches develop and new approaches are introduced. Ultimately, many different methods will be combined to achieve a move complete picture of age-related neurocognitive changes. This is definitely a neuroscience frontier in cognitive aging research.

Author's note

Supported in part by the National Institutes of Health (Grant AG-19731).

References

Anderson, N. D., and Craik, F. I. M. (2000). Memory in the aging brain. In E. Tulving and F. I. M. Craik (eds), *Handbook of Memory*. Oxford: Oxford University Press.

Bäckman, L., Almkvist, O., Andersson, J., Nordberg, A., Windblad, B., Rineck, R., and Lågström, B. (1997). Brain activation in young and older adults during implicit and explicit retrieval. *Journal of Cognitive Neuroscience*, 9, 378–391.

Bäckman, L., Andersson, J. L., Nyberg, L., Winblad, B., Nordberg, A., and Almkvist, O. (1999). Brain regions associated with episodic retrieval in normal aging and Alzheimer's disease. *Neurology*, 52, 1861–1870.

Bäckman, L., Ginovart, N., Dixon, R. A., Wahlin, T. B., Wahlin, A., Halldin, C., and Farde, L. (2000a). Age-related cognitive deficits mediated by changes in the striatal dopamine system. *American Journal of Psychiatry*, 157, 635–637.

Bäckman, L., Small, B. J., and Fratiglioni, L. (2000b). Stability of the preclinical episodic memory deficit in Alzheimer's disease. *Brain*, 124, 96–102.

Baltes, P. B., and Lindenberger, U. (1997). Emergence of a powerful connection between sensory and cognitive functions across the adult life span: A new window to the study of cognitive aging? *Psychology and Aging*, 12, 12–21.

Bookheimer, S. Y., Strojwas, M. H., Cohen, M. S., Saunders, A. M., Pericak-Vance, M. A., Maxxiotta, J. C., and Small, G. W. (2000). Patterns of brain activation in people at risk for Alzheimer's disease. *The New England Journal of Medicine*, 343, 450–456.

Buckner, R. L. (2002). *Age-related changes in neural activity during episodic memory*. Paper presented at the Symposium on Neuroscience, Aging and Cognition, San Francisco.

Cabeza, R. (2001a). Cognitive neuroscience of aging: Contributions of functional neuroimaging. *Scandinavian Journal of Psychology*, 42, 277–286.

Cabeza, R. (2001b). Functional neuroimaging of cognitive aging. In R. Cabeza and A. Kingstone (eds), *Handbook of Functional Neuroimaging of Cognition* (pp. 331–377). Cambridge, MA: MIT Press.

Cabeza, R. (2002). Hemispheric asymmetry reduction in old adults: The HAROLD Model. *Psychology and Aging*, 17, 85–100.

Cabeza, R., Anderson, N. D., Houle, S., Mangels, J. A., and Nyberg, L. (2000). Age-related differences in neural activity during item and temporal-order memory retrieval: A positron emission tomography study. *Journal of Cognitive Neuroscience, 12*, 1–10.

Cabeza, R., Anderson, N. D., Kester, J., and McIntosh, A. R. (2002). Aging gracefully: Compensatory brain activity in high-performing older adults. *Neuroimage, 17*, 1394–1402.

Cabeza, R., Grady, C. L., Nyberg, L., McIntosh, A. R., Tulving, E., Kapur, S., Jennings, J. M., Houle, S., and Craik, F. I. M. (1997a). Age-related differences in neural activity during memory encoding and retrieval: A positron emission tomography study. *Journal of Neuroscience, 17*, 391–400.

Cabeza, R., McIntosh, A. R., Tulving, E., Nyberg, L., and Grady, C. L. (1997b). Age-related differences in effective neural connectivity during encoding and recall. *Neuroreport, 8*, 3479–3483.

Cao, Y., Vikingstad, E. M., Paige George, K., Johnson, A. F., and Welch, K. M. A. (1999). Cortical language activation in stroke patients recovering from aphasia with functional MRI. *Stroke, 30*, 2331–2340.

Chiarello, C., and Maxfield, L. (1996). Varieties of interhemispheric inhibition, or how to keep a good hemisphere down. *Brain and Cognition, 36*, 81–108.

Dixit, N. K., Gerton, B. K., Dohn, P., Meyer-Lindenberg, A., and Berman, K. F. (2000). *Age-related changes in rCBF activation during an N-Back working memory paradigm occur prior to age 50.* Paper presented at the Neuroimage Human Brain Mapping.

Golomb, J., Kluger, A., de Leon, M. J., Ferris, S. H., Convit, A., Mittelman, M., Cohen, J., Rusinek, De Santi, S., and George, A. E. (1994). Hippocampal formation size in normal human aging: A correlate of delayed secondary memory performance. *Learning and Memory, 1*, 45–54.

Grady, C. L., Bernstein, L. J., Beig, S., and Siegenthaler, A. L. (2002). The effects of encoding strategy on age-related changes in the functional neuroanatomy of face memory. *Psychology and Aging, 17*, 7–23.

Grady, C. L., Maisog, J. M., Horwitz, B., Ungerleider, L. G., Mentis, M. J., Salerno, J. A., Pietrini, P., Wagner, E., and Haxby, J. V. (1994). Age-related changes in cortical blood flow activation during visual processing of faces and location. *Journal of Neuroscience, 14*, 1450–1462.

Grady, C. L., McIntosh, A. R., Horwitz, B., and Rapoport, S. I. (2000). Age-related changes in the neural correlates of degraded and nondegraded face processing. *Cognitive Neuropsychology, 217*, 165–186.

Gunning-Dixon, F. M., and Raz, N. (submitted). Age-related differences in cortical volumes and white matter hyperintensities independently predict age-related cognitive declines.

Haist, F., Shimamura, A. P., and Squire, L. R. (1992). On the relationship between recall and recognition memory. *Journal of Experimental Psychology: Learning, Memory, and Cognition, 18*, 691–702.

Head, D., Raz, N., Gunning-Dixon, F. M., Williamson, A., and Acker, J. D. (in press). Age-related shrinkage of the prefrontal cortex is associated with executive but not procedural aspects of cognitive performance. *Psychology and Aging.*

Katzman, R. (1993). Education and the prevalence of dementia and Alzheimer's disease. *Neurology, 43*, 13–20.

Kohler, S., Black, S. E., Sinden, M., Szekely, C., Kidron, D., Parker, J. L., Foster, J. K., Moscovitch, M., Winocur, G., Szalai, J. P., and Bronskill, M. J. (1998). Hippocampal and parahippocampal gyrus atrophy in relation to distinct anterograde memory impairment in Alzheimer's disease: An MR volumetric study. *Neuropsychologia*, **26**, 129–142.

Li, S.-C., and Lindenberger, U. (1999). Cross-level unification: A computational exploration of the link between deterioration of neurotransmitter systems dedifferentiation of cognitive abilities in old age. In L.-G. Nilsson and H. J. Markowitsch (eds), *Cognitive Neuroscience of Memory* (pp. 103–146). Seattle, WA, US: Hogrefe and Huber Publishers.

Logan, J. M., Sanders, A. L., Snyder, A. Z., Morris, J. C., and Buckner, R. L. (2002). Under-recruitment and nonselective recruitment: Dissociable neural mechanisms associated with aging. *Neuron*, **33**, 827–840.

Madden, D. J., Turkington, T. G., Provenzale, J. M., Denny, L. L., Hawk, T. C., Gottlob, L. R., and Coleman, R. E. (1999). Adult age differences in functional neuroanatomy of verbal recognition memory. *Human Brain Mapping*, **7**, 115–135.

McArdle, J. J., Hamgami, F., Jones, K., Jolesz, F., Sandor, T., Kikinis, R., Spiro, R., and Albert, M. S. (under review). Structural modeling of dynamic changes in memory and brain structure: Longitudinal data from the normative aging study.

McIntosh, A. R., Sekuler, A. B., Penpeci, C., Rajah, M. N., Grady, C. L., Sekuler, R., and Bennett, P. J. (1999). Recruitment of unique neural systems to support visual memory in normal aging. *Current Biology*, **9**, 1275–1278.

Morcom, A. M., Good, C. D., Frackowiak, R. S., and Rugg, M. D. (2002). Age effects on the neural correlates of successful encoding. *Manuscript submitted for publication*.

Moscovitch, M., and Winocur, G. (1995). Frontal lobes, memory, and aging. *Annals of the New York Academy of Sciences*, **769**, 119–150.

Nielson, K. A., Langenecker, S. A., and Garavan, H. P. (2002). Differences in the functional neuroanatomy of inhibitory control across the adult lifespan. *Psychology and Aging*, **17**, 56–71.

Nolde, S. F., Johnson, M. K., and Raye, C. L. (1998). The role of prefrontal cortex during tests of episodic memory. *Trends in Cognitive Sciences*, **2**, 399–406.

Prull, M. W., Gabrieli, J. D. E., and Bunge, S. A. (2000). Memory and aging: A cognitive neuroscience perspective. In F. I. M. Craik and T. A. Salthouse (eds), *Handbook of Aging and Cognition II*. Mahwah, NJ: Erlbaum.

Raz, N. (2000). Aging of the brain and its impact on cognitive performance: Integration of structural and functional findings. In F. I. M. Craik and T. A. Salthouse (eds), *Handbook of Aging and Cognition – II*. Mahwah, NJ: Erlbaum.

Raz, N. (2002). *Anatomical measures of cognitive aging*. Paper presented at the Symposium on Neuroscience Aging and Cognition, San Francisco.

Raz, N., Gunning-Dixon, F. M., Head, D., Dupuis, J. H., and Acker, J. D. (1998). Neuroanatomical correlates of cognitive aging: evidence from structural magnetic resonance imaging. *Neuropsychology*, **12**, 95–114.

Raz, N., Williamson, A., Gunning-Dixon, F. M., Head, D., and Acker, J. D. (2000). Neuroanatomical and cognitive correlates of adult age differences in acquisition of a perceptual-motor skill. *Microscopy Research and Technique*, **51**, 85–93.

Reuter-Lorenz, P., Jonides, J., Smith, E. S., Hartley, A., Miller, A., Marshuetz, C., and Koeppe, R. A. (2000). Age differences in the frontal lateralization of verbal and spatial working memory revealed by PET. *Journal of Cognitive Neuroscience,* **12**, 174–187.

Schacter, D. L. (1987). Memory, amnesia, and frontal lobe dysfunction. *Psychobiology,* **15**, 21–36.

Silvestrini, M., Cupini, L. M., Placidi, F., Diomedi, M., and Bernardi, G. (1998). Bilateral hemispheric activation in the early recovery of motor function after stroke. *Stroke,* **29**, 1305–1310.

Small, B. J., Fratiglioni, L., Viitamen, M., Winblad, B., and Bäckman, L. (2000). The course of cognitive impairment in preclinical Alzheimer's disease: 3- and 6-year follow-up of a population-based sample. *Archives of Neurology,* **57**, 839–844.

Spencer, W. D., and Raz, N. (1994). Memory for facts, source, and context: can frontal lobe dysfunction explain age-related differences? *Psychology and Aging,* **9**, 149–159.

Stebbins, G. T., Carrillo, M. C., Dorman, J., Dirksen, C., Desond, J., Turner, D. A., Bennett, D. A., Wilson, R. S., Glover, G., and Gabrieli, D. E. (2002). Aging effects on memory encoding in the frontal lobes. *Psychology and Aging,* **17**, 44–55.

Stuss, D. T., Eskes, G. A., and Foster, J. K. (1994). Experimental neuropsychological studies of frontal lobe functions. In F. Boller and J. Grafman (eds), *Handbook of Neuropsychology,* (Vol. 9, pp. 149–185). Amsterdam: Elsevier.

Volkow, N. D., Gur, R. C., Wang, G. J., Fowler, J. S., Moberg, P. J., Ding, Y. S., Hitzemann, R., Smith, G., and Logan, J. (1998). Association between decline in brain dopamine activity with age and cognitive and motor impairment in healthy individuals. *American Journal of Psychiatry,* **155**, 344–349.

Volkow, N. D., Logan, J., Fowler, J. S., Wang, G. J., Gur, R. C., Wong, C., Felder, C., Gatley, S. J., Ding, Y. S., Hitzemann, R., and Pappas, N. (2000). Association between age-related decline in brain dopamine activity and impairment in frontal and cingulate metabolism. *American Journal of Psychiatry,* **157**, 75–80.

West, R. L. (1996). An application of prefrontal cortex function theory to cognitive aging. *Psychological Bulletin,* **120**, 272–292.

Part 4

Frontiers of biological and health effects in cognitive aging

Chapter 10

Modeling longitudinal changes in old age: From covariance structures to dynamic systems

Ulman Lindenberger

Paolo Ghisletta

Methods in cognitive aging

A major goal in aging research is to identify the structural dynamics and causal mechanisms of senescent changes in behavior. This goal is pursued within and across psychometric, cognitive-experimental, and cognitive-neuroscience research traditions, among others (Lindenberger and Baltes, 1994a; Li and Lindenberger, 1999). Each of these traditions has developed modal research strategies. For instance, the psychometric tradition often applies variance-partitioning procedures to cross-sectional data sets; the cognitive-experimental tradition produces predominantly ordinal age-by-treatment interactions; and aging researchers within the emerging field of cognitive neuroscience try to establish links between age differences in behavior and age differences in patterns of brain activation, which are generally obtained by subtracting patterns of baseline activation from patterns of activation observed under experimental conditions.

Each of these methods has its strengths and weaknesses. Variance-partitioning techniques applied to age-heterogeneous cross-sectional data are a useful heuristic for identifying variables that share large amounts of variance with other variables including age. However, such variables may function remarkably well as 'mediators' (alleged proximal causes) of age differences in other variables for reasons that are unrelated to the structure and mechanisms of age-based changes in cognition (Hertzog, 1996; Lindenberger and Pötter, 1998). Ordinal age-by-condition interactions revealed by the cognitive-experimental research tradition, such as greater negative age differences for the more difficult of two task conditions, cannot be taken as firm evidence that the mechanisms underlying performance in different task conditions age independently or at different rates (cf. Dunn and Kirsner, 1988; Kliegl, Mayr, and Krampe, 1994). Rather, such interactions need to be interpreted with reference to parameterized theoretical models that predict over- or underadditivity of age and condition effects for specific scalings of the dependent variable. Finally, the existence of vast differences in functional connectivity between young and older adults revealed by recent neuroimaging studies (Schreurs *et al.*, 2001) adds complexity to the functional interpretation of age-based activation differences in specific areas of the brain (cf. Cabeza, 2001, 2002).

Latent growth models and multilevel models

In this chapter, we discuss yet another set of methods aimed at discerning structural dynamics and causal mechanisms of ontogenetic changes: the multivariate analysis of longitudinal changes by means of latent growth models (LGM) and multilevel models (MLM). Similar to other methods, LGM and MLM have specific strengths, limitations, and problems. The aim of the present chapter is to highlight central characteristics, using recent examples from our own research for illustration (Ghisletta and Lindenberger, in press, 2002; Lindenberger and Ghisletta, 2002).

LGM evolved in psychometrics, biometrics, and behavior genetics, and can be considered as variants of structural equation modeling aimed at longitudinal data analysis. MLM evolved independently of LGM, and are extensively used in educational research (Laird and Ware, 1982; Bryk and Raudenbush, 1987). When applied to the analysis of longitudinal data, LGM and MLM are closely related and sometimes identical (Chou, Bentler, and Pentz, 1998; McArdle and Hamagami, 1996; MacCallum *et al.*, 1997; Little, Schnabel, and Baumert, 2000). However, as will be shown later on, some research questions are more easily addressed with MLM, whereas others can only be formalized with LGM.

LGM and MLM enable researchers to explore the structure of change, and to test hypotheses about the underlying dynamics that drive this structure. In the context of research on behavioral aging, an important feature of LGM and MLM is to further examine, and potentially disambiguate, the functional status of correlations observed in age-heterogeneous cross-sectional data. Take, for instance, the strong correlations between sensory and intellectual functioning in old and very old age observed in various cross-sectional data sets (Anstey, Lord, and Williams, 1997; Lindenberger and Baltes, 1994b). On the one hand, these correlations may indicate a functional connection between sensory and intellectual domains in advanced old age. On the other, they may result from the superimposition of functionally independent age-linked processes (Bäckman *et al.*, 2000: 505; for a formal treatment, see Lindenberger and Pötter, 1998). Here, LGM and MLM help to discern the relative importance of the two alternatives by examining whether, and to what degree and in which manner, changes are correlated (coupled) across domains.

If the analyses, perhaps due to the nature of available data (e.g., many individuals, few occasions), focus on interindividual differences, the investigation of correlated change corresponds to asking the question whether individuals who show more decline in one domain also show more decline in others. Of course, this question only makes sense if rates of change differ reliably across individuals; if individuals change at similar rates in the domains involved, these domains may still be linked *within* subjects, but between-subject methods are unable to inform us about it. Conversely, the existence of a link between two variables at the level of interindividual differences in change does not necessarily imply a functional coupling within each individual, especially if crucial statistical assumptions are violated (e.g., sample homogeneity, ergodicity; cf. Molenaar, Huizenga, and Nesselroade, 2003). Despite these complications, longitudinal data generally provide more valid information about the functional relation between different age changes than cross-sectional data.

LGM and MLM are general and adaptive tools for testing hypotheses about dynamic structural relations. In contrast to alternative standard data-analytic procedures, LGM and MLM impose fewer restrictions on the shape and variability of the change phenomena under study. As an example, take empirical situations in which variances or covariances change over time. Such situations violate the variance–covariance homogeneity assumption underlying repeated measures ANOVA. That is, changes in variance and covariance cannot be examined using repeated measures ANOVA because use of this method assumes their constancy. In contrast, LGM and MLM permit time-dependent changes in variances and covariances, and empower researchers to formally specify and test hypotheses about their magnitude, direction, and dynamics (LGM), in conjunction with or independent of hypotheses about changes in level. In addition, shapes, variances, and covariances of change are controlled for error, according to the error structure specified by the user.

In sum, LGM and MLM allow researchers to represent a wide range of change processes in a flexible and reliable manner. To make optimal use of these benefits, researchers need to provide a formal expression of guiding hypotheses and plausible competitors, and to choose an appropriate representation of available data. That is, they need to specify which questions to ask to the data, and to arrange the available data in a manner that maximizes the chances of obtaining a meaningful answer. Depending upon the questions asked and the data at hand, this process is either facilitated by LGM or MLM. In the following, we first focus on notation and commonalities between LGM and MLM, and then list their discriminating features.

Latent growth and multilevel models: Commonalities

In the simplest longitudinal case, LGM and MLM aim at estimating the parameter values of a specified function representing the longitudinal change of the sample analyzed. The parameters ought to minimize the discrepancies between the shape of the assumed change function and observed individual trajectories. All individuals' change trajectories are assumed to follow the same curve. Individual differences are expressed as deviations from average (population) parameters.

A popular expression for the change function is a linear curve, defined as the sum of a time-independent intercept and a time-dependent slope:

$$Y_{i,j} = \beta_{0,i} + \beta_{1,i} \cdot T_{i,j} + E_{i,j} \tag{1}$$

The measurement $Y_{i,j}$ for individual i at time j is the sum of an intercept $\beta_{0,i}$ plus the linear slope coefficient $\beta_{1,i}$ multiplied by time plus the error component $E_{i,j}$. Note however that both $\beta_{0,i}$ and $\beta_{1,i}$ and $E_{i,j}$ have subscripts i. This indicates that each individual's change function is represented as a deviation from the population. The error component and the time indicator are both time-dependent. In the most common application the change function in equation (1) will lead to the estimation of six parameters:

1 The average intercept (the average of $\beta_{0,i}$);
2 The average slope (the average $\beta_{1,i}$);
3 The variance of the intercept (the variance of $\beta_{0,i}$);
4 The variance of the slope (the variance of $\beta_{0,i}$);
5 The covariance between intercept and slope (the covariance between $\beta_{0,i}$ and $\beta_{1,i}$); and
6 The error variance (the variance of $E_{i,j}$).

More parameters may be estimated by modeling the error structure. In the most usual application the error is assumed constant across time and uncorrelated (e.g., no autocorrelations over time).

Note that these six parameters are named differently in LGM and MLM terminology. In LGM, the six parameters are called in the order of presentation:

1 Average of the level factor,
2 Average of the change factor,
3 Variance of the level factor,

4   Variance of the change factor,

5   Covariance between level and change factors, and

6   Variance of the error factors.

In MLM the respective terms are:

1   Fixed intercept effect,

2   Fixed slope effect,

3   Random intercept effect,

4   Random slope effect,

5   Intercept-slope covariance (or level 2 covariance); and

6   Residual variance (or level 1 variance).

The change function of equation (1) can be used to evaluate basic hypotheses about change. Often, the covariance between level and change is of theoretical interest (do individuals with higher levels of performance show more positive change?). In interpreting the magnitude of this correlation, however, two things need to be kept in mind. First, this covariance is limited by the corresponding variances of level and change. Specifically, the covariance between level and change is not defined if level, change, or both do not display individual differences. Second, the correlation between level and change is dependent upon the point in time at which time equals zero, that is, the placement of the intercept. Caution is thus required when substantive interpretations of the correlation between level and change are being made.

With LGM and MLM, time can be represented in any possible way such as time in study, age from birth, or time to onset of disease. For each of these representations, the intercept can be shifted to the beginning, the center, or the end of the observation period, or to any other point in time. For most applications of MLM and LGM, it is advantageous to center the intercept at the middle of the observation period (Kreft, de Leeuw, and Aiken, 1995; Mehta and West, 2000; Wainer, 2000; see Figure 10.1 for an example).

Another generally overlooked property of change functions of the type in equation (1) is that several statistical variations are feasible. Both level and change may display one of four combinations of effects: only a fixed, average effect different from zero, only a random, variance effect different from zero, neither effect different from zero, or both effects different from zero. Many research applications of equation (1) simply assume that both level and change have a fixed, average effect different from zero, *and* a random, variance effect different from zero. However, while many permutations of level and change effects are possible ($4^2 = 16$), only those allowing random, variance effects for both level and change can define the covariance effect between level and change. Hence, only four of the possible 16 permutations define the covariance effect! To simply assume that both level and change have both fixed, average effect and random, variance effect may lead to flawed conclusions. Specifically, it is not meaningful to interpret covariances based on variances that do not reliably differ from zero.

Latent growth and multilevel models: Differences

Despite their overall similarity, researchers sometimes may prefer MLM over LGM and vice versa. Both LGM and MLM can accommodate incomplete data and unbalanced data structures (under missing at random assumptions). LGM require extra efforts for this adjustment because time is defined as a series of discrete variables, so that each measurement point has to be specified. If the data structure is highly unbalanced, if many data points are missing, or both, this results in a large number of missing observations (for an application in which each individual contributed at most three measurements to a curve covering 26 possible measurement occasions, see Ghisletta and McArdle, [2001]). To reduce missing data points, the time variable needs to be rounded into discrete bins (e.g., days, months, or years of age). With MLM, this problem does not exist because time is treated as a single continuous variable (Hedeker and Gibbons, 1997).

In most applications of LGM and MLM, the shape of average change is specified through the researcher. However, the relation between time and the variable of interest Y, which is linear in equation (1), can also be optimized in a data-driven manner. This exercise is straightforward with LGM because the loadings defining the change factor do not have to be specified a priori but can be estimated, as in ordinary factor analysis. Technically, two loadings still need to be specified (e.g., fixed) for identification purposes (see Ghisletta and McArdle, 2001). In MLM, this exercise is cumbersome but possible (see McArdle and Woodcock, in preparation).

At times, researchers may wish to specify the error structure. In equation (1) it is assumed that the error is constant in time and uncorrelated. This need not be the case. Substantive considerations may dictate an in-depth analysis of the error structure as well as nested comparisons between alternative structures. Depending upon the structures in question, this is more easily accomplished with LGM or with MLM. However, only LGM provides all possible degrees of freedom in the specification of the error structure.

In multivariate applications, relations among different variables are generally of greatest interest. In MLM, relations among time-varying variables are typically confined to covariances. For instance, the level of one variable may be found to correlate significantly with the change of another variable, or various changes may be found to correlate. With LGM, as with any other structural equation model, relations among time-varying variables can be freely specified. The level of one variable may thus be specified to exert a unidirectional, regression-type effect onto the change of another variable (as compared to a bidirectional covariance relation). With more advanced models and more complex theories (see Examples 2 and 3 below), greater flexibility currently mandates an LGM approach.

Time-invariant covariates are often included in the study of change. In the multilevel modeling tradition, which is strictly hierarchical (top-down) in orientation, time-invariant covariates are conceived as predictors or antecedents of time-varying variables. In contrast, LGM does not prescribe the relation between the two sets of variables. For instance, instead of assuming that SES predicts interindividual differences in cognitive change, the researcher may 'turn the arrow around' and posit that interindividual differences in cognitive change predict SES.

In summary, if there are many incomplete data and the design results in highly unbalanced data, if the change function is rather common (e.g., linear, polynomial, logistic, exponential), if the theory does not call for unusual error structures, if the multivariate application focuses on covariances among the variables' change features, and if time-invariant covariates are included as predictors, then MLM may be the preferred method of analysis. Note that these conditions cover a wide range of applications in the psychological literature. However, if the analyzer is able to accommodate unbalanced and incomplete data structure by a series of discrete variables without producing too many missing data points, if the shape of the change function is to be estimated by the data, if the error structure is of primary interest, if directional relations among the variables' change features are posited, and if time-invariant covariates are also considered as predicted variables or correlates, and not only as predictors, then LGM may be the preferred. Both methods are rather easily implemented thanks to new software (see Zhou, Perkins, and Hui, 1999). However, advanced applications of LGM, such as Examples 2 and 3 reported below, still require more than common familiarity with structural equation modeling software.

Research examples: Participants, observations, and variables

The following three illustrations all concern various aspects of the longitudinal cognitive and sensory test batteries of the Berlin Aging Study (BASE) (Baltes and

Mayer, 1999). BASE is a multidisciplinary study of aging, involving psychology, sociology and social policy, internal medicine and geriatrics, and psychiatry. The sample originated from a random draw of addresses from the city registry of West Berlin. On the first occasion, it comprised 516 individuals and was stratified by age and gender (mean age = 85 years; age range = 70 − 103 years) (cf. Lindenberger *et al.*, 1999). For a summary of research on intellectual functioning in the context of BASE, see Lövdén, Ghisletta, and Lindenberger (in press).

Started in 1989, the BASE longitudinal design currently consists of five measurement occasions. Data collection and data entry has been completed up to the fourth occasion. The first, third, and fourth measurement occasions include a reduced multidisciplinary measurement protocol (Intake assessment) followed by an in-depth, discipline-specific follow-up (Intensive protocol); the second occasion was limited to the Intake assessment. Table 10.1 displays the longitudinal design up to the fourth measurement occasion. For each occasion, the relevant variables and the effective sample sizes are specified. The average distance in time to the first occasion is also provided. As is generally true for longitudinal studies of aging populations, the effective sample decreased considerably over occasions (see also Lindenberger, Singer, and Baltes, 2002 and Singer, *et al.*, 2003).

Four intellectual abilities were included in the longitudinal test battery, represented by two variables each: Perceptual speed was marked by Digit Letter

Table 10.1 Description of cognitive and sensory variables from the BASE longitudinal design

	IA_1	IP_1	IA_2	IA_3	IP_3	IA_4	IP_4
			Occasion of measurement				
Variables							
Perceptual speed	DL	DL, IP	DL	DL	DL, IP	DL	DL, IP
Memory	PA, MT			PA, MT			PA, MT
Fluency		CA, WB	CA	CA	CA, WB	CA	CA, WB
Knowledge		VO, SW			VO, SW		VO, SW
Vision		CV, DV	CV,DV		CV, DV		CV, DV
Hearing		H	H		H		H
Time in study	0.00	0.13	1.95	3.76	3.99	5.55	6.03
N	516	516	361	244	208	164	132

Note. IA = Intake Assessment; IP_n = Intensive Protocol on the n-tn longitudinal measurement occasion; DL = Digit Letter; IP = Identical Pictures; PA = Paired Associates; MT = Memory for Text; CA = Categories; WB = Word Beginnings; VO = Vocabulary; SW = Spot-a-Word; CV = close visual acuity; DV = distance visual acuity; H = hearing. Time in study is calculated as average in years.

(DL) and Identical Pictures (IP), verbal knowledge by Vocabulary (VO) and Spot-a-Word (SW), episodic memory by Memory for Text (MT) and Paired Associates (PA), and fluency by Categories (CA) and Word Beginnings (WB) (for details, see Lindenberger, Mayr, and Kliegl, 1993). The sensory variables included close visual acuity (CV) and distant visual acuity (DV), assessed with regular Snellen reading tables, as well as auditory acuity, measured by pure-tone thresholds across four frequencies in both ears (H; for details see Marsiske *et al.*, 1999).

Research example number 1

Covariance structures of level and change analyzed by means of MLM followed by exploratory factor analysis

In this first example, we will describe an analysis of interrelations of change among cognitive and sensory variables of BASE (Lindenberger and Ghisletta, 2002). The focus of the analysis was on exploring the amount of shared variance among cognitive and sensory variables, especially with respect to change. The eight cognitive and two vision variables in Table 10.1 were analyzed; auditory measurements were aggregated into a single hearing indicator. We first wished to obtain the ideal specification of the change function for each variable according to equation (1). Then we wanted to calculate the amount of shared random, variance effects among the variables' changes. We assumed, for each variable, that error variances are constant and uncorrelated. As mentioned above, dropout caused the data to be incomplete, and the fact that participants were not measured at identical time intervals implied unbalanced data. Hence, the MLM approach proved ideal. Change was defined as the passing of time in years since the beginning of the study. *We thus applied the time = time in study definition.* To provide unbiased estimates of covariances between level and change, the data were linearly transformed for each individual such that the time in study summed over all available data points was zero (centering; see Figure 10.1).

At first we investigated the functional expression of each variable's change, in particular testing for random, variance effects of change. This implied 11 separate univariate growth models. All 11 variables displayed reliable fixed, average as well as random, variance level effects. Nine (that is, all but VO and HE) displayed reliable fixed, average change effects while only six (DL, IP, PA, CA, CV, and DV) displayed significant random, variance effects of change over the six years of observations. Hence, only six variables could define their correlation between level and change and could potentially share change variance among each other.

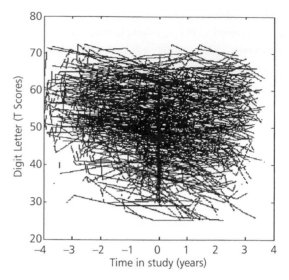

Fig. 10.1 Performance on the Digit Letter, a test of perceptual speed, as a function of time in study. For each individual, data are centered in time. Individuals with incomplete data are included in the analysis.

In a second step, we specified one multivariate growth model with 11 variables, which defined 17 random, variance effects (11 for the level and six for the change components). Besides estimating the analogous parameters of the 11 separate univariate models, this model also contained the relations among the 11 variables. In particular, it estimated a 17 by 17 covariance matrix expressing the relations among all non-zero level and change components. The previous univariate analyses were restricted to the diagonal of the random, variance effects matrix, that is, the variance of the random, variance effects, plus the covariances between level and change within each variable. The additional 130 ($= 17^* 18/2 - 17 - 6$) elements can only be estimated through multivariate analysis. The parameters analogous to the 11 univariate models of the previous step were very closely approximated by the estimates of the multivariate model.

The resulting multivariate covariance matrix was finally analyzed in a third step by exploratory factor analysis. The two factors with eigenvalues greater than one were extracted and obliquely rotated. Generally, the level variables had positive, moderate to high loadings on the first factor, whereas the six change variables showed positive, moderate to high loadings on the second factor. The two factors were positively correlated ($r = 0.41$), suggesting that individuals with higher levels of performance showed less negative change. Taken together, the two factors explained 61 per cent of the total variance across the 17 measures. Thus, this analysis suggests that a sizeable portion of the variance in level and change is shared across intellectual and visual domains.

Research example number 2

Testing the dedifferentiation hypothesis of old-age cognition

The second research example refers to a formal test of the dedifferentiation of cognitive abilities hypothesis in old and very old-age (Ghisletta and Lindenberger, in press). According to this hypothesis (Baltes *et al.*, 1998; Lindenberger, 2001), behavioral aging is marked by a contraction of 'functional cerebral space' (Kinsbourne and Hicks, 1978), or by decreasing specificity and increasing overlap among representations, induced by biological changes in the aging brain. With respect to the distinction between broad fluid and broad crystallized abilities (Horn, 1989), or the mechanics and pragmatics of cognition (Baltes, 1987), the dedifferentiation hypothesis of old-age cognition predicts that changes in the mechanics *drive* (i.e., temporally precede and causally influence) age changes in the pragmatics.

Thus far, evidence regarding dedifferentiation is cross-sectional and indirect. In contrast to cross-sectional data, longitudinal data allow for a direct test of age based dedifferentiation dynamics. We addressed the dedifferentiation hypothesis by concentrating on perceptual speed as a marker of the mechanics, and knowledge as a marker of the pragmatics of cognition. Each of the two abilities was represented by two variables, DL and IP for perceptual speed, Vo and SW for knowledge.

Unfortunately, standard LGM or MLM do not allow for the specification of lead – lag relations because relations among time-dependent processes are modeled symmetrically. However, a recently developed variant of LGM, called the Dual Change Score Model (DCM) (McArdle, 1986, 2001a, 2001b; McArdle, Hamagami, Meredith *et al.*, 2000; McArdle and Hamagami, 2001), can be used for this purpose. In addition to modeling the time-invariant (stationary and often linear) change process, DCM has a 'dynamic' parameter, expressing the effect of a variable's true score at t-1 time on the true change of that variable from t-1 to t. This extra parameter is accommodated by respecification and extension of the standard LGM approach; the MLM approach cannot be adapted correspondingly.

The dedifferentiation hypothesis is clearly longitudinal in nature and is usually formulated in relation to chronological age; the process of dedifferentiation is assumed to unfold with advancing age. Therefore, in the present case, and in

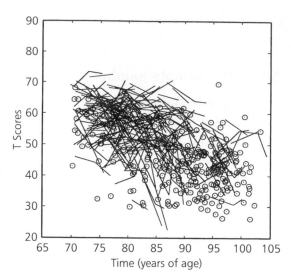

Fig. 10.2 Performance on perceptual speed, a unit-weighted composite of Digit Letter and Identical Pictures, as a function of chronological age. Individuals with incomplete data are included in the analysis. The resulting age trajectory is influenced by both cross-sectional and longitudinal data components.

contrast to the previous example, time was defined in terms of chronological age (see Figure 10.2; cf. Raudenbush and Chan, 1992). Within the DCM, the expression of the variable Y at any time point is directly dependent upon its expression at the previous time point:

$$Y_{i,j} = (1 + \beta)Y_{i,j-1} + \bar{S} \qquad (2)$$

where $Y_{i,j}$ is the true value Y of individual i at time j, β is the dynamical, autoregressive parameter, $Y_{i,j-1}$ is the true value Y of individual i at time $j - 1$, and $\bar{S}$ is the average of the slope factor (McArdle, 2001b). The multivariate extension of the DCM easily adds a similar dynamic parameter, say γ, quantifying the effect of another variable for individual i at time j − 1, say $Z_{i,j-i}$ on the value of Y at time t. Hence equation (2) is expanded to

$$Y_{i,j} = (1 + \beta)Y_{i,j-1} + \gamma \cdot Z_{i,j-1} + \bar{S} \qquad (3)$$

Equation 3 estimates the strength of the auto-proportion (β) as well as that of the proportion of the second variable (γ). In such a system of two equations we can compare the effect sizes of β and γ and draw conclusions on the relative importance of each variable upon its change and upon the change of the other variable. Hence, within the system analyzed, possible 'leading' and 'lagging' variables may be statistically identified.

The bivariate DCM applied to perceptual speed and knowledge clearly indicated that perceptual speed is the leader of the system and knowledge the lagger (for statistical tests, see Ghisletta and Lindenberger, in press). As a consequence, the variance of knowledge is increasingly saturated by variance in perceptual speed with advancing age. Thus, this application provides strong longitudinal evidence for the hypothesis of age-based directional dedifferentiation.

Research example number 3

Time-based structural dynamics between intellectual and visual changes in old age

The final example refers to the longitudinal exploration of relations between intellectual and sensory abilities (Ghisletta and Lindenberger, 2002). Specifically, we examined three current hypotheses about the link between intellectual and sensory domains in old age: the mediation hypothesis (Anstey, 1999), the common cause hypothesis (Lindenberger and Baltes, 1994b), and the cascade hypothesis (Birren, 1964). Two intellectual abilities, perceptual speed and knowledge, and two sensory abilities, close and distance visual acuity, were included in the analysis to yield a quadrivariate DCM. In contrast to the second research example, the basic time dimension was defined in terms of measurement occasion instead of chronological age. This focus on measurement occasions was in part motivated by practical considerations; given the large amount of missing data and the maximum longitudinal observation period of six years spread out over 34 years of age, a model with age as the basic time dimension would have run the risk of empirical under-identification. Instead, age was specified as a covariate of the level factors and as a possible direct influence on latent changes of each of the four variables. In this manner, we were able to examine whether a variable is changing, whether its change is affected by itself, by one of the other three variables, and by chronological age.

The results indicated that individuals changed on all four variables across occasions. The average, group changes were more marked for close vision and perceptual speed than for distance vision and knowledge. Occasion-based changes in perceptual speed were reliably affected by chronological age and close vision, changes in knowledge by chronological age and itself, changes in close vision by itself and distance vision, and changes in distance vision by perceptual speed and knowledge. Intellectual and sensory abilities were intimately connected in time, but neither one was dominating the other. Thus, contrary to the previous age-based specification of the DCM for perceptual speed and knowledge, no single leader of change emerged. As argued in detail elsewhere (Ghisletta and Lindenberger, 2002), this finding provides limited support for the common-cause hypothesis, and no support for the mediation and cascade hypotheses.

Concluding remarks

The study of age changes in behavior requires the concerted use of different statistical tools and research designs (Baltes, Reese, and Nesselroade, 1988; Hertzog, 1996). By structuring longitudinal change, LGM and MLM make a unique contributions towards a better understanding of the structural dynamics and causal mechanisms of behavioral aging. However, as is true for other methods, LGM and MLM are not without problems and limitations. In the context of longitudinal investigations of behavioral aging, four issues seem especially relevant.

First, LGM and MLM generally assume sample homogeneity (cf. Molenaar *et al.*, 2003). Each individual's change is described as the deviation from a single average curve. This procedure makes only limited sense if the shape of the average curve differs from the shape of individual curves, or if the sample consists of a mixture of subsamples with different change trajectories (for an early treatment of this issue in the gerontological literature, see Baltes and Labouvie, 1973: 146; cf. Wohlwill, 1970). For instance, modal shapes of change appear to differ between individuals with and without a dementing illness before this illness has reached a clinical threshold (Bäckman, Small, and Fratiglioni, 2001; Sliwinski *et al.*, 1996). Uncritical use of the full-information approach, in which each individual is included in the estimation of the overall curve regardless of how much data are missing, may hide sample heterogeneity and distort shapes of change. Thus, an important goal in longitudinal research is to identify early markers of subgroup membership, and to examine group differences in change trajectories. A useful means to this end is to separately model change in the total sample and in subgroups to examine the existence of systematic differences in shape of change (Singer *et al.*, 2003).

Second, a more general but related assumption of LGM and MLM is ergodicity, or the assumption that the structure of interindividual differences is governed by the same regularities as the structure of within-person changes. If the ergodicity assumption does not hold, the analysis of interindividual differences may yield an invalid picture of within-person changes. Unfortunately, lack of ergodicity is not detected easily (Molenaar *et al.*, 2003). Innovative formal analyses and quantitative simulations are needed to determine whether certain violations of the ergodicity assumption are more detrimental to the validity of between-person differences in the study of ontogenetic change than others (Lövdén and Lindenberger, in press).

Third, both LGM and MLM assume that data are missing at random (MAR). In longitudinal studies of aging, this assumption is often violated. In dealing with this fundamental problem, several strategies seem productive. For example, one may consider, in each particular case, whether violation of the MAR assumption precludes an unbiased and meaningful test of the relevant guiding hypothesis. Also, attempts should be made to explicitly model sample selectivity by including key markers such as onset of disease or distance to death. This may require multiple representations of time within the same model. For instance, time in study may serve as the basic time dimension, and chronological age, distance to death, or distance to onset of disease may be specified as antecedents or consequents of change.

Finally, with typical longitudinal data, variances and covariances of change are generally small in relation to variances and covariances in level. As argued above, variances that differ reliably from zero are a necessary condition for investigating structural hypotheses about covariances. However, the sampling distributions of covariances may be overly wide with small variances, even if they differ significantly from zero. Again, formal analyses and statistical simulations are needed to examine the robustness of LGM and MLM under such conditions.

To a large degree, the problems listed above refer to fundamental aspects of behavioral aging and ontogenetic change in general. Thus, working on these problems in the context of LGM and MLM represents not only a methodological but also a conceptual challenge. Both seem well worth the effort.

Author note

Preparation of this chapter was financially supported by a grant from the Deutsche Forschungsgemeinschaft to the Ulman Lindenberger; SFB 378, project: Aging, Resources, and Cognition (ARC).

References

Anstey, K. J. (1999). Construct overlap in resource theories of memory aging. *Gerontology,* **45**, 348–350.

Anstey, K. J., Lord, S. R., and Williams, P. (1997). Strength in the lower limbs, visual contrast sensitivity and simple reaction time predict cognition in older women. *Psychology and Aging,* **12**, 137–144.

Bäckman, L., Small, B. J., Wahlin, A., and Larsson, M. (2000). Cognitive functioning in very old age. In F. I. M. Craik and T. A. Salthouse (eds), *The Handbook of Aging and Cognition* (2nd ed., pp. 499–558). Mahwah, NJ: Lawrence Erlbaum Associates.

Bäckman, L., Small, B. J., and Fratiglioni, L. (2001). Stability of the preclinical episodic memory deficit in Alzheimer's disease. *Brain,* **124**, 96–102.

Baltes, P. B. (1987). Theoretical propositions of life-span developmental psychology: On the dynamics between growth and decline. *Developmental Psychology,* **23**, 611–626.

Baltes, P. B., and Labouvie, G. V. (1973). Adult development of intellectual performance: Description, explanation, modification. In C. Eisdrofer and M. P. Lawton (eds), *The Psychology of Adult Development and Aging.* Washington, DC: Americal Psychological Association.

Baltes, P. B., Lindenberger, U., and Staudinger, U. M. (1998). Life-span theory in developmental psychology. In R. M. Lerner (ed.), *Theoretical Models of Human Development. Vol. 1 of the Handbook of Child Psychology* (pp. 1029–1143). New York: Wiley.

Baltes, P. B., and Mayer, K. U. (1999). *The Berlin Aging Study: Aging from 70 to 100.* New York: Cambridge University Press.

Baltes, P. B., Reese, H. W., and Nesselroade, J. R. (1988). *Life-span Developmental Psychology: Introduction to research methods* (reprint of 1977 ed.). Hillsdale, NJ: Erlbaum.

Birren, J. E. (1964). *The Psychology of Aging.* Englewood Cliffs, N.J.: Prentice-Hall.

Bryk, A. S., and Raudenbush, S. W. (1987). Application of hierarchical linear models to assessing change. *Psychological Bulletin, 101*, 147–158.

Cabeza, R. (2001). Functional neuroimaging of cognitive aging. In R. Cabeza and A. Kingstone (eds), *Handbook of Functional Neuroimaging of Cognition* (pp. 331–377). Cambridge, MA: MIT Press.

Cabeza, R. (2002). Hemispheric asymmetry reduction in old adults: The HAROLD Model. *Psychology and Aging, 17*, 85–100.

Chou, C.-P., Benter, P. M., and Pentz, M. A. (1998). Comparisons of two statistical approaches to study growth curves: The multilevel model and latent curve analysis. *Structural Equation Modeling, 5*, 247–266.

Dunn, J. C., and Kirsner, K. (1988). Discovering functionally independent mental processes: The principle of reversed association. *Psychological Review, 95*, 91–101.

Ghisletta, P., and Lindenberger, U. (in press). Age-based structural dynamics between perceptual speed and knowledge in the Berlin Aging Study: Direct evidence for ability dedifferentiation in old age. *Psychology and Aging.*

Ghisletta, P., and Lindenberger, U. (2002). Exploring the structural dynamics of the link between sensory and cognitive functioning in old age: Longitudinal evidence from the Berlin Aging Study. Manuscript in preparation.

Ghisletta, P., and McArdle, J. J. (2001). Latent growth curve analyses of the development of height. *Structural Equation Modeling, 8*, 531–555.

Hedeker, D., and Gibbons, R. D. (1997). Application of random-effects pattern-mixture models for missing data in longitudinal studies. *Psychological Methods, 2*, 64–78.

Hertzog, C. A. (1996). Research design in studies of aging and cognition. In J. E. Birren and K. W. Schaie (eds), *Handbook of the Psychology of Aging* (pp. 24–37). San Diego, CA: Academic Press.

Horn, J. L. (1989). Models of intelligence. In R. L. Linn (ed.), *Intelligence: Measurement, theory, and public policy* (pp. 29–73). Urbana, IL: University of Illinois Press.

Kinsbourne, M., and Hicks, R. E. (1978). Functional cerebral space: A model for overflow, transfer and interference effects in human performance: A tutorial review. In J. Requin (ed.), *Attention and Performance VII.* Hillsdale, New Jersey: Lawrence Erlbaum Associates.

Kliegl, R., Mayr, U., and Krampe, R. T. (1994). Time-accuracy functions for determining process and person differences: An application to cognitive aging. *Cognitive Psychology, 26*, 134–164.

Kreft, I. G. G., de Leeuw, J., and Aiken, L. S. (1995). The effect of different forms of centering in hierarchical linear models. *Multivariate Behavioral Research, 30*, 1–21.

Laird, N. M., and Ware, J. H. (1982). Random-effects models for longitudinal data. *Biometrics*, **38**, 963–974.

Li, S.-C., and Lindenberger, U. (1999). Cross-level unification: A computational exploration of the link between deterioration of neurotransmitter systems and dedifferentiation of cognitive abilities in old age. In L.-G. Nilsson and H. Markowitsch (eds), *Cognitive Neuroscience of Memory* (pp. 104–146). Toronto: Hogrefe and Huber.

Lindenberger, U. (2001). Lifespan theories of cognitive development. In N. J. Smelser and P. B. Baltes (eds), *International Encyclopedia of the Social and Behavioral Sciences*. Oxford, UK: Elsevier.

Lindenberger, U., and Baltes, P. B. (1994a). Aging and intelligence. In R. J. Sternberg (ed.), *Encyclopedia of Human Intelligence* (Vol. 1, pp. 52–66). New York: Macmillan.

Lindenberger, U. and Baltes, P. B. (1994b). Sensory fuctioning and intelligence in old age: A strong connection. *Psychology and Aging*, **9**, 339–355.

Lindenberger, U., Gilberg, R., Nuthmann, R., Pötter, U., Little, T. L., and Baltes, P. B. (1999). Sample selectivity and generalizability of results from the Berlin Aging Study. In P. B. Baltes and K. U. Mayer (eds), *The Berlin Aging Study: Aging from 70 to 100* (pp. 56– 82). New York: Cambridge University Press.

Lindenberger, U., and Ghisletta, P. (2002). *Cognitive and sensory changes in the Berlin Aging Study: Longitudinal analyses of the total sample.* Paper presented at the Cognitive Aging Conference, Atlanta, Georgia.

Lindenberger, U., Mayr, U., and Kliegl, R. (1993). Speed and intelligence in old age. *Psychology and Aging*, **8**, 207–220.

Lindenberger, U., and Pötter, U. (1998). The complex nature of unique and shared effects in hierarchical linear regression: Implications for developmental psychology. *Psychological Methods*, **3**, 218–230.

Lindenberger, U., Singer, T., and Baltes, P. B. (2002). Longitudinal selectivity in aging populations: Separating mortality-associated versus experimental components in the Berlin Aging Study (BASE). *Journal of Gerontology: Psychological Science*.

Little, T. D., Schnabel, K. U., and Baumert, J. (eds) (2000). *Modeling Longitudinal and Multilevel Data: Practical issues, applied approaches, and specific examples.* Mahwah, NJ: Lawrence Erlbaum Associates.

Lövdén, M., Ghisletta, P., and Lindenberger, U. (in press). Cognition in the Berlin Aging Study: The first ten years. *Aging, Neuropsychology, and Cognition.*

Lövdén, M., and Lindenberger, U. (in press). Development of intellectual abilities in old age: From age gradients to individuals. In O. Wilhelm and R. W. Engle (Eds.), *Understanding and measuring intelligence.* Thousand Oaks, CA: Sage.

McArdle, J. J. (1986). Latent growth within behavior genetic models. *Behavior Genetics*, **16**, 163–200.

McArdle, J. J. (2001a). Growth curve analysis. In N. J. Smelser and P. B. Baltes (eds), *The International Encyclopedia of the Behavioral and Social Sciences*. New York, NY: Pergamon Press.

McArdle, J. J. (2001b). A latent difference score approach to longitudinal dynamic structural analyses. In R. Cudeck, S. duToit, and D. Sorbom (eds), *Structural Equation Modeling: Present and future* (pp. 342–380). Lincolnwood, IL: Scientific Software International.

McArdle, J. J. and Hamagami, F. (1996). Multilevel models from a multiple group structural equation perspective. In G. A. Marcoulides and R. E. Schumaker (eds),

Advanced Structural Equation Modeling. Issues and techniques (pp. 89–124). Mahwah, NJ: Lawrence Erlbaum Associates.

McArdle, J. J. and Hamagami, F. (2001). Linear dynamic analyses of incomplete longitudinal data. In L. M. Collins and M. Sayer (eds), *New Methods for the Analysis of Change*. Washington, DC: American Psychological Association.

McArdle, J. J., Hamagami, F., Meredith, W., and Bradway, K. P. (2000). Modeling the dynamic hypotheses of Gf-Gc theory using longitudinal life-span data. *Learning and Individual Differences*, **12**, 53–79.

McArdle, J. J., and Woodcock, R. W. (in preparation). Longitudinal multilevel analyses of test-retest data of the growth and decline of cognitive abilities.

MacCallum, R. C., Kim, C., Malarkey, W. B., and Kiecolt-Glaser, J. K. (1997). Studying multivariate change using multilevel models and latent curve models. *Multivariate Behavioral Research*, **32**, 215–253.

Marsiske, M., Delius, J., Maas, I., Lindenberger, U., Scherer, H., and Tesch-Römer, C. (1999). Sensory systems in old age. In P. B. Baltes and K. U. Mayer (eds), *The Berlin Aging Study: Aging from 70 to 100*. London, UK: Cambridge University Press.

Mehta, P. D., and West, S. G. (2000). Putting the individual back into individual growth curves. *Psychological Methods*, **5**, 23–43.

Molenaar, P. C. M., Huizenga, H. M., and Nesselroade, J. R. (2003). The relationship between the structure of inter-individual and intra-individual variability: A theoretical and empirical vindication of developmental systems theory. In U. M. Staudinger and U. Lindenberger (eds), *Understanding Human Development: Lifespan psychology in exchange with other disciplines* (pp. 339–360). Dordrecht, NL: Kluwer Academic Publishers.

Raudenbush, S. W., and Chan, W. (1992). Growth curve analysis in accelerated longitudinal designs. *Journal of Consulting and Clinical Psychology*, **61**, 941–951.

Schreurs, B. G., Bahro, M., Molchan, S. E., Sunderland, T., and McIntosh, A. R. (2001). Interactions of prefrontal cortex during exeblink conditioning as a function of age. *Neurobiology of Aging*, **22**, 237–246.

Singer, T., Verhaeghen, P., Ghisletta, P., Lindenberger, U., and Baltes, P. B. (2003). The fate of cognition in very old age: Six-year longitudinal findings in the Berlin Aging Study (BASE). *Psychology and Aging*, **18**, 318–331.

Sliwinski, M., Lipton, R. B., Buschke, H., and Stewart, W. (1996). The effects of preclinical dementia on estimates of normal cognitive functioning in aging. *Journal of Gerontology: Psychological Sciences*, **50B**, P162–P170.

Wainer, H. (2000). The centercept: An estimable and meaningful regression parameter. *Psychological Science*, **11**, 434–436.

Wohlwill, J. F. (1970). The age variable in psychological research. *Psychological Review*, **77**, 49–64.

Zhou, X.-H., Perkins, A. J., and Hui, S. L. (1999). Comparisons of software packages for generalized linear multilevel models. *The American Statistician*, **53**, 282–290.

Chapter 11

Exploring the relationships between sensory, physiological, genetic and health measures in relation to the common cause hypothesis

Helen Christensen and Andrew Mackinnon

However slowly and clumsily it has sometimes been
approached, the main goal of research in cognitive
gerontology has always been the relation of patterns of
cognitive and behavioural change to corresponding
alterations in brain function
(Rabbitt 1993: 431)

Specifying the new frontier

Performance on speeded tasks and general ability tests is known to decline from
relatively early in life. Sensory, respiratory, cardiovascular, muscular and skeletal
functioning also deteriorates, commencing in late adulthood and continuing into
late old age (Anstey, Lord, and Smith, 1996). Many of the processes underlying
changes in these different areas of functioning have similar developmental paths
(see Deary, 2000). Accordingly, it has been suggested that a single causal mechanism may be responsible for changes across certain domains of performance
(Lindenberger and Baltes, 1994). The new challenge in cognitive aging is to
determine the cause or causes of these demonstrated associations.

One of the most interesting findings in this field is that associations between
changes across domains encompass such a broad range of physiological and
psychological functions, and that these systems do not seem to be strongly
linked with one another or related directly to a common brain system. To
illustrate, grip strength and lung capacity are both correlated with memory
decline (Christensen, Mackinnon, Korten *et al.*, 2001), a finding that has,
arguably, greater theoretical impact on this field than the observation that the

changes in the hippocampus and memory decline are related. This is primarily because the finding cannot be explained by straightforward appeal to brain function. As discussed in detail below, one of the major implications of these associations is the suggestion that the causes of age-related decline in cognitive performance may be the same as or related to those that determine changes in sensory and physiological functioning.

Figure 11.1 shows age-related performance on cognitive and non-cognitive measures across four age ranges from the Canberra Longitudinal Study (Christensen *et al.*, 2001). The variables included were reaction time, vision, grip strength, forced expiratory volume (FEV), blood pressure, memory, crystallized intelligence and a symbol letter modalities test (SLMT). With the exception of crystallized intelligence and systolic blood pressure which did not differ significantly as a function of age cognitive and marker variables were significantly lower in the older groups. In this data set, variables correlated with each other moderately to strongly (range 0.20 to 0.70).

This chapter outlines the state of research surrounding the common cause hypothesis, interpretations of the findings in the light of the substantial methodological and design limitations of much of the available research, and the implications for future research. A number of conceptual issues need to be addressed first.

It is important to distinguish between the observation of associations of change over time in variables and the theoretical hypotheses that these observations generate. A correlation does not imply a causal connection.

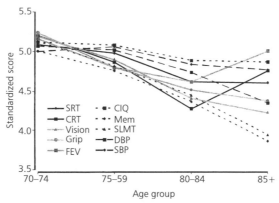

Fig. 11.1 Cognitive and non-cognitive variables as a function of age group. Note: SRT = Simple reaction time, CRT = Choice reaction time, Vision = Snellen chart, Grip = Grip strength, FEV = Forced expiratory volume, CIQ = Crystallized intelligence, Mem = Memory, SLMT = Symbol letters modality test, DBP = Diastolic blood pressure, SBP = Systolic blood pressure.

Indeed, intercorrelations may be due to one cause, many causes, or many unlinked causes. It is useful to think about what might be required in order to establish the existence of a 'common factor'. The requirements could include:

1 The reliable concordance of cognitive and non-cognitive changes – equivalent to the identification of a 'syndrome',

2 The identification of a higher order factor of change on which these cognitive and non-cognitive changes load,

3 The identification of similar risk factors for each of the changes, including the possible identification of shared 'markers' of change, and

4 The identification of an association of a theoretically plausible causal mechanism with both the cognitive and non-cognitive measures.

It is also fundamentally important to distinguish between the common cause or causes and any statistically-derived common cause factor (CCF). In keeping with Salthouse's (1999) distinction between statistical and causal mediators, the term 'common cause factor' will be used here to refer to a latent variable (factor) identified empirically by factor analytic procedures. The term 'common cause' will refer to the conditions or processes that are hypothesized to 'drive' the common factor, and that are responsible for the conjoint decline with age of the variables associated with the factor.

Current status of the new frontier

Findings in support of the common factor hypothesis

Raw correlations

Cross-sectional studies have demonstrated clearly that cognitive and non-cognitive factors are significantly inter-correlated across the lifespan (see Salthouse, 1999). In cross-sectional studies of elderly persons (where the age range of the sample extends across 30 years) raw correlations ranging from 0.15 to 0.70 have been found of age with sensory, motor and cognitive measures. To provide a specific example, in a study of community-dwelling elderly women aged 65 to 91, Anstey, Stankov, and Lord (1993) reported correlations with chronological age of 0.37 for reaction time, 0.62 for visual acuity, 0.15 for vibration sense and −0.34 for Cattell's Matrices. Intercorrelations were of a similar order and provided 'evidence for a decline in Gf [fluid intelligence] related to biological changes in the brain, central nervous system, and motor system' (Starkov and Lord, 1993: 568). In a follow-up study (Anstey, Lord, and Williams, 1997), correlations with age were 0.34 for reaction time, −0.39 for visual contrast sensitivity, and −0.45 for knee extension.

Mediational models

Most research on the relationship between age and sensory, speed and cognitive factors has gone beyond the reporting of raw correlations to the examination of relationships among variables. Mediational models involve examining the extent to which age effects can be accounted for by other variables of interest. For example, investigators have been concerned with the extent to which changes in cognitive performance are accounted for by changes in sensory performance. This model is illustrated in Figure 11.2 (a). In this example, age predicts a sensory functioning latent factor (Sen) (indicated by two tests, S_1 and S_2), and Sen predicts a cognitive latent factor (Cog) (indicated by two tests, C_1 and C_2). The need for a direct path from age to cognitive performance is then evaluated. The argument has been that if the direct path from age to cognition is significant and its inclusion improves model fit, the sensory variable is not the sole mediator of cognitive performance. Findings from studies using this methodology suggest that age has only a small direct role in predicting cognitive performance over its effect via sensory functioning or speed of processing (see, for example, Lindenberger and Baltes, 1994; Anstey, Luszcz, and Sanchez, 2001). Lindenberger and Baltes (1994) reported that 49 per cent of the total and 93 per cent of the shared variance in intellectual functioning was accounted for by a composite variable measuring visual and auditory ability. The finding of large proportions of shared age-related variance and relatively little to no specific age-related variance has been interpreted as suggesting that the same processes determines both sensory functioning, physiological functioning and cognitive performance.

Modeling of a common cause factor in cross-sectional data sets

A number of studies have indicated that a common factor can be identified in cross-sectional datasets. Age associations can be modeled through this factor for most or all age-related cognitive and physiological variables included (see Figure 11.2 (b)). For example, Salthouse, Hambrick, and McGuthry (1998) estimated a common factor directly, with the effect of age being regressed onto both the factor and onto its indicators. Fitting this model to five datasets, Salthouse *et al.* (1998) found that speed, cognitive functioning, grip strength, and visual tests loaded on a common factor. Age had an (additional) independent relationship with sensory functioning but not with the other indicators of the common factor. Using two sets of data, Salthouse and Czaja (2000) evaluated four models that described the underlying basis for the relationship between age and a range of cognitive and non-cognitive variables. These were labeled: complete independence, single common factor, independent factors and hierarchical. Individuals aged from late teens to late eighties or early nineties were included.

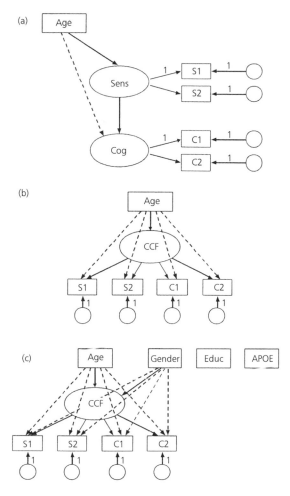

Fig. 11.2 Mediational models.

Schematic illustration of a mediational model (a) with cognitive function (indicated by C1 and C2) predicted by a sensory latent factor (indicated by S1 and S2) which is predicted by age; a common cause model with both sensory and cognitive factors loading on a common factor (b) and a common factor model with multiple pre-dictors (paths shown for age and gender but not shown for education and APOE) (c). Sen = Sensory latent factor; Cog = Cognitive latent factor; CCF = Common cause factor, Educ = Education.

The single factor model and the hierarchical model, both of which postulated a single first- or second-order factor, accounted for a considerable proportion of the variance and better fitted the data than the other models.

Allen, Hall, Druley *et al.* (2001) undertook a re-analysis of these data sets. They concluded that

> Our results suggest that these tests do not unequivocally support a strong common factor explanation of age-related declines. Alternative models in which age effects are carried through multiple latent factors . . . provide at least equally good, and in several cases better, explanations of the observed age-cognitive indicator relationships
> (Allen *et al.* 2001: 534).

Their re-analysis also suggested that there are substantial direct effects of age and that these were often in the opposite direction to the negative age effects on the general factor. This analysis demonstrates the difficulty of determining which of a number of possible models best fit the data arising from cross-sectional studies and using current modeling techniques (see the section methodological considerations below).

Christensen, Mackinnon, Korten *et al.* (2001) used a multiple indicator, multiple cause (MIMIC) model to examine the factor structure of a variety of physiological and other indicators. In their model, a common cause factor (CFF) was defined and fitted, and then a MIMIC structure (Muthén, 1988; Bollen, 1989; Gallo *et al.*, 1994) was used to examine the direct, differential relationships between age and the CCF, and between age and each indicator of the CCF. Figure 11.2 (c) shows the form of the model as it was applied to the established CCF. All variables loaded on a single latent variable representing the common factor. The critical elaboration of this from model (b) was the introduction of a number of demographic and genetic predictor variables. In model (c) the covariates were age, gender, education and APOE. In addition to estimating the effect of the covariates on the latent factor, the model allows the effects of age (and other covariates) on each of the items to be assessed directly (these paths are shown for age and gender only, but were also estimated for other covariates (see Figure 11.2 (c)). The effects of the covariates (e.g., age) were assessed by a direct path from the covariate to the indicator test and can be detected even if there is an overall decline in the common factor with age.

All measures except blood pressure loaded on a single latent factor – the CCF. The CCF was negatively associated with age and could be modeled in two sub-groups comprising (narrow) age ranges. Age was associated with two variables – grip strength and visual acuity – beyond the association mediated by the CCF. Thus, like the study of Salthouse *et al.* (1998), this study found that visual acuity had an additional association with age, independent of the effect mediated by the CCF. However, alternative correlated factor models were not tested.

Longitudinal studies

Data from longitudinal studies are critical to the resolution of the issue of the common cause (see methodological considerations below). A small number of recent longitudinal studies have reported that changes within individuals over time in physiological, sensory and cognitive measures are correlated. Using latent change modeling techniques, Christensen, Mackinnon, Korten *et al.* (1999) reported moderately strong correlations among changes in grip strength, speed and memory, indicating that these variables moved together over the 3.5 year period of their study. Changes in sensory disability correlated with age, but not with changes in speed, grip, memory or Crystallized intelligence (CIQ). These relationships held after adjustment for age and sex. Speed change correlated 0.24 with grip change, grip change correlated approximately 0.30 with memory change, and speed 0.23 with memory change.

In a more recent study, using three waves of data covering 7.5 years, we used a Factor of Curves model (McArdle, 1988) to evaluate associations among rates of change and to examine age, gender, education, pre-morbid intelligence and to the ApoE genotype as predictors of common and specific rates of change (Christensen *et al.*, in press). Latent growth models were developed for each of reaction time, Symbol letter modalities test (SLMT), grip strength, self-reported sensory disability and memory from three waves of data. Second-order latent level and slope factors were fitted as individual factor growth curve models. Five predictors – established risk factors for poor aging outcome – were added to the individual growth curve and second-order factor models to determine whether they were associated with the developmental trajectory of the common factor and each of the lower-order cognitive and non-cognitive trajectories (see Figure 11.3). The risk factors were chronological age, the presence of at least one ApoE ε4 allele, years of education, pre-morbid intelligence, and gender. ApoE, a gene that is involved in central and peripheral lipid metabolism and neuronal repair, is an established risk factor for Alzheimer's disease (AD) and for cardiovascular disease. Additionally, ApoE ε4 has been found to predict cognitive decline in those who do not meet criteria for dementia (see Anstey and Christensen, 2000; Dik, Jonker, Bouter *et al.*, 2000; Hofer, Christensen, Mackinnon *et al.*, 2002). Those carrying the ApoE ε4 allele may

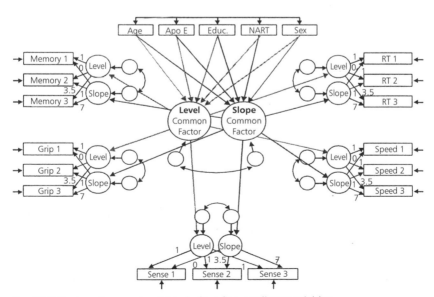

Fig. 11.3 Factor of curves model including five predictor variables.
Note: RT = Simple reaction time (SRT), Sense = Sensory disability, Speed = SLMT.

have more rapid overall brain deterioration once they reach old age, and/or specific hippocampal atrophy (see Bookheimer *et al.*, 2000).

Three main findings emerged. Cognitive and non-cognitive processes changed together across time, although the degree to which they covaried differed considerably. For example, changes in cognitive variables such as simple reaction time (SRT), memory and SLMT were strongly correlated with each other and shared up to 50 per cent of the variance in change in functioning. Associations between cognitive and non-cognitive factors were also moderately strong, with grip strength correlating significantly with SLMT. Sensory disability was less likely than the other measures to 'move together' with other non-cognitive or cognitive variables. This may have been due to the self-report nature of this measure.

All five individual growth curves loaded significantly on the common slope and level factors. These factors accounted for a considerable amount of the variance of some, but not all, of the individual growth curves. Clearly this model demonstrates that, for some variables, a substantial amount of variation in change over time is unique and not accounted for by a common slope factor. Finally, the common slope factor shared only one significant predictor (age) with the slopes of individual growth curves. Even this predictor was not significantly associated with one growth curve (sensory functioning). This indicates that age-related changes across functions are accelerated in later life with the possibility that such changes are related to unspecified health-related causes or other variables not measured in our study. Other predictors were associated with the common cause factors but with only one or two of the individual growth curves. For example, ApoE was significantly associated with the common cause slope factor and with both Memory and SLMT slope factors; sex correlated with the common cause slope factor, and also with Grip slope. One predictor (the NART) was significantly correlated with the common slope factor but not with the slopes of any individual variables, although it had weak and near-significant correlations with a number of the individual growth curves in the expected direction.

Anstey and colleagues (Anstey, Lusczc, and Sanchez, 2001), using data from the Australian Longitudinal Study, have reported findings of some positive correlations between changes in sensory measures and cognitive decline. The sample from the Australian Longitudinal Study of Ageing (N = 2087) was assessed in 1992 and 1994 on measures of sensory and cognitive function as part of a larger clinical assessment. Decline in visual acuity had a significant effect on memory decline, but not on decline in verbal ability or processing speed. Decline in hearing was not associated with decline in any cognitive domain.

The conclusions that can be drawn from these longitudinal studies are complex. In a general sense it is clear that both cognitive and non-cognitive variables change over time, and that change in one type of functioning is related, to some extent, to change in other domains of functioning. The association of the growth curves with a common factor was moderate to strong for some but not all variables, suggesting that the common factor may reflect only one of a number of underlying processes. For example, it may be related to systemic decline associated with health and with age-related increases in risk. In evaluating these conclusions, the impact of measurement error must be considered. It is possible that certain underlying processes might be perfectly correlated but poorly measured. This will lead to weaker correlations.

Data from cohort sequential studies

An unresolved issue to date is the age at which these associations are manifest. Salthouse and colleagues (1998) suggested that there is evidence that the common factor is operating through most of the adult years. However, this has yet to be demonstrated conclusively. Cross-sectional studies have usually involved samples spanning broad age ranges and hence findings from them are subject to possible artifacts (see below). Further, these associations have not been demonstrated longitudinally. Hofer and Sliwinski (2001) have suggested that narrow age-range cohort sequential studies may be a preferred design to investigate these relationships.

We have some preliminary data from three large samples of community-dwellers drawn from narrow age ranges – 20–24 years, 40–44 years and 60–64. These data have been collected over the last three years on 7,500 individuals. The fit of a common factor model was compared to a correlated factors model within each age range, and for men and for women separately. For all three age groups, the correlated factor model (cognitive, speed and biological factors) provided a more satisfactory fit than a common factor model. In the oldest group, vision correlated slightly more strongly with the biological factor. Associations between factors also increased. These results are consistent with the possibility that the common factor may be absent in middle or early old age groups. Given cross-sectional and longitudinal evidence for the emergence of the common factor in older samples together with reports of dedifferentiation in late older age, these findings suggest that the cause or causes of the common factor may begin to exert themselves more strongly after 60–64 years of age.

Methodological considerations

There has been concern that the findings of substantial associations in changes across domains of function reported in the studies discussed above might be artifacts of their design. Mediational and common factor models using cross-sectional data have been particularly criticized for a variety of reasons: these include problems with variance partitioning (see Lindenberger and Potter, 1998; Sliwinski and Hofer, 1999); inadequacy of common factor modeling techniques, as demonstrated by recent Monte Carlo simulation studies (Allen *et al.*, 2001); and limited interpretation of factor modeling, such as the need to examine the direction of direct and indirect age effects. Allen *et al.* (2001) reported that the structural equation modeling investigations of simulated data sets did not clearly indicate the 'true' model but, rather, demonstrated the potential to accept false models. Common factor models may be difficult to falsify (Allen *et al.*, 2001) and, as noted above, the nature of the common factor is dependent on the choice of indicators of these latent factors. In more complex modeling including possible markers of the common causal mechanism the choice of relevant risk factor variables is equally critical. Relevant risk factors and latent variables may not be included because they were not measured in the study or may be excluded due to numerical problems with model estimation.

Recent years have seen growth in attempts to overcome some of these difficulties. From a theoretical perspective, there is a need to choose the indicators for any factor carefully, to be aware that the common cause factors identified within and across studies do not necessarily represent the same construct. It must also be appreciated that the broad explanatory mechanisms underlying the common factor require more detailed specification, and that the inclusion of 'marker' indicator variables for the common factor is important (Allen *et al.*, 2001: 544).

Hofer and Sliwinski (2001) have demonstrated that cross-sectional studies, based on age heterogeneous samples, are confounded in terms of associations between age-related variables in that population mean trends (i.e., age-related differences) will produce an association even when no association between processes is present. However, they note that an alternative cross-sectional design based on narrow age-cohorts permits an evaluation of associational hypotheses without the confound of mean trends.

Are the available data supportive of the existence of a common cause?

To summarize briefly: there are data to suggest that cognitive change is associated with change in physiological, motor, sensory and other areas of functioning. Although data from cross-sectional studies needs to be interpreted cautiously, there is evidence from longitudinal studies that, within individuals, changes correlate with changes, and that these changes are likely to begin in later old age. Not all variance is accounted for by the higher order factor (Christensen *et al.*, in press). Recently, it has been established that few of the predictors of cognitive change are shared with predictors of physiological or other factors, or indeed with the higher order factor. However, since only a few predictors have been examined, this may not be conclusive. There is no clear evidence as to when these correlated changes begin, but it may not be until very late adulthood.

We interpret these findings to suggest that a number of specific and general processes accompany aging, and one of these *may* be a causal process of considerable generality in the functional systems it affects.

Plausible candidates for the common cause

Given the empirical findings presented above, it is worthwhile to consider what mechanisms are plausible candidates for the common cause. The identification of an actual causal mechanism acting in more than one domain of functioning would significantly accelerate progress in this field of research.

Investigators have attempted to explain the findings of large proportions of shared age-related variance across cognitive and noncognitive functions as a change in a physiological process or processes, for example, the 'aging brain' (Lindenberger and Baltes, 1994), changes in the central nervous system and general fitness of the organism (Anstey, Lord, and Williams, 1997), and the aging-related changes to the physiology of the entire organism (Anstey and Smith, 1999). Baltes and Lindenberger (1997: 13) broadened the brain hypothesis to include other bodily functions. 'The ensemble of common cause factors promoting the strong connection between the two domains of functioning may not only involve age-related changes in brain integrity, but also age-based changes in other functions.' These explanations are essentially metaphorical and run the risk of being circular. More recently, Salthouse and Czaja (2000) have suggested specific mechanisms that could be tested. They suggest two types of shared causal mechanisms that may not be mutually exclusive. The first type is cognitive. It could be either a particular type of process or a property of processing, such as speed of processing or the involvement of working memory. The second type of mechanism they propose is neurophysiological or neuroanatomical (either an area of processing, such as the dorso-lateral prefrontal cortex) or a specific process, (such as the dopaminergic system). Salthouse and Czaja (2000: 54) note:

> the results of . . . analyses impose clear constraints on the nature of plausible explanations for cognitive aging phenomena. That is, because many age-related effects seem to operate at relatively broad levels, which affect a wide variety of cognitive variables, researchers must apparently postulate some general or nonspecific explanatory mechanisms.

There are many such mechanisms that could be involved. Theories of aging of the brain include both molecular and neurotransmitter hypotheses. These include:

1   The oxidation and free radical hypothesis (that the production of free-radicals occurs in aging, these then damage cell lipids, proteins and

DNA, and cause neuronal dysfunction and cell death) (see Barzilai and Shuldiner, 2001);

2   The calcium hypothesis, in which changes in calcium homeostasis are postulated to occur with age, and leads to cell death;

3   The gene expression hypotheses, a set of hypotheses concerning genes that are expressed differently with age, thereby influencing oxidative stress, inflammatory processes and DNA repair;

4   Mitochondrial dysfunction, resulting in mutations in the mitochondrial genome;

5   The glucocorticoids hypothesis, in which it is proposed that the production of glucocorticoids may adversely affect hippocampal neurones;

6   The homocysteine hypothesis, whereby increasing levels of homocysteine are associated with cardiovascular disease and stroke.

Neurotransmitter hypotheses involve (i) acetylcholine – a neutotransmitter system that is heavily affected in AD but only modestly affected in normal aging (see Troller and Valenzuela, 2001); (ii) dopamine, in which changes in normal aging are well documented, including a reduction in the density of striatal D2 receptors.

Any of the above cell processes is likely to influence all systems. To illustrate, people with progeria, a rare hereditary disorder that resembles 'accelerated aging', have changes in a group of 15 genes that control cell mitosis (see Marx, 2000). This suggests that genes that control cell mitosis may be involved in an aging process. It is known that cells in culture undergo a limited number of cell divisions and then stop in a state known as replicative senescence (see Lundberg, Hahn, Gupta *et al.*, 2000). Progressive telomere shortening has been proposed as a cause of cell senescence. Within the framework of this hypothesis a critical task for proponents of the common cause hypothesis is to establish telomere length correlates across a variety of systems. This would demonstrate that cellular senescence is linked across brain and bodily systems. Friedrich, Griese, Schwab *et al.*, 2000, suggest that different tissues from the same donor have similar telomere length, perhaps indicating that regulation of telomere length is tissue independent. Conclusions drawn for this study must, however, be tentative due to its small sample size.

Our findings suggest that the underlying process of change may not be linked to Alzheimer-type processes. The ApoE ε4 allele confers risk of AD dementia, a disorder associated with excess plaque and neurofibrillary tangles in cortical cells. If ApoE-linked processes underlie the common factor, presence of the ApoE ε4 genotype would have been expected to correlate with changes in other variables that also correlate with the common cause factor, such as grip and reaction time. For this field to progress, there is a clear need to investigate specific brain and cell processes together with their relationship with cognitive decline and other motor and physiological processes.

Knowledge about the structure and function of the brain is increasing rapidly (see Troller and Valenzuela, 2001) as is the development of brain imaging techniques and genetic analysis. It is now possible to investigate associations at the anatomical and functional level systematically. However, to date, very little of such research has been conducted, particularly longitudinally. At present most of the research conducted in cognitive aging has examined the relationship between cognitive change and brain volume using MRI imaging. This type of investigation is necessarily crude. The correlation between age and brain volume observed in MRI studies is approximately -0.40 (Raz, 2000), with selective shrinkage of the frontal lobe. The cause of brain shrinkage is no longer considered to be the result of neuronal death (although the hippocampus may be an exception).

We recently conducted a review of epidemiological studies using brain MRIs to examine the association of cognitive change with brain volume. Table 11.1 shows longitudinal studies examining the association between various areas of the brain and measures of cognitive performance as a function of the cognitive status of the individuals: normal individuals; those with Alzheimer's disease (AD) or probable AD; and those assessed as having Mild Cognitive Decline, (MCI) or described as being 'at risk'. This table summarizes the number of subjects, the length of the study, the age of the participants, the brain area under study, whether the study found significant changes in brain area volumes and whether the study found evidence for change in cognitive performance across a range of measures. Findings from each study were classified according to whether significant volume change or cognitive change was identified.

Over time there were changes in brain volumes for normal individuals, those with risk of AD, those with MCI and for those with AD. The volume loss was greater in those with AD than those with other conditions (Fox, Cousens, Schahill et al., 2000) and in older subjects (Jack, Petersen, Xu et al., 1998). Evidence collected longitudinally also supports the position that cognitive change is particularly evident for individuals who were diagnosed with MCI and AD at baseline. Over the range of follow-ups, normal individuals also show cognitive change. At shorter intervals, there is less clear evidence for cognitive decline in this group. What is of particular interest, however, was the finding in three studies (in which the association was examined directly) of no significant correlation found between MRI volume changes and cognitive change.

This lack of association cannot be readily attributed to length of follow-up since these measures were taken over long intervals (up to five years). However,

Table 11.1: Longitudinal Studies reporting MRI changes and their associations with cognitive change

Study	Number of Subjects	Length of Study (years)	Age (years)	Brain Area	Change in Brain Area	Change in Cognition	Correlation
Alzheimer's Disease (AD) or Probable AD							
Fox 1996	11	1	53.8	B	Yes	?	?
Jack 1998	24	1	80.42	H	Yes	?	?
Fox 1999	29	6	58.1	B	Yes	Yes	Yes
Fox 2000	18	1	65	B	Yes	Yes	?
Jack 2000	28	3	73.8	H	Yes	Yes	?
Cognitive Decline, Mild Cognitive Impairment (MCI), or 'at risk							
Kaye 1997	12	3.6	84	B, H, TL	Yes	Yes	Yes
Fox 1998	63	6	44.7	H	Yes	?	?
Jack 2000	43	3	77	H	Yes	Yes	?
Normal individuals							
Wahlund 1996	24	5	79	B, WML	Yes	Psychomotor but not other	No
Fox 1996	11	1	51.3	B	?	No	?
Kaye 1997	30	3.6	84	B,H,TL	Yes	No	?
Mueller 1998	46	5	>65	B	Yes	?	?
Jack 1998	24	1	81.04	H	Yes	?	?
Fox 1999	15	6	55.3	B	Yes	?	?
Schmidt 1999	273	3	60	WML	Yes	?	No
Ylikoski 2000	35	5	55–70	WML, TL	Yes	Yes	No
Fox 2000	18	1	65	B	Yes	No	?
Jack 2000	58	3	80.4	H	Yes	Yes	?
Garde 2000	68	16	80.7	WML	Yes	Yes	?
Moffat 2000	26	2.7	68	H	Yes	?	?

Note: WML = White matter lesions, B = Whole brain or other brain regions, H = Hippocampal area, TL = Temporal lobe area. ? = Evidence not provided.

one explanation is that the age range of the subjects was restricted (i.e., there was only a small range of ages in those examined), thereby reducing the likelihood of finding a significant association. Similarly, it is possible that floor or ceiling effects in the tests resulted in a restricted range of test scores, thus reducing the likelihood of finding a significant correlation. This might well be the case in many of these studies, because screening tests rather than comprehensive memory or neuropsychological measures were the only outcome measures examined. Another possible explanation of the absence of association is that reliable tracing of brain structures is only possible once these structures show significant involution or shrinkage. The possibility of more sophisticated longitudinal analyses using functional magnetic imaging and the new proton magnetic spectroscopy (a method that allows *in vivo* estimations of brain chemical profiles) will provide tools to better understand the connection between physiological, brain and cognitive changes.

Next steps to be taken in charting the new frontier

Useful future directions for understanding the cognitive aging process will come from the development of hypotheses about specific potential causal agents and their association with both cognitive and non-cognitive processes. A number of plausible candidates have been considered above and it is now possible to test a number of these mechanisms. There is a need to use a greater variety of measures of cognitive and non-cognitive performance and to incorporate brain indices, such as white matter hyperintensities and brain volume measures, genes other than ApoE that are involved in 'aging processes,' as well as measures, such as telomere length, that predict cell senescence. A shift is needed to examine relationships more broadly, from the investigation of cognitive change and brain mechanisms, to the investigation of brain mechanisms, cellular mechanisms and physiological processes as well as cognitive changes.

Risk factors and markers other than those tested in studies to date could readily be examined to give additional insights into the possible mechanisms underlying both the common factor and specific sensory, cognitive and physiological processes. These analyses could readily be extended to other predictors, including health, disability, time from death, and mortality. In this respect, it is important to consider the distinction drawn by Birren and Cunningham (1985) between 'maturational' and 'health' factors. The role of disease processes on 'biological' aging must be considered. For example, cerebrovascular changes begin in the fourth decade, and may directly affect the facilitation of glucose and oxygen to the total brain.

The frontier is likely to be advanced by large scale epidemiological studies over the lifespan. The reasons for this are numerous: complex dynamic models such as latent growth curve models can be applied to large samples and individual differences in patterns of performance can be identified. Cognitive change begins early in the lifespan for fluid and speeded tasks, so studies encompassing this stage of life are required. It is clearly the case that cognitive aging processes are likely to be complex. There may be distinct individual patterns of aging and clusters of aging profiles.

Cognitive research must broaden its framework to incorporate more extensive measures across a broad range of domains. Multidisciplinary and cross-disciplinary research, incorporating, for example, genetic and cellular aging expertise, is likely to accelerate progress in this field. Methodological advances in the analysis of longitudinal and cross-sectional analysis must be applied to currently available and new data.

Authors' note

This study was supported by grant 973302 from the National Health and Medical Research Council and by the Australian Rotary Health Research Fund.

Thanks are due to A.F. Jorm, S. Easteal, Ailsa Korten, and R. Kumar for their contribution to the reported empirical studies, and to P.A. Jacomb the survey design and management.

References

Allen, P. A., Hall, R. J., Druley, J. A., Smith, A. F., Sanders, R. E. and Murphy, M. D. (2001). How shared are age-related influences on cognitive and non cognitive variables? *Psychology and Aging*, **16**, 532–549.

Anstey, K. J. and Christensen, H. (2000). Education, activity, health, BP and APOE as predictors of cognitive change in old age: A review. *Gerontology*, **46**, 163–177.

Anstey, K. J., Lord, S. R., and Smith (1996). Measuring human functional age: A review of empirical findings. *Experimental Aging Research*, **22**, 245–266.

Anstey, K. J. and Smith, G. A. (1999). Interrelationships among biological markers of aging, health, activity, acculturation and cognitive performance in older adults. *Psychology and Aging*, **14**, 615–618.

Anstey, K. J., Lord, S. R., and Williams, P. (1997). Strength in the lower limbs, visual contrast sensitivity and simple reaction time predict cognition in older women. *Psychology and Aging*, **12**, 137–144.

Anstey, K. J., Luszcz, M. A., and Sanchez, L. (2001). A reevaluation of the common factor theory of shared variance among age, sensory function, and cognitive function in older adults. *Journal of Gerontology: B Psychological Sciences*, **56**, P3–11.

Anstey, K. Stankov, L., and Lord, S. (1993). Primary aging, secondary aging, and intelligence. *Psychology and Aging*, 562–570.

Baltes, P. and Lindenberger, U. (1997). Emergence of a powerful connection between sensory and cognitive functions across the adult life span: a new window to the study of cognitive aging? *Psychology and Aging*, **12**(1), 12–21.

Barzilai, N. and Shuldiner, A. R. (2001). Searching for human longevity genes: the future history of gerontology in the post-genomic era. *Journal of Gerontology: A Medical Sciences*, **56**, M83–7.

Birren, J. E. and Cunningham, W. (1985). Research on the psychology of aging: Principles, concepts and theory. In J.E. Birren and W. Schaie (eds), *Handbook of the Psychology of Aging* (2nd ed, pp. 3–34). New York: Van Nostrand Reinhold.

Bookheimer, S. Y., Strojwas, M. H., Cohen, M. S., Saunders, A. M., Pericak-Vance, M. A., Mazziotta, J. C., and Small, G. W. (2000). Patterns of brain activation in people at risk for Alzheimer's disease. *New England Journal of Medicine*, **343**, 450–6.

Bollen, K. A. (1989). *Structural Equations with Latent Variables*. New York: Wiley.

Christensen, H., Mackinnon, A. J., Korten, A., and Jorm, A. F. (2001). The 'common cause hypothesis' of cognitive aging: Evidence for a common factor but also specific associations of age with vision and grip strength in a cross-sectional analysis. *Psychology and Aging*, **16**, 588–599.

Christensen, H., Mackinnon, A. J., Jorm, A. F., Korten, A. E., Jacomb, P., Hofer, S. M., and Hendersen, S. (in press). The Canberra Longitudinal Study: Design, aims, methodology, outcomes, and recent empirical investigations. *Aging, Neuropsychology and Cognition.*

Christensen, H., Mackinnon, A. J., Korten, A. E, Jorm, A. F., Henderson, A. S., Jacomb, P. A., and Rodgers, B. (1999). Are changes in sensory disability, reaction time, and grip strength associated with changes in memory and crystallized Intelligence? A longitudinal analysis in an elderly community sample. *Gerontology*, **46**, 276–292.

Deary, I. J. (2000). *Looking Down on Human Intelligence.* Oxford, UK: Oxford University Press.

Dik, M. G., Jonker, C., Bouter, L. M., Geerlings, M. I., van Kamp, G. J., and Deeg, D. J. (2000). APOE-epsilon4 is associated with memory decline in cognitively impaired elderly. *Neurology*, **54**, 1492–1497.

Fox, N. C., Counsens, S., Scahill, R., Harvey, R. J., Rossor, M. N. (2000). Using serial registered brain magnetic resonance imaging to measure disease progression in Alzheimer's disease. Power calculations and estimates of sample size to detect treatment effects. *Archives of Neurology*, **57**, 339–344.

Fox, N. C., Freeborough, P. A., and Rossor, M. N. (1996). Visualization and quantification of rate of atrophy in Alzheimer's disease. *Lancet*, **348**, 94–97.

Fox, N. C., Warrington, E. K., Seiffer, A. L., Agnew, S. K., and Rossor, M. N. (1998). Presymptomatic cognitive deficits in individuals at risk of familial Alzheimer's disease. A longitudinal study. *Brain*, **121**, 1631–1639.

Fox, N. C., Scahill, R. I., Crum, W. R., and Rossor, M. N. (1999). Correlation between rates of brain atrophy and cognitive decline in AD. *Neurology*, **52**, 1687–1689.

Friedrich, U., Griese, E., Schwab, M., Fritz, P., Thon, K., and Klotz, U. (2000). Telomere length in different tissues of elderly patients. *Mechanisms of Ageing Development*, **119**, 89–99.

Gallo, J. J., Anthony, J. C., and Muthén, B. O. (1994). Age differences in the symptoms of depression: a latent trait analysis. *Journal of Gerontology: Psychological Sciences*, **49**, 251–264.

Garde, E., Mortensen, E. L., Krabbe, K., Rostrup, E., and Larsson, H. B. W. (2000). Relation between age-related decline in intelligence and cerebral white matter hyperintensities in healthy octogenarians: a longitudinal study. *Lancet*, **356**, 628–634.

Hofer, S. M. and Sliwinski, M. J. (2001). Understanding ageing: An evaluation of research designs for assessing the interdependence of ageing-related changes. *Gerontology*, **47**, 341–352.

Hofer, S. M., Christensen, H., Mackinnon, A. J., Korten, A. E., Jorm, A. F., Henderson, A. S, and Easteal, S. (2002). Change in cognitive functioning associated with apoE genotype in a community sample of older adults. *Psychology and Aging*, **17**, 194–208.

Jack, C. R., Petersen, R. C., Xu, Y., O'Brien, P. C., Smith, G. E., Ivnik, R. J., Tangalos, E. G., and Kokmen, E. (1998). Rate of median temporal lobe atrophy in typical aging and Alzheimer's disease. *Neurology*, **51**, 993–999.

Jack, C. R., Petersen, R. C., Xu, Y., O'Brien, P. C., Smith, G. E., Ivnik, R. J., Boeve, B. F., Tangalos, E.G., and Kokmen E. (2000). Rates of hippocampal atrophy correlate with change in clinical status in aging and AD. *Neurology*, **55**, 484–489.

Kaye, J. A., Swihart, T., Howieson, D., Dame, A., Moore, M. M., Karnos, T., Camicioli, R. M., Ball, M., Oken, B., and Sexton, G. (1997). Volume loss of the hippocampus and temporal lobe in healthy elderly persons destined to develop dementia. *Neurology*, **48**, 1297–1304.

Lindenberger, U. and Baltes, P. (1994). Sensory functioning and intelligence in old age: A strong connection. *Psychology and Aging*, **9**, 339–335.

Lindenberger, U. and Potter, U. (1998). The complex nature of unique and shared effects in hierarchical linear regression: Implications for developmental psychology. *Psychological Methods*, **3**, 218–230.

Lundberg, A. S., Hahn, W. C., Gupta, P., and Weinberg, R. A. (2000). Genes involved in senescence and immortalization. *Current Opinion in Cell Biology*, **12**, 705–709.

Marx, J. (2000). Chipping away at the causes of aging. *Science*, 287, 2390.

McArdle, J. J. (1988). Dynamic by structural equation modeling of repeated measures data. In J. R. Nesselroade and R. B. Cattell (eds), *Handbook of Multivariate Experimental Psychology* (pp. 561–614). New York: Plenum.

Moffat, S. D., Szekely, C. A., Zonderman, A. B., Kabani, N. J., and Resnick, S. M. (2000). Longitudinal change in hipoocampal volume as a function of apolipoprotein E genotype. *Neurology*, **55**, 134–136.

Mueller, E. A., Moore, M. M., Kerr, D. C. R., Sexton, G., Camicioli, R. M., Howieson, D. B., Quinn, J. F., and Kaye, J. A. (1998). Brain volume preserved in healthy elderly through the eleventh decade. *Neurology*, **51**, 1555–1562.

Muthén, B. (1988). Some uses of structural equation modelling in validity studies: extending IRT to external variables. In H. Wainer and H.I. Braun (eds), *Test Validity* (pp. 213–238). Hillsdale, NJ: Lawrence Erlbaum.

Rabbitt, P. M. (1993). Does it all go together when it goes? The Nineteenth Bartlett Memorial Lecture. *Quarterly Journal of Experimental Psychology*, A, **41**, 385–434.

Raz, N. (2000). Aging of the brain and its impact on cognitive performance: integration of structural and functional findings. In F. Craik and T. Salthouse *et al. The Handbook of the Psychology of Aging and Cognition* (pp. 1–90). New Jersey: Lawrence Erlbaum Associates.

Salthouse T. A. and Czaja S. J. (2000). Structural constraints on process explanations in cognitive aging. *Psychology and Aging*, **15**, 44–55.

Salthouse, T. A. (1999). From the present to the future. *Gerontology*, **45**, 345–347.

Salthouse, T. A., Hambrick, D. Z., and McGuthry, K. E. (1998). Shared age-related influences on cognitive and noncognitive variables. *Psychology and Aging*, 13, 486–500.

Sliwinski, M. and Hofer, S. (1999). How strong is the evidence for mediational hypotheses of age-related memory loss? *Gerontology*, **45**, 351–354.

Schmidt, R., Fazekas, F., Kapeller, P., Schmidt, H., and Hartung, H. (1999). MRI white matter hyperintensities. Three year follow-up of the Austrian Stroke Prevention Study. *Neurology*, **53**, 132–139.

Troller, J. N. and Valenzuela, M. J. (2001). Brain ageing in the new millennium. *Australian and New Zealand Journal of Psychiatry*, **35**, 788–805.

Wahlund, L., Almkvist, O., Basun, H., and Julin, P. (1996). MRI in successful aging, A 5-year follow-up study from eighth to ninth decade of life. *Magnetic Resonance Imaging*, **14**, 601–608.

Ylikosky, R., Salonen, O., Mantyla, R., Ylikosky, A., Keskivaara, P., Leskela, M., and Erkinjuntti, T. (2000). Hippocampal and temporal lobe atrophy and age-related decline in memory. *Acta Neurologica Scandinavica*, **101**, 273–278.

Chapter 12

New frontiers in genetic influences on cognitive aging

Nancy L. Pedersen

Introduction

During the past 30 years considerable strides have been made in demonstrating that genetic effects are of importance for cognitive abilities. The first steps taken were typically to demonstrate that genetic variation contributed significantly to individual differences for various measures of cognitive functioning, both specific and general abilities. Most of the early studies were based on cross-sectional analyses of either twins or family members. Very few of these studies ever looked at age-related differences and even fewer focused on the consequences of finding genetic influences for cognitive aging. During the 1980s and 1990s a number of longitudinal studies of aging in twins were established, and at the same time considerable methodological advances were made for analyzing true age-related change. As a consequence, the new frontier of genetic influences on cognitive aging will be focused on the interface between methodological advancements in modeling cognitive change, topics that are of relevance for cognitive aging, and applications to genetically informative populations.

In this chapter I focus on providing a brief overview of some of the models and results that have emanated from twin studies of aging, and then proceed to describing the areas that represent new frontiers.

Genetic influences

In contrast to most studies of behavioral phenotypes that focus on normative differences in means across the lifespan, quantitative and behavioral genetic approaches focus on variances, that is to say individual differences, and sources of interindividual variation. The student of general genetics will know that with a simple additive model, that is to say with additive affects between alleles of locus, and having only two or three loci available that may be influencing a trait, a normal distribution of the trait will arise in the population. On top of this there may be environmental factors that are also contributing to variation in a trait and these environmental factors may be working in interaction with the genetic factors. Thus, there are both multiple genes and multiple environments, each with a small effect, which may be influencing a trait at the intracellular, extracellular and organismic level. Thus far the focus has been on looking at these genetic and environment influences in an anonymous fashion, characterizing the extent to which the aggregate of genetic effects contribute to variation in a population, without specifying a particular locus, a specific allele, or a specific environmental influence. Thus the total variation is divided into anonymous genetic and environmental variation and the proportion of the total variation that is due to genetic variation is termed to heritability. Heritability tells us the extent to which individual differences among us are due to genetic differences. This is a population-based parameter that tells nothing about the individual, nor does it say anything about mean group differences. However, it does give us an effect size indicating the extent to which genetic effects might be of import-ance in a population. There are numerous textbooks that describe how heritability can be quantified using genetically informative populations (Plomin, DeFries, McClearn *et al.*, 2001). In essence the design as applied to family, twin and adoption studies is to fit a model of expected correlations to observed correlations. An example of the model as applied to twins is described in Figure 12.1. The covariation between twin A and twin B can be due to sharing genetic variation, having in common environmental influences attributable to the rearing environment (Es) or due to other types of shared environments post rearing (Ec). Note that there are also non-shared environ-mental influences that do not contribute to covariation among family

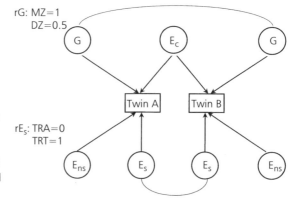

Fig. 12.1 Path model for analysis of twin data. Squares represent measured phenotypes in twin 1 and twin 2. Circles represent latent variables, in this case genetic, shared environmental and non-shared environmental sources of variation.

members and hence have no correlation or path between them. These are also called within-family influences.

Evidence from twin studies of cognitive aging

There are currently five longitudinal studies of cognitive aging in twins, all of which are in Scandinavia (McClearn *et al.*, 1997; Pedersen *et al.*, 1991; Gold, Malmberg, McClearn *et al.*, 2002; McGue and Christensen, 2001). In Sweden there is the Swedish Adoption Twin Study of Aging (SATSA), a study of twins reared apart and reared together, the OCTO-Twin Study of origins of variation in the oldest old with intact twin pairs tested at the age of 80 or older, the GENDER study of sex differences in normal aging using unlike sex twins, and a longitudinal study of aging in Danish twins. In the United States there is also a study of aging, the Minnesota Twin Study of Adult Development and Aging (Finkel, Whitfield, and McGue, 1995).

The first step in evaluating genetics of cognitive aging is to demonstrate that genetic influences are indeed important for the trait of interest. Figure 12.2 summarizes the results for general cognitive abilities and for aggregates of specific cognitive abilities from SATSA, OCTO-Twin and the Danish study. Note that SATSA twins represent the 'young-old' as the age range was from 50 to 85 at the first measurement occasion, whereas in the Danish study the twins were 75 or older and in OCTO-Twin the pairs were 80 years of age or older. Furthermore, the Danish study did not have specific tests of cognitive abilities and hence the results are reported only for the general ability composite. In the figure we see that there are differences both across studies (which may represent proxies for age groups) as well as across measures within the same domain. Hence, it appears as though the relative importance of genetic effects is greater for the younger old in SATSA than the older old in Denmark and OCTO-Twin for the first principle component as well as for spatial abilities. For verbal and speeded measures, there

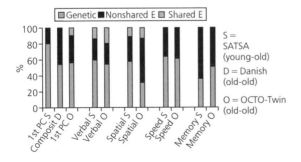

Fig. 12.2 Relative proportions of total variance due to genetic, nonshared environmental, and shared environmental influences from three twin studies of aging.

appear to be few age-related differences in heritability whereas for memory, heritability is lower for the younger than the older old.

There are some important principles to keep in mind when reviewing cross-sectional results of this nature. First, the importance of genetic effects is genotype-specific even within a domain. Thus, just because genetic effects may be of one importance for spatial abilities does not mean that they need to be of the same importance for verbal abilities or memory. Second, it is important to realize that the relative importance of genetic effects can change across the lifespan. Genes can turn on and turn off or be expressed differently depending on the phase in life. Similarly, there may be new environmental influences that are coming into play or we may be accumulating environmental experiences as we age. Thus, what we can expect to see is an even more complex causal nexus in which both genetic and environmental factors may be changing considerably in their importance throughout the lifespan.

The fact that genetic and environmental influences can change with age makes studies of their relative importance particularly challenging when evaluating twins. One particular challenge has to do with dealing with missing data. In order to provide information about covariation within a pair, both members of a pair must be participating. Thus, early longitudinal studies of heritability in cognitive aging evaluated pairs where both members had participated at both occasions (Plomin, Pedersen, Lichtenstein *et al.*, 1994). Analyses from this study suggested that heritability was quite stable across a three year period of time. Furthermore, the authors concluded that there were some changes not in the *relative* importance of environmental affects but in *which* environmental effects were of importance across the three-year interval. However, as mentioned before these data were based on SATSA-twins where both had participated at both points in time. Further exploration of this data set suggested that those twin pairs in which both members continued to participate across up to three occasions were the most stable both in their mean levels as well as in their similarity. In fact, the pattern of correlations for these pairs compared to those pairs in which both participated at only two occasions or both participated at only one occasion reassembles a pattern of terminal decline (Pedersen and Lichtenstein, 1997). During the mid-1990s, further developments in modeling techniques for twin and family studies were developed such that information from single responders as well as intact pairs could be included in the analyses. Finkel, Pedersen, Plomin *et al.*, (1998) applied such a technique to three occasions of measurement in SATSA (Figure 12.3). Rather than dividing total variation into proportions of genetic environmental variance, the results were depicted in terms of raw variance components. Furthermore, the sample was divided into age-cohorts that were

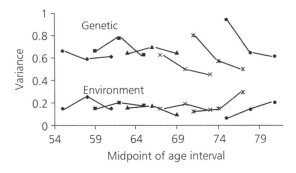

Fig. 12.3 Raw genetic and environmental variances for general cognitive abilities in a sliding interval analysis of SATSA. Adapted from SATSA.

slightly overlapping and moved these age-cohorts through the sample such that there were six cohorts evaluated, of which the first two and the last two are non-overlapping. A totally new conclusion arose from this presentation of the data. In the youngest cohorts both genetic and environmental variance was stable across the six year period of time. A very different pattern was seen for the older cohorts. In agreement with lifespan developmental theories (Baltes, Reese, and Lipsett, 1980), environmental variance increased somewhat across this period of time. However, quite unexpectedly, genetic variance within these cohorts decreased longitudinally. These longitudinal changes in genetic and environmental variance are consistent with the cross-sectional differences we see across the SATSA, Danish OCTO-Twin cohorts, suggesting that indeed environmental influences may be of somewhat greater importance in the oldest old, but that genetic influences are of less importance for general cognitive abilities in the oldest old.

Thus far none of the analyses for cognitive abilities have evaluated *decline* in cognitive function per se. Remember that twin analyses evaluate similarities within pairs. The similarity in any given twin pair might be a function not only of the individual twins' levels at any one point in time, but of entrance into a period of decline. Hence, there may be several factors that are contributing to dissimilarity within a pair such as, (a) timing of the onset of decline and (b) the slope of the decline. Furthermore, both the timing and the slope of decline may be a function of terminal decline (Berg, 1996). In Figure 12.4, three different hypothetical twins' trajectories are depicted. All three twins start at approximately the same baseline level. Twin A has a slight decline prior to the age of 70, after which there is more decline at a relatively shallow rate. Twin B has a very stable trajectory until the age of 73 at which point the twin declines sharply. Twin C has the same trajectory as twin B; however the timing of the onset of decline is shifted some five years later than twin B. If one was to evaluate age at onset, twins A and B would be more similar than twins B and C.

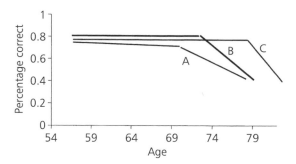

Fig. 12.4 Three hypothetical trajectories of cognitive ability.

However, if one was to evaluate slope, twins B and C would be much more similar. Thus, it is clear that techniques such as latent growth curve models (McArdle and Epstein, 1987) that evaluate not only intercept but also slope are essential for the appropriate evaluation of individual differences in cognitive aging. The application of these models to genetically informative populations with measures of cognition is clearly of foremost frontier for cognitive aging and will be discussed later in this chapter.

Multivariate analyses

Thus far the analyses that have been described have been univariate and evaluated the relative importance of genetic environmental factors at one point in time or in a longitudinal prospective. Parallel with demonstrating that genetic effects were indeed important for cognitive abilities, advancements were made in models for evaluating the extent to which genetic effects could explain the associations among measures. Thus, rather than taking separate measures and looking at them cross-sectionally or longitudinally there have also been attempts to assess the structure of cognitive aging and the associations within and among domains. Finkel *et al.*, using data from SATSA and MTSADA (Finkel, Pedersen, McGue *et al.*, 1995), used a multivariate quantitative genetic model to characterize the factor structure of cognitive abilities in young old and older old. At the same time that the phenotypic factor structure was evaluated, the genetic structure of the general cognitive abilities factor was also evaluated. The phenotypic structure differed by age groups. The loading of the speeded measure on the general factor was greater in the older than in the younger age group. Furthermore, the genetic influences were to a greater extent explained by genetic influences for speed than the other specific abilities. In a similar vain, a series of papers (Pedersen, Plomin, and McClearn, 1994), (Finkel, Pedersen *et al.*, 1995), (Petrill *et al.*, 1998) demonstrated that the more a cognitive ability loads on the general 'g' factor, the greater the proportion of variance in this measure is explained by genetic variance for general cognitive abilities. Furthermore, the extent to which genetic variance for speeded measures is shared with genetic variance for general abilities increases across age groups (Figure 12.5). In sum, these results using multivariate techniques indicate that genetic influences for speeded measures are increasingly important across the lifespan.

The role of speed in explaining age-related cognitive functioning was further explored in analyses of SATSA with a model (Figure 12.6) that separately tested paths between speeded measures and other cognitive measures, age and the cognitive measures, and age through speed to cognitive measures. Individual differences in speed were the most important predictor of individual differences in the other cognitive abilities. Age also was a significant contributor; however, much of the age related variation was mediated through

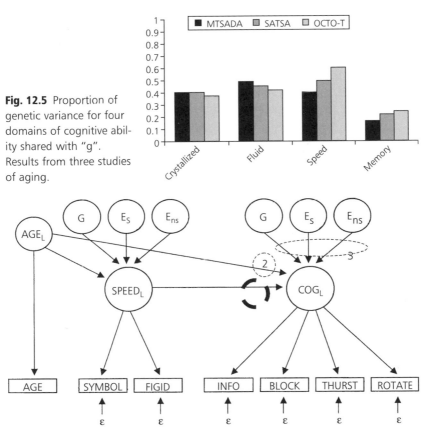

Fig. 12.5 Proportion of genetic variance for four domains of cognitive ability shared with "g". Results from three studies of aging.

Fig. 12.6 Path diagram describing the speed-age-cognitive abilities association.

speed. Finally, there were genetic and environmental influences on the separate ability measures independent of that for speed. These are three examples
of how multivariate analyses in a genetic perspective can contribute to our
understanding of the structure of cognitive abilities late in life. Clearly one
of the frontiers of cognitive aging would be to apply such an approach in
a longitudinal framework.

New frontiers

The future is incredibly exciting, as there are numerous new frontiers in which
the genetics of cognitive aging can be explored. Among those to be discussed
in the following are applications of latent growth curve models, inclusion of
covariates into these models, multivariate analyses in a longitudinal prospective, studying intraindividual variability, incorporating mortality into our
considerations and finally, molecular genetic analyses.

Latent growth modeling

It is difficult not to notice the burgeoning use of latent growth curve models in
studies of aging in general, and in some studies of cognitive aging in particular.
These models are very appealing as they provide the opportunity not only to
look at the intercept per se (baseline level) but also the slope of potential
change. From the behavior genetics point of view, characterizing the intercept
and slope in terms of group intercepts, group means and group slopes is
important. However, perhaps more interesting is to understand the nature of
individual differences about these parameters. In order to truly be informative
about change, these models require at least three points of measurement.
Fortunately, most of the studies of aging in twins have now at least three
points of measurement and as a consequence we are seeing many analyses
being applied to the data, the first of which is to characterize the data from
a phenotypic point of view.

Four occasions of measurement would be optimal in order to test whether
or not there is non-linear change and to test whether or not there is some
turning point at which decline accelerates. Thus far none of the existing twin
studies of aging have applied latent growth curve models to all four points of
time. However, researchers working with SATSA have adapted a spline model,
based on the latent growth curve model described by McArdle (McArdle,
Prescott, Hamagami *et al.*, 1998), in order to test whether or not there are two
slopes that describe cognitive functioning. If there are two slopes at what age
do these slopes differ? If they differ is there an acceleration of the decline in
the aging process? This model is depicted in Figure 12.7 and examples of the

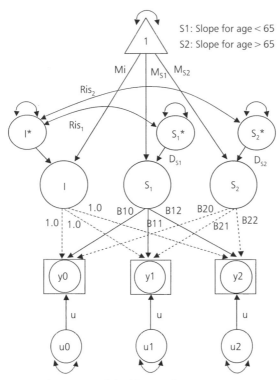

Fig. 12.7 Latent growth curve model with two slopes.

results of this model are summarized in Figure 12.8. In the upper left hand quadrant of Figure 12.8 the raw data on general cognitive ability scores from 40 per cent of the SATSA sample are plotted. There appears to be considerable variability and although mean values appear to be decreasing across age, the variability appears to be relatively stable. Application of the model depicted in Figure 12.7 to these data (Finkel, Reynolds, McArdle *et al.*, 2003) demonstrates that two slopes are indeed the most appropriate for describing the data. Mean levels are relatively stable until the age of 65, after which there is considerable decline. However, the variance is not changing significantly across the age range. Similarly, total variance did not change in the cohort sequential analysis described by Finkel earlier (Finkel *et al.*, 1998). Nevertheless, even with stable total variance there were age-related changes in genetic variance in the older cohort. A more pertinent question for further explanation of individual differences in the slopes is to ask whether or not there is significant slope variance, which would indicate systematic individual differences. Indeed, there was significant variance around the group slope both on slope

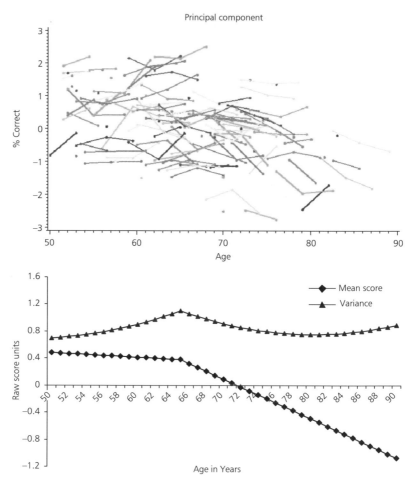

Fig. 12.8 Random sample of individual trajectories (upper left hand corner) and predicted means and variance from two spline growth model of the first principal component.

one and slope two for principal component. Of the ten cognitive measures that showed a slope, seven showed marked individual variation around the group decrement rate. Analyses using the spline model provided evidence for accelerating decline in some measures, evidence that the typical age at which decline accelerates is typically around 65 depending on the measure, and that there were different patterns of decline for different cognitive abilities. Furthermore, the analyses indicated that there was more systematic variation in change for some measures than for others, and it is this variation in change that would be particularly interesting to evaluate in terms of genetic and environmental influences.

Having demonstrated that there are individual differences about the intercept and about the slope or slopes, the next obvious step is to apply a growth curve model that uses information from both members of a pair. Using data from the landmark New York twin study by Kallmann and Jarvik from the 1960s, McArdle and colleagues (McArdle *et al.*, 1998) applied a single slope growth curve model to the WAIS measures of block design and vocabulary. The results provide a very poignant demonstration of how very different genetic effects can influence decline versus overall (baseline) cognitive functioning. For example, for block design the rate of decline (slopes) shows substantial genetic variation. However, the overall heritability decreased across age from 63 per cent at age 60 to 35 per cent at age 90. This pattern of decrease in overall heritability for the measure is very similar to that found by SATSA researchers and that seen when contrasting cross-sectional results from SATSA and OCTO-Twin. Thus, for the first time we have an indication that not only may genetic effects be decreasing in the overall relative importance but that genetic effects are at the same time important for rate of decline, at least for this particular cognitive measure. In contrast, for vocabulary, rate of decline showed substantial environmental influences. In other words, genetic effects were not as important for individual variation in the slopes of this crystallized measure. Also in contrast to the results for block design, there was a relative stability of overall heritable variance across time going from 73 per cent at age 60 to 71 per cent at age 90. Not only are the means for vocabulary relatively stable, but the individual differences and the relative importance of genetic effects for these individual differences are stable across time. Nevertheless, decline – should there be any – appears to be mostly reflecting individual specific perhaps random environmental influences.

Similar analyses of the SATSA data, which although they cover a broad age range reflect longitudinal follow-ups of only six years per individual, suggest that the major source of variance contributing to individual differences in the intercept was genetic, whereas individual variation and slopes is primarily due to environmental influences (Reynolds, Gatz, and Pedersen, 1998). Indeed, for a block design there were *no* significant genetic influences on slopes. These findings differ considerably from those reported by McArdle *et al.* for the longitudinal New York study. It is unlikely that cultural differences alone explain the differences across studies as SATSA results have previously been shown to be quite consistent with findings in Minnesota and in Denmark. Methodological differences may describe the discrepancies. The model used in SATSA examines change over time within two age groups whereas the model based on the New York data considers change over age. Certainly further exploration of the consequences of different model parameterization such as the choice of centering ages, the choice of focusing on change over age versus change over time, whether or not subjects would become demented are to be kept into model etc. should be explored and new comparisons between studies made. Nevertheless, even though the SATSA analyses are very preliminary, these studies provide exciting indications of the potential for understanding the nature of individual differences in the cognitive aging process.

Considering covariates

Thus far, longitudinal growth curve models that have been applied to twin study data have addressed issues of centering on age, of centering on time, of the presence or absence of one or two slopes and variability around intercept and these slopes. These are certainly important first steps. However there are number of advancements that can be made as well. One clear extended model would be that which would include covariates where we not only evaluate the nature of mean levels and cognitive change but also the importance of a specified covariate, be it a measure of health, environmental exposure or genotypic exposure. One could imagine, for example, using education as a covariate where education could be correlated with the intercept or with the slope. Similarly one could evaluate whether or not individual differences around the slopes or around the intercepts are correlated with individual differences in education. Furthermore, one could test the extent to which the genetic influences on variability in intercepts and slopes differ as a function of educational level. These models are also closely related to issues of dynamic change. Models are being developed to test whether or not change in one measure is driving change in another measure. For example, do changes in fluid abilities drive changes in crystallized abilities or do changes in speed drive changes in other types of cognitive performance? Although complex, it would be most interesting to see what happens when these dynamic change models are incorporated into a twin framework.

Multivariate analyses in a longitudinal perspective

The multivariate analyses that were described earlier have thus far only been performed on cross-sectional data, despite the fact that many of the consequences results have been extrapolated to be descriptive of age-related changes. Clearly, longitudinal analyses that utilize multivariate designs are necessary in order to make true conclusions that are descriptive of aging processes and structural change. Thus, a third major new frontier would be developing multivariate models, whether they are a latent growth curve model or other structural models that incorporate both multivariate as well as longitudinal aspects. Only in this way will we truly understand what is happening with regard to the apparent speed related change in cognitive abilities with age.

Terminal decline

Another very important covariate that should be considered in the aging process is mortality. Many of the studies of cognitive aging are plagued by the confounds and selection biases that are inherent in studies where mortality is expected to be an aspect. The phenomenon of terminal decline has been characterized for a number of cognitive measures. Individuals who are close to death show a noticeable increasing trajectory with poorer performance the closer they are to death. Although there are a number of studies that have described the phenomenon of terminal decline, there are few studies that have evaluated what may be the mediators of terminal decline and how the terminal decline phenomenon per se may be influencing the results from analyses of cognitive aging (Berg, 1996). One way to approach this issue is to test whether or not measurable environmental or medical factors are contributing to the cognitive decline that is associated with mortality. Using such a model, Hassing *et al.* (2002) could demonstrate that much of the mortality-related cognitive decline in OCTO-Twin was related to cardiovascular health.

Another approach would be to evaluate the extent to which time to death is an important covariate for the shape of the growth curve function. One could imagine in principle centering the model on death rather than centering the model on age if one simply aggregated the data so that the last time of measurement for every individual would be the time of measurement closest to death and then set up the model backwards, so to speak. One might see that much what was thought of as random environmental variation around the slope could instead be viewed as systematic variation due to age at death. Unfortunately, it is difficult to implement such a latent growth curve model, particularly when the entire sample has not yet died; there are few methods by which one can accommodate censoring in such models.

Frailty models

Within the field of epidemiology and biostatistics, survival models are typically used to analyze age-related events. These models are able to take into account both left truncation and censoring. Yashin and colleagues have further developed these models such that the frailty or the underlying susceptibility to death can be evaluated in a twin-based model (Yashin and Iachine, 1995). Recently Ripatti and colleagues have developed a three stage frailty model such that the hazards of developing a disease, dying, or the combined frailty of going from a disease to death can be evaluated (Ripatti, Gatz, Pedersen *et al.*, 2003). The new frontier for cognitive aging will be the application of this kind of frailty model to evaluate cognitive decline. At present the models are only developed to evaluate dichotomous outcomes such as onset of a disease or death. However, one could imagine applying various criteria such as the standard error of the measurement indicator of cognitive decline (Schaie, 1989). With such models, one can ask whether or not genetic variation for decline actually reflects to some extent genetic influences on mortality.

Intraindividual variability

Thus far most of the descriptions of new frontiers have been focused on individual differences across the life span and/or spanning a great number of longitudinal occasions over a long time period. Nesselroade and colleagues have been at the forefront in considering aspects of intraindividual variability, that is to say whether or not there are recognizable, systematic patterns for an individual when measured at multiple occasions with a short intra-test interval (Nesselroade and Jones, 1991). Not only should this field of inquiry be considered at the phenotypic level as a frontier of cognitive aging but the interface between this topic and issues of genetic influences on intraindividual variability should be developed. Important questions should be answered whether or not the recognizable patterns of intraindividual variability themselves reflect the aging processes or whether or not they represent genetic variability. Are the same genetic influences that are reflected in interindividual differences responsible for the recognizable individual fluctuations that we see? Data concerning intraindividual variability have recently been collected in SATSA. Hopefully this information will give us an opportunity to address these issues for the first time in genetically informative samples.

Classical cognitive aging and information processing

Most of the studies of cognitive aging in genetically informative populations have used paper-and-pencil tests that were developed during the era of psychometric testing. Behavioral geneticists used these instruments because they were easily administered to large samples and because their very nature was well-adapted to an individual differences approach. Relatively few studies have focused on experiment-based assessments of cognitive aging. Hence, rather global measures of memory, verbal, spatial and perceptual speed performance have been utilized. One of the challenges that lie ahead is to incorporate measures that are typically assessed in a laboratory environment or that involved manipulations such as presentation of different stimuli in order to test for responses in particular brain areas. Both fields, cognitive aging as well as behavioral genetics, will benefit by incorporation of each others' methods into their designs. Studies of information processing, for example, could provide added information on individual differences by including family members in the study. Similarly, longitudinal studies of aging twins should incorporate experiment-based instruments. The greatest challenge, however, will be to meet the sample size requirements necessary to obtain adequate power in the behavioral genetic design but at the same time be able to perform adequately the arduous test taking procedures inherent in the experimental process.

Genes and cognitive aging

Ever since APOE-4 was demonstrated to be associated with Alzheimer's disease there have been numerous attempts to demonstrate that this susceptibility gene is related to cognitive impairment and cognitive decline. There currently several ongoing attempts, such as the work reported by Lars-Göran Nilsson, to test whether APOE-4 is associated with specific aspects of cognitive function and episodic memory. Genetic association studies evaluate whether mean levels in a trait differ as a function of a specific gene. In contrast to association studies, the behavioral genetic studies discussed earlier focus on variation rather than the mean. However, behavioral genetic analyses can also be used to evaluate the importance of a genetic association, that is to say how much of the genetic variance can be accounted for by any specific gene.

There are currently numerous attempts to identify genes that may be associated with cognitive abilities, however very few of these attempts are focused on elderly samples. Thus far these studies have been disappointed by the lack of significant, replicable findings. Despite our enthusiasm based on the substantial effect found for APOE, as well as the substantial heritability estimated for most cognitive abilities, none of the genes being evaluated thus far has demonstrated a significant affect of notable size. Why are we failing to demonstrate significant associations when we have already shown that one gene, APOE-4, is so important, at least for Alzheimer's disease? The problem lies in effect sizes and the very nature of additive genetic influences. The variation seen is most likely a result of many genes, each of small effect that is adding up to contribute to the variation in the traits of interest. Furthermore, these genes may be interacting with each other or interacting with the environment. Thus, it is unlikely that we will find any one gene of substantial effect and perhaps not even clusters of say two or three genes that are of importance for cognitive decline. Rather we may need to be focusing on genes in pathways that we feel may be of importance for brain functioning, realizing that there is a complex nexus such that any single gene or any single environment is expected to result in a relatively small effect. Furthermore, we should take lessons from the twin studies of aging, which demonstrate that for some aspects of cognitive aging genetic effects actually decrease in their importance later in life. Hence, we would do well to be using different approaches to studying influences on baseline level versus those that may be contributing to change.

Despite disappointments thus far, efforts to explore this new frontier should not be discouraged. However, their efforts should perhaps be put into perspective. When genes are found that influence specific aspects of the aging process we will gain a much greater understanding of the mechanisms by which neurological and physiological processes are important. These findings and the hope of these findings should not be seen as a panacea. One might liken the process to that of great the explorers traveling across the North American continent. After considerable encouragement by finding the St Lawrence Seaway, they were convinced that if they traveled further westward they would find a short-cut to the Pacific. Instead they encountered massive prairies, forests and then mountains: none of which, however, were insurmountable.

In conclusion

The interface between genetics and cognitive aging is a new frontier that has both multiple starting points and numerous crossroads. It is a field with enormous potential that can only be enhanced by further incorporation of sound studies of cognitive science in genetically informative populations.

Acknowledgements

Supported in part by grants from NIA (AG04563, AG10175)

References

Baltes, P. B., Reese, H. W., and Lipsett, L. P. (1980). Life span developmental psychology. *Annual Review of Psychology*, **31**, 65–110.

Berg, S. (1996). Aging, behavior, and terminal decline. In J. E. Birren and K. W. Schaie (eds), *Handbook of the Psychology of Aging* (4th ed., pp. 323–337). San Diego, CA: Academic Press.

Finkel, D., Pedersen, N. L., McGue, M., and McClearn, G. E. (1995). Heritability of cognitive abilities in adult twins: Comparison of Minnesota and Swedish data. *Behavior Genetics*, **25** (5) 421–431.

Finkel, D., Pedersen, N. L., Plomin, R., and McClearn, G. E. (1998). Longitudinal and cross-sectional twin data on cognitive abilities in adulthood: The Swedish Adoption/Twin Study of Aging. *Developmental Psychology*, **34** (6), 1400–1413.

Finkel, D., Reynolds, C. A., McArdle, J. J., Gatz, M., and Pedersen, N. L. (2003). Latent growth curve analyses of accelerating decline in cognitive abilities in late adulthood. *Developmental Psychology,* **39**, 535–550.

Finkel, D., Whitfield, K., and McGue, M. (1995). Genetic and environmental influences on functional age: A twin study. *Journal of Gerontology: Psychological Sciences,* **50B** (2), P104–P113.

Gold, C. H., Malmberg, B., McClearn, G. E., Pedersen, N. L., and Berg, S. (2002). Gender and health: A study of older unlike-sex twins. *Journal of Gerontology: Social Sciences,* **57B**, 168–176.

Hassing, L. B., Johansson, B., Berg, S., Nilsson, S. E., Pedersen, N. L., Hofer, S. M., and McClearn, G. (2002). Terminal decline and markers of cerebro- and cardiovascular disease: Findings from a longitudinal study of the oldest old. *Journal of Gerontology: Psychological Sciences,* **57**, 268–276.

McArdle, J. J. and Epstein, D. (1987). Latent growth curves within developmental structural equation models. *Child Development,* **58**, 110–133.

McArdle, J. J. Prescott, C. A., Hamagami, F., and Horn, J. L. (1998). A contemporary method for developmental-genetic analyses of age changes in intellectual abilities. *Developmental Neuropsychology,* **14**, 69–114.

McClearn, G. E., Johansson, B., Berg, S., Pedersen, N. L., Ahern, F., Petrill, S. A., and Plomin, R. (1997). Substantial genetic influence on cognitive abilities in twins 80 or more years old. *Science,* **276,** 1560–1563.

McGue, M., and Christensen, K. (2001). The heritability of cognitive functioning in very old adults: Evidence from Danish twins aged 75 years and older. *Psychology and Aging,* **16**, 272–280.

Nesselroade, J. R. and Jones, C. J. (1991). Multi-modal selection effects in the study of adult development: A perspective on multivariate, replicated, single-subject, repeated measures designs. *Experimental Aging Research,* **17** (1), 21–27.

Schaie, K. W. (1989). The hazards of cognitive aging. *The Gerontologist,* **29**, 484–493.

Pedersen, N. L. and Lichtenstein, P. (1997). Biometric analyses of human abilities. In C. Cooper and V. Varma (eds), *Processes in Individual Differences* (pp. 125–147). London: Routledge.

Pedersen, N. L., McClearn, G. E., Plomin, R., Nesselroade, J. R., Berg, S., and de Faire, U. (1991). The Swedish Adoption Twin Study of Aging: An update. *Acta Geneticae Medicae et Gemellologiae (Roma),* **40,** 7–20.

Pedersen, N. L., Plomin, R., and McClearn, G. E. (1994). Is there G beyond g? (Is there genetic influence on specific cognitive abilities independent of genetic influence on general cognitive ability?). *Intelligence,* **18,** 133–143.

Petrill, S. A., Plomin, R., Berg, S., Johansson, B., Pedersen, N. L., Ahern, F., and McClearn, G. E. (1998). The genetic and environmental relationship between general and specific cognitive abilities in twins age 80 and older. *Psychological Science,* **9** (3), 25–31.

Plomin, R., DeFries, J. C., McClearn, G. E., and McGuffin, P. (2001). *Behavioral Genetics* (4th ed.). New York: Worth Publishers.

Plomin, R., Pedersen, N. L., Lichtenstein, P., and McClearn, G. E. (1994). Variability and stability in cognitive abilities are largely genetic later in life. *Behavior Genetics,* **24** (3), 207–215.

Reynolds, C. A., Gatz, M., and Pedersen, N. L. (1998). Sources of individual variation contributing to change in cognitive abilities. *Behavior Genetics,* **28 (6),** 479.

Ripatti, S., Gatz, M., Pedersen, N. L., and Palmgren, J. (2003). Three-state frailty model for age at onset of dementia and death in Swedish twins. *Genetic Epidemiology,* **24,** 139–149.

Yashin, A. I., and Iachine, I. A. (1995). Genetic analysis of durations: Correlated frailty model applied to survival of Danish twins. *Genetic Epidemiology,* **12 (5),** 529–538.

Chapter 13

Hormonal effects on cognition in adults

Agneta Herlitz and Julie E. Yonker

In the search for biological influences on cognition, steroid hormones have proven to be engaging variables in psychological research for over two decades. Hormones have been claimed to influence a variety of cognitive abilities from spatial and verbal abilities to various forms of memory. Hormones and cognition have been compared both within and between men and women. The goal of this present chapter is to present the rationale for studying sex hormones in relation to cognition and to review and discuss hormonal influences on cognitive functioning in adulthood and old age. We will focus on the potential role of steroid hormones on sex differences in cognitive function across the adult life span. Testosterone (T), in particular, will be examined for its possible influence on spatial abilities in both men and women. Additionally, we will address questions regarding the effect on cognition of endogenous estrogen levels in pre- and postmenopausal women, the contribution of hormone replacement therapy (HRT) on cognition in postmenopausal women, and the potentially protective effect of estrogen for the development of Alzheimer's disease. Promising areas for future research will also be highlighted.

Why are hormones appealing with respect to cognition?

Studies on the relation between hormones and cognition have focused not only on the organizational role steroid hormones may play during brain development, but also on the activational role they are hypothesized to have on behavior throughout life. In the present chapter we will concentrate primarily on the activational role hormones may have on behavior.

Before presenting the rationale behind theories claiming an activational role of hormones, we will briefly outline the evidence for hormonal influence on brain organization and thereby hormonal influence on cognition. As is well known, the sex chromosomes (XX and XY) determine genetic sex in humans. An important prenatal function of these chromosomes is to determine whether the primordial gonads will differentiate as ovaries or testes. The subsequent secretions from the differentiated gonads start a chain of events leading to phenotypic sexual differentiation, including the development of internal and external genitalia, as well as the neural and behavioral characteristics associated with the two sexes (Collaer and Hines, 1995; MacLusky and Naftolin, 1981; Wilson, George, and Griffin, 1981). In general, the organizing effect of gonadal sex hormones is believed to influence feminization and masculinization. In mammals, very early exposure to androgens (i.e., masculinizing hormones) is believed to result in defeminization and masculinization of anatomy and behavior (Arnold and Gorski, 1984), whereas prevention or reduction of androgen exposure feminizes and prevents masculinization (MacLusky and Naftolin, 1981).

In humans, female masculinization from excessive fetal androgen exposure is evident in girls with congenital adrenal hyperplasia (CAH). CAH is a rare disorder in which a genetic mutation on the short arm of chromosome 6 results in a deficient enzyme in the adrenal cortex. This deficiency results in unusually high levels of androgens during gestation in the affected CAH boys and girls. When the cognitive performance of CAH girls has been studied, results show they perform at a higher level than their female controls on tasks assessing visuospatial performance (i.e., tasks in which men typically outperform women), but lower on tasks assessing perceptual speed (i.e., tasks in which women usually outperform men) (Berenbaum, 2001; Hampson, Rovet, and Altmann, 1998). Girls with CAH have also been found to prefer masculine toys rather than feminine toys, and have more male playmates than non-affected girls (Berenbaum and Hines, 1992; Servin, Nordenström *et al.*, 2003).

For many animal behaviors, activational and organizational effects are believed to act in concert, meaning the appropriate adult activating hormone is necessary to reveal the underlying organizational contributions of that hormone during development (Collaer and Hines, 1995). Most research has focused on the activational role of estrogen (i.e., estradiol), but androgens (i.e., testosterone (T), dihydrotestosterone, and androstenedione) have also attracted some interest. In addition to the empirical evidence we will subsequently present, there are also plausible biological mechanisms to support a role for estrogen and T in cognitive function. For example, estrogen receptors can be found in a variety of brain areas, such as the cerebral cortex, hypothalamus, pituitary, and the limbic system, including the amygdala and the hippocampus (Bixo, Bäckström, Winblad *et al.*, 1995; Ciocca and Vargas Roig, 1995). T receptors can be found in the hypothalamus (Krithivas, *et al.*, 1999). The general rationale for androgens' and estrogens' activational role on cognition is that they act by binding to their specific receptors within brain cells, thereby influencing the actions of the brain area in which the receptors are located. Much research has therefore focused on the localization of such receptors in the brain.

Estrogen and T are common for both sexes, although the levels are markedly different in men and women. Women undergo large variations in estrogen and progesterone levels across the natural menstrual cycle, with estrogen levels high in mid-cycle (i.e., the preovulatory phase). Approximately five to ten days before menstruation, progesterone levels are high, and estrogen levels dip just slightly from their mid-cycle peak. Both estrogen and progesterone levels are very low at the onset of menstruation and stay low for several days, before estrogen starts rising again. Men experience changes in T levels not only across the seasons, but also within the course of the day. Typically, the levels of T are higher in the morning than in the afternoon (Moffat and Hampson, 1996), and higher in the autumn than in the spring (Kimura and Hampson, 1994). In addition, there are great hormonal variations across the life span for both men and women. For women, levels of estrogen are low before menarche, relatively high during their reproductive years, and decrease at menopause to levels as before menarche. It is interesting to note that women's estrogen levels are often lower after menopause than are adult men's estrogen levels (Greenspan and Strewler, 1997). T levels are similar in boys and girls before puberty, but after puberty T increases drastically for men with only a modest increase for girls, where it basically stays throughout life. T levels decrease with increasing age for men, with mean values being approximately two-thirds of those at age 25 (Vermeulen, 1991), although all male T levels are substantially higher than the levels for women.

Sex differences in cognition

It is common knowledge that men and women differ in their performance on certain cognitive tasks. The prevailing opinion has been that women perform at a higher level than men on tasks assessing verbal ability, and that men typically perform at a higher level than women on visuospatial and mathematical tasks (Halpern, 1992). However, the picture is slightly more complicated. Assuming a female advantage in verbal abilities, it is clear that women are not performing at a higher level than men on all verbal tasks (Hyde and Linn, 1988). There is female superiority on tasks assessing verbal production (e.g., verbal fluency and speeded articulation), as well as on speed and proficiency of solving anagrams. By contrast, there are typically no differences between men and women on tasks measuring vocabulary and reading comprehension, and men may even perform at a higher level than women on analogies. Thus, the advantage women have over men with regard to verbal ability appears to be restricted to verbal production tasks and anagram solving.

Men are reported to perform at a higher level than women on most visuospatial tasks (Voyer, Voyer, and Bryden, 1995). Visuospatial tasks may divided into mental rotation (i.e., the ability to mentally rotate an object in space), spatial perception (i.e., the ability locate the horizontal or the vertical while ignoring distracting information), and spatial visualization (i.e., the ability to manipulate complex spatial information when several stages are needed to produce the correct solution). Although men perform at a higher level than women on all these tasks, mental rotation tasks typically yield the largest sex difference, with the effect size, d,[1] around -0.90. The overall difference is also substantial in tasks assessing spatial perception ($d = -0.64$), but much less pronounced in spatial visualization ($d = -0.13$).

We have shown that women outperform men in verbal episodic memory tasks (see Herlitz, Nilsson and Bäckman, 1997, for an overview). The episodic memory tasks where women have excelled include word recall (Kramer, Delis, and Daniel, 1988), word recognition (Hill *et al.*, 1995), story recall (Hultsch, Masson, and Small, 1991; Zelinski, Gilewski, and Schaie, 1993), name recognition (Larrabee and Crook, 1993), face recognition (Wahlin *et al.*, 1993), and concrete picture recall and recognition of concrete pictures (Herlitz, Airaksinen, and Nordström, 1999).

In contrast, we have demonstrated that men perform at a higher level than women on episodic memory tasks requiring visuospatial processing (see Figure 13.1a; Lewin, Wolgers, and Herlitz, 2001). In addition, there are typically no sex differences on non-verbal episodic memory tasks (see Figure 13.1b; Herlitz *et al.*, 1999). These data seem to suggest that the higher performance by women on episodic memory tasks with a verbal component could be a result of the female advantage seen in verbal abilities, and especially in verbal production (Hyde and Linn, 1988). However, the few studies investigating the impact of verbal fluency on episodic memory tasks have found only partial support for this hypothesis, since the sex differences in verbal episodic memory tasks remain after controlling for verbal fluency (Herlitz *et al.*, 1997, 1999). Contrary to the verbal ability hypothesis are findings that no differences exist between men and women in the equally verbal primary and semantic memory tasks (Herlitz *et al.*, 1997).

---

[1] Effect size, $d = (M_{women} - M_{men})/Sd_{total}$. A positive value of d indicates that women performed at a higher level than men; a negative value indicated that men performed at a higher level than women.

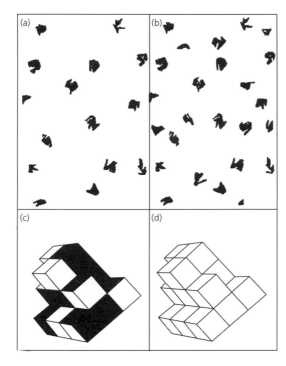

Fig. 13.1 Examples of non-verbal (a, b) and visuospatial episodic memory tasks (c, d) at presentation (a, c) and rest (b, d). Permission sought.

Another finding that runs counter to the verbal ability hypothesis is that women have repeatedly been shown to perform at a higher level than men on non-verbal face recognition tasks (Lewin and Herlitz, in press; McKelvie, 1987). Although faces could be hypothesized to have a verbal component, or be verbalizable (e.g., 'a handsome, young, dark man'), this does not assist women in their face recognition performance. By contrast, men seem to rely more than women do on their verbal abilities (Lewin and Herlitz, 2002). In the same study, evidence suggested that women's higher performance in face recognition was due to an advantage in recognizing female faces. Specifically, men and women recognized male faces with the same proficiency, and men performed similarly for male and female faces. Why women recognize female faces with such expertise remains unclear. It is also not apparent why face recognition is highly correlated with intelligence in men, whereas there is a zero order correlation between face recognition performance and intelligence in women (Herlitz and Yonker, 2002).

When discussing hormones as a link to cognitive sex differences across the adult lifespan, periods of hormonal alteration are particularly relevant to consider. Results showing that there are no, or very small, sex differences before puberty would seem to indicate that the hormonal changes associated with puberty (ages 11 to 18) are tied to the emergence of sex differences in cognition. Similarly, decreasing sex differences around menopause (ages 45 to 55) would also point in that direction.

However, very few studies have addressed this issue. A meta-analysis on sex differences in visuospatial abilities investigated the magnitude of such sex differences before age 13, between 13 and 18 years of age, and over 18 years of age (Voyer et al., 1995). The results showed that the effect sizes increased with age for mental rotation, spatial perception, and spatial visualization, but that mental rotation tasks were the only tasks that yielded significant sex differences in cognition prior to the age of 13. The authors of this study did not take into consideration whether there is a sex difference decrease as a result of menopause. Another meta-analysis investigating potential age trends in verbal abilities found no consistent pattern of data; however, tasks assessing verbal production were not included in the analysis (Hyde and Linn, 1988).

Investigating the development of sex differences in episodic memory, Kramer and colleagues (Kramer, Delis, Kaplan et al., 1997) found that differences between boys and girls on a verbal episodic memory task were evident from age 5. In the Betula prospective study of memory, health, and aging (Nilsson et al., 1997), we have investigated a potential decrease in the magnitude of sex differences in episodic memory around the time of menopause. The Betula participants were randomly sampled from the healthy population in Umeå, Sweden. At time 1, there were 100 participants in each of 10 age groups (35-year-olds, 40-year-olds, 45-year-olds . . . 80-year-olds etc.), adding up to a total of 1000 subjects. Five years later, the original sample was reassessed, together with additional participants in age groups ranging between 35 and 85. Approximately half of the 2858 subjects were women. The participants were tested on several episodic memory tasks, a few semantic memory tasks, two verbal fluency tasks, and a spatial visualization task (Herlitz et al., 1997). Instead of analyzing each task separately, we formed one composite measure of episodic free recall, episodic recognition, semantic memory, and verbal fluency.

Looking at the cross-sectional analysis in Figure 13.2, there is no evidence of decreasing sex differences in episodic recall around menopause, neither do we see such tendencies in verbal fluency or in the visuospatial task. The longitudinal data in Figure 13.3 show a slightly different pattern. Women appear to show a 10 year earlier age-related decline in episodic recall than do men, as evidenced by the crossing lines. Whereas women appear to start declining from age 60 to 65, men start declining from age 70 to 75. The same pattern of data is seen for semantic memory, although the age-related decline for both men and women occurs at a much later point in time.

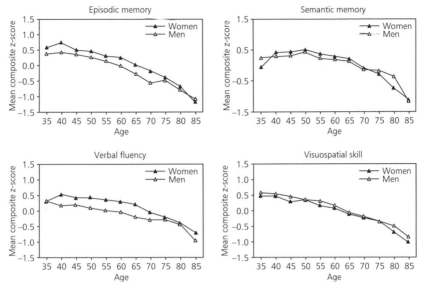

Fig. 13.2 The cross-sectional performance of approximately 1000 women and 900 men on tasks assessing episodic memory, semantic memory, verbal fluency, and visuospatial skill.

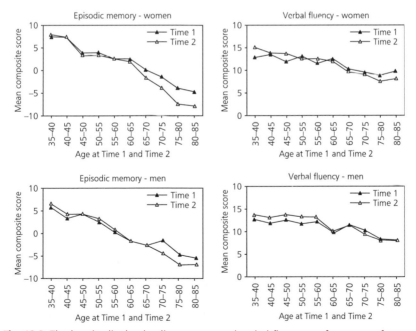

Fig. 13.3 The longitudinal episodic memory and verbal fluency performance of 470 women and 400 men assessed at Time 1 and five years later at Time 2.

All things considered, there appears to be scant evidence of a relationship between hormones and sex differences in cognition when the relationship is inferred from group data from a particular developmental period, such as puberty or menopause. One exception may be mental rotation. On the other hand, since both puberty and menopause take place for an extended time period, varying between individuals, the influence of hormones would need to be large to be detected amidst the noise of other variables. A better test of the hormone–cognition hypothesis would be to use a within subjects design for direct investigation of individual hormone levels and cognition.

Testosterone and cognition

The relationship between circulating T levels and cognitive functions has attracted attention since the 1970s, although in early studies, actual T levels were only estimated by means of bodily characteristics in young men (Petersen, 1976). Petersen reported that for boys, relatively less masculine physical characteristics were positively associated with spatial abilities and negatively associated with verbal production performance. The opposite was true for boys with more masculine appearance. Although no objective measures of T were taken in Petersen's study, it was followed by others, reporting that high spatial performance was found in young men with relatively low levels of T (Gouchie and Kimura, 1991; Moffat and Hampson, 1996; Shute, Pellegrino, Hubert, and Reynolds, 1983). In an effort to decipher brain laterality and its possible influence on visuospatial performance, Moffat and Hampson (1996) found that T levels in right-handed young men showed a negative correlation with spatial performance, yet for right-handed female subjects, there was a positive relation between spatial visualization and T. These studies seem to indicate that there is a relationship between T and visuospatial performance in both young men and women.

The only study investigating the relation between prenatal T level and later visuospatial performance (Grimshaw, Sitarenios, and Finegan, 1995) found a positive correlation between prenatal T levels and speed of mental rotation in girls and a less clear negative correlation in boys. These data indicate that there could be an optimal level of childhood T with regard to visuospatial performance for each sex. In older adults, most studies have examined exogenous T in men. Two clinical trials that studied T supplementation and cognitive function in older men found that T enhanced visuospatial functioning (Cherrier et al., 2001; Janowsky, Oviatt, and Orwoll, 1994). All of these cross-sectional studies, with subjects of widely varying ages, seem to imply that T has the ability to influence spatial performance throughout life span.

In the Betula study, we had the opportunity to investigate the relationship between endogenous T levels in 452 men between 35 and 80 years of age (Yonker, Eriksson, Hellstrand *et al.*, 2003). Like many other studies, we found that the level of T decreased as a function of increasing age. We divided each of the five age groups (35–40, 45–50 etc.), into groups of men with either relatively high or relatively low T values, based on the age mean of T. All these men had participated in two visuospatial tasks, the Block design task from the Wechsler Adult Intelligence Scale-revised (Wechsler, 1981) and the visuospatial sub-task from the Mini-mental state examination (MMSE) (i.e., draw a figure; Folstein *et al.*, 1975). These two tasks were combined to form a composite measure of visuospatial ability. Like all participants in the Betula study, they were also tested in episodic and semantic memory tasks, together with fluency tasks. As can be seen in the Figure 13.4, men with high T performed at a lower level on the visuospatial composite score than men who had relatively low levels of T. No such effects seem to be present for the other cognitive tasks.

Another interesting issue, which to our knowledge has not been reported previously, is the tendency towards a negative association between education and T. Does the level of T influence education, or does education level influence T? We do not know, but it has been shown that men with relatively high levels of T are more impatient and irritable, which may lead to an increased

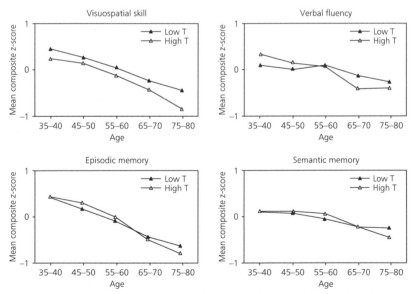

Fig. 13.4 The performance of 452 men with either relatively high, or relatively low levels of T, in tasks assessing visuospatial skill, verbal fluency, episodic memory, and semantic memory. Adapted from Yonker, Eriksson, Nilson *et al.* (2003).

propensity to engage in aggressive behavior, than men with relatively low levels of T (Olweus, Mattson, Schalling *et al.*, 1988). Speculatively, such behavior may not be optimal in educational settings. In our data, men with low levels of T had higher visuospatial performance and also higher education. The natural explanation for the higher visuospatial performance would be that level of education, rather than T, influenced visuospatial performance. However, since there is no association between T and performance on all other cognitive tasks, we do not believe that education, in this case, is responsible for the effect of T seen in visuospatial performance.

The notion of an overall optimal level of T for high visuospatial performance, as argued by Hampson (2000; Moffat and Hampson, 1996), is not fully supported by our data. Instead, it seems as if for men there are age dependent optimum T levels for visuospatial performance, not one optimal level for all age groups. The differences in results are likely due to most previous studies being conducted in young men, not being population based, and not assessing the wide age range we had the opportunity to investigate. As an explanation for our data, we speculate that individuals with genetically more sensitive androgen receptors have lower levels of T in their serum. These men are still hypoandrogen, but their receptors are very sensitive to T. At present, we are awaiting the genetic analyses that could shed some light on this question.

Estrogen and cognition

Men and estrogen

Very few studies have examined the relationship between estrogen and cognition in men, and the few studies examining this issue have typically failed to find an effect. Kampen and Sherwin (1996) studied young men on a number of visual and verbal episodic memory tasks. Although they found a positive effect of estrogen on two of the visual episodic memory tasks, there were no effects on most of the other measures. Older men who had higher levels of estradiol (the active form of estrogen) at a point in time five years before participating in cognitive testing, performed better on the Blessed Information-Memory-Concentration Test and MMSE (Barrett-Connor, Goodman-Gruen, and Patay, 1999). These results are of course difficult to interpret because of the substantial time lag between hormonal and cognitive assessment.

With the intention to investigate the effect of estrogen on potential sex differences in the cognitive tasks used in the Betula study, we examined 18 men and 18 women in their sixties, who were matched on estradiol level (Yonker, Eriksson, Nilsson, and Herlitz, 2003). That is, we specifically selected men and women with similar levels of estradiol, and matched them on age and MMSE

Table 13.1 Correlation coefficients between estradiol and composite memory measures for women and men, r values

	Estradiol	
	Women	Men
Episodic Memory (composite of 13)	.37	.06
Verbal free recall (composite of 8)	.30	.02
Verbal cued Recall (composite of 2)	−.02	.11
Verbal Recognition (composite of 2)	.32	.17
Face recognition	.55*	−.20
Semantic Memory (composite of 2)	.35	−.06

* <.05.

Adapted from Yonker, Eriksson, Nilsson, *et al.* (2003).

score. We found the typical sex differences favoring women on tasks assessing episodic memory. Additionally, we found the typical tendency for the men to perform at a higher level than women did on the visuospatial task. However, as can be seen in Table 13.1, there was no association between estradiol level and any of the composite measures of episodic memory in men, whereas there was a reliable association between estradiol level and episodic recognition, especially so for face recognition in females. We believe that our results, and the results by Kampen and Sherwin (1996), show that the effect of estrogen on cognitive performance in men is non-existent. The conclusions are less clear with regard to women. Although the results are ambiguous, based on these studies it appears as if estradiol is weakly related to episodic and semantic memory measures in women, but not to visuospatial performance or verbal fluency. In addition, based on our study alone, estrogen does not appear to be an important contributing factor for sex differences in episodic memory.

Women and estrogen

Up to this point in time, several studies have investigated the impact of estrogen on cognition in healthy non-demented women. One line of research has studied the impact of endogenous estrogens on cognitive functions in women, whereas another line of research has concentrated on the influence of hormone replacement therapy (HRT) on cognitive functions.

Naturally cycling young women

In the late 1980s, Elizabeth Hampson conducted a series of interesting studies showing that cognitive performance of normally cycling women varied as a function of phase of menstrual cycle (Hampson, 1990a, b; Hampson and

Kimura, 1988). The results showed that women tested during the high estrogen phases of their menstrual cycle performed at a higher level on verbal production tasks and fine motor tasks, than women did during the low estrogen phase (i.e., menstruation). In contrast, women in the low estrogen phase performed at a higher level on visuospatially oriented cognitive tasks. Since mood changes related to the menstrual cycle are common (Golub, 1980; cited in Hampson, 1990a), it could be surmised that concurrent mood changes influenced cognitive performance, but this was not the case. The finding that hormonal variation throughout the menstrual cycle has an effect on visuospatial functioning has since been replicated by others (Hausmann, Slabbekoorn, van Goozen *et al.*, 2000; Moody, 1997; Phillips and Silverman Saveier and Kimura, 1998,), although some studies have failed to replicate the effects (Gordon and Lee, 1993; Postma, Winkel, Tuiten *et al.*, 1999).

Thus, some studies (Hampson, 1990a, b; Hampson and Kimura, 1988) suggest that estrogen may have an inhibitory influence on visuospatial functioning, whereas it has a facilitating effect on tasks in which women typically excel, such as articulation and manual speed and coordination. However, the effects are not always found and are typically rather small. The lack of effect could be due to the fact that the menstrual cycle is difficult to control, and women are sometimes incorrect in their statements regarding cycle phase. In addition, cycle length is individually determined and is not always stable, especially in young women, making young women less suitable as subjects. Certainty regarding menstrual phase can only be reached through blood sampling which, of course, is more expensive and requires, among other things, laboratory access. Before the conclusion can be drawn that cognition is affected by fluctuating levels of estrogen associated with the menstrual cycle, studies must be conducted in which the experimenter is unaware of the participants' cycle phase and the hormone levels are carefully assessed.

Menopausal women

Researchers have investigated the relation between endogenous levels of estrogen and cognition in older women and studied the cognitive performance of women with varying levels of endogenous estrogen. Most studies in this area have failed to show an effect of endogenous estrogen values and cognition (Barrett-Connor and Goodman-Gruen, 1999; Portin, Polo-Kantola, Polo *et al.*, 1999; Yaffe, Grady, Pressman *et al.*, 1998).

However, there are three exceptions to this pattern. One recent study by Drake and colleagues (2000) reported that high estrogen levels were associated with higher verbal memory performance, whereas low levels were associated with higher visual memory. Although 17 cognitive measures were assessed in this study, and many were found to be unrelated to estrogen, the data seem appropriate because several cognitive measures with a non-verbal or visuospatial profile were negatively associated with estrogen as in Hampson's studies (1990a, b). Additionally, associations failing to reach statistical significance pointed in the same direction. From the same research group, Smith *et al.* (1999) reported that lifelong estrogen exposure was related to cognitive performance. Lifetime estrogen exposure was based on factors that are known to affect estrogen levels, such as duration of estrogen treatment, age at menopause, nulliparity, postmenopausal weight, age at menarche, and time since menopause. Although the results were inconsistent, lifelong exposure was positively related to performance on a global screening instrument and to digit span forward and backward, but not to other cognitive measures. Another study (Carlson *et al.*, 2001) investigating lifetime HRT in over 2000 elderly women found that lifetime HRT exposure was not only related to improved performance on the modified MMSE (Teng and Chui, 1987), but also to attenuated decline of cognitive function over a three-year interval. These effects were largest in the oldest age group (i.e., over 85). However, actual hormonal values were not reported in the Smith *et al.* and Carlson *et al.* studies.

Thus, there are methodological problems in the research on endogenous estrogen in postmenopausal women. For example, serum was collected for hormonal analysis before cognitive testing took place, either four to five years (Barrett-Connor and Goodman-Gruen, 1999), five months (Drake *et al.*, 2000), or two years (Yaffe *et al.*, 1998) prior to the cognitive testing taking place. Some studies did not conduct hormonal analyses (Carlson *et al.*, 2001; Smith *et al.*, 1999). To expect reliable associations between estrogen and cognition to be found is perhaps to be overly optimistic. Thus, additional well-controlled studies, with blood sampling concurrent with cognitive testing, are needed in this area.

Another line of research has focused on treatment effects of estrogen on cognition in postmenopausal, non-demented women. After reviewing the observational studies in this area, it becomes clear that the majority of studies claim positive effects of HRT on cognition (Grodstein *et al.*, 2000; Jacobs *et al.*, 1998; Kampen and Sherwin, 1994; Kimura, 1995; Maki, Zonderman, and Resnick, 2001; Robinson Friedman, Marcus, Tinklenberg and Yesavage, 1994; Schmidt *et al.*, 1996; Steffens *et al.*, 1999), although one study (Barrett-Connor and Kritz-Silverstein, 1993: 2637) reports that there was no 'compelling or internally consistent evidence for an effect of estrogen on cognitive function'.

In a cross-sectional comparison in the Betula study, we investigated the relation between HRT and cognitive performance in 79 HRT users and 79 non-users (Yonker, Adolfsson *et al.*, 2003). The selected HRT users were randomly matched to women in the non-users group on age and education. Since we collected data on medication use in the Betula study, we ensured that, besides HRT, the only medication used were periodic pain relievers and cold/flu preparations. The women, ranging in age from 45 to 85, were assigned to one of three age groups: middle-aged (45–55), young old (60–70), and old (75–85). As can be seen in Figure 13.5, we found an effect of HRT use on episodic memory and a tendency in that direction on the verbal fluency tasks. In the young old group, we found that HRT was very weakly associated with performance on both the semantic memory tasks and the verbal fluency tasks. There were no differences between HRT users and non-users in the old age group. What we found especially interesting was the reliable correlation between serum estradiol levels and episodic memory performance in the middle-aged group, and the tendency in that direction for verbal fluency. None of the correlations for the young old and old age groups were reliable. However, when we investigated the actual serum values of estrogen, we discovered that 6 out of 27 women in the middle-aged group had very low estrogen values, indicating that these 6 women were non-compliant with their HRT medication. Similarly, there was non-compliance with HRT medication in the young old group, 21 out of 40, and 6 out of 8 for the old age group. Finding any relation between estrogen and cognition, or differences between HRT users and non-users, seem very unlikely if the users, in fact, are non-users.

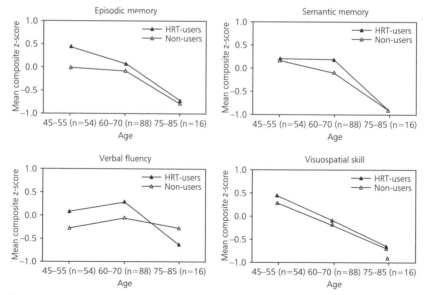

Fig. 13.5 The performance of 79 HRT users and 79 non-users on tasks assessing episodic memory, semantic memory, verbal fluency, and visuospatial skill. Adapted from Yonker, Adolfsson, Eriksson, *et al.* (2003).

The results from this study underscore the need for careful assessment of true estrogen values and not presumption of HRT usage.

From the above review it would appear as if there is a positive effect of HRT on cognition in postmenopausal women. However, the observational design of the studies can be severely criticized. One of the problems associated with these studies is that women on HRT typically have higher education than non-users (Jacobs et al., 1998; Kampen and Sherwin, 1994; Robinson et al., 1994; Schmidt et al., 1996; Steffens et al., 1999). In some studies, level of education was not reported (Barrett-Connor and Kritz-Silverstein, 1993), and it is clear that very few studies report naturally matched groups on education level (Kimura, 1995; Maki et al., 2001). Although most studies have statistically controlled for differences in education, other factors related to inherent differences could, of course, contribute to the results. For example, if women who take estrogen have higher education than non-users and education is statistically controlled for, it is still possible that the more educated subjects are healthier, have better access to health care facilities, and are more cognitively intact than non-users. That is, they differ on factors unrelated to estrogen use or education. Thus, the unequal education levels among HRT users and non-users puts serious restrictions to the conclusions that can be drawn.

From a cognitive psychology perspective, another serious methodological problem is that many different cognitive tasks have been used, assessing a variety of cognitive abilities. This would not be a problem had the reported effects by estrogen been consistent, but this is rarely the case. For example, positive effects on verbal fluency were reported in the absence of effects on three measures of verbal memory and on an overall measure of cognition (Grodstein et al., 2000). Schmidt and colleagues (1996) reported positive effects on one measure of conceptualization and on one measure of visuo-practical skill, in the absence of effects on tasks assessing episodic memory, attention, speed, and reaction time (i.e., positive effects were found in only two out of 18 measures). In contrast, Kimura (1995) reported overall positive effects on eight out of ten measures of verbal fluency, perceptual speed, spatial ability, and articulatory and motor skills. Episodic memory was one of the two tasks not showing an effect of HRT use. Further, Kampen and Sherwin (1994) reported that the estrogen users in their study performed at a higher level than non-users in two out of six verbal episodic memory tasks. This list could be made longer. In addition, there are some studies that have used very crude measures of cognitive performance, thereby denying an analysis of estrogen's potential effect on cognitive functions (Steffens et al., 1999). Rarely are any attempts made at explaining or discussing the effect, or lack of effect, for any given cognitive task.

In addition to problems associated with inherent differences in demographic variables and inconsistencies with regard to cognitive measures, there are also problems relating to retrospective reports and medication compliance. Many studies have divided women into groups of current users of estrogen, ever users, or never users. Such data rely on retrospective reports, which can be problematic. Unfortunately, as our data analysis on women participating in the Betula study illustrated, it is important to have objective measures of serum levels of estrogen, since women can report being HRT users, when their serum levels of estrogen speak in another direction. Objective measures on serum estrogen values were not available in any of the other studies (Barrett-Connor and Kritz-Silverstein, 1993; Grodstein *et al.*, 2000; Jacobs *et al.*, 1998; Kampen & Sherwin, 1994; Kimura, 1995; Maki *et al.*, 2001; Robinson *et al.*, 1994; Schmidt *et al.*, 1996; Steffens *et al.*, 1999).

Although the conclusions drawn from the data have often been overly optimistic, there are also studies showing more consistent and reliable positive effects of HRT use. Maki and colleagues (2001) compared age and education matched HRT users and non-users. They found that presumed HRT users performed at a higher level than non-users on 13 of 15 verbal episodic memory measures, whereas there were no effects on digit span forward or backward, Benton visual retention test, or a mental rotation test. Robinson *et al.* (1994) reported positive effects of presumed HRT use on two out of two episodic memory tasks in the age and education matched HRT users and non-users. Taken together, it is evident that positive effects of estrogen have been found in many tasks assessing a wide variety of cognitive functions, although there may be a slight advantage favoring, as hypothesized from basic quasi-experimental studies, estrogen's positive effects on episodic memory and verbal fluency performance. However, further studies in this area should be done with randomized controlled treatment designs.

There are less methodological problems in randomized controlled treatment studies, although results have been far from conclusive. Duka, Tasker, and McGowan (2000) found positive effects of a three-week HRT treatment on three episodic memory measures and on a mental rotation task, in the absence of effects on frontal lobe tests. Although Shaywitz and colleagues (1999) failed to find performance differences on their verbal and non-verbal working memory tasks as a result of HRT treatment, they did find differential brain activation patterns using functional magnetic resonance imaging. Clear-cut negative results were reported by Polo-Kantola *et al.* (1998) and by Phillips and Sherwin (1992) who found no effect of HRT treatment in women with previous hysterectomy.

The results in this area are difficult to interpret. It is clear that many studies have reported positive effects of HRT on cognition, but too many method-ological problems are associated with the studies for firm conclusions to be drawn. It seems clear that observational studies are of less value for the research field. If research is to be pursued in this area, carefully controlled treatment studies should be the goal.

Estrogen and Alzheimer's disease

Studies examining possible positive effects of estrogen on Alzheimer's disease (AD) have looked either at the protective role estrogen can have on the risk of acquiring AD, or at the therapeutic effect of estrogen on AD symptoms. The hypothesis that estrogen deficiency associated with menopause may contribute to the development of AD comes from studies reporting lower serum estrogen values in women with AD than in age-matched controls (Honjo *et al.*, 1989). Studies also show an increased risk for women to develop AD, as compared to men (Fratiglioni *et al.*, 1997), suggesting that estrogen may be of interest.

Estrogen and risk for AD

A meta-analysis conducted a few years ago concluded that the risk of AD among postmenopausal women taking HRT was reduced by 29 per cent compared to women never exposed to exogenous estrogen (Yaffe, Sawaya, Lieberburg *et al.*, 1998). However, the 10 studies reviewed in the meta-analysis reported conflicting results. Some investigations showed a protective role of HRT (Henderson *et al.*, 1994; Kawas *et al.*, 1997; Tang *et al.*, 1996), others showed a non-significant protective effect of HRT (Broe *et al.*, 1990; Paganini-Hill and Henderson, 1994; Mortel and Meyer, 1995), still others illustrated no difference (Brenner *et al.*, 1994; Graves *et al.*, 1990), and finally, some demonstrated a non-significant increased risk for AD (Amaducci *et al.*, 1986). Since then, three additional studies have been conducted, finding a protective role of HRT (Baldereschi *et al.*, 1998; Waring *et al.*, 1999), but also a non-protective role (Seshadri, 2001). Although these studies, similar to observational studies on estrogen and cognition in non-demented women, are contaminated with problems concerning level of education, medical access, and the retrospective nature of the reports, the general notion is that HRT may reduce the risk for AD (Marder and Sano, 2000). However, future studies need to be prospective in order to control for inherent differences in the samples and quality of reports. It is also important to address the issue of time on HRT and at what age the treatment was initiated. Such studies are currently under way.

Estrogen as treatment for AD

There are an increasing number of studies investigating the therapeutic effect of estrogen on cognition in AD. The small, early studies found a positive relation between short estrogen treatment periods (i.e., between three and six weeks) and improved cognition (Fillit *et al.*, 1986; Honjo *et al.*, 1989; Ohkura *et al.*, 1994). Very few women participated in these studies (i.e., 6 to 15) and the cognitive instruments were typically not very specific (e.g., rating or screening instruments). Later studies have been less positive, although there are exceptions here also.

Recently, five randomized placebo-controlled studies have been conducted. Asthana and colleagues (1999; 2001) have performed two trials, with either six (1999) or 10 (2001) women in the treatment groups, with eight weeks of treatment. The pattern of results was similar in both studies, showing positive effects on some measures of a Stroop task, and on both a verbal and visual episodic memory task. However, there were also measures from these cognitive tasks that did not yield positive effects of estrogen (e.g., paragraph recall, total recall, Stroop interference condition).

Three other large, double blind, placebo-controlled trials investigating the effect of estrogen treatment in AD (Henderson *et al.*, 2000; Mulnard *et al.*, 2000; Wang *et al.*, 2000) have been rather negative in the effects reported. These three recently published papers used treatment periods ranging from three months to one year and included 42, 50, and 120 subjects respectively. The conclusions drawn from these studies were that neither short-term estrogen therapy (Henderson *et al.*, 2000; Wang *et al.*, 2000) nor long-term estrogen treatment (Mulnard *et al.*, 2000) could slow disease progression or improve cognitive functions in AD. Therefore, it seems as if the earlier positive expectations of estrogen as a treatment for AD have become rather negative. The discrepancies in the results of earlier and later studies are most likely due to earlier studies often highlighting one or two significant results, rarely controlling for multiple comparisons, while later studies demand more systematic and reliable effects before positive conclusions are drawn.

General conclusions

Many studies on hormonal influences on cognition have focused on the potentially protective role of estrogen in age-related cognitive decline and AD. For several years, HRT constituted a hope for many health afflictions of post-menopausal women: cognitive deterioration, AD, osteoporosis, or cardiovascular disease. Although the results are not conclusive, the general data pattern does not meet the expectations. The positive expectations from basic neural mechanisms, suggesting that estrogen can beneficially affect brain areas associated with cognition and AD, taken together with the relative ease of conducting observational studies, led to less than rigorous research being pursued in this area. However, the methodological problems common in the early research are not seen in the recent studies, thereby promising interesting findings for the future.

A striking observation is that few areas of this research have obtained clear-cut evidence of a hormonal influence on cognition. In spite of the inconsistency in results across studies, however, there is an interesting consistency among groups of researchers obtaining evidence either for or against a relation between hormones and cognition. In a research area where the result is a matter of either finding an association between two factors or not, such patterns can easily arise. Nevertheless, it weakens the strength of evidence in the studies.

With these problems in mind, the following tentative conclusions can be drawn:

1   There is not much evidence to suggest that hormonal changes associated with puberty and menopause should change the magnitude of sex differences in verbal production and episodic memory tasks, visuospatial tasks being a possible exception.

2   Testosterone appears to be negatively associated with spatial performance in men, irrespective of age. Whether the opposite is true for women remains unclear.

3   Although very few studies have been done, estrogen does not appear to affect cognitive performance in men.

4   In naturally cycling women, estrogen seems to positively affect verbal production performance and fine motor tasks, although blinded studies need to be done before definite conclusions can be drawn.

5   In spite of the many studies showing a positive effect of HRT on cognition in non-demented menopausal women, there is little evidence to support strong conclusions. Additional carefully controlled treatment studies are needed.

6   Estrogen as a protective factor for AD seems promising, but the studies from which such conclusions are drawn are contaminated by methodological problems similar to those encountered in the studies on non-demented women.

7   There is, at present, no evidence of a treatment effect of estrogen in clinical AD.

References

Amaducci.L. A., Fratiglioni, L., Rocca, W., Fieschi, C., Livrea, P., Pedone, D., Bracco, L., Lippi, A., Gandolfo, C., Bino. G., Prencipe, M., Bonatti, M. L., Girotti, F., Carella, F., Tavolato, B., Ferla, S., Lenzi, G. L., Crolei, A., Gambi, A., Grigoletto, F., and Schoenberg, B. S. (1986). Risk factors for clinically diagnosed Alzheimer's disease: A case-control study of an Italian population. *Neurology,* **36**, 922–931.

Arnold, A. P., and Gorski, R. A. (1984). Gonadal steroid induction of structural sex differences in the central nervous system. *Annual Review of Neuroscience*, 7, 413–442.

Asthana, S., Baker, L. D., Craft, S., Stanczyk, F. Z., Veith, R. C., Raskind, M. A., and Plymate, S. R. (2001). High-dose estradiol improves cognition for women with AD: Results of a randomized study. *Neurology*, 57, 605–612.

Asthana, S., Craft, S., Baker, L. D., Raskind, M. A., Birnbaum, R. S., Lofgreen, C. P., Veith, R. C., and Plymate, S. R. (1999). Cognitive and neuroendocrine response to transdermal estrogen in postmenopausal women with Alzheimer's disease: results of a placebo-controlled, double-blind, pilot study. *Psychoneuroendocrinology*, 24, 657–677.

Baldereschi, M., Di Carlo, A., Lepore, V., Bracco, L., Maggi, S., Grigoletto, F., Scarlato, G., and Amaducci, L. (1998). Estrogen-replacement therapy and Alzheimer's disease in the Italian Longitudinal Study on Aging. *Neurology*, 50, 996–1002.

Barrett-Connor, E., and Goodman-Gruen, D. (1999). Cognitive function and endogenous sex hormones in older women. *Journal of the American Geriatric Society*, 47, 1289–1293.

Barrett-Connor, E., Goodman-Gruen, D., and Patay, B. (1999). Endogenous sex hormones and cognitive function in older men. *Journal of Clinical Endocrinology and Metabolism*, 84, 3681–3685.

Barrett-Connor, E., and Kritz-Silverstein, D. (1993). Estrogen replacement therapy and cognitive function in older women. *Journal of the American Medical Association*, 269, 2637–2641.

Berenbaum, S. A., (2001). Cognitive function in congenital adrenal hperplasia. *Endocrinology and Metabolism Clinics of North America*, 1, 173–192.

Berenbaum, S. A., and Hines, M. (1992). Early androgens are related to childhood sex-typed toy preferences. *Psychological Science*, 3, 203–206.

Bixo, M., Bäckström T., Winblad, B., and Andersson, A. (1995). Estradiol and testosterone in specific regions of the human female brain in different endocrine states. *Journal of Steroid Biochemistry and Molecular Biology*, 55, 297–303.

Brenner, D. E., Kukull, W. A., Stergachis, A., Vanbelle, G., Bowen, J. D., McCormick, W. C., Teri, T., and Larson, E. B. (1994). Postmenopausal estrogen replacement therapy and the risk of Alzheimer's disease. A population-based case-control study. *American Journal of Epidemiology*, 140, 262–267.

Broe, G. A., Henderson, A. S., Creasey, H., McCusker, E., Korten, A. E., Jorm, A. F., Longley, W., and Anthony, J. C. (1990). A case-control study of Alzheimer's disease in Australia. *Neurology*, 40, 1698–1707.

Carlson, M. C., Zandi, P. P., Plassman, B. L., Tschanz, J. T., Welsh-Bohmer, K. A., Steffens, D. C., Bastian, L. A., Mehta, K. M., and Breitner, J. C. S. (2001). Hormone replacement therapy and reduced cognitive decline in older women. The Cache County Study. *Neurology*, 57, 2210–2216.

Cherrier, M. M., Asthana, S., Plymate, S., Baker, L., Matsumoto, A. M., Peskind, E., Raskind, M. A., Bodkin, K., Bremner, W., Petrova, A., LaTendresse, S., and Craft, S. (2001). Testosterone supplementation improves spatial and verbal memory in healthy older men. *Neurology*, 57, 80–88.

Ciocca, D. R., Vargas Roig, L. M. (1995). Estrogen receptors in human non-target tissues: Biological and clinical implications. *Endocrine Reviews*, 16, 35–62.

Collaer, M. L., and Hines, M. (1995). Human behavioral sex differences: A role for gonadal hormones during early development? *Psychological Bulletin*, 118, 55–107.

Drake, E. B., Henderson, V. W., Stanczyk, F. X., McCleary, C. A., Brown, W. S., Smith, C. A., Rizzo, A. A., Murdock, G. A., and Buckwalter, J. G. (2000). Associations between circulating sex steroid hormones and cognition in normal elderly women. *Neurology,* **54**, 599–603.

Duka, T., Tasker, R., and McGowan, J. F. (2000). The effects of 3-week estrogen hormone replacement on cognition in elderly healthy females. *Psychopharmacology,* **149**, 129–139.

Fillit, H., Weinreb, H., Cholst, I, Luine, V., McEwen, B., Amador, R., Zabriskie, J. (1986). Observations in a preliminary open trial of estradiol therapy for senile dementia – Alzheimer's type. *Psychoneuroendocrinology,* **11**, 337–345.

Folstein, M. F., Folstein, S. E., and McHugh, P. R. (1975). 'Mini-Mental State': A practical method for grading the cognitive state of the patient for the clinician. *Journal of Psychiatric Research,* **12**, 189–198.

Fratiglioni, L., Viitanen, M., von Strauss, E., Tontodonati, V., Herlitz, A., and Winblad, B. (1997). Very old women at highest risk of dementia and Alzheimer's disease: Incidence data from the Kungsholmen Project, Stockholm. *Neurology, 1997, 48*, 132–138.

Gordon, H. W. and Lee, P. A. (1993). *Psychoneuroendocrinology,* **18**, 521–X.

Gouchie, C., and Kimura, D. (1991). The relationship between testosterone levels and cognitive ability patterns. *Psychoneuroendocrinology,* **16**, 323–334.

Graves, A. B., White, E., Koepsell, T. D., Reifler, B. V., Vanbelle, G., Larson, E. B., Raskind, M. (1990). A case-control study of Alzheimer's disease. *Annals of Neurology,* **28**, 766–774.

Greenspan, F. S., and Strewler, G. J. (1997). *Basic and Clinical Endocrinology.* (5th ed.) London: Prentice Hall International.

Grimshaw, G. M., Sitarenios, G., and Finegan, J.-A. (1995). Mental rotation at 7 years: Relations with prenatal testosterone levels and spatial play experiences. *Brain and Cognition,* **29**, 85–100.

Grodstein, F., Chen J., Pollen, D. A., Albert, M. S., Wilson, R. S., Folstein, M. F., Evans, D. A., and Stampfer, M. J. (2000). Postmenopausal hormone therapy and cognitive function in healthy older women. *Journal of the American Geriatrics Society,* **48**, 746–752.

Halpern, D. (1992). *Sex Differences in Cognitive Abilities.* (2nd ed.) Hillsdale, NJ: LEA.

Hampson, E. (1990a). Estrogen-related variations in human spatial and articulator-motor skills. *Psychoneuroendocrinology,* **15**, 97–111.

Hampson, E. (1990b). Variations in sex-related cognitive abilities across the menstrual cycle. *Brain and Cognition,* **14**, 26–43.

Hampson, E. (2000). Sexual differentiation of spatial functions in humans. In A. Matsumoto (ed.) *Sexual Differentiation of the Brain.* London: CRC Press.

Hampson, E. and Kimura, D. (1988). Reciprocal effects of hormonal fluctuations on human motor and perceptual-spatial skills. *Behavioral Neuroscience,* **102**, 456–459.

Hampson, E., Rovet, J. F., and Altmann, D. (1998). Spatial reasoning in children with congenital adrenal hyperplasia due to 21-hydroxylase deficiency. *Developmental Neurpsychology,* **14**, 299–320.

Hausmann, M., Slabbekoorn, D., van Goozen, S. H., Cohen-Kettenis, P. T., and Gunturkun, O. (2000). Sex hormones affect spatial abilities during the menstrual cycle. *Behavioral Neuroscience,* **114**, 1245–1250.

Henderson, V. W., Paganini-Hill, A., Emanuel, C. K., Dunn, M. E., and Buckwalter, G. (1994). Estrogen replacement therapy in older women. *Archives of Neurology,* **51**, 896–900.

Henderson, V. W., Paganini-Hill, A., Miller, B. L., Elble, R. J., Reyes, P. F., Shoupe, D., McClearly, C. A., Klein, R. A., Hake, A. M., and Farlow, M. R. (2000). Estrogen for Alzheimer's disease in women: Randomized, double-blind, placebo-controlled trial. *Neurology,* **54**, 295–301.

Herlitz, A., Airaksinen, E., and Nordström, E. (1999). Sex differences in episodic memory: The impact of verbal and visuospatial ability. *Neuropsychology,* **13**, 590–597.

Herlitz, A., Nilsson, L.-G., and Bäckman, L. (1997). Gender differences in episodic memory. *Memory and Cognition,* **25**, 801–811.

Herlitz, A., and Yonker, J. (2002). Sex differences in episodic memory: The influence of intelligence. *Journal of Clinical and Experimental Psychology,* **24**, 107–114.

Hill, R. D., Grut, M., Wahlin, Å., Herlitz, A., Winblad, B., and Bäckman, L. (1995). Predicting memory performance in optimally healthy very old adults. *Journal of Mental Health and Aging,* **1**, 57–67.

Honjo, H., Ogino, Y., Naitoh, K., Urabe, M., Kitawaki, J. Yasuda, J., Yamamoto, T., Ishihara, S., Okada, H., Yonezawa, T., Hayashi, K., and Nambara, T. (1989). *In vivo* effects by estrone sulfate on the central nervous system – senile dementia (Alzheimer's type). *Journal of Steroid Biochemistry and Molecular Biology,* **34**, 521–525.

Hultsch, D. F., Masson, M. E. J., and Small B. J. (1991). Adult age differences in direct and indirect tests of memory. *Journal of Gerontology: Psychological Sciences,* **46**, 22–30.

Hyde, J. S., and Linn, M. C. (1988). Gender differences in verbal ability: A meta-analysis. *Psychological Bulletin,* **104**, 53–69.

Jacobs, D. M., Tang, M.-X., Stern, Y., Sano, M., Marder, K., Bell, K. L., Schofield, P. Dooneief, G., Gurland, B., and Mayeux, R. (1997). Cognitive function in nondemented older women who took estrogen after menopause. *Neurology,* **50**, 368–373.

Janowsky, J. S., Oviatt, S. K., and Orwoll, E. S. (1994). Testosterone influence spatial cognition in older men. *Behavioral Neuroscience,* **108**, 325–332.

Kampen, D. L., and Sherwin, B. B. (1994). Estrogen use and verbal memory in healthy postmenopausal women. *Obstetrics and Gynecology,* **83**, 979–983.

Kampen, D. L., and Sherwin, B. B. (1996). Estradiol is related to visual memory in healthy young men. *Behavioral Neuroscience,* **110**, 613–617.

Kawas, C., Resnick, R., Morrison, A., Brookmeyer, R., Corrada, M., Zonderman, A., Bacal, C., Lingle, D. D., and Metter, E. (1997). A prospective study of estrogen replacement therapy and the risk of developing Alzheimer's disease: The Baltimore Longitudinal Study of Aging. *Neurology,* **48**, 1517–1521.

Kimura, D. (1995). Estrogen replacement therapy may protect against intellectual decline in postmenopausal women. *Hormones and Behavior,* **29**, 312–321.

Kimura, D., and Hampson, E., (1994). Cognitive pattern in men and women is influenced by fluctuations in sex hormones. *Current Directions in Psychological Science,* **3**, 57–61.

Kramer, J. H., Delis, D. C., and Daniel, M. (1988). Sex differences in verbal learning. *Journal of Clinical Psychology,* **44**, 907–915.

Kramer, J. H., Delis, D. C., Kaplan, E., O'Donnell, L., and Prifitera, A. (1997). Developmental sex differences in verbal learning. *Neuropsychology,* **4**, 577–584.

Krithivas, K., Yurgalevitch, S. M., Mohr, B. A., Wilcox, C. J., Batter, S. J., Brown, M., and Longcope, C., McKinlay, J. B., and Kantoff, P. W. (1999). Evidence that the CAG repeat in the androgen receptor gene is associated with the age-related decline in serum androgen levels in men. *Journal of Endocrinology,* **162**, 137–142.

Larrabee, G. J., and Crook, T. H. (1993). Do men show more rapid age-associated decline in simulated everyday verbal memory than do women? *Psychology and Aging*, 8, 68–71.

Lewin, C., and Herlitz, A. (2002). Sex differences in face recognition: Women's faces make the difference. *Brain and Cognition*, 50, 121–128.

Lewin, C., Wolgers, G., and Herlitz, A. (2001). Sex differences favoring women in verbal but not in visuospatial episodic memory. *Neuropsychology*, 15, 165–173.

MacLusky, N. J., and Naftolin, F. (1981). Sexual differentiation of the central nervous system. *Science*, 211, 1294–1303.

Maki, P. M., Zonderman, A. B., and Resnick, S. M. (2001). Enhanced verbal memory in nondemented elderly women receiving hormone-replacement therapy. *American Journal of Psychiatry*, 158, 227–233.

Marder, K., and Sano, M. (2000). Estrogen to treat Alzheimer's disease: Too little, too late? So what's a woman to do? *Neurology*, 54, 2035–2037.

McKelvie, S. J. (1987). Recognition memory for faces with and without spectacles. *Perceptual and Motor Skills*, 65, 705–706.

Moffat, S. D., and Hampson, E. (1996). A curvilinear relationship between testosterone and spatial cognition in humans: Possible influence of hand preference. *Psychoneuroendocrinology*, 21, 323–337.

Moody, M. S., (1997). Changes in scores on the Mental Rotations Test during the menstrual cycle, *Perceptual Motor Skills*, 84, 955–961.

Mortel, K. F., and Meyer, J. S. (1995) Lack of postmenopausal estrogen replacement therapy and the risk of dementia. *Journal of Neuropsychiatry and Clinical Neurosciences*, 7, 334–337.

Mulnard, R. A., Cotman, C. W., Kawas, C., van Dyck, C. H., Sao, M., Doody, R., Koss, E., Pfeiffer, E., Jin, S., Gamst, A., Grundman, M., Thomas, R., and Thal, L. J. (2000). Estrogen replacement therapy for treatment of mild to moderate Alzheimer disease. *Journal of American Medical Association*, 283, 1007–1016.

Nilsson, L.-G., Bäckman, L., Erngrund, K., Nyberg, L, Adolfsson, R., Bucht, G., Karlsson, S., Widing, M., and Winblad, B. (1997). The Betula prospective cohort study: Memory, health, and aging. *Aging, Neuropsychology, and Cognition*, 4, 1–32

Ohkura, T., Isse, K., Akazawa, K., Hamamoto, M., Yaoi, Y., and Hagino, N. (1994). Evaluation of estrogen treatment in female patients with dementia of the Alzheimer type. *Endocrine Journal*, 41, 361–371.

Olweus, D., Mattsson, Å., Schalling, S., and Löw, H. (1988). Circulating testosterone levels and aggression in adolescent males: A causal analysis. *Psychosomatic Medicine*, 50, 261–272.

Pagainin-Hill, A., and Henderson, V. W. (1994). Estrogen deficiency and risk of Alzheimer's disease in women. *American Journal of Epidemiology*, 140, 256–261.

Petersen, A. (1976). Physical androgyny and cognitive functioning in adolescence. *Developmental Psychology*, 12, 524–533.

Phillips, S. M., and Sherwin, B. B. (1992). Effects of estrogen on memory function in surgically menopausal women. *Psychoneuroendocrinology*, 17, 485–495.

Phillips, K., and Silverman, I. (1997). Differences in the relationship of menstrual cycle phase to spatial performance on two-and three-dimensional tasks. *Hormones and Behavior*, 32, 167–X.

Polo-Kantola, P., Portin, R., Polo, O., Helenius, H., Irjala, K., and Erkkola, R. (1998). *Obstetric Gynecology*, 91, 459–466.

Portin, R., Polo-Kantola, P., Polo, O., Koskinen, T., Revonsuo, A., Irjala, K., and Erkkola, R. (1999). Serum estrogen level, attention, memory and other cognitive functions in middle-aged women. *Climacteric, 1999*, **2**, 115–123.

Postma, A., Winkel, J., Tuiten, A., and van Honk, J. (1999). Sex differences and menstrual cycle effects in human spatial memory. *Psychoneuroendocrinology*, **24**, 175–192.

Robinson, D., Friedman, L., Marcus, R., Tinklenberg, J., and Yesavage, J. (1994). Estrogen replacement therapy and memory in older women. *Journal of the American Geriatrics Society*, **42**, 919–922.

Saucier, D. M., and Kimura, D. (1998). Intrapersonal motor but not extrapersonal targeting skill is enhanced during the midluteal phase of the menstrual cycle. *Developmental Neuropsychology*, **14**, 385–398.

Schmidt, R., Fazekas, F., Reinhart, B., Kapeller, P., Fazekas, G., Offenbacher, H., Eber, B., Schumacher, M., and Freidl, W. (1996). Estrogen replacement therapy in older women: A neuropsychological and brain MRI study. *Journal of the American Geriatrics Society*, **44**, 1307–1313.

Servin, A., Nordenström, A., Larsson, A., and Bohlin, G. (2003). Prenatal androgens and gender-typed behavior: A study with mild and severe forms of congenital adrenal hyperplasia. *Developmental Psychology*, **39**, 440–450.

Seshadri, S., Zornberg, G. L., Derby, L. E., Myers, M. W., Jick, H., Drachman, D. A. (2001). Postmenopausal estrogen replacement therapy and the risk of Alzheimer disease. *Archives of Neurology*, **58**, 435–440.

Shaywitz, S. E., Shaywitz, B. A., Pugh, K. R., Fullbright, R. K., Skudlarski, P., Mencl, W. E., Constable, R. T., Naftolin, F., Palter, S. F., Marichione, K. E., Katz, L., Shankweiler, D. P., Fletcher, J. M., Lacadie, C., Keltz, M., and Gore, J. C. (1999). Effect of estrogen on brain activation patterns in postmenopausal women during working memory tasks. *Journal of the American Medical Association*, **281**, 1197–1202.

Shute, V., Pellegrino, J. W., Hubert, L., and Reynolds, R. W. (1983). The relationship between androgen levels and human spatial abilities. *Bulletin of the Psychonomic Society*, **21**, 465–468.

Smith, C. A., McCleary, C. A., Murdock, G. A., Wilshire, T. W., Buckwalter, D. K., Bretsky, P. Marmol, L., Gorsuch, R. L., and Buckwalter, J. G. (1999). Lifelong estrogen exposure and cognitive performance in elderly women. *Brain and Cognition*, **39**, 203–218.

Steffens, D. C., Norton, M. C., Plassman, B. L., Tschanz, J. T., Wyse, B. W., Welsh-Bohmer, K. A., Anthony, J. C., and Breitner, J. C. (1999). Enhanced cognitive performance with estrogen use in nondemented community-dwelling older women. *Journal of the American Geriatric Society*, **47**, 1267–1268.

Tang, M. X., Jacobs, D., Stern, Y., Marder, K., Schofield, P., Gurland, B., Andrews, H., and Mayeux, R. (1996). Effect of oestrogen during menopause on risk and age at onset of Alzheimer's disease. *Lancet*, **348**, 429–432.

Vermeulen, A. (1991). Clinical review 24. Androgens in the aging male. *Journal of Clinical Endocrinology and Metabolism*, **73**, 221–224.

Voyer, D., Voyer, S., and Bryden, M. P. (1995). Magnitude of sex differences in spatial abilities: A meta-analysis and consideration of critical variables. *Psychological Bulletin*, **117**, 250–270.

Wahlin, Å., Bäckman, L., Mäntylä, T., Herlitz, A., Viitanen, M., and Winblad, B. (1993). Prior knowledge and face recognition in a community-based sample of healthy, very old adults. *Journal of Gerontology: Psychological Sciences*, **48**, 54–61.

Wang, P. N., Liao, S. Q., Liu, R. S., Liu, C. Y., Chao, H. T., Lu, S. R., Yu, H. Y., Wang, S. J., Liu, H. C. (2000). Effects of estrogen on cognition, mood, and cerebral blood flow in AD. A controlled study. *Neurology, 54,* 2061–2066.

Waring, S. C., Rocca, W. A., Petersen, R. C., O'Brien, P. C., Tangalos, E. G., and Kokmen, E. (1999). Postmenopausal estrogen replacement therapy and risk of AD. *Neurology, 52,* 965–970.

Wechsler, D. (1981). *Manual for the Wechsler Adult Intelligence Scale-Revised* (WAIS-R). San Antonio, TX: Psychological Corporation.

Wilson, J. D., George, F. W., and Griffin, J. E. (1981, March 20). The hormonal control of sexual development. *Science, 211,* 1278–1284.

Yaffe, K., Grady, D., Pressman, A., and Cummings, S. (1998). Serum estrogen levels, cognitive performance, and risk of cognitive decline in older community women. *Journal of American Geriatric Society, 46,* 816–821.

Yaffe, K., Sawaya, G., Lieberburg, I., and Grady, D. (1998). Estrogen therapy in pos-menopausal women. Effects on cognitive function and dementia. *Journal of American Medical Association, 279,* 688–695.

Yonker, J. E., Adolfsson, R., Eriksson, E., Hellstrand, M., Nilsson, L.-G., and Herlitz, A. (2003). Effects of postmenopausal estrogen use on episodic memory performance.

Yonker, J. E., Eriksson, E., Hellstrand, M. Nilsson, L.-G., and Herlitz, A. (2003). Androgens and visuospatial ability in 35 to 80 year old men.

Yonker, J. E., Eriksson, E., Nilsson, L. G., and Herlitz, A. (2003). Sex differences in episodic memory: Minimal influence of estradiol. *Brain and Cognition, 52,* 231–238.

Zelinski, E. M., Gilewski, M. J., and Schaie, K. W. (1993). Individual differences in cross-sectional and 3-year longitudinal memory performance across the adult life span. *Psychology and Aging, 8,* 176–186.

Chapter 14

Health, disease, and cognitive functioning in old age

Åke Wahlin

The accumulation of multiple chronic illnesses with advancing age is well established, and characterizes a significant proportion of the elderly population. This chapter discusses how this is commonly dealt with in cognitive aging research. The absence of a comprehensive view about cognition-associated diseases may result in failures to take into consideration health conditions that are critical to cognitive functioning, sometimes selectively, and this may be particularly true in the study of old age. Different approaches to the definition of health and disease are discussed, followed by examples of research explicitly focused on the relation between health-related variations and cognitive performance. Finally, possible ways to expand this research are proposed. The main message of the chapter is the need for clarity about what it means that participants in cognitive aging research are rarely free of disease.

Introduction

At this moment most of us are aware of the accumulation of elderly persons in many of the world's societies. Because of the political recognition of aging societies as a potential for causing a breakdown of welfare systems, a multitude of aging studies were initiated during the latter part of the twentieth century. The primary concern lies with another related change: the shift from acute to chronic disease as a major cause of death. For the first time in human history, conditions such as heart disease, cancer, and stroke are leading causes of morbidity and mortality. Importantly, most chronic diseases are not just slow in developing; they are also long lasting. Obviously there are many consequences from this apart from its economical impact, and this chapter will discuss some of the implications from a relatively narrow perspective: the impact of physical health/disease on individual variation in cognitive functioning. We have all heard the old adage that 'Aging is not a disease', and most cognitive aging researchers are consciously positioned somewhere between the endpoints of a thought scale where the opposite end reads 'Aging is a disease' (among others). This positioning is of concern because the related distinction between biological and pathological aging is troublesome. Thus, a safer position might be to assume a continuum between the biological changes of the aging human body and the point at which diseases are diagnosed. The chapter is not intended to present a medical frame of reference, nor is the ambition to provide any complete overview of the literature – dementia and psychiatric diseases are not covered. Medical health will principally be discussed at the level of variables and data collection. The main intentions are to discuss, first, some common practices in the cognitive aging research with respect to inclusion of medical health information among the independent variables, and to provide examples of medical health indicators that are known to be associated with cognitive functioning in old age. Second, some examples of as yet under-utilized approaches to the examination of health-related cognitive variation are provided.

What is health?

At a very general level, most researchers probably agree on the World Health Organization definition, which says that health is a state of complete physical, mental, and social well-being but not necessarily the absence of disease or infirmity. Also, further subdivision of physical health into medical, psychological, and functional aspects might seem unproblematic at a first glance. Yet much confusion exists at the level of measurement. For example, the concepts of physical or medical health are not always differentiated from their measures which may be anamnestic self-reports, physical examination scores, laboratory tests, or even proxies such as self-evaluated health status or functional aspects of health. A selection of issues related to the assessment of medical health will be discussed below.

What does 'healthy' mean?

Before doing that, it might be worthwhile to stop at the opposite to disease, that is, health. Looking up 'healthy' in a dictionary, the word implies full strength and vigor as well as freedom from signs of disease, which in the case of elderly persons is a rather exclusive condition (Fozard, Metter, and Brant, 1990). However, many cognitive aging studies describe their participants as relatively healthy, and this statement is often based on the participants' self-reports or after having applied some exclusion criteria based on information about medical status. Still, the variety of meaning assigned to the word 'healthy' across studies may be large and, importantly, result in quite diverging descriptions of cognitive aging (see Bäckman, Small, Wahlin *et al.*, 1999, for an overview). Furthermore, with respect to 'disease' (and to complicate matters further) this concept represents a condition in which functions are disturbed in comparison with some 'normal' reference condition. The related diagnostic problem here is what should be regarded as normal in old age. Also, disease is often perceived as being potentially avoidable through preventive measures or therapeutic agents, and thus, disease may indicate a condition that is not necessarily static (or progressing), not even chronic disease. Although the argument here is not that we have to agree on the exact meaning of 'healthy', it would be of great value to agree at a general level, or at a minimum to recognize the diversity of operationalizations that do exist in the cognitive aging literature. As will be exemplified later on, disease may affect not just the overall level of cognitive performance, but also mimic patterns of deficits typically assigned to biological aging itself or, in some cases, act on select cognitive abilities.

Assessment of medical health – some examples

As indicated above, quite different instruments are sometimes used as if they were assessing the same type of information. In the next paragraphs, some commonly used methods for collection of health data will be discussed: self-evaluations, administrative medical register data, and self-reports.

Subjective or self-evaluated health

A subjective health rating is the individual's perception and evaluation of his or her overall physical health. Such evaluations are often made in reference to the perceived health status of others or one's previous health condition. Sometimes, these measures are substituted for more 'objective' indicators of health such as physician's ratings or self-reported illnesses. Research on subjective health spans a vast literature about, for example, the strong predictive value of subjective health ratings for future death (see Benyamini and Idler, 1999; Idler and Benyamini, 1997, for overviews) that will not be discussed here. However it is important to realize that subjective health ratings take on different meanings in the individual and the frame of reference may be dependent upon, for example, the age (Hays, Schoenfeld, and Blazer, 1996), gender (Jylhä, Guralnik, Ferrucci *et al.*, 1998), nationality (Appels, Borma, Grabauskas *et al.*, 1996), income level (Franks, Clancy, Gold *et al.*, 1993), or sense of control and well-being (Helmer, Barber-Gateau, Letenneur *et al.*, 1999;

Menec, Chipperfield, and Perry, 1999) of the individual. It may be particularly notable that elderly in general tend to rate their overall health more positively as compared to younger persons, in spite of the higher prevalence figures across most medical diseases among the elderly. There is some evidence to indicate that these seemingly inaccurate health evaluations of elderly persons may be accounted for by other factors such as selective survivorship or cohort differences (Idler, 1993) where the elderly may be accepting a deterioration of their medical status as a consequence of aging, and not as an aspect of poor health. Additionally, there is some evidence that self-evaluated health ratings are based differentially on different medical conditions (Hoeymans, Feskens, Kromhout *et al.*, 1999; Kempen, Ormel, Brilman *et al.*, 1997). In sum, in any study, it may not be entirely accurate to substitute assessment of self-rated health for a medical assessment of some sort. Interestingly enough, subjective health ratings may predict memory decline, independently of differences in nationality and related demographic, changing physical health status, and subjective memory decline (Wahlin, Maitland, Bäckman *et al.*, 2004).

Medical health

Ideally, any study involving medical health data should be based on standardized medical diagnoses. Although large-scale multidisciplinary projects examining memory and other cognitive functions have tended to screen for potentially critical aspects of physical health (Fratiglioni, Viitanen, Bäckman *et al.*, 1992; Nilsson *et al.*, 1997; Steinhagen-Thiessen and Borchelt, 1993), this is of course not possible. In addition to asking the participant about his or her health status and history (as described in the next paragraph), a researcher may at times have access to medical records, usually from some central administrative database. Such registers will, for each individual and on each hospital contact, hold diagnostic codes based on the ICD (International Classification of Diseases); (World Health Organization, 1987) coding system for the primary and additional diagnoses present at a particular occasion. Thus, administrative data may provide a wealth of information even on whole populations, and at a relatively low cost. Having stated this, it is necessary to mention some notes of caution. First, diagnoses have, at least until recent years, been assigned retrospectively based on medical records and discharge summaries, and by staff other than the examining physician. If the medical record is incomplete, relevant diagnoses may be omitted or miscoded. Also, it is important to realize that clinical register data do not provide information on all health problems. One reason for this is that persons admitted to hospitals are generally more severely ill than persons who seek help in primary care or private practices. Thus, data may represent more severe conditions, and not all conditions present in a particular population. Second, the ordering of diagnoses (primary, secondary, etc.) is not necessarily based on severity judgements but on clinical as well as financial considerations. Third, although this varies across systems, the number of diagnoses allowed per record may result in loss of diagnostic information. Finally, most systems do not include information on whether a particular diagnosis was present upon admission to the hospital which is why the time span covered in the collection of register data may be crucial for considerations such as disease duration.

Self-reported health

As a rule, collection of medical health data in research includes, at least to some extent, anamnestic or survey data, which is not surprising given the costs of performing a complete clinical examination. In survey research, participants are typically questioned about their health problems and specific illnesses. Although there may be reasons to doubt the accuracy of self-reports, it is important to realize that the information provided by such queries is most likely derived from previous medical diagnoses explained by a physician. Thus, an individual's knowledge of many types of medical conditions is possible only through interaction with a practitioner (Ferraro, 1987). However, it is known that the reporting of easily comprehended diagnoses tends to be somewhat more reliable than the reporting of less conceptually clear-cut diagnoses (Paganini-Hill and Chao, 1993) and also that the agreement between medical and self-reported information is higher for chronic and long-lasting conditions than for less serious or unstable diseases (Kriegsmann, Penninx, van Eijk et al., 1996). Additionally, the tendency to report a disease might be dependent on the extent to which the condition in question has been traumatic, incapacitating and long-lasting (see Schach, 1976), or even on what social class the individual belongs to (Blane, Power, and Bartley, 1996). Finally, most individuals recall general information about their medical conditions rather than the detailed descriptions and specific diagnoses required for accurate ICD coding. Thus, these biases may influence the level of detail available to researchers and subsequently, the number of possible analytic methods to determine the impact of health on an outcome.

General concerns about health and individual differences

One of the main messages of this chapter is that we have as yet relatively limited knowledge about the extent to which variations in medical health account for variations in cognitive functioning among elderly persons.

For some groups of diseases, such as dementing and other psychiatric conditions or aspects of the circulatory system, the literature is extensive, while many diseases have rarely been examined other than perhaps as components of a disease summary score. There are of course reasons for that, some of which are outlined in this chapter.

It is premature to state any conclusions about how health relates to the common subdivision of cognitive variations into age-related and other variations. Still it may be realistic to assume that diseases account for relatively little of the age-related variation in cognitive performance (Earles and Salthouse, 1995), although biological markers of aging may account for most of the very same variations (Anstey and Smith, 1999). Such a pattern of findings may illustrate the distinction between biological and pathological aging as mentioned above, where chronological age taps into the biological age but not necessarily to the same extent into diseased age (although dementia is an exception to this). This line of reasoning relates mainly to the old adult age range, because there is little evidence of a linear increase of individual diseases in this range, although comorbidity rates appear to be highest among the oldest. To the contrary, in research involving young-old comparisons, the subdivision of performance differences into age-related and others is complicated by the existence of higher disease prevalence rates among the old participants.

Another concern is the possible existence of any Age X Disease interaction effects, that is, if disease affects level of cognitive performance differently in, for example, 70-79 year olds than in 80-89 year olds. Although sometimes examined, most available evidence indicates that this is not the case (see Bäckman *et al.*, 1999, for a summary). This again has to be a tentative conclusion, since relatively few diseases have been examined in this respect and also because many studies lack statistical power to detect Age X Disease interaction effects (see the section on the problem of rare and common diseases below).

Finally, yet another aspect of age by health interaction effects concerns the inclusion of oldest old among the participants of a study. While examinations of such interaction effects across most of the adult age range might prove significant in the end, it may well be the case that the greatest impact of health is found among the oldest old. Available evidence indicates both that demographic characteristics have a reduced impact among the oldest (Hassing, Wahlin, and Bäckman, 1998) and that biological factors become increasingly important in this group (Lindenberger and Baltes, 1997). It remains to be explored whether the shift generalizes from biological factors (e.g., hearing, vision, and balance) to diseases.

Do we really know what matters?

A straightforward answer is: no. Thus, the topic calls for inspection from a variety of angles, some of which are discussed here. One approach is to focus on those conditions that are most common among the elderly. Although prevalence rates vary across countries, even in the western world, a list of such diseases would include arthritis, hypertension, heart disease, depression, and type 2 diabetes (Fried, 2000). Indeed, the literature is to some extent populated by studies on the cognitive repercussions of such diseases, which is reasonable due to the relevance for public health. Also, even if the effects may be small on the individual basis, such as is sometimes found to be the case with circulatory diseases such as coronary heart disease or hypotension, on a population basis they still account for a considerable proportion of the cognitive deficits (Breteler, Claus, Grobbee *et al.*, 1994). From another angle, there are diseases that are somewhat less common but where the effects on cognitive performance may be dramatic in the individual. One example is hyperthyroidism (Haggerty *et al.*, 1990; Osterweil *et al.*, 1992). Note however that diagnosis of this condition may be particularly difficult in the case of elderly persons. Unfortunate blind inclusion of hyperthyroid subjects in a particular cognitive aging study may thus result in disturbing variation or, more seriously, in distorted conclusions. Additionally, even in the normal range, biochemical markers of thyroid functioning, such as thyroid stimulating hormone or free thyroxine, have been found to account for sizable portions of cognitive variation (Wahlin, Robins Wahlin, Small *et al.*, 1998; Prinz *et al.*, 1999).

Rare and common diseases

As discussed in the previous section, whether a particular disease may be regarded as an important predictor or not is dependent on how one looks at the problem. On the level of analysis, there are still other issues that call for attention. One such issue is statistical power, which in this case depends on mean differences in the outcome of interest (cognitive performance), sample size, and distribution of subjects suffering from a particular disease. Thus, the power to detect an association or effect increases as the mean differences in the outcome (e.g., episodic memory) increases, the sample size increases, or the number of affected subjects increases (up to the point of a balanced distribution among those who are affected and those who are not). While acknowledging the validity of power considerations in many types of research contexts, the concern here is with detection of cognitive deficits (or decline) related to physical disease. Hence, the failure to recognize that a particular disease has an impact on cognitive performance may depend on the fact that the impact is small on the mean level, that there are too few affected individuals available for analysis, or that the available total sample is too small, or a combination of these. Insufficient statistical power may also be one reason for the relative lack of studies examining interaction effects of disease combinations (see the section on additive and multiplicative effects below). At times, it may prove valuable to calculate power before specifying tests of disease interactions (see also Ferraro and Wilmoth, 2000).

Severity and comorbidity

Among elderly persons, multiple diseases is a rule rather than an exception, and among those who are 80 and above the majority of both men and women suffer from more than one condition (Cauley, Dorman, and Ganguli, 1996). The distinction between severity of illness and comorbidity is not always clear, however. Severity of illness may refer to the severity of a specific illness or to severity of illness across diseases, where it is difficult to disentangle severity of illness from comorbidity. To solve the latter issue, various scales, including scales applying different weights to individual diagnoses, have been constructed, some of which are in the public domain (e.g., The Duke University Severity of Illness Scale) (Parkerson, Broadhead, and Tse, 1993). Note however, that such scales are usually constructed for the purpose of calculating risk of mortality or in-hospital use.

For the grading of specific illnesses there are available instruments as well. Examples include grading of arthritis (Meenan, Gertman, and Mason, 1980), diabetes mellitus (Kuzuya, 2000), or heart disease (Mosterd *et al.*, 1997). The appropriateness of these and other gradings is dependent on, among other things, the type of outcome of interest and it is not possible to design a generic severity-of-illness measure that will encompass all outcomes or serve all purposes. Thus, for most diseases, it remains unclear what particular scale is the most appropriate for use in the context of cognitive performance examinations. Importantly though, variations of disease severity may be reflected in the size of cognitive deficits observed (Kalmijn, Feskens, Launer *et al.*, 1995).

Duration

For some diseases the impact on cognitive performance may be determined by how long the individual has suffered from the condition in question. Although systematic examination of this statement is lacking for most diseases, there are indications that duration is predictive of cognitive performance in, for example, diabetics (Elias *et al.*, 1997; Croxon and Jagger, 1995), or individuals suffering from B vitamin deficiency (Martin, Francis, Protetch *et al.*, 1992). Given the purpose of this chapter I will not go into details here but rather note a few problems. Indexing duration of a chronic disease may seem unproblematic and duration is typically counted as the distance between clinical diagnosis and the point of reference (e.g., cognitive testing). Although such a procedure may serve pragmatic purposes, one should be aware that in most cases we are able to recognize a disease clinically only at an advanced stage in its development. Thus, the true duration includes both the preclinical (or undetectable) period and the clinical phase. Additionally, the time point of clinical significance may vary both across diseases and subjects due to available diagnostic technology. For example, the same disease may, in one individual, be diagnosed at a stage where clinical symptoms are evident. In another person the same disease is diagnosed on the basis of laboratory or histological testing even though no clinical symptoms are yet evident.

Sex and age

Personal characteristics including age and sex are critical to our understanding of health as a predictor of cognitive functioning. A recent report noted that 'sex matters' in the study of all levels of biomedical and health related research, and being male or female is an important variable that affects health and illness throughout the life span (Institute of Medicine, 2001). Women generally live longer than men, but also tend to report more illnesses overall (Brayne, Matthews, McGee *et al.*, 2001). Thus, sex may be viewed as a potential confound in all studies of illness-related effects. It is also known that the incidence and severity of diseases vary between the sexes and several specific diseases are known to occur more commonly in either of the sexes. Examples of this are the greater prevalence of heart disease in men (Godsland, Wynn, Crook *et al.*, 1987) and higher frequencies of diseases such as hypertension, osteoporosis or hip fracture reported by women (Johnson and Wolinsky, 1994).

Concerning age it is, as we have already said, well established that the frequency of chronic diseases increases dramatically in old age (Fozard *et al.*, 1990). It is similarly well known that, in the medical health context, sex interacts with age so that men tend to die at a younger age than women and that the main causes of death among men are heart disease, cancers, and respiratory diseases. Whereas women suffer from the same illnesses, onset of disease is often later for women (e.g., developing coronary heart disease), and they tend to survive longer, resulting in higher disease prevalence figures among older women (Wylie, 1984). Studies focusing age by gender interaction effects on cognitive performance have both documented such effects and concluded that survival effects vary by gender (Perls, Morris, Ooi *et al.*, 1993; Stewart, Zelinski, and Wallace, 2000). Thus, it is tempting to state that many aging studies suffer to some extent from survivor bias that may be active across the entire age range studied depending on the distribution of sex among the participants.

Some common approaches

A common practice in the cognitive aging literature is to create a summary score of all disease indicators as an index of comorbidity for use as a predictor or control variable. Depending on what type of information is included, this may result in the additions of quite independent diseases and, perhaps needless to say, affects negatively the resulting summary variable's ability to discriminate among variations in many outcome measures. At the same time this procedure has the advantage of making use of information even from rare conditions (see the previous section on rare and common diseases). Another major approach is to use dummy variables for each illness in order to avoid the summation of very different conditions, where a major argument often is that the correlations among various disease indicators is typically modest (Chapell, 1981). Variations to this include counts of chronic conditions, serious illnesses, or aggregation of conditions within ICD categories and thus classifying conditions of related pathology and preserving variations in morbidity within bodily systems. Yet another approach is to use factor analysis to reduce the number of predictors to consider in the analyses, an approach that may be appropriate provided that the selection of conditions permits such a procedure (Wahlin, Nilsson, and Fastbom, 2002). Each of the mentioned approaches may have advantages and disadvantages depending on the research questions of interest.

There is no consensus about how to best conceptualize patterns of illness nor the appropriateness of the practice to study diseases in isolation, applying extreme group comparisons where effects on cognitive performance is typically studied (Wahlin, Hill, Winblad *et al.*, 1996). In this type of research, a primary concern is to control for related conditions as is the case in, for example, diabetes research where at minimum the associated impact of cardiovascular disease should be accounted for (see Strachan, Ewing, Deary *et al.*, 1997). It is important to realize that decisions about what potential confounds are worthy of consideration in a particular study are to a large extent based on clinical experience and such strategies, while rarely empirically driven, are commonly applied in research. For illustrative purposes, a short review of cognitive research on the impact of some common diseases follows next.

Extreme group comparisons

Perhaps the most common approach to examination of cognitive effects due to disease is extreme group comparisons. In this type of study, cognitive performance in a group of persons diagnosed with a particular disease is typically compared with a control group that is found to be free of the disease in question but comparable in other supposedly critical aspects.

B vitamin status is commonly assessed by analysis of serum concentrations. The diagnostic techniques have improved in recent years and there is at present some consensus that assessment of the metabolites methylmalonic acid and/or homocysteine are needed in order to diagnose deficiency (Carmel, 2000). The association between B vitamins and cognition has become a topic of increasing interest (see Calvaresi and Bryan, 2001, for a review). This may also be of particular relevance for aging studies, since prevalence of both clinical and subclinical B vitamin deficiency appears to be most common in old age (Baik and Russel, 1999; Olivares, Hertrampf, Capurro *et al.*, 2000), and since chronological age is the only factor known to correlate with presumedly normal levels of vitamin B_{12}, where vitamin levels decline linearly across the adult age range (Wahlin, Bäckman, Hultdin *et al.*, 2002), independently of other demographic differences, variations in gastric and intestinal health, and lifestyle.

Vitamin B deficiency states may, if untreated, lead to severe consequences such as depression, psychosis or dementia (see Hutto, 1997). But also subclinical stages of deficiency result in dysfunction and cognitive repercussions are perhaps the best-documented outcome. To date, most studies are cross-sectional and one of the first (and perhaps most cited) to document such associations was that of Goodwin *et al.* (1983). An important finding in this study, later confirmed by others (Wahlin *et al.*, 1996) was that there seem to be critical thresholds above or below which biochemical indicators of vitamin status exert their effects on cognitive performance. A second conclusion to be drawn from the available literature is that, among B_{12} and folate, the latter indicator may be the most critical for cognitive functioning (Hassing, Wahlin, Winblad *et al.*, 1999; Lindeman *et al.*, 2000), and homocysteine seems to be a better marker of B vitamin status-related cognitive deficits (Riggs, Spiro, Tucker *et al.*, 1996). Third and finally, although most studies have involved a relatively small number of dependent cognitive variables, recent research indicates that the cognitive deficits due to B vitamin status are selective, and that the abilities that are most affected are the same as those abilities most affected by chronological age itself (Robins Wahlin, Wahlin, Winblad *et al.*, 2001). In sum, vitamin B status represents a disease where the cognitive repercussions mimic those commonly ascribed to biological aging, although the cognitive variation accounted for by B vitamin status may not necessarily be age-related. This has, however, not been systematically examined.

Diabetes mellitus is a metabolic old age disease, mainly because the non-insulin dependent form (type 2) is characterized by late life onset. The disease is associated with structural and functional alterations of various organ systems, and affects the brain in several ways, for example by changing blood flow and brain metabolism (McCall, 1992). The effects of diabetes on cognitive performance were examined very early on (Miles and Root, 1922), and although it may be rather difficult to identify any clear patterns in the results yet reported, some of the most common findings are that diabetes is associated with deficient performance on tests of episodic memory (U'Ren, Riddle, Lezak et al., 1990), verbal fluency (Lowe, Tranel, Wallace et al., 1994), and speeded tasks (Tun, Perlmuter, Russo et al., 1987). The disease causes much disability in the later years of life, mainly as a result of the associated complications, and predisposes to atherosclerosis, ischemic heart disease, cerebrovascular disease and peripheral vascular disease (Elliot and Viberti, 1993). Thus, for any study of diabetes-related effects it is crucial to control for associated morbidity (Strachan et al., 1997) which may also exert an impact on cognitive performance. In this context, it should be noted that even less severe signs of cardiovascular disease are known to be negatively associated with cognitive functioning (Fahlander et al., 2000). In two recent studies where the impact of associated diseases were taken into account, it was found that diabetes among very old persons negatively affects global cognitive ability as assessed by the MMSE (Nilsson, Fastbom, and Wahlin, 2002) and, second, that although diabetes is associated with deficient performance on tests of verbal fluency and episodic memory, the effects on both types of abilities are less pronounced in tasks involving higher degrees of semantic structure. Thus, the effects are pronounced on letter fluency but not category fluency, on recall of random words but not recall of organizable words. Furthermore, taking preclinical dementia and impending death into account it was shown that cognitive deficits among very old diabetics are most likely detected by letter fluency tests (Wahlin, Nilsson et al., 2002). Thus, diabetes mellitus is an example where available evidence suggests that the disease may act selectively on cognitive abilities, and not independently of methodological variations.

Some less common analytic approaches

In addition to many of the methodologically oriented paragraphs, the chapter will end by proposing some possible ways by which this type of research may be expanded on the level of analysis. Thus, leaving the previously discussed conceptual and methodological questions aside for a moment I would like to outline some approaches that take into account, among other things, the lack of comprehensive views about what matters in terms of health variations, the fact that many elderly are affected by more than one disease, that the effects may not be additive only, and that information about future events may provide additional ideas about how disease relates to cognitive functioning.

The structure of health

Health is usually conceptualized in a multi-dimensional manner. As indicated in the beginning of the chapter, three major approaches to subdivision of health are commonly discussed: the medical model also known as the physical definition, the social definition or functional model, and the subjective evaluation or psychological model of health. The validity of and interrelations among these constructs have been evaluated empirically in a number of studies utilizing structural equation modeling procedures (Johnson and Wolinsky 1994; Liang, 1986; Liang, Bennett, Whitelaw et al., 1991; Whitelaw and Liang, 1991). In short, such studies indicate that whereas the three dimensions of health receive support empirically, and that the directions of interrelationships among such broad constructs may be specified, there is as yet little success in the specification of structures within the medical/physical dimension, at least as shown by available publications. However, we have recently completed a study based on two samples aged 55-80 years and assessed in Sweden and Canada. The results lend support to an ICD-related structure of medical health, and invariance across samples but (as expected from the previous section on sex and age) the model was not invariant across sexes or age (Maitland, Wahlin, Nyberg et al., 2003). Although there are studies that have included aspects of health (e.g., biomarkers, subjective health, number of self-reported diseases) in a modeling framework (Anstey and Smith, 1999; Earles and Salthouse, 1995), there are as yet no studies examining both cognitive performance and diseases within a modeling framework including comprehensive models of both constructs.

Additive and multiplicative effects

Old ways of thinking give diseases an ontological existence of their own. However, the fact that among the elderly multiple pathology is a rule rather than an exception calls for different modes of thinking. As discussed above, the reality of multiple diseases can be thought of in terms of severity and comorbidity but there may be more to it than that. An alternate approach to those already mentioned is to view diseases as belonging to different sets or combinations of conditions, depending on the extant patterns of overlap among the participants in a particular study (Thompson, 1996). Extending on this, one may hypothesize the existence of combinations among diseases and/or other physical indicators that produce (cognitive) effects that are larger than what would be expected from the sum of effects resulting from the predictors one by one. Interaction effects on cognitive performance are rarely examined in the literature on disease and cognition but there are some studies that report both absence (e.g., liver disease × alcoholism) (Edvin, Flynn, Klein *et al.*, 1999), and presence of such effects (e.g., hypertension × Diabetes) (Elias *et al.*, 1997). In general, however, it is unclear whether the effects, if any, represent the additive effects of two or more diseases or something beyond that. Therefore, I would like to discuss disease interaction effects in terms of additive and multiplicative effects. For this purpose, Figure 14.1 will serve as an illustration.

Here, Panel A represents comorbidity-related additive effects, where Condition 1 produces a deficit of -2, Condition 2 a deficit of -2, and the combination of Conditions $1 + 2$ a deficit of -4. Thus, although both conditions adds to the observed cognitive deficits, an interaction effect will most likely not indicate this, at least not in an analysis with factorial design. Also, in most cases the deficit resulting from Condition $1 + 2$ is somewhat smaller than the sum of deficits in subjects with either Condition 1 or 2 (Hassing *et al.*, 1999) probably because of the overlap in behavioral outcome due to the fact that most complex cognitive abilities depend on similarly complex neural networks in the brain and (relatedly) due to the fact that two distinctly different diseases may produce an identical outcome (see the section on future events below). Here, the set theory approach proposed by Thompson (1996) might prove useful, grouping subjects on the basis of what combinations of diseases they are diagnosed with and analysing their results separately, group by group.

Panel B represents a multiplicative effect where the reasons for the multiplicative effects of Conditions $1 + 2$ may simply be an expression of disease burden or a multiplicative interaction where either of the conditions predisposes for larger than expected effects of the other. Before discussing this possibility, the last panel will be commented on. Panel C represents a special case that has been found in several studies where dementia constitutes Condition 1. Here, Condition 2 adds nothing to the deficits resulting from Condition 1, in spite of that Condition 2 has an effect when occurring alone (Fahlander, Berger, Wahlin *et al.*, 1999). One reason for the lack of additive effects as illustrated in Panel C is thought to be due to the size of the effects related to Condition 1. This is not to say that there are no comorbidity effects of Condition 2, but that they are not detectable by the cognitive instruments.

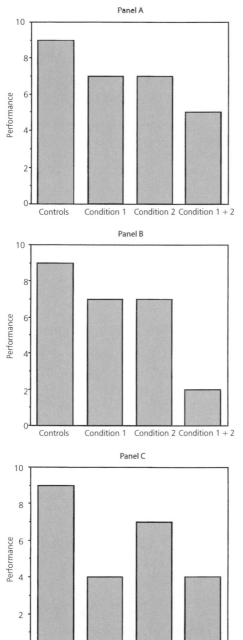

Fig. 14.1 An illustration of additive and multiplicative interaction effects of diseases on levels of cognitive performance

As noted, a multiplicative effect that is not simply due to disease burden may be due to a combination of conditions where at least one of them predisposes for a larger than expected effect of the other. A particularly interesting combination of predictors is that of gene–disease indicators. Apolipoprotein E (ApoE) is a plasma protein that is determined by the combination of three alleles, ε2, ε3, ε4, which are involved in cholesterol transportation. While the physiological mechanisms by which the genotype is expressed are still unclear, there is accumulating evidence that carriers of the ε4 allele, relative to their non-ε4 carrying age-matched cohort, display inferior cognitive function (O'Hara *et al.*, 1998; Yaffe, Cauley, Sands *et al.*, 1997), although there are conflicting results (Small *et al.*, 2000). It is however less controversial that ApoE ε4 is associated with a greater likelihood of developing Alzheimer's disease or other dementias. Although ApoE is not a specific disease locus, it may act as a vulnerability factor in interaction with several other physiological conditions and cause larger than expected cognitive decline. One mechanism for such effects might be that ApoE affects the rate of disease progression (Fazekas *et al.*, 2001). There are as yet few studies on interaction effects on cognitive functioning of ApoE ε4 and physical disease, although available data indicate the existence of effects, such as the combination with atherosclerosis, peripheral vascular disease, and diabetes mellitus (Haan, Shemanski, Jagust *et al.*, 1999), or impaired olfactory functioning (Borenstein Graves *et al.*, 1999). Given the small number of studies and limited aspects of cognitive functioning examined thus for, it is premature to speculate on whether multiplicative effects may act qualitatively differently than do the main effects.

Future events

Although dementias are not covered in this chapter, there are several good reasons for considering the preclinical phases of this group of diseases at the level of analysis. First, the fact that some medical diseases may be risk factors of dementia calls for attention. Apart from the well known association between vascular diseases and development of dementia, there are reports that other very common old age diseases such as diabetes (Ott *et al.*, 1999) or vitamin B deficiency (Wang *et al.*, 2001) constitute risk factors as well. Thus, recognizing both that dementia has a long preclinical phase during which cognitive effects may be observed (Bäckman, Small, and Fratiglioni, 2001) and that there are associations between some common diseases with a known impact on current cognitive performance *and* future dementia diagnosis does not automatically mean that subjects in a preclinical phase of dementia are to be excluded from the analysis (see Wahlin, Nilsson *et al.*, 2002, for a different approach). Relatedly, the bulk of studies on cognitive comorbidity effects in dementia show that an additional chronic disease adds very little to the cognitive deficits associated with dementia once it is diagnosed (Breen, Larson, Reifler *et al.*, 1984; Fahlander *et al.*, 1999). Although less well examined, this pattern of results may apply to the preclinical period of dementia as well (Fahlander, Wahlin, and Bäckman, 2003). This does not mean that the dementia disease eliminates the effects related to other diseases. Realizing that, in most research, we rely on diagnoses and measures of cognitive performance it may be impossible to disentangle the strictly other-disease related effects from those resulting from, say, preclinical dementia if the effects covary as they tend to do in the assessment of complex cognitive abilities that depend on complex neural networks in the brain. Thus, two poor test performances caused by different failures in the network may be indistinguishable at the behavioral level. A challenge for the future is to collect brain-imaging data in order to do that separation.

An inevitable future event is death, and the fact that some of the participants in our cognitive aging studies will die for reasons other than accidents and within the next couple of years requires some consideration. The main reason for that is the terminal decline phenomenon (Berg, 1996) that is known to occur several years before death (Small and Bäckman, 1999). Until we know whether the mechanisms of the accentuated cognitive decline among those who face their impending death are disease related (Smits, Deeg, Kriegsman *et al.*, 1999) or caused by some other mechanism, proximity to death has to be taken into account as a potential confound in any disease–cognition study. As with preclinical dementia, it may be a mistake to exclude subjects known to die in relative proximity to the time of cognitive testing. These participants may carry valuable information with respect to the patterns of the disease–cognition associations under scrutiny.

Taking both impending death and preclinical dementia into account, available reports are yet somewhat contradictory as to whether they affect the age-associated cognitive variations (Bäckman, Jonsson Laukka, Wahlin *et al.*, 2002; Sliwinski, Lipton, Buschke *et al.*, 1996), although it is clear that the non age-related variation is affected.

Concluding remarks

The main message here is that within cognitive aging research, the medical health of the participants is a relatively neglected factor, in spite of the rather dramatic prevalence figures among elderly persons. Although the chapter was mainly methodologically oriented, I would like to end by again highlighting some of the main points.

- While acknowledging the problems associated with gathering thorough information about medical health, at the same time we need to recognize that we do not know yet what matters.

- Physical health may (within the old adult age range) be of less concern for the study of age-related cognitive variation than non age-related variation.

- Still, the cognitive repercussions of pathology may mimic those typically assigned to chronological age, causing ideas about accentuated aging as a result of a particular disease (cf. common discussions on diabetes mellitus). Relatedly, because the effects of some diseases seem to be selective, the results of any study with a different focus may be distorted.

- Although it is informative to focus on single pathologies, it is also important to realize that we do not yet know the extent to which examinations of the structure of medical health may provide different information.

- Multiplicative disease interaction effects on cognitive performance may exist, but are under-explored. Such effects are most likely found in the context of factors known to influence the vulnerability of the biological systems in humans.

References

Anstey, K. J. and Smith, G. A. (1999). Interrelationships among biological markers of aging, health, activity, acculturation, and cognitive performance in late adulthood. *Psychology and Aging*, 14, 605–618.

Appels, A., Borma, H., Grabauskas, V., Gostaukas, A., and Sturmans, F. (1996). Self-rated health and mortality in a Lithuanian and a Dutch population. *Social Science and Medicine*, 42, 681–689.

Bäckman, L., Jonsson Laukka, E., Wahlin, Å., Small, B. J., and Fratiglioni, L. (2002). Influences of preclinical dementia and impending death on the magnitude of age-related cognitive deficits. *Psychology and Aging*, 17, 435–442.

Bäckman, L., Small, B. J., and Fratiglioni, L. (2001). Stability of the preclinical episodic memory deficit in Alzheimer's disease. *Brain*, 124, 96–102.

Bäckman, L., Small, B. J., Wahlin, Å., and Larsson, M. (1999). Cognitive functioning in very old age. In F. I. M. Craik and T. A. Salthouse (eds), *Handbook of Cognitive Aging* (Vol. 2, p. 499–558). Hillsdale, NJ: Erlbaum.

Baik, H. W. and Russel, R. M. (1999). Vitamin B_{12} deficiency in the elderly. *Annual Review of Nutrition*, 19, 257–377.

Benyamini, Y. and Idler, E. L. (1999). Community studies reporting associations between self-rated health and mortality: Additional studies, 1995–1998. *Research on Aging*, 21, 392–401.

Berg, S. (1996). Aging, behavior, and terminal decline. In J. E. Birren and K. W. Schaie (eds), *Handbook of the Psychology of Aging* (4th ed., pp. 323–337). San Diego, CA: Academic Press.

Blane, D., Power, C., and Bartley, M. (1996). Class differential in morbidity, illness bahaviour and the measurement of differentials in morbidity. *Journal of the Royal Statistical Society Series A*, 159, 77–92.

Borenstein Graves, A., Bowen, J. D., Rajaram, L., McCormick, W. C., McCurry, S. M., Schellenberg, G. D., and Larson, E. B. (1999). Impaired olfaction as a marker for cognitive decline: Interaction with apolipoprotein E e4 status. *Neurology*, 53, 1480–1487.

Brayne, C., Matthews, F. E., McGee, M. A., and Jagger, C. (2001). Health and ill-health in the older population in England and Wales: The Medical Research Council Cognitive Function and Ageing Study (MRC CFAS). *Age and Ageing*, 30, 53–62.

Breen, A. R., Larson, E. B., Reifler, B. V., Vitaliano, P. P., and Lawrence, G. L. (1984). Cognitive performance and functional competence in coexisting dementia and depression. *Journal of the American Geriatrics Society*, 32, 132–137.

Breteler, M. M. B., Claus, J. J., Grobbee, D. E., and Hofman, A. (1994). Cardiovascular disease and distribution of cognitive function in elderly people: The Rotterdam Study. *British Medical Journal*, 308, 1604–1608.

Calvaresi, E. and Bryan, J. (2001). B vitamins, cognition, and aging: A review. *Journal of Gerontology: Psychological Sciences*, 56B, P327–P339.

Carmel, R. (2000). Current concepts in cobalamin deficiency. *Annual Review of Medicine*, 51, 357–375.

Cauley, J. A., Dorman, J. S., and Ganguli, M. (1996). Genetic and aging epidemiology: The merging of two disciplines. *Neurology Clinics*, 14, 467–475.

Chapell, N. L. (1981). Measuring functional ability and chronic health conditions among the elderly: A research note on the adequacy of three instruments. *Journal of Health and Social Behavior*, 22, 90–102.

Croxon, S. C. M. and Jagger, C. (1995). Diabetes and cognitive impairment: A community-based study of elderly subjects. *Age and Ageing*, 24, 421–424.

Earles, J. L. and Salthouse, T. A. (1995). Interrelations of age, health, and speed. *Journal of Gerontology: Psychological Sciences*, 50B, P33–P41.

Edvin, D., Flynn, L., Klein, A., and Thuluvath, P. J. (1999). Cognitive impairment in alcoholic and nonalcoholic cirrhotic patients. *Hepatology*, 30, 1363–1367.

Elias, P. K., Elias, M. F., D'Agostino, R. B., Cupples, L. A., Wilson, P. W., Silbershatz, H., and Wolf, P. A. (1997). NIDDM and blood pressure as risk factors for poor cognitive performance: The Framingham Study. *Diabetes Care*, 20, 1388–1395.

Elliot, T. G. and Viberti, G. (1993). Relationship between insulin resistance and coronary heart disease in diabetes mellitus and the general population: A critical appraisal. *Baillieres Clinical Endocrinology and Metabolism*, 7, 1079–1103.

Fahlander, K., Berger, A.-K., Wahlin, Å., and Bäckman, L. (1999). Depression does not aggravate the episodic memory deficits associated with Alzheimer's disease. *Neuropsychology*, 13, 532–538.

Fahlander, K., Wahlin, Å., and Bäckman, L. (2003). *The relationship between vitamin B status and cognitive performance in preclinical and clinical Alzheimer's disease: Data from the Kungsholmen Project*. Manuscript submitted for publication.

Fahlander, K., Wahlin, Å., Fastbom, J., Grut, M., Forsell, Y., Hill, R. D., Winblad, B., and Bäckman, L. (2000). The relationship between signs of cardiovascular deficiency and cognitive performance in old age: A population-based study. *Journal of Gerontology: Psychological Sciences*, 55B, P259–P265.

Fazekas, F., Strasser-Fuchs, S., Kollegger, H., Berger, T., Kristoferitsch, W., Schmidt, H., Enzinger, C., Schiefermeier, M., Schwarz, C., Kornek, B., Reindl, M., Huber, K., Grass, R., Wimmer, G., Vass, K., Pfeiffer, K. H., Hartung, H. P., and Scmidt, R. (2001). Apolipoprotein E ε4 is associated with rapid progression of multiple sclerosis. *Neurology*, 57, 853–857.

Ferraro, K. F. (1987). Double jeopardy to health for black older adults? *Journal of Gerontology*, 42, 528–533.

Ferraro, K. F. and Wilmoth, J. M. (2000). Measuring morbidity: Disease counts, binary variables, and statistical power. *Journal of Gerontology: Social Sciences*, 55B, S173–S189.

Fozard, J. L., Metter, E. F., and Brant, L. J. (1990). Next steps in describing aging and disease in longitudinal studies. *Journal of Gerontology: Psychological Sciences*, 45, 116–127.

Franks, P., Clancy, C. M., Gold, M. R., and Nutting, P. A. (1993). Health insurance and subjective health status: Data from the 1987 National Medical Expenditure Survey. *American Journal of Public Health*, 83, 1295–1299.

Fratiglioni, L., Viitanen, M., Bäckman, L., Sandman, P.-O., and Winblad, B. (1992). Occurence of dementia in advanced age: The study design of the Kungsholmen Project. *Neuroepidemiology*, 11, *(Suppl. 1)*, 29–36.

Fried, L. P. (2000). Epidemiology of aging. *Epidemiology Reviews*, 22, 95–106.

Godsland, I. F., Wynn, V., Crook, D., and Miller, N. E. (1987). Sex, plasma lipoproteins, and artherosclerosis: Prevailing assumptions and outstanding questions. *American Heart Journal*, 114, 1467–1503.

Goodwin, J. S., Goodwin, J. M., and Garry, P. J. (1983). Association between nutritional status and cognitive functioning in a healthy elderly population. *JAMA*, 249, 2917–2921.

Haan, M. N., Shemanski, L., Jagust, W. J., Manolio, T. A., and Kuller, L. (1999). The role of APOE ε4 in modulating effects of other risk factors for cognitive decline in elderly persons. *JAMA*, 282, 40–46.

Haggerty, J. J., Garbutt, J. C., Evans, D. L., Golden, R. N., Pedersen, C., Simon, J. S., and Nemeroff, C. B. (1990). Subclinical hypothyroidism: A review of neuropsychiatric aspects. *International Journal of Psychiatry in Medicine*, 20, 193–208.

Hassing, L., Wahlin, Å., and Bäckman, L. (1998). Minimal influence of age, education, and gender on episodic memory functioning in very old age: A population-based study of nonagenarians. *Archives of Gerontology and Geriatrics*, 27, 75–87.

Hassing, L., Wahlin, Å., Winblad, B., and Bäckman, L. (1999). Further evidence for the effects of vitamin B_{12} and folate status on episodic memory functioning: A population-based study of very old adults. *Biological Psychiatry*, 45, 1472–1480.

Hays, J. C., Schoenfeld, D. E., and Blazer, D. G. (1996). Determinants of poor self-rated health in late life. *American Journal of Geriatric Psychiatry*, 4, 188–196.

Helmer, C., Barberger-Gateau, P., Letenneur, L., and Dartigues, J.-F. (1999). Subjective health and mortality in French elderly women and men. *Journal of Gerontology: Social Sciences*, 54B, S84–S92.

Hoeymans, N., Feskens, E. J. M., Kromhout, D., and van den Bos, G. A. M. (1999). The contribution of chronic conditions and disabilities to poor self-rated health in elderly men. *Journal of Gerontology: Medical Sciences*, 54A, M501–M506.

Hutto, B. R. (1997). Folate and cobalamin in psychiatric illness. *Comprehensive Psychiatry*, 38, 305–314.

Idler, E. L. (1993). Age differences in self-assessments of health: Age changes, cohort differences, or survivorship? *Journal of Gerontology: Social Sciences*, 48, S289–S300.

Idler, E. and Benyamini, Y. (1997). Self-rated health and mortality: A review of twenty-seven community studies. *Journal of Health and Social Behavior*, 38, 21–37.

Institute of Medicine (2001). *Exploring the Biological Contributions to Human Health: Does sex matter?* T. M. Wizeman and M. L. Pardue (eds). Wahington, DC: National Academy Press.

Johnson, R. J. and Wolinsky, F. D. (1994). Gender, race and health: The structure of health status among older adults. *The Gerontologist*, 34, 24–35.

Jylhä, M., Guralnik, J. M., Ferrucci, L., Jokela, J., and Heikkinen, H. (1998). Is self-rated health comparable across cultures and genders? *Journal of Gerontology: Social Sciences*, 53B, S144–S152.

Kalmijn, S., Feskens, E. J. M., Launer, L. J., Stijnen, T., and Kromhout, D. (1995). Glucose intolerance, hyperinsulinaemia and cognitive function in a general population of elderly men. *Diabetologia*, 38, 1096–1102.

Kempen, G. I. J. M., Ormel, J., Brilman, E. I., and Relyveld, J. (1997). Adaptive responses among Dutch elderly: The impact of eight chronic medical conditions on health-related quality of life. *American Journal of Public Health*, 87, 38–44.

Kriegsmann, D. M. W., Penninx, B. W. J. H., van Eijk, J. T. M., Boeke, A. J. P., and Deeg, D. J. H. (1996). Self-reports and general practioner information on the presence of chronic diseases in community dwelling elderly. A study on the accuracy of patient's self-reports and on determinants of inaccuracy. *Journal of Clinical Epidemiology*, 49, 1407–1417.

Kuzuya, T. (2000). Early diagnosis, early treatment and the new diagnostic criteria of diabetes mellitus. *British Journal of Nutrition*, 84, *(Suppl. 2)*, S177–S181.

Liang, J. (1986). Self-reported physical health among aged adults. *Journal of Gerontology*, 41, 248–260.

Liang, J., Bennett, J., Whitelaw, N., and Maeda, D. (1991). The structure of self-reported physical health among the aged in United States and Japan. *Medical Care*, 29, 1161–1180.

Lindenberger, U. and Baltes, P. B. (1997). Intellectual functioning in old and very old age: Cross-sectional results from the Berlin Aging Study. *Psychology and Aging*, 12, 410–432.

Lindeman, R. D., Romero, L. J., Koehler, K. M., Liang, H. C., LaRue, A., Baumgartner, R. N., and Garry, P. J. (2000). Serum Vitamin B12, C, and folate concentrations in the New Mexico Elder Health Survey: Correlations with cognitive and affective functions. *Journal of the American College of Nutrition*, 19, 68–76.

Lowe, L. P., Tranel, D., Wallace, R. B., and Welty, T. K. (1994). Type II diabetes and cognitive function: A population-based study of native Americans. *Diabetes Care*, 17, 891–896.

McCall, A. L. (1992). Perspectives in diabetes: The impact of diabetes on the CNS. *Diabetes*, 41, 557–570.

Maitland, S. B., Wahlin, Å., Nyberg, L., Bäckman, L., Dixon, R. A., and Nilsson, L.-G. (2003). A five-factor model of medical health: Generality across age, sex, and nations. Manuscript submitted for publication.

Martin, D. C., Francis, J., Protetch, J., and Huff, F. J. (1992). Time dependency of cognitive recovery with cobalamin replacement: Report of a pilot study. *Journal of the American Geriatrics Society*, 40, 168–172.

Meenan, R. F., Gertman, P. M., and Mason, J. H. (1980). Measuring health status in arthritis: The AIMS. *Arthritis and Rheumatism*, 23, 146–152.

Menec, V. H., Chipperfield, J. G., and Perry, R. P. (1999). Self-perceptions of health: A prospective analysis of mortality, control, and health. *Journal of Gerontology: Psychological Sciences*, 54B, P85–P93.

Miles, W. R., and Root, H. F. (1922). Psychologic tests applied to diabetic patients. *Archives of Internal Medicine*, 30, 767–777.

Mosterd, A., Deckers, J. W., Hoes, A. W., Nederspel, A., Smeets, A., Linker, D. T., and Grobbee, D. E. (1997). Classification of heart failure in population based research: An assessment of six heart failure scores. *European Journal of Epidemiology*, 13, 491–502.

Nilsson, L.-G., Bäckman, L., Erngrund, K., Nyberg, L., Adolfsson, R., Bucht, G., Karlsson, S., Widing, M., and Winblad, B. (1997). The Betula Prospective Cohort Study: Memory, health, and aging. *Aging, Neuropsychology, and Cognition*, 4, 1–32.

Nilsson, E., Fastbom, J., and Wahlin, Å. (2002). Cognitive functioning in very old non-demented and non-depressed persons: The impact of diabetes. *Archives of Gerontology and Geriatrics*, 35, 95–105.

O'Hara, R., Yesavage, J. A., Kraemer, H. C., Mauricio, M., Friedman, L. F., and Murphy, G. M. (1998). The APOE epsilon 4 allele is associated with decline on delayed recall performance in community-dwelling older adults. *Journal of the American Geriatrics Society*, 46, 1493–1498.

Olivares, M., Hertrampf, E., Capurro, M. T., and Wegner, D. (2000). Prevalence of anemia in elderly subjects living at home: Role of micronutrient deficiency and inflammation. *European Journal of Clinical Nutrition*, 11, 834–839.

Osterweil, D., Syndulko, K., Cohen, S. N., Pettler-Jennings, P. D., Hershman, J. M., Cummings, J. L., Tourtellotte, W. W., and Solomon, D. H. (1992). Cognitive function in non-demented older adults with hypothyroidism. *Journal of the American Geriatrics Society*, 40, 325–335.

Ott, A., Stolk, R. P., van Harskamp, F., Pols, H. A. P., Grobbee, D. E., Hofman, A., and Breteler, M. M. B. (1999). Diabetes mellitus and the risk of dementia: The Rotterdam Study. *Neurology*, 53, 1937–1942.

Paganini-Hill, A. and Chao, A. (1993). Accuracy of recall of hip fracture, heart attack, and cancer: A comparison of postal survey data and medical records. *American Journal of Epidemiology*, 138, 101–106.

Parkerson, G. R. Jr, Broadhead, W. E., and Tse, C.-K. J. (1993). The Duke Severity of Illness Checklist (DUSOI) for measurement of severity and comorbidity. *Journal of Clinical Epidemiology*, 46, 379–393.

Perls, T. T., Morris, J. N., Ooi, W. L., and Lipsitz, L. A. (1993). The relationship between age, gender and cognitive performance in the very old: The effect of selective survival. *Journal of the American Geriatrics Society*, 41, 193–201.

Prinz, P. N., Scanlan, J. M., Vitaliano, P. P., Moe, K. E., Borson, S., Toivola, B., Merriam, G. R., Larsen, L. H., and Reed, H. L. (1999). Thyroid hormones: Positive relationships with cognition in healthy, euthyroid older men. *Journal of Gerontology: Medical Sciences*, 3, 111–116.

Riggs, K. M., Spiro, A., Tucker, K., and Rush, D. (1996). Relations of Vitamin B-12, folate, and homocysteine to cognitive performance in the Normative Aging Study. *American Journal of Clinical Nutrition*, 63, 306–314.

Robins Wahlin, T.-B., Wahlin, Å., Winblad, B., and Bäckman, L. (2001). The influence of serum vitamin B_{12} and folate status on cognitive functioning in very old age. *Biological Psychology*, 56, 247–265.

Schach, E. (1976). *Reliability in Sociomedical Research: Implications for cross-national studies*. Series 90-032, vol. 4. Beverly Hills, CA: Sage Publications.

Sliwinski, M., Lipton, R. B., Buschke, H., and Stewart, W. (1996). The effects of preclinical dementia on estimates of normal cognitive functioning in aging. *Journal of Gerontology: Psychological Sciences*, 51, 217–225.

Small, B. J. and Bäckman, L. (1999). Time to death and cognitive performance. *Current Directions in Psychological Science*, 8, 168–172.

Small, B. J., Graves, A. B., McEvoy, C. L., Crawford, F. C., Mullan, M., and Mortimer, J. A. (2000). Is APOE-ε4 a risk factor for cognitive impairment in normal aging? *Neurology*, 54, 2082–2088.

Smits, C. H. M., Deeg, D. J. H., Kriegsman, D. M. W., and Schmand, B. (1999). Cognitive functioning and health as determinants of mortality in an older population. *American Journal of Epidemiology*, 150, 978–986.

Steinhagen-Thiessen, E. and Borchelt, M. (1993). Health differences in advanced old age. *Ageing and Society*, 13, 619–655.

Stewart, S. T., Zelinski, E. M., and Wallace, R. B. (2000). Age, medical conditions, and gender as interactive predictors of cognitive performance: The effects of selective survival. *Journal of Gerontology: Psychological Sciences*, 55B, P381–P383.

Strachan, M. W. J., Ewing, F. M. E., Deary, I. J., and Frier, B. M. (1997). Is type II diabetes associated with an increased risk of cognitive dysfunction? *Diabetes Care*, 20, 438–445.

Thompson, M. K. (1996). The need for a new biological model in Geratology. *Age and Ageing*, 25, 168–171.

Tun, P. A., Perlmuter, L. C., Russo, P., and Nathan, D. M. (1987). Memory self-assessment and performance in aged diabetics and non-diabetics. *Experimental Aging Research*, 13, 151–157.

U'Ren, R., Riddle, M. C., Lezak, M. D., and Bennington-Davis, M. (1990). The mental efficiency of the elderly person with type 2 diabetes mellitus. *Journal of the American Geriatrics Society*, 38, 505–510.

Wahlin, Å., Bäckman, L., Hultdin, J., Adolfsson, R., and Nilsson, L.-G. (2002). Reference values for serum levels of vitamin B_{12} and folic acid in a population-based sample of adults between 35 and 80 years of age. *Public Health Nutrition*, 5, 505–511.

Wahlin, Å., Hill, R. D., Winblad, B., and Bäckman, L. (1996). Effects of serum vitamin B_{12} and folate status on episodic memory performance in very old age: A population-based study. *Psychology and Aging*, 11, 487–496.

Wahlin, Å., Maitland, S. B., Bäckman, L., and Dixon, R. A. (2004). Interrelations between subjective health and episodic memory change in Swedish and Canadian samples of older adults. *International Journal of Aging and Human Development*, 57, 21–35.

Wahlin, Å., Nilsson, E., and Fastbom, J. (2002). Cognitive performance in very old diabetic persons: The impact of semantic structure, preclinical dementia, and impending death. *Neuropsychology*, 16, 208–216.

Wahlin, Å., Robins Wahlin, T.-B., Small, B. J., and Bäckman, L. (1998). Influences of Thyroid Stimulating Hormone on cognitive functioning in very old age. *Journal of Gerontology: Psychological Sciences*, 53B, P234–P239.

Wang, H.-X., Wahlin, Å., Basun, H., Fastbom, J., Winblad, B., and Fratiglioni, L. (2001). Low levels of vitamin B_{12} and folate in relation to the incidence of Alzheimer's disease: Results from the Kungsholmen Project. *Neurology*, 56, 1188–1194.

Whitelaw, N. A. and Liang, J. (1991). The structure of the OARS physical health measures. *Medical Care*, 29, 332–347.

World Health Organization (1987). *International Classification of Diseases, Injuries, and Cause of Death, ninth revision (ICD-9)*. Geneva, Switzerland.

Wylie, C. M. (1984). Contrasts in the health of elderly men and women: An analysis of recent data for whites in the United States. *Journal of the American Geriatrics Society*, 32, 670–675.

Yaffe, K., Cauley, J., Sands, L., and Browner, W. (1997). Apolipoprotein E phenotype and cognitive decline in a prospective study of elderly community women. *Archives of Neurology*, 54, 1110–1114.

Chapter 15

Broadening the context of cognitive aging: A commentary

Peter Graf

The majority of empirical investigations on changes in cognition that accompany old age have focused on the main and interaction effects that occur among high-level abilities, especially memory, attention and perception. The chapters in this section serve to situate this type of research in a broader context. Christensen and Mackinnon summarize recent work on age-related declines in sensory, respiratory and physiological functions. Wahlin's chapter discusses various aspects of health, difficulties with the definition and objective measurement of health, and age-associated declines in health that are likely to impact cognitive functions. Herlitz and Yonker review research on hormonal influences on cognitive functions in adulthood and old age, and finally, Pedersen provides an overview of genetic factors that have come under investigation as potential contributors to individual and gender differences in cognitive aging. Together, these chapters cover a large domain, the biological and health context that shapes cognitive aging. They provide a status report of progress that has been achieved in these different areas while highlighting interesting questions for future research.

These chapters were not intended as an exhaustive survey of all variables that are known or suspected to influence cognitive aging, but by emphasizing sensory, physiological, biological and genetic factors, they focus research on potential 'hardware' causes of this process. Research with this type of focus must proceed with full awareness that other factors modify the impact of hardware contributions to cognitive aging. Prominent among these other factors are personality, marital status, social–cultural variables as well as economic circumstances. It is well established, for example, that an individual's response to health problems and to injury and disease depends on their personality, that social-group and cultural variables are correlated with the manner and effectiveness of coping with stress, and that there is a well-documented link between health and socio-economic status (Cairney, 2001; Friedman, 1993;

Heslop *et al.*, 2001; Livneh and Antonak, 1997; Perilla, Norris and Lavizzo, 2002; Tseng, 2001). Investigations that ignore these social and psychological influences are likely to distort the true impact on cognitive aging due to hardware causes. Therefore, if the goal of research is to develop a comprehensive understanding of the causes of cognitive aging, it will be necessary to investigate the influence of hardware causes in combination with the influence of social and psychological factors.

By situating cognitive aging in the broad context of health, physiological and biological processes, the chapters in this section seem to underscore the need for large-scale, comprehensive investigations that are able to tease apart the often subtle main and interaction effects among the multitude of causes of cognitive aging. These kinds of investigations will need to be longitudinal in order to ferret out changes that occur within individuals, and cutting-edge statistical methods will be required for data analysis. The chapters by Pederson and by Lindenberger and Ghisletta make the strongest argument in favor of comprehensive longitudinal investigations, and they provide highly readable overviews of the novel data handling methods that go along with them.

While there can be no doubt that comprehensive longitudinal studies will be required in order to develop a complete understanding of the causes of cognitive aging, I am convinced that the time for these types of studies has not yet come. My conviction is based on four related observations. First, comprehensive investigations are expensive, and they tend to concentrate scarce resources in a few centers while stifling essential propaedeutic research endeavors. Second, in order to make comprehensive studies feasible and fundable, it is often necessary to rely on screening instruments that may be economical but which fail to capture critical nuances of the core constructs under investigation. Third, many of the core constructs that seem implicated in cognitive aging are still too poorly understood and defined. The chapter by Wahlin makes this point especially thoroughly in connection with health. Fourth, we have not yet developed adequately valid and reliable methods and instruments for assessing many of the core constructs that seem central to cognitive aging. I will elaborate briefly on each of these points in the remainder of this commentary.

Keeping focused on preparatory research

Contemporary cognitive aging research makes use of a variety of approaches, including small group experiments that tend to compare young with older adults, medium-sized cross-sectional experiments often involving representative samples of adults beyond the middle age, plus a scattering of much more involved, larger multi-cohort longitudinal studies. This mixture of research approaches has served us well because each makes a distinct and valuable contribution to the advancement of the field. The small group experiment is an ideal, relatively inexpensive vehicle for exploring questions about age-group differences in cognition. The larger cross-sectional studies with representative samples of participants are able to provide insight into relationships among variables and how they change across the lifespan, and they have been used to generate a wealth of valuable normative data and hypotheses. But only longitudinal studies can reveal change that occurs within individuals, and to separate this type of change from that due to specific cohorts.

The extent to which cognitive aging research has relied on small group, cross-sectional and longitudinal studies seems governed by a symbiotic relationship that would be threatened by the premature, increased use of larger and more comprehensive longitudinal investigations. Small-group experiments and cross-sectional studies provide the data and the compelling hypotheses that are required to justify relatively large-scale comprehensive longitudinal studies. The former are also required, and clearly much better suited, for developing and fine-tuning the assessment instruments that are essential for the latter. A number of the chapters in this section have discussed the currently still ill-defined nature of core constructs such as health and the relatively primitive stage of research on hormones and cognition, thereby underscoring the need for more preparatory research. The field of cognitive aging is not yet ready for larger, more comprehensive investigations. Large-scale investigations that aim to be even more comprehensive than current or recent longitudinal projects (e.g., the Betula project, the Berlin Aging Study and the Victoria Longitudinal Study) are extremely expensive and thus ought to be undertaken only when compelled by specific testable hypotheses, and when supported by valid and reliable instruments, that is, the products of extensive preliminary work. In the absence of specific testable hypotheses, comprehensive investigations tend to turn into superficial surveys whose results are unlikely to replicate. They consume the financial and intellectual resources that could have been invested more productively in strengthening the knowledge and method foundation upon which they ought to be built.

Not all comprehensive investigations are alike except perhaps by being expensive. In order to minimize expenses as well as the time required for a comprehensive assessment of each participant, some investigations have used global screening instruments such as the modified mini-mental state exam (Teng and Chui, 1987) or the North American Adult Reading Test (Nelson, 1982; Spreen and Strauss, 1991) for estimating cognitive functions and intelligence, coupled with various self-rating instruments and questionnaires for estimating health and socio-economic status. These types of instruments are easy and inexpensive to administer, and in some instances suitable as tools for distinguishing, for example, between individuals with and without cognitive impairments. However, they provide only a superficial, inexact and insensitive estimate of the critical constructs that are implicated in cognitive aging. These instruments are not sufficiently sensitive for tracking cognitive changes that occur in normal aging individuals, and cannot be used for testing hypotheses about specific cognitive-aging constructs (e.g., fluid intelligence, processing speed) that have emerged from previous research. An investigation that covers any domain of cognitive aging by means of these types of screening instruments is doomed to failure, to yield misleading information about the true impact of the various causes of cognitive aging.

Many of the core constructs that are involved in cognitive aging have not yet been precisely defined and operationalized. Wahlin's chapter underscores the need for better definitions of health and disease in the context of aging. The chapter by Herlitz and Yonker calls for improved methods for tracking various hormone levels. There is room for improvement even in the operationalization of various aspects of perception and cognition. Although in this domain there is fairly good agreement on the meaning of some terms like verbal fluency and explicit episodic memory, this type of agreement does not exist for terms like working memory, processing resources or sensory skills. To illustrate, a recent review by De Ribaupierre (2002) highlighted, on one hand, the different ways in which processing resources and working memory have been operationalized by developmental and cognitive aging researchers, and on the other hand, the absence of correlations among various measures of inhibition, one of the core constructs of working memory. In the absence of precise definitions of core constructs, their operationalization is poorly constrained, and assessment instruments tend to be chosen on the basis of personal preference, availability, etc.

The attempt to derive constructs statistically is not a solution to this problem either; it only serves to hide it. Statistically derived 'latent' constructs are the products of the data gathering instruments that were employed, and thus, these constructs will differ according to the choice of assessment instruments that has been made. In the absence of clear definitions and operationalizations of potentially critical constructs, no investigation will be able to reveal the true pattern of causal influences involved in cognitive aging. Instead, the outcome of such premature investigations will be an accident determined by arbitrarily chosen assessment instruments.

To set the stage for future comprehensive investigations of cognitive aging, there is a need to develop assessment instruments that yield valid and reliable data. An enormous amount of work has gone into developing these kinds of instruments, for example, for various aspects of cognition (e.g., memory, attention, perception, sensation and language). Do we have equally valid and reliable ways for assessing health, physiological functions and hormone levels? Do brain-imaging methods (e.g., fMRI) yield reliable results? Clear answers to such questions are difficult to obtain, especially because our measures need to produce similarly valid and reliable data across a large segment of the adult lifespan. One cause for serious concern about validity and reliability comes from the verbal paired associates test of the widely used Wechsler Memory Scale (Wechsler, 1997). According to the published normative data, the top-performing 25 per cent of subjects who are under 25 years of age are expected to score perfectly on the delayed version of this test, and the top-performing 25 per cent of all subjects who are under 55 years of age are expected to score within one standard deviation of the maximum (see Uttl, Graf and Richter, 2002). The presence of these types of performance ceiling effects limits the test's ability to ferret out differences among high-scoring individuals and it lowers the magnitude of any correlations that may be computed. More importantly, these limits on the reliability of the Wechsler Memory Scale, one of the most widely used assessment instruments, should provoke serious investigations into the validity, reliability and suitability of less well-established assessment instruments. Unless all constructs targeted by a comprehensive investigation are assessed by means of comparably reliable instruments, its outcome will be misinforming.

Conclusion

A frontier in science may be defined as the farthermost limits of knowledge in an area, as a field of inquiry where a few discoveries have been made but have not yet organized into a coherent theoretical system. In this sense, the chapters in this section define one of the frontiers of research on cognitive aging. My commentary has identified a few of the most obvious preliminary steps that will need to be taken in order to connect isolated discoveries about potential 'hardware' causes of cognitive aging with those that have dominated theoretical proposal and previous psychological investigations. The kind of preparatory work that is underscored in my commentary is mundane, 'grunt' work that makes use of well-tried methods, but it is essential in order to set the stage for more comprehensive investigations in the future. My fear is that we will try to take a short cut, attempt to proceed without doing the necessary preparatory research, by relying on cutting edge statistical methods such as latent growth curve models. These models are not a panacea; the quality of insights we derive from their use depends entirely on the quality of the data we feed into them and on the quality of theorizing that guides their application.

References

Cairney, J. (2000). Socio-economic status and self-rated health among older Canadians. *Canadian Journal on Aging*, **19**, 456–478.

De Ribaupierre, A. (2002). Working memory and attentional processes across the lifespan. In P. Graf and N. Ohta (eds). *Lifespan Development of Human Memory* (pp. 59–80). Cambridge, MA: MIT Press.

Friedman, R. S. (1993). When the patient Intrudes on the treatment: The aging of personality types in medical management. *Journal of Geriatric Psychiatry*, **26**, 149–177.

Heslop, P., Davey-Smith, G., Carroll, D., MacLeod, J., Hyland, F., and Hart, C. (2001). Perceived stress and coronary heart disease risk factors: The contribution of socio-economic position. *British Journal of Health Psychology*, **6**, 167–178.

Livneh, H. and Antonak, R. F. (1997). *Psychosocial Adaptation to Chronic Illness and Disability*. Gaithersburg, MD: Aspen Publishers.

Nelson, H. E. (1982). *National Adult Reading Test (NART): Test Manual*. Windsor, UK: NFER Nelson.

Perilla, J. L., Norris, F. H., and Lavizzo, E. A. (2002). Ethnicity, culture, and disaster response: Identifying and explaining ethnic differences in PTSD six months after Hurricane Andrew. *Journal of Social and Clinical Psychology*, **21**, 20–45.

Spreen, O. and Strauss, E. (1991). *A Compendium of Neuropsychological Tests*. New York, NY: Oxford University Press.

Teng, E. L. and Chui, H. C. (1987). A modified mini-mental state (3MS) examination. *Journal of Clinical Psychiatry*, **48**, 314–318.

Tseng, W. S. (2001). *Handbook of Cultural Psychiatry*. San Diego, CA: Academic Press.

Uttl, B., Graf, P., and Richter, L. K. (2002). Verbal paired associates tests: Limits on validity and reliability. *Archives of Clinical Neuropsychology*, **17**, 569–583.

Wechsler, D. (1987). *Wechsler Memory Scale-Revised*. San Antonio, TX: Pscyhological Corporation.

Chapter 16

Commentary: Framing fearful (a)symmetries: Three hard questions about cognitive aging

Paul Verhaeghen

Two opposite forces drive researchers' thinking (and hence their research practice) concerning cognitive aging. The first driving force is towards strong reduction. The monograph that exemplifies this approach best is probably Salthouse's 1991 *Theoretical perspectives on cognitive aging*. The preferred method is a correlational, individual-differences approach, in which a set of antecedent variables is used to predict age differences (in a cross-sectional design) or age changes (in a longitudinal design) in some aspect of cognition – often measured by a small set of tasks assumed to tap into relatively broad psychometric concepts. The current dream among reductionists is of cross-level unification (see, for example, the strong claims in Li, Lindenberger, and Frensch, 2000, and Park, Polk, Mikels *et al.*, 2001); the aspiration is to build up explanations for cognitive aging from the bottom up, referring to changes in brain structure, in neuronal functioning, or both. This dream is inherent in the quintet of excellent papers offered in this section: they either explicitly investigate biological mechanisms (Herlitz and Yonker, Pedersen, and Wahlin), or suggest that a foray into biology would be a desirable next step (Christensen and Mackinnon, Lindenberger and Ghisletta).

A second school of cognitive aging, perhaps best represented by Kausler's 1991 monograph *Experimental psychology, cognition, and human aging*, aims at high precision, and examines aging at the process level. The current front line approach in the process-oriented camp is computational, that is, aging is modeled mathematically by borrowing existing models from cognitive psychology and searching for age-relatedness in specific parameters of those models (see, for example, the strong positions taken by Byrne, 1998; Kahana, Howard, Zaromb *et al.*, 2002; Meyer, Glass, Mueller *et al.*, 2001; and Ratcliff, Spieler, and McKoon, 2000); the aspiration is to reproduce the pattern of age-effects observed in a particular set of tasks by modifiying as few of the general-cognitive model parameters as possible. The preferred method for obtaining human data is the experimental method, in which performance (latency or accuracy) is compared between a baseline version of a task and a version in which the process of interest is manipulated.

In many ways, the two approaches are diametrical opposites: the first operates at a macro-level (three of the papers in this section use broad concepts such as 'cognition', 'cognitive functioning', or 'cognitive aging' in their titles, suggesting that the results generalize across all aspects of cognitive performance; one title does not even mention cognition, but merely 'old age'), the second is decidedly micro with only occasional broad claims (Meyer *et al.*, 2001). The ambitions differ: the former approach goes broad, the latter deep. The former seems to suggest that cognitive aging is orderly and simple; the latter that it is diverse and quite messy.

Shall, or even *can* the twain meet? Meso-approaches exist in which cognitive aging is considered in much more detail that is typically done in the macro-approach, but still at much coarser resolutions than those obtained in the micro-approach (Kliegl, 1996; Hale and Myerson, 1996; Verhaeghen *et al.*, 2002), but this meso-approach may be a theoretical alternative rather than a bridge. Still, questions emerge from the meso-approach that are relevant as background questions to the wider epistemology as exemplified by the papers in this section. It docs not exactly *answer* those questions, but in a book that wants to push new frontiers, it might well be worth while to keep some unanswerables at the horizon of our vision . . .

The first question concerns the integration of research findings across approaches. It is my feeling that cognitive aging is best described by the terrifying beauty – terrifying at least to the researcher trying to understand them – of two almost paradoxically opposed phenomena: first, the existence of strong and reliable across-phenomenon regularities between the cognitive behavior of younger and older adults, and, second, the existence of equally strong and reliable dissociations along presumed (but currently ill-understood) fault lines in the cognitive system. This terrifying beauty, these fearful symmetries and asymmetries between the cognitive system as implemented in a young adult and an older adult body, seem to speak against any dream of quick and easy unification through single-parameter models.

The second question deals with the nature of aging itself. What exactly is it that cognitive aging researchers try to explain? Are our methods, our models, and our favorite explanatory variables aimed at the aging process itself, or at age differences? More specifically, the field has a pretty good grip on the major variables that explain age-related variance in a cross-sectional context (i.e., we understand age differences pretty well), but these same methods, models, and variables fall drastically short when predicting or describing global age-related change or individual differences in change.

The third question is related to the second question. It inquires as to what makes the study of aging special, that is, what makes our explanation for aging distinct from other explanations invoking the same variables to explain other aspects of group or individual differences?

The first hard question: What is the complexity dimension of cognitive aging?

Aging is not programmed. Humans posses a genetic blueprint for development, but it seems likely that we are not equipped with a blueprint for aging. Therefore, the effects of aging might be expected to be any (and maybe even any combination) of the following: (a) the system breaks down in a global fashion in all individuals (but not necessarily at identical rates); (b) the system breaks down randomly (i.e., some components become defective earlier than others, but which components break down is a matter of chance), leading to global changes when perceived at the group level; or (c) the system breaks down along predictable lines. Scenario A will occur if all elements of the system are equally vulnerable; scenario B will occur if some randomness is involved in system component vulnerability, or if the integrity of the components is compromised differently due to life history and/or life circumstances (e.g., vascular damage due to tobacco use); scenario C will occur if particular system components are particularly vulnerable or invulnerable. Different methods will pick up different aspects of the reality of cognitive aging. Unfortunately, the correlational approach is not helpful in distinguishing the alternatives. If change is correlated, that is, if the rank ordering of individuals remains largely identical over time, then by necessity a common factor will emerge; this is under either scenario A or scenario C. If has been demonstrated analytically that even scenario B can lead to the emergence of a common factor. Experimental research, however, can help in detecting predictable dissociations (scenario C).

One of the accomplishments of the meso-approach is that it points both at similarities between performance of young and older adults and at crucial differences. In the next section, I will briefly review five sample cases, and conclude that single-parameter models by necessity fall short in explaining such (a)symmetries. The first four sample cases show that regularities can be detected between different systems or different subject groups when examined at a deeper level, that is, when the data are parameterized according to underlying performance models rather than merely being examined at the level of age-by-condition or age-by-subject-group interactions. The fifth sample case makes the opposite point, namely that there exist breaking points in the system that are specifically associated with age, and that cannot be reduced to any single-parameter explanation. In other words, the message is that there are between-task-domain asymmetries with regard to aging effects, but that within the boundaries of those domains, remarkable regularities surface.

Sample case 1: Regularities between recall accuracy obtained from different types of processing

Figure 16.1 presents an example of a regularity in the young-old relation between two types of processes (viz., effortful vs. automatic) for the same stimuli (viz., disconnected words). This graph combines the results of two meta-analyses (Verhaeghen, 2000; Verhaeghen and Marcoen, 1993). The data are presented in Brinley plot format, that is, each point represents mean performance of a group of older adults plotted against mean performance of a corresponding group of younger adults. Performance is scaled such that 0 is chance, and 1 is perfect performance. The open circles represent data from 81 independent young-old subject samples, obtained from studies on explicit,

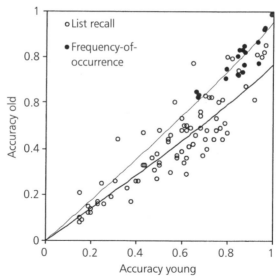

Fig. 16.1 Results from a meta-analysis reported in Verhaeghen (2000): proportion recalled by older adults from word list and frequency-of-occurrence information studies, plotted against proportion recalled by younger adults from the same studies, along with best fitting curves.

effortful list recall. The filled circles represent data from 18 independent young-old subject samples, obtained from studies examining a frequency-of-occurrence task. In the frequency-of-occurrence task, word stimuli are presented in list format; some of the words are presented more than once. The participant's task is to remember the words; after study, he or she is also asked to provide an estimate of the frequency of occurrence of each word. Frequency-of-occurrence is supposed to be coded automatically and without awareness (Hasher and Zacks, 1979). The curved lines in the figure present non-linear fits to the data according to a model outlined in Verhaeghen (2000). This model explains the curvature of the function through age-related slowing; the intercept of the function at $x = 1$ (i.e., when recall is perfect for younger adults) indicates ultimate, asymptotic differences in performance. The results indicate identical curvature for the two lines (indicating 9 per cent slowing), but marked differences in the $x = 1$ intercept: for frequency-of-occurrence, older adults are 96 per cent correct when younger adults are 100 per cent correct; for list recall, older adults are 77 per cent correct when younger adults are 100 per cent correct. The message is that the (small) age difference for frequency-of-occurrence information originates from an identical age deficit in processing dynamics as the (large) age difference in list recall, and that only the task difficulty differs – in other words, there is a regularity in age deficits for this type of processing, namely recall for disconnected material.

Sample case 2: Regularities between groups differing in task-related expertise

The second illustration (Figure 16.2) concerns a regularity across two different groups of older adults, using the same task. The data are from a single study (Lindenberger, 1990), in which 48 different lists of disconnected words were administered to three different groups, namely one group of young subjects and two groups of older participants: a group of randomly selected older persons ('non-experts') and a group of older graphic designers ('experts'). The lists were studied using the method of loci. This mnemonic technique consists of building visual associations between each to-be-remembered word and a place taken from a route that the subject has learned by heart. In the original study, it was assumed that expertise in forming mental images would lead to smaller age differences when study and recall were guided by a visual mnemonic. The different points plotted in Figure 16.2 represent performance averaged across subjects on the 48 word lists, administered at different points in time after training and using different presentation times. Data of the older

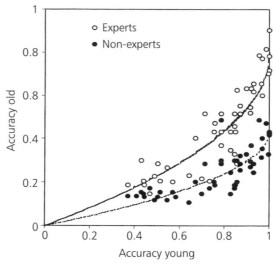

Fig. 16.2 Proportion recalled from 48 lists studied under the method of loci by older experts (graphic designers) and non-experts as a function of proportion recalled by a group of younger adults (data from Lindenberger, 1990), along with best fitting curves.

non-experts and older experts are plotted against the data of the group of younger subjects. Verhaeghen (2000) fitted these data to the curvilinear model mentioned above. It was found that the same curvature was present across both groups (indicating 104 per cent slowing), but that the groups differed in x = 1 intercept (80 per cent and 44 per cent for experts and non-experts, respectively). Thus, in this study, it seems that the age deficits in the dynamics of processing are identical across two groups of older adults, and that the locus of expertise is situated solely in an increase in asymptotic performance. This suggests that lifelong experience may influence the carrying capacity of the episodic memory system, but that mental slowing may be a direct function of aging.

Sample case 3: Regularities between short-term memory tasks differing in complexity demands

Figure 16.3 shows results from a large meta-analysis concerning aging effects in working memory/short-term memory measures (Bopp and Verhaeghen, 2002). A number of different models were fitted to these data (including a model with freely estimated linear slopes and intercepts for each task, and the curvilinear information-loss model; Myerson, Hale, Wagstaff *et al.*, 1990). Ultimately what proved to be the best-fitting model consists of three parallel

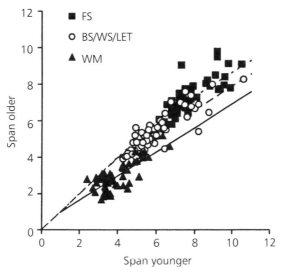

Fig. 16.3 Results from a meta-analysis reported in Bopp and Verhaeghen (2002). Memory span of older adults as a function of memory span of younger adults, along with the best fitting linear model (FS = forward digit span; LET = letter span; WS = word span; BS = backward digit span; CS = computation span; LS = listening span; RS = reading span; SS = sentence span).

lines (one for forward digit span, one for backwards digit span, word span, and letter span, and one for working memory tasks such as reading span, listening span, and computation span). The common slope shared by all tasks is 0.66.

At first blush, this linear model is quite strange: it is characterized by a positive intercept (varying with task type) and a slope smaller than 1. The implication is that higher spans of younger adults are associated with larger age differences, an implication which goes against the empirically well-grounded complexity hypothesis (Cerella, Poon, and Williams, 1980; Salthouse, 1991), which states that more complex or difficult tasks yield larger age differences. Here, within each of the three span types, the tasks yielding the largest span – the easiest tasks – result in the larger age differences. Another unusual aspect of the model is that its positive intercept implies that when the tasks are very difficult and very small span scores are obtained, the line will lie above the diagonal, indicating that older adults will perform *better* than younger adults. Our interpretation of the linear model is to consider the lines as starting off at the diagonal, and then showing increasing age differences with increasing span of the young. One possible interpretation is that short-term memory consists of two portions: (a) a portion that is impervious (or near-impervious) to aging, its size being described by the intersection of the line with the diagonal (for forward span: at 6.1, for the backward span, word span and letter span: at 3.9; and for working memory: at 1.0); and (b) a portion that is age-sensitive, showing a proportional decrement (i.e., within this portion, the span of the old equals a given percentage of the span of the young, and that percentage is equal to the slope of the function, viz., 66 per cent). What varies across task types is the size of the age-impervious portion of the short-term buffer: it is close to six items for forward span, four items for other primary memory measures, and close to one item for working memory. The latter two numbers raise the intriguing possibility that the portion of working memory that is age-insensitive may be the size of the focus of attention. The focus of attention is often defined as the number of items that is immediately available and accessible for processing. Recent work has shown that this number is close to four when passive storage is required (Cowan, 2001), but shrinks to one when continuous updating has to be performed, as in most working memory tasks (Garavan, 1998; McElree, 2001). It is then possible that the size of the focus of attention changes little or not at all with aging, but that age differences only emerge for super-attention-span tasks, that is, when it is necessary to swap items in and out of the focus of attention. Once the number of items to be stored and manipulated exceeds the number of immediately available items, older adults consistently retain 66 per cent of the number of items retained by younger adults, regardless of the type of processing required. An ad hoc interpretation is that the 66 per cent age-related loss is due to slower processing in older adults; see Salthouse's (1996) simultaneity mechanism. That is, if speed-of-processing is crucial for manipulation of items in and out of the focus of attention, then the 66 per cent age-related item loss may simply be the expression of an age-related slowing factor of 1.5 (viz., $1/0.66 = 1.5$), a value that is indeed quite close to slowing factors derived from the literature (Cerella, Poon, and Williams, 1980).

Sample case 4: Coupled young-old systems in mnemonic strategy training

Figure 16.4 shows results obtained from a study in which 19 younger and 16 older participants were trained in the method of loci (Verhaeghen and Kliegl, 2000; original data collected by Baltes and Kliegl, 1992). Participants were pretested, were trained in the mnemonic, and then underwent a long period of repeated training and practice, and repeated post-testing. At each testing occasion, participants studies several lists of 30 concrete, unrelated words; each list was presented using a different presentation time. The data

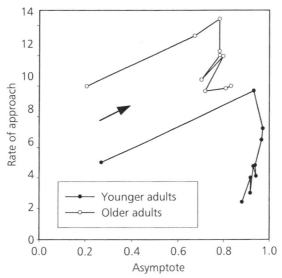

Fig. 16.4 Time-series plot from Verhaeghen and Kliegl (2000). Younger and older adults were pretested on episodic memory, and then received instruction in the method of loci. Data were fitted to a time-accuracy function. The plot shows evolution over time of the rate of approach as a function of asymptotic performance. The two points in the left-hand portion of the graph represent performance at pretest; the arrow indicates the direction of time; successive sessions are connected with lines.

were analyzed using time-accuracy functions, that is, performance was captured in a mathematical function described by three parameters: onset time (minimum presentation time needed to rise above chance); rate of approach (the steepness of the rise of the curve, an indicator of the speed of encoding processes); and the asymptote (the level of performance that can ultimately be reached, as indicated by projected accuracy when presentation time is infinite; this can be considered a measure of the carrying capacity of the memory system under the given circumstances).

Figure 16.4 shows a phase portrait of the data (i.e., a connected time series) in the coordinate system described by the asymptote and the rate of approach; separate lines are provided for younger and older adults. The first data point indicates pretest performance, which is characterized by low asymptotic performance (around 20 per cent correct) and fast encoding speed (note that lower rates denote faster encoding speeds). After training, the system rapidly moves to a high asymptote (around 80 per cent correct for older adults and 90 per cent correct for younger adults) and slow encoding speeds. After the peak asymptotic level is reached, the main change in performance is a speed-up of encoding processes, indicated in the figure by a vertical drop of the time series. The drop continues until the speed of encoding matches speed of encoding at pretest. In sum, the effects of instruction were to immediately and permanently boost asymptotic performance and to initially slow down the rate of approach to the asymptote; after extensive practice, rate of approach returned to the initial fast level. What is remarkable is that the time series of younger and older adults is qualitatively near-identical, that is, even though age differences were found in both asymptotic performance and rate of approach at all levels, the phase portrait of older adults is just a translation and a slight compression of the phase portrait of younger adults. After a history of more than a year of practice, age differences return to the pretest settings, suggesting not only plasticity (i.e., performance enhancement as captured in the asymptote), but also elasticity, that is, after the perturbation of training, the coupled young-old system relaxes back into the original parameter settings. Note, however, that older adults reach the peak in the graph only at the second testing occasion, showing that while the system described by the rate and asymptotic parameters is indeed similar in older and younger adults, the older system moves slower through state space.

Sample case 5: Symmetry breaking – efficiency modes

Older theories of age-related latency differences have posited general age effects (see Cerella, 1990, for an overview). In more recent studies, however, distinct age-related slowing functions have emerged for different types or domains of tasks. Such bifurcations have been termed dissociations (Perfect and Maylor, 2000). Figure 16.5 shows data from a study by Verhaeghen *et al.* (2002), set up to investigate the possible interplay of two such dissociations, namely: (a) the dissociation found by Hale, Myerson, and colleagues (Hale and Myerson, 1996; Jenkins, Myerson, Joerding *et al.*, 2000) between lexical and nonlexical tasks; and (b) the dissociation found by Mayr, Kliegl, and colleagues (Kliegl, Mayr, and Krampe, 1994; Mayr and Kliegl, 1993; Verhaeghen, Kliegl, and Mayr, 1997) between tasks involving simultaneous storage-and-processing, and task without such concurrent requirements. It is important to note that in each of those theories, the dissociations are proposed to be binary-valued rather than graded, that is, within any one dimension, the age deficit is uniform.

In our experiment, we used a large set of verbal and spatial tasks with high and low demands for executive control (the latter was our more general translation of the Mayr-type dissociation). We found three distinct age-related deficits, plotted in Figure 16.5a. The smallest deficit (defined by an age-related slowing factor of about 1.0, i.e., no age difference) was tied to lexical tasks

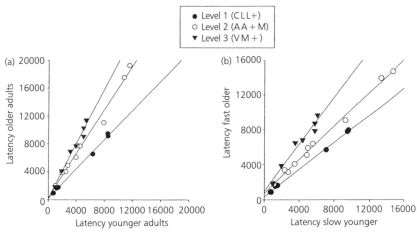

Fig. 16.5 Brinley plots of the latency data reported in Verhaeghen *et al.* (2002). (a) Plot of averages of all participants in eight tasks, sorted in three efficiency modes (C = category judgement; L = lexical decision; L+ = lexical decision plus letter transposition; A = anagrams; A+ = anagrams plus letter transposition; M = matrices [a pattern identification task]; M+ = matrices plus location transposition; V = visual search); (b) plot of the average of the fastest 15 older participants versus those of the 15 slowest younger participants (median splits on the average latency across all tasks).

with low executive involvement. The largest deficit (with a slowing factor of about 2.2) was tied to visuospatial tasks with high executive involvement. An intermediate level of deficit (with a slowing factor of about 1.7) was found for two types of tasks, visuospatial tasks with low executive load, and verbal tasks with high executive load. As predicted from previous theories, the stratification of points in the Brinley plot suggested qualitative, all-or-none jumps in processing speed, to the exclusion of intermediary values. To underscore the quantal character of the deficits, Verhaeghen *et al.* labeled these levels efficiency modes.

Can the diversity in efficiency modes sprout from a single, common mechanism? Figure 16.5b presents an examination of this hypothesis. The original motivation for this analysis comes from Salthouse (1996). He argued that dissociations may be due to a loss of information from working memory, in memory-dependent conditions. As Salthouse points out, this can be caused by a decline in processing speed, even without age change in memory function. With slower processing, intermediate results must be retained over longer intervals, and will hence be lost more frequently, assuming equal decay rates across age groups. Loss of intermediate results necessitates recomputation.

A higher frequency of recalculation would lead to a disproportionate increase in older subjects' response times. A Brinley analysis on subsamples of younger and older adults matched for overall speed provides a test of Salthouse's theory. If a dissociation were due to slowing-induced loss of information, it should disappear in samples matched for speed (Hale and Myerson, 1996). If a dissociation re-emerges in this context, however, it would refute not only Salthouse's speed/retention theory, but any other reductionist account that sought to explain higher-order deficits in terms of the compounded effects of a lower-order deficit. If (selected) older adults perform better than (selected) younger adults in a lower-order condition, then they cannot perform worse in a higher-order condition, unless the second condition draws on a cognitive function not operating in the first condition, and unless that function is negatively affected by age. Indeed, the technique of selection on average performance may help to surmount the more general interpretation problems that arise with ordinal interactions in group comparison research (Faust *et al.*, 1999; Loftus, 1978). Figure 16.5b shows that the dissociation remains in the selected groups.

The complexity of the reality of aging and the simplicity of theories

For anyone trying to theorize about cognitive aging, the symmetries and asymmetries are fearful indeed. How can they be framed adequately? In the previous paragraph, I argued that single-parameter models of aging (Hasher and Zacks, 1988; Li *et al.*, 2000; Salthouse *et al.*, 1996; West, 1996) cannot adequately capture the complexity of age-related dissociations. That is, while such models may well explain a large amount of the age-related variance in cognitive measures, no single-mechanism theory is sufficient to explain the *pattern* of results mentioned above, that is: (a) the existence of an elegant manifold of distinct efficiency modes, each governed by a distinct age-related slowing factor; coupled with (b) general age-related effects within these efficiency modes. A truly broad conspiracy of mechanisms is necessary to explain such patterns (Park *et al.*, 2001, for an attempt at a unifying multi-factor approach). Given that the age-associated dissociations are relatively large-scale and few, our hope should be that their number is finite enough to make a unifying approach viable.

One recent theory (see Christensen and Mackinnon, Chapter 11 and Lindenberger and Ghisletta Chapter 10 in the present volume) states that one common cause may be responsible for the age deficits seen across a large set of cognitive variables. The reasoning is that many cognitive variables load

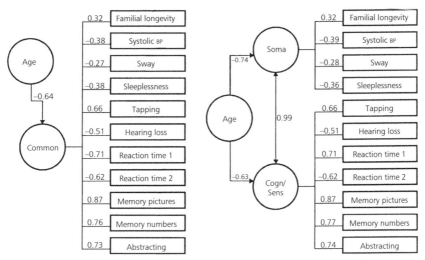

Fig. 16.6 Results from fitting (a) a single-factor model, and (b) a two-factor model to data collected by Jalavisto *et al.* (1964).

together with many biological markers (such as perceptual measures; Lindenberger and Baltes, 1994) to form a common factor.

This approach comes with its own problems. Figure 16.6, for instance, illustrates just how far a common factor/common cause will stretch. The figure represents results from two confirmatory factor analyses I conducted on a data set collected in the 1960s by Jalavisto, Lindquist, and Makkonen (1964). The data were obtained from 130 women between the ages of 44 and 93; a wide spectrum of variables was examined. The left-hand side of the figure shows the fit of a single-factor model to a subset of the data; the right-hand side shows an attempt at separating out a somatic and a cognitive/sensory factor (all coefficients are standardized). The data speak strongly for the existence of a single factor; in the two-factor model, the two factors correlate 0.99 with each other. (In fact, the two-factor model mainly shows that the cognitive variables are measured with higher reliability than the somatic variables.) The meaning of this single factor is entirely unclear, because so many disparate variables load on it: the presumably genetic influences associated with familial longevity; the peace of mind or bladder to get a good night's sleep; the speed at which one can tap one's fingers; and one's ability for abstract reasoning. It seems unlikely to me that *any* single mechanism, apart from the global concept of biological sturdiness, can capture all this diversity. This then means that we have come full circle: in order to explain aging, we have invoked the concept of a common cause, which turns out to be a measure of biological integrity – in fact, we are explaining cognitive aging by invoking the accumulation of biological damage, which in turn is an obvious marker for functional aging.

My proposal would be to stop invoking the common factor as an explanation (it is as empty of meaning as the concept of chronological age), or to keep wanting to define its contours, but rather to use the common factor model the way many experimental psychologists in the aging field currently treat general age-related slowing, namely as a null hypothesis (Faust, Balota, Spieler *et al.*, 1999; Perfect and Maylor, 2000). That is, the starting assumption of any kind of correlational research should be that there is a common factor, and the real work involves either showing that mediational models fit the data better than the common factor (see, for example, Verhaeghen and Salthouse, 1997), or that the common factor is mis-specified for specific variables (*ibidem*).

The second hard question: What does cognitive aging research tell us about cognitive aging?

One cannot help but make the observation that cognitive aging researchers are quite good at explaining differences between persons of different ages, as observed at one point in time, but that we are having much more difficulty explaining what affects individual differences in *change*. For instance, a series of studies have now demonstrated that the cornerstone variable of 1990s cognitive aging theory, speed-of-processing (Salthouse, 1991, 1996) indeed explains some of the individual differences in change in other variables (i.e., changes in speed are related to changes in other variables, or level of speed predicts subsequent change), but that speed's power for predicting change is alarmingly smaller than its power for predicting individual differences (see, for example, Lindenberger and Ghisletta, Chapter 10 this volume; Sliwinski and Buschke, 1999).

Figure 16.7 (adapted from Verhaeghen, Borchelt, and Smith, in press) provides a different example. This figure presents data from the Berlin Aging Study (BASE), in which adults age 75 or older were tested longitudinally; the present data concern the four-year period between the first and the third measurement point. Verhaeghen *et al.* found that, at the first measurement point, four somatic diagnoses were related to cognition, namely coronary heart disease, congestive heart failure, diabetes, and stroke. In the analyses presented in the figure, two groups of participants were selected for each of the diagnoses: (a) those who were diagnosed with the particular condition prior to the first measurement point (diagnosis-present); and (b) those who were found to be free of this condition both at the first and third measurement point (diagnosis-absent). The number of participants varies between 126 and 194, depending on

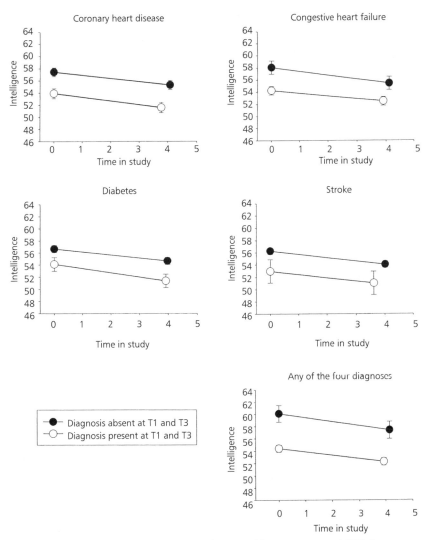

Fig. 16.7 Four-year longitudinal changes (corrected for age, sex, and SES) for diagnosis-absent and diagnosis-present cases for four selected somatic as well as for any combination of the four cognition-related diagnoses (data from the Berlin Aging Study; Verhaeghen *et al.*, in press). Error bars represent one standard error.

the diagnosis. The x-axis shows time in study, the y-axis performance on an intelligence composite (based on two perceptual speed tests, two episodic memory tests, two verbal fluency tests, and two knowledge tests). The figure strikingly demonstrates that health status explains some of the individual differences at both the first and the third measurement point (in the sense that individuals without the diagnosis consistently outperform afflicted individuals), but also that none of the individual differences in long-term change are accounted for by health status (i.e., the lines are nearly parallel). In other words, a set of variables that are strong predictors of individual differences turns out to be utterly useless in explaining change. The simple explanation is that even though aging increases susceptibility to disease, and disease has a knock-down effect on cognition, these conditions are superimposed on (and maybe even independent of) the negative effects on cognition of the aging process proper.

This phenomenon of differences in level of performance coupled with parallel rates of decline is remarkably common. Within the BASE data-set, the same disparity between cross-sectional and longitudinal results has been noted for gender differences (cross-sectionally, females scored higher than males on memory, fluency, and the intelligence composite, but the longitudinal slopes were not significantly different) and SES differences (cross-sectionally, participants scoring 1 SD above the mean on an SES composite scored higher on all intelligence variables than participants scoring 1 SD below the mean on the SES composite, but the longitudinal trajectories were statistically parallel) (Singer, Verhaeghen, Ghisletta *et al.*, 2003; see Carmelli, Swan, LaRue *et al.*, 1997; Gribbin, Schaie, and Parham, 1989; Hultsch, Hertzog, Dixon *et al.*, 1998, for similar results). Other studies have shown that individual differences in the rate of decline may be due to the presence of preclinical dementia, rather than to individual differences in the aging process (Sliwinski, Hofer, and Hall, 2002).

All of this raises disturbing questions. Is our current obsession with explaining individual-differences variance warranted? Where does aging truly reside? Is it situated in individual differences in longitudinal slopes? Or rather in the (relatively) immutable and maybe inscrutable universal change underlying it all?

The third hard question: Do the mechanisms of cognitive aging depend on the point in the lifespan they operate on?

Many single-parameter models used in the context of aging (speed-of-processing, inhibition, neuromodulation, health, dopamine system dysfunction, frontal lobe damage) have also been invoked to explain group differences in non-aging populations. For instance, speed-of-processing (see Salthouse, 1996, for an overview of this theory) is a variable used in explaining cognitive development (Kail, 2000), mental retardation (for a meta-analysis, see Kail, 1992), depression (Tsouros, Thompson, and Stough, 2002), and even individual

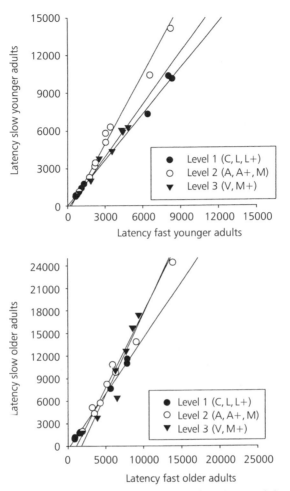

Fig. 16.8 Brinley plot of a subset of the data from Verhaeghen *et al.* (in press). (a) Mean latency of the slower half of the younger participants as a function of mean latency of the faster half of the younger participants; and (b) mean latency of the slower half of the older participants as a function of mean latency of the faster half of the older participants, organized by efficiency mode (C = category judgement; L = lexical decision; L+ = lexical decision plus letter transposition; A = anagrams; A+ = anagrams plus letter transposition; M = matrices [a pattern identification task]; M+ = matrices plus location transposition; V = visual search).

differences in general intelligence (Nettelbeck, 1987). Yet, the average seventy-year old clearly does not behave like a seven-year old (those two groups are matched on central processing speed; Cerella and Hale, 1994) and like a mentally retarded or depressed person. Likewise, neurocomputational models that explain aging effects through changes in the dopamine system have been borrowed explicitly from schizophrenia research (Braver and Cohen, 2001; Li *et al.*, 2000). Yet, older adults do not show schizophrenic symptoms. Clearly, mental slowing or dysfunctions in the dopamine system, even though they do explain a large amount of variance or an impressive array of experimental patterns, are only part of a multi-faceted, multilevel story.

As an illustration, Figure 16.8 presents data from the aforementioned study by Verhaeghen *et al.* (2002). It examines one corrolary of speed theory, namely that the dissocations are caused not by age, but by slow processing speed. This implication was tested on our data by comparing not young and old adults (as in Figure 16.5), but faster and slower individuals within each age group. If the dissociations were due to being slower (as opposed to being older), then the age-related dissociations should replicate as a fast-young/slow-young dissociation and as a fast-old/slow-old dissociation. Clearly, this is not the case: within the group of younger adults, it is the middle mode that dissociates reliably from the low and high modes; within the group of older adults, the three levels are statistically indistinguishable. Therefore, we concluded that a single-parameter model – any single-parameter model – is insufficient to capture the data, and that an age-related decline in working memory capacity, working memory functioning, or both, combined with differential age-related effects on task domains are the most likely explanation for the age effects.

Summary

In this paper, three questions were raised, none of which can currently be answered. I argued for examining age effects at the meso-level, that is, the behavioral level where large-scale dissociations become visible. I suggested using the common factor model as a null hypothesis, rather than as an explanans or an explanandum. I argued for the construction of models of change, as opposed to models for individual differences, and for the examination of aging as *aging*, that is, of a unique constellation of factors that distinguishes the aging process from reverse development or ailing mental or physical health. It is hoped that such approaches might lead to an integration between research findings obtained from experimental research and those obtained from individual differences research.

Author's note

This research was supported in part by a grant from the National Institute on Aging (AG-16201).

References

Baltes, P. B., and Kliegl, R. (1992). Further testing of limits of cognitive plasticity: Negative age differences in a mnemonic skill are robust. *Developmental Psychology*, **28**, 121–125.

Bopp, K. L., and Verhaeghen, P. (2002). *Aging, short-term memory span and working memory span: A meta-analysis*. Manuscript submitted for publication.

Byrne, M. D. (1998). Taking a computational approach to aging: The SPAN theory of working memory. *Psychology and Aging*, **13**, 309–322.

Carmelli, D., Swan, G. E., LaRue, A., and Eslinger, P. J. (1997). Correlates of change in cognitive function in survivors from the western Collaborative Group Study. *Neuroepidemiology*, **16**, 285–295.

Cerella, J., and Hale, S. (1994). The rise and fall in information-processing rates over the life span. *Acta Psychologica*, **86**, 109–197.

Cerella, J., Poon, L. W., and Williams, D. H. (1980). Age and the complexity hypothesis. In L. W. Poon (ed.), *Aging in the 1980s* (pp. 332–340). Washington, DC: American Psychological Association.

Cowan, N. (2001). The magical number 4 in short-term memory: A reconsideration of mental storage capacity. *Behavioral and Brain Sciences*, **24**, 87–185.

Faust, M. E., Balota, D. A., Spieler, D. H., and Ferraro, F. R. (1999). Individual differences in information-processing rate and amount: Implications for group differences in response latency. *Psychological Bulletin*, **125**, 777–799.

Garavan, H. (1998). Serial attention within working memory. *Memory and Cognition*, **26**, 263–276.

Gribbin, K., Schaie, K. W., and Parham, I. A. (1989). Complexity of life style and maintenance of intellectual abilities. *Journal of Social Issues*, **36**, 47–61.

Hale, S., and Myerson, J. (1996). Experimental evidence for differential slowing in the lexical and nonlexical domains. *Aging, Neuropsychology, and Cognition*, **3**, 154–165.

Hasher, L., and Zacks, R. T. (1979). Automatic and effortful processes in memory. *Journal of Experimental Psychology: General*, **108**, 356–388.

Hasher, L., and Zacks, R. T. (1988). Working memory, comprehension, and aging: a review and a new view. In G. H. Bower (ed.), *The Psychology of Learning and Motivation* (Vol. 22, pp. 193–225). San Diego, CA: Academic Press.

Hofer, S. M., and Sliwinski, M. J. (2001). Understanding ageing: An evaluation of research designs for assessing interdependence of ageing-related changes. *Gerontology*, **47**, 341–352.

Hultsch, D. F., Hertzog, C., Dixon, R. A., and Small, B. J. (1998). *Memory Change in the Aged*. New York: Cambridge University Press.

Jalavisto, E., Lindquist, C., Makkonen, T. (1964). Assessment of biological age III. *Annales Academiae Scientiarum Fennicae, A(V)* **106**, *1*, 1–20.

Jenkins, L., Myerson, J., Joerding, J. A., and Hale, S. (2000). Converging evidence that visuospatial cognition is more age-sensitive than verbal cognition. *Psychology and Aging*, **15**, 157–175.

Kahana, M. J., Howard, M. W., Zaromb, F., and Wingfield, A. (2002). Age dissociates recency and lag recency effects in free recall. *Journal of Experimental Research: Learning, Memory, and Cognition*, **28**, 530–540.

Kail, R. (1992). General slowing of information-processing by persons with mental retardation. *American Journal in Mental Retardation*, **97**, 333–341.

Kail, R. (2000). Speed of information processing: Developmental change and links to intelligence. *Journal of School Psychology, 38*, 51–61.

Kausler, D. H. (1991). *Experimental Psychology, Cognition, and Human Aging,* (2nd ed.). New York: Springer-Verlag.

Kliegl, R. (1996). *Cognitive development and cognitive complexity: A psychophysics approach.* Paper presented at the Max Planck Institute for Psychological Research, Munich, Germany.

Kliegl, R., Mayr, U., and Krampe, R. T. (1994). Time-accuracy functions for determining process and person differences: An application to cognitive aging. *Cognitive Psychology, 26*, 134–164.

Li, S.-C., Lindenberger, U., and Frensch, P. A. (2000). Unifying cognitive aging: From neuromodulation to representation to cognition. *Neurocomputing, 32–33*, 879–890.

Lindenberger, U. (1990). *The effects of professional expertise and cognitive aging on skilled memory performance.* Unpublished doctoral dissertation, Freie Universität, Berlin, Germany.

Lindenberger, U., and Baltes, P. B. (1994). Sensory functioning and intelligence in old age: A strong connection. *Psychology and Aging, 9*, 339–355.

Loftus, G. R. (1978). On interpretation of interactions. *Memory and Cognition, 6*, 312–319.

McElree, B. (2001). Working memory and focal attention. *Journal of Experimental Psychology: Learning, Memory, and Cognition, 27*, 817–835.

Mayr, U., and Kliegl, R. (1993). Sequential and coordinative complexity: Age-based processing limitations in figural transformations. *Journal of Experimental Psychology: Learning, Memory, and Cognition, 19*, 1297–1320.

Meyer, D. E., Glass, J. M., Mueller, S. T., Seymour, T. L., and Kieras, D. E. (2001). Executive-process interactive control: A unified computational theory for answering 20 questions (and more) about cognitive aging. *European Journal of Cognitive Psychology, 13*, 123–164.

Myerson, J., Hale, S., Wagstaff, D., Poon, L. W., and Smith, G. A. (1990). The information-loss model: A mathematical theory of age-related cognitive slowing. *Psychological Review, 97*, 475–487.

Nettelbeck, T. (1987). Inspection time and intelligence. In P. A. Vernon (ed.), *Speed of Information Processing and Intelligence* (pp. 295–346). Norwood, NJ: Ablex.

Park, D. C., Polk, T. A., Mikels, J. A., Taylor, S. F., and Marshuetz, C. (2001). Cerebral aging: Integration of brain and behavioral models of cognitive function. *Dialogues in Clinical Neuroscience, 3*, 151–165.

Perfect, T. J., and Maylor, E. A. (2000). Rejecting the dull hypothesis: The relation between method and theory in cognitive aging research. In T. J. Perfect and E. A. Maylor (eds), *Models of Cognitive Aging* (pp. 1–18). Oxford, UK: Oxford University Press.

Ratcliff, R., Spieler, D., and McKoon, G. (2000). Explicitly modeling the effects of aging on response time. *Psychonomic Bulletin and Review, 7*, 1–25.

Salthouse, T. A. (1991). *Theoretical Perspectives on Cognitive Aging.* Hillsdale, NJ: Erlbaum.

Salthouse, T. A. (1996). General and specific speed mediation of adults age differences in memory. *Journal of Gerontology: Psychological Sciences, 51B*, P30–42.

Singer, T., Verhaeghen, P., Ghisletta, P., Lindenberger, U., and Baltes, P. B. (2003). The fate of cognition in very old age: Six-year longitudinal findings in the Berlin Aging Study (BASE). *Psychology and Aging, 18*, 318–331.

Sliwinski, M., and Buschke, H. (1999). Cross-sectional and longitudinal relationships among age, cognition, and processing speed. *Psychology and Aging*, 14, 18–33.

Sliwinski, M. J., Hofer, S. M., and Hall, C. B. (2002). *Distinguishing between-person correlations from within-person coupling: A multilevel, multivariate analysis of cognitive change.* Paper presented at the Cognitive Aging Conference, Atlanta, GA.

Tsourtos, G. Thompson, J. C., and Stough, C. (2002). Evidence of an early information processing speed deficit in unipolar major depression. *Psychological Medicine*, 32, 259–265.

Verhaeghen, P. (2000). The parallels in beauty's brow: Time-accuracy functions and their implications for cognitive aging theories. In T. J. Perfect and E. A. Maylor (eds), *Models of Cognitive Aging* (pp. 50–86). Oxford: Oxford University Press.

Verhaeghen, P., Borchelt, M., and Smith, J. (in press). The relation between cardiovascular health and cognition in very old age: Cross-sectional and longitudinal findings from the Berlin Aging Study. *Health Psychology*.

Verhaeghen, P., Cerella, J., Semenec, S. C.; Leo, M. E., Bopp, K. L., and Steitz, D. W. (2002). Cognitive efficiency modes in old age: Performance on sequential and coordinative verbal and visuospatial tasks. *Psychology and Aging*, 17, 558–570.

Verhaeghen, P., and Kliegl, R. (2000). The effects of learning a new algorithm on asymptotic accuracy and execution speed in old age: A reanalysis. *Psychology and Aging*, 15, 648–656.

Verhaeghen, P., Kliegl, R., and Mayr, U. (1997). Sequential and coordinative complexity in time-accuracy function for mental arithmetic. *Psychology and Aging*, 12, 555–564.

Verhaeghen, P., and Marcoen, A. (1993). Memory aging as a general phenomenon: Episodic recall of older adults is a function of episodic recall of the young. *Psychology and Aging*, 8, 380–388.

Verhaeghen, P., and Salthouse, T. A. (1997). Meta-analyses of age-cognition relations in adulthood: Estimates of linear and non-linear age effects and structural models. *Psychological Bulletin*, 122, 231–249.

West, R. (1996). An application of prefrontal cortex function theory to cognitive aging. *Psychological Bulletin*, 120, 272–292.

Part 5

Final frontiers? New research directions, perspectives and imperatives

Chapter 17

Future directions in cognitive aging research: Perspectives from the National Institute on Aging

Daniel B. Berch and Molly V. Wagster

The National Institute on Aging (NIA) has had a long-standing interest in supporting both mainstream and cutting-edge research in the field of cognitive aging. In this chapter, we outline the NIA's perspective on future directions in this continually evolving field. We begin by describing the overall mission of the NIA, the two extramural programs at the Institute that fund cognitive aging research, and the domains of study under this broad rubric that we currently support. Next, we present several cognitive aging initiatives recommended by the National Academy of Sciences. This is followed by a discussion of the rationale underlying the use of workshops as one of the means of developing scientific road maps for future research directions. Pursuing this approach in more detail, we provide summaries of several recently held, NIA-sponsored workshops that covered various domains of cognitive aging and present some of the suggestions and recommendations that emerged from these meetings. In addition, we describe some planned workshops and initiatives, as well as several workshops that addressed aspects of cognitive aging though not focusing exclusively on this topic. Finally, we outline several future directions for research, focusing on issues of theory development, the cognitive neuroscience of aging, neuroplasticity and behavioral adaptability, epidemiology and demography of cognitive aging, cognitive interventions, and translational research.

Mission of the NIA

The mission of the NIA is to improve the health and well-being of older Americans through research, and specifically to:

1 Support and conduct high quality research on aging processes, age-related diseases, and special problems and needs of the aged;

2 Train and develop highly skilled research scientists from all population groups;

3 Develop and maintain state-of-the-art resources to accelerate research progress; and

4 Disseminate information and communicate with the public and interested groups on health and research advances and on new directions for research.

As the other chapters in this volume clearly demonstrate, exciting developments are taking place in the field of cognitive aging, driven by advances in measurement, methodology, statistics, and biotechnology. Additionally, fields such as cognitive neuroscience are being cultivated for what they can reveal about both normal cognitive aging and neurodegenerative diseases of aging such as Alzheimer's disease. Finally, the study of genetic factors is shedding new light on individual differences in brain structure and function.

Extramural program support at the NIA

The two extramural programs at the NIA that support the vast majority of research in cognitive aging are the Behavioral and Social Research (BSR) Program and the Neuroscience and Neuropsychology of Aging (NNA) Program. With respect to the domain of cognitive aging, BSR primarily has funded research in the areas of higher-order cognition, judgement and decision-making, cognition and intellectual development, cognition in context, social cognition, emotional reasoning, language comprehension, metacognition, memory strategies, attention, expertise, and cognitive interventions. A wide range of methodological approaches to the study of cognitive aging are supported, including experimental laboratory techniques, longitudinal designs, psychometric measures, observational methods, surveys and interviews, and simulations of real-life tasks and settings. The area of ergonomics or human factors has received support for the study of cognitive performance in older drivers and older pilots, as well as computer usage, searching the World Wide Web, and skill acquisition with respect to other types of technology increasingly used by older adults in everyday settings. Additional areas of interest include the contribution of workplace and economic factors to cognitive aging, as well as the cognitive demands of instrumental activities of daily living. Finally, a sizable number of longitudinal studies have been funded that provide a life course perspective on normal cognitive changes in adulthood and old age, as well as developmental precursors of Alzheimer's disease.

In a largely complementary fashion, NNA has traditionally funded research aimed at the understanding of the processes and mechanisms, both behavioral and biological, that characterize the aging mind. Research foci include the areas of attention, learning, memory, executive function, spatial orientation, language, emotion, mood, and reasoning. The application of a vertical framework for research funding has proved advantageous for the exploitation of models from drosophila to humans and for the inclusion of diverse approaches, such as behavioral science, molecular and cellular neuroscience, computational neuroscience, and neuroimaging. In addition, NNA supports research on the processes and mechanisms of dementias of aging. As well as basic research, areas of interest include the identification and testing of pre-clinical and ante-mortem biological, chemical, neuroimaging, and behavioral markers for cognitive decline, mild cognitive impairment, and Alzheimer's disease; refinement of methods for diagnostic assessment and tracking of clinical course, including studies employing neuropsychological batteries and neuroradiological techniques; clinical and neuropathological concordance studies; and preclinical and clinical intervention studies. Both BSR and NNA support investigations into the impact of age-related diseases (e.g., hypertension, diabetes, sleep disorders) on cognition, studies of the genetic bases of cognitive change and stability, and research into the appropriate assessments and characterization of cognitive function in older minority groups.

Sources of ideas for developing funding initiatives at the NIA

The NIA has at its disposal a variety of both formal and informal vehicles for gathering information and developing ideas concerning the kinds of research it will eventually choose to fund in the field of aging in general and in the area of cognitive aging in particular. These sources include, but are not limited to, reports issued by the National Academy of Sciences (which are often commis-sioned by the Institute), exploratory and advisory workshops sponsored by the Institute, suggestions from members of the NIA's National Advisory Council on Aging, directives and advisories from the United States Congress, recommendations put forward by professional scientific organizations, assessment of the current literature by staff, and suggestions generated from informal meetings, exchanges, and discussions between staff and individual researchers. As funding initiatives are developed, NIA program staff may com-bine some of the recommendations emanating from these various sources, modify others, and/or provide some of their own perspectives, as for example when attempting to: (1) jump start a new area of research; (2) seed innovative opportunities for collaborative efforts that require combinations of expertise from somewhat disparate domains; or (3) rejuvenate a field by supporting the application of state-of-the-art of approaches that could yield novel directions for future research. As the process continues, drafts of the initiatives are reviewed by other program staff, senior Institute staff, and members of the National Advisory Council on Aging, prior to obtaining final approval from the NIA Director.

The aging mind: Opportunities in cognitive research (NRC report, 2000)

In a presentation made to the National Research Council's (NRC) Board on Behavioral, Cognitive, and Sensory Sciences in 1998, the NIA requested a reappraisal of research opportunities that would enhance the understanding of how cognition develops and changes with age. Through follow-up efforts of this Board, the NRC established the Committee on Future Directions for Cognitive Research on Aging. Their charge was

> To identify a small number of significant and promising research opportunities in cognition and aging in neuroscience, cognitive science and behavioral science, in some cases emphasizing research opportunities that would have the added benefit of linking these three approaches in new ways.

> (Carstensen, 2000: ix–x)

A subsequent study by the Committee produced several recommendations for expanding cognitive aging research as outlined in its ensuing report, *The Aging Mind: Opportunities in Cognitive Research* (http://www.nap.edu/). Specifically, the committee recommended that the NIA undertake major research initiatives in three areas: neural health, cognition in context, and structure of the aging mind.

Neural health

The NIA was advised to try to build the scientific basis for promoting neural health in the aging brain. Four major goals of this initiative were outlined by the committee: to develop quantitative functional and performance indicators, including behavioral tests, for neuronal health and neuronal dysfunction; to identify factors that influence neural health during the aging process, especially disparities in homeostatic processes, such as inflammation, apoptosis, and oxidative activity; to develop interventions for the maintenance of healthy neurons and the recovery and restoration of neural networks; and to evaluate the effectiveness of intervention strategies.

Cognition in context

The committee also recommended that the NIA undertake an initiative to understand the effects of behavioral, social, cultural, and technological contexts on the cognitive functioning and life-performance of aging individuals. In addition, it was suggested that this initiative should build the knowledge base needed to produce effective interventions in these contexts, thereby providing assistance for older adults. More specifically, the report suggests that research is needed in several areas: understanding the adaptive processes that influence age-related changes in cognitive functioning and performance; determining how differences in social, cultural, economic, and experiential contexts lead to systematic variation in cognitive functioning and perform-ance; developing the knowledge needed to devise effective technologies for supporting adaptability in older adults; and understanding the relationships among these contexts and their effects on neural and behavioral systems.

Structure of the aging mind

Finally, it was recommended that the NIA undertake an initiative to improve understanding of the structure of the aging mind, including the uncovering of mechanisms at the neural and behavioral levels that contribute to normal and abnormal age-related changes in cognitive functioning. The aim here would be to identify patterns of variation in cognitive functioning which occur during the aging process and to specify the mechanisms that contribute to age-linked stability and change at levels of analysis from the molecular to the cultural. Additionally, the report recommends three method-based strategies: linking high-resolution measures of neural functioning to measures of cognitive functioning; broadening mathematical and theory-based models; and performing and evaluating large-scale multivariate studies.

NIA-sponsored scientific workshops

New frontiers in research are often initiated by individual investigators pursuing answers to questions posed by themselves or their colleagues. While this time-honored approach continues to yield important breakthroughs, the NIA along with other Federal funding agencies frequently organize workshops in an effort to draw upon the collective wisdom of the scientific community to generate road maps for charting future research directions. According to Galvin (1998: 803), 'The optimal process for gathering and selecting the content of road maps is to include as many practicing professionals as possible in workshops periodically in order to allow all suggestions to be considered'. ... The resultant road maps that get constructed 'communicate visions, attract resources from business and government, stimulate investigations, and monitor progress. They become *the* inventory of possibilities for a particular field, thus stimulating earlier, more targeted investigations. They facilitate more interdisciplinary networking and teamed pursuit' (Galvin, 1998).

The NIA categorizes workshops as exploratory or advisory, using the former primarily as a means of educating extramural staff on the latest advances in a given area, and the latter as a source of expert recommendations. Both types of workshops frequently bring together very different groups from the research community that rarely interact with one another, thus facilitating not only direct communication among these individuals but also assisting the Institute in synthesizing diverse perspectives. In addition, these meetings (and their ensuing summaries or reports) help educate the research community with respect to the NIA's interests as well as to the viewpoints of other disciplines.

Recommendations emanating from NIA-sponsored workshops may be used by the Institute to develop priorities for future funding and form part of the foundation for crafting Program Announcements (PAs) or Requests for Applications (RFAs). PAs are comparatively broad in scope (e.g., targeting the area of higher-order cognitive functioning), have a shelf-life of approximately three years, and typically do not have designated set-aside funds. In contrast, RFAs tend to have a comparatively narrow focus (e.g., exploring how social relationships may be protective against the risk of dementia), constitute a one time only competition, and furnish specific set-aside funds.

In the following section, we offer examples of some of the workshops recently convened by the NIA that guide us in our job of stimulating and supporting cognitive aging research. Accompanying each description is a brief explanation of the stimulus for the workshop.

Existing evidence indicates that a large segment of our aging population in the U.S. is at substantial risk for cognitive and emotional impairment from a number of causes. A priority at the NIA is to promote translational research that will move basic research into practical approaches that can be used to prevent or diminish these changes. To further this goal, the Cognitive and Emotional Health Project was conceived at the NIH, through the combined efforts of three Institutes: the NIA, the National Institute of Neurological Disorders and Stroke (NINDS), and the National Institute of Mental Health (NIMH). To launch this project, the three Institutes held a workshop, 'Cognitive and emotional health project: The healthy brain'. In July 2001, approximately 100 participants gathered for plenary presentations, focused discussions, and generating recommendations.

Relevant recommendations included:

◆ Finalize the reviews of existing data on predictive factors for cognitive and emotional health by completing four bibliographies that were created for the workshop as well as the catalogue (also created for the workshop) of large-scale epidemiological, NIH-supported and international studies that include measures of cognitive and emotional functioning.

◆ Convene a panel to conduct a critical analysis of existing studies, with the objectives of identifying weaknesses and gaps in existing data and determining opportunities for secondary analysis as well as add-on studies.

◆ Create a trans-Institute RFA focused on cognitive and psychosocial health in adults.

Cognitive health in aging depends on a complex mix of environment, genes, and life experiences. One type of event that may impact future cognitive health is whether the individual undergoes particular forms of surgery at an advanced age. For example, untoward neurologic sequelae have emerged as a complication of cardiac surgery, particularly coronary artery bypass graft surgery (CABG), an increasingly common procedure in persons aged 50 and older. Furthermore, there is wide variation in the frequency of reported cognitive complications following CABG. In order to highlight the issue and explore the underlying mechanisms and potential treatments, a trans-NIH workshop was held in April 2002, 'Neurocognitive change after cardiac surgery.' Jointly sponsored by the National Heart, Lung, and Blood Institute (NHLBI), the NIA, and the NINDS, the meeting brought together clinical and basic scientists from different disciplines to address issues related to the impact of cardiac surgery and resulting neurological injury. The workshop was organized around three consecutive sessions encompassing:

1 A review of the characteristics of normal cognitive change with age as well as the cognitive sequelae and neuropathological changes following cardiac surgery;

2 A review of current surgical techniques, approaches, and factors that may be relevant and modifiable in relation to neurologic outcomes; and

3 A discussion of potential methods of neuroprotection in order to determine how best to reduce adverse neurological events following surgery.

Recommendations generated by the participants are currently being reviewed by Institute staff prior to public dissemination.

Another workshop focusing on the factors that may positively or negatively impact successful cognitive aging was organized and sponsored by the NIA in April 2002, 'Cognition in context.' As noted in the NRC report, *The aging mind: Opportunities in cognitive research*, much can be learned from increased research attention to the aging mind in context: to factors such as cultural expectations and differences, changes in living situations and motives in late life, maximizing function in everyday situations, and emerging technologies to assist individuals in daily performance. Our exploratory workshop included participants with expertise in cognitive psychology, developmental psychology, social cognition, motivation and emotion, ethnicity and culture, human factors, and behavioral neuroscience. Attendees included program staff from the NIA, as well as from the NIMH, the NINDS, the National Institute on Drug Abuse (NIDA), the Office of Behavioral and Social Sciences Research (OBSSR), and the NRC.

A number of questions were posed to the participants:

1   What theoretical constructs are important in providing an overarching framework for understanding the effects of cognition in context?

2   What are the implications of cognition in context for theoretical conceptions of cognitive aging?

3   What kinds of obstacles, if any, have precluded more concerted, programmatic efforts to conduct research on the topic of cognition in context?

Selected ideas and issues emerging from this meeting include:

◆   A need for theory and model development to form the basis for designing ways to approach important research questions.

◆   Motivation and states of arousal should be factored into the study of contexts and older adults.

◆   Cognition in context brings with it more of a functional outcome focus that has been missing from a lot of cognitive aging research.

◆   Even subtle shifts in context may put older adults at adaptive risk.

◆   Focusing on contexts turns the question around from saying how is the person failing to how is the environment failing the older person.

One context that the NIA considered in need of a new look and more focused research attention was that of cultural expectations and differences and how they may impact cognitive aging, particularly cognitive assessment in minority elders. Diverse ethnic, social, economic, environmental, and geographic/cultural factors frequently are not taken into account when individuals are assessed for cognitive performance. To date, many of the standardized neuropsychological tests and instruments and cognitive tasks that assess cognitive function have not been developed along culturally fair or appropriate lines and, with the exception of a few, have not been translated into and standardized for other languages. To explore these issues, the NIA and the Alzheimer's Association hosted a workshop in October 2001 entitled 'Racial and cultural effects on measurement of cognition.' The workshop assembled experts from a wide range of fields including geriatric neurology, epidemiology, psychiatry, neuropsychology, and cognitive psychology. Work group participants discussed cognitive measures and evaluations that currently are used in elderly and minority populations. The major purpose of the workshop was to understand adaptive processes that affect cognitive functioning and performance during aging, and to determine how differences in racial, ethnic, and sociocultural context can impact them. A second purpose of the workshop was to generate a set of recommendations on how to proceed to develop valid and useful measures that would allow accurate neuropsychological assessments of defined age, racial, and ethnic groups. Some of the recommendations were:

- Create a document that provides guidelines for important issues in designing cognitive tests and adapting them to different cultures.
- Continue to expand the compendium of existing tests that were compiled for the workshop.
- Promote research to characterize the domain of executive function. This may be the best cognitive domain to distinguish between normal cognitive aging and early dementia; assess whether declines in executive function are precursors to dementia. Work on developing new executive function tests and refining current ones.
- Consider developing a brief cognitive battery for use by clinicians.
- Provide support for secondary data analysis of large studies with good cognitive and neuropsychological data and oversampling of minorities.
- Include appropriate measures of education and designation of ethnicity in large studies.
- Consider the utility of establishing normative data for age, racial, and ethnic groups.

The social context of older adults recently has received renewed interest as a possible factor in the mediation of cognitive health. Long considered important for emotional as well as the physical health of older adults (Berkman and Syme, 1979; House, Landis, and Umberson, 1988; Seeman, 1996), social relationships have been less frequently examined as a potential protective factor against risk of cognitive decline and dementia. However, Fratiglioni et al. (2000)

recently published a study demonstrating a strong relationship between social networks and incidence of dementia. The large effect size reported by these investigators served as the impetus for an exploratory workshop organized by the NIA on this topic, 'Social relationships and risk of cognitive decline in the elderly,' which was held in December 2000.

The plenary address by Dr. Laura Fratiglioni included her findings indicating that while infrequent contact with children, relatives, and friends is predictive of the onset of dementia, lack of satisfaction with these relationships is an even more important predictor (Fratiglioni *et al.*, 2000). The participants discussed a variety of issues, such as current gaps in our knowledge concerning various mechanisms that may be responsible for this association. In particular, they pointed out the consideration that prodromal cognitive decline may precipitate exclusion from existing social relationships, thus necessitating careful assessment as to whether dementia is a cause, or effect, of the breakdown in social relationships. Additional topics discussed were issues in measuring social relationships (e.g., social density, types of social support, varieties of social participation and engagement) and the optimal timing of interventions. The workshop generated a number of useful suggestions for future research directions, including ways to unpack the construct of social engagement that would permit us to make further headway toward pinning down the most crucial facets of interpersonal relationships that might impact cognitive status downstream.

Several actions were suggested, including: provide support for studies that nest biological and social psychological studies within large-scale surveys; solicit research aimed at assessing roles of social organizations in maintaining psychosocial functioning of the elderly; utilize social networks in promoting cognitive health. The participants also posed a number of questions for future research: What types of theoretical development(s) are needed in order to move this area forward? For example, are existing conceptions of social relationships adequate for this purpose? How necessary are more integrative, multilevel theoretical perspectives for advancing this field? Are extant measures of interpersonal relationships adequate for substantial progress to be made in this area in the near future?

Beyond the traditionally considered social milieu of family and friends, there are other important ways in which the older adult interfaces with society and deals with information that helps him/her function in that context. One aspect of that interface is the increasing reliance of our society on numerical information for the purposes of decision-making. As Steen (1997) has noted, 'Numeracy is the currency of modern life.' He also points out that 'Literacy is no longer just a matter of words, sentences, and paragraphs, but also of data, measurements, graphs, and inferences. Pattern and number lurk behind words and sentences, in machines and computers, in organizations and networks.' Several dimensions of numeracy or quantitative literacy have been articulated, including: (a) *practical* – for immediate use in the routine tasks of life; (b) *civic* – for understanding major public policy issues (e.g., making sense of election polls, taxes, census data, and other societal indices; (c) *professional* – providing skills necessary for employment; and (d) *recreational* – to appreciate games, sports, etc. (Steen, 1990). Many everyday judgement tasks involve reasoning, including estimating how much the groceries will cost or ascertaining the interest rate on a mortgage. Similarly, a comparatively high level of numerical comprehension and reasoning is required for accurate interpretation of medical and scientific news, for wise investment and retirement decisions, and for making prudent decisions about health-related matters (Sanfey and Hastie, 2000). Unfortunately, however, little is known about the maintenance or decline of these types of quantitative reasoning skills in older adults.

With the growing importance of the need to rely on quantitative reasoning skills for purposes of decision-making in our society, the NIA organized an exploratory workshop on this topic, 'Quantitative reasoning in adult development and aging' (July 2002), that included researchers with expertise in numerical cognition, quantitative and document literacy, judgement and decision-making, mathematics, neuropsychology, and behavioral economics. The specific topics covered at the workshop included: age-related changes in numerical processing strategies, proportional and probabilistic reasoning processes, estimation skills, investment and risk-taking behaviors, and financial abilities in patients with Alzheimer's disease.

Prior to the meeting, participants were asked to respond to a number of questions, including:

1   What kinds of quantitative reasoning skills are most important for cognitively demanding, instrumental activities of daily living (e.g., financial management, meal preparation, medication management, transportation, etc.)?

2   What research approaches are needed to clarify the factors contributing to age-related declines in both quantitative and document literacy that may be compromising the ability of older adults to interpret information crucial for their physical health, as well as for their psychological and financial well-being?

3   What can the NIA do to help foster collaborative efforts between psychologists and economists that might yield novel, integrative approaches to the study of probabilistic reasoning skills?

The responses to these questions have been compiled, and will be reviewed along with the ideas generated from the presentations and plenary discussions to provide potential next steps that should be taken in developing an initiative in the area of quantitative reasoning.

Other higher thought processes such as planning, sequencing, and abstraction are known to be disproportionately affected by the aging process. Yet the underlying mechanisms of decline in these so-called 'executive' functions in older individuals, and how to prevent the decline, need to be further elucidated. Several issues have hampered progress toward evaluation and understanding of changes in executive functions in older adults. One factor affecting our understanding is the lack of consensus on operational definitions of what constitutes executive function, which in turn affects comparability of methods/instruments for evaluation. Another factor is the complex interactions among these higher-order functions and education, SES, language use and ethnicity, making older persons of diverse backgrounds vulnerable to possible misinterpretations and/or misdiagnosis when evaluated. A third factor is the complexity of existing measures of executive functions, limiting their usefulness for evaluating, staging, and tracking changes in higher-order cognitive functions in older populations.

In order to define the specific research needs in this area for an aging population, the NIA held a small advisory workshop in January 2003, 'Research needs in the evaluation of executive functions from cognitive aging to dementias.' In part, the idea for this workshop stemmed from recommendations from one of our recently held workshops, 'Racial and cultural effects on measurement of cognition.' Participants encouraged the NIA to promote the refinement of current executive function tests/tasks and the development of new tests/tasks. In addition, the NIA was encouraged to pursue the potential of executive function assessment as a means of distinguishing between normal age-related change in cognition and early dementia. The focus of the workshop was on measurement of executive functions in older individuals and measurement comparability through the use of brain imaging. Brain imaging provides a powerful tool for characterizing age-related changes in uniformly acquired data that can facilitate comparability across disparate populations. Specifically, experts in the field were assembled to discuss the feasibility of using animal models and imaging measurement paradigms to compare age-related changes in executive functions in groups with varying cognitive ability, education, language, and ethnicity.

Other workshops with cognitive components

'Genetics, behavior and aging': the purpose of this workshop, held in March 2002, was to review current research in behavior genetics and aging, to discuss important areas for future research development as applied to the study of aging, and to generate new ideas regarding optimal strategies and the most fruitful avenues for new initiatives. The participants included researchers with expertise in an array of fields, including psychology, evolutionary theory, statistical methodology, economics, and animal systems, bringing together diverse perspectives to explore prevailing research questions. While the focus of this meeting was not on cognition per se, some findings pertaining to cognitive impairment were discussed.

A workshop entitled, 'Disability and aging,' was organized by the NIA in November 2001 for the purpose of discussing some of the most recent research on the declining disability among older Americans. Among other relevant findings, evidence was presented indicating that as a group, older adults, especially those well into their 80s, may have better cognitive functioning today than was the case for comparably aged adults in the early 1990s (for more details, see the section on Epidemiological and demographic studies of cognition).

With support from the NIA, the NRC is in the process of planning two workshops on 'Adaptive aging: From gerontology to technology' that will examine the potential of recent technological advances for improving the lives of older adults.

Future directions

The role of theory

It is clear that theories of cognitive aging play a crucial heuristic role in a variety of sub-areas within this broad field, and as such are worthy of continued and even increasing emphasis and support. By some accounts, however, methodological and empirical advances in the field of cognitive aging far outweigh progress in the development and adequate testing of theories capable of encompassing the vast accumulation of empirical findings in this field (Burke, 1997; MacKay and James, 2001). Testable models are vital not only for understanding the mechanisms underlying age-related cognitive changes, but also for providing a solid conceptual foundation for the design, development, and execution of intervention studies to enhance cognitive function in older adults.

As noted in the NRC report, *The aging mind*, research that is based on theoretically justified measures of specialized congitive functions will enable a closer examination of associations between the functioning of specific neural circuits and performance on behavioral indicators, as well as between the latter and performance on everyday tasks. In addition, the report suggests that the study of cognitive aging can benefit from advances in the development of various mathematical modeling and analytic techniques for characterizing the 'structure and evolution of behavior over time' (NRC, 2000: 47). Suggested examples include: dynamical systems theory, hidden Markov models, adaptive control theory, structural equation modeling, and dynamic factor analysis for informing the study of 'short-term variability, long-term stability and change, and multisystem causal linkages involving or affecting cognitive linkages in older adults (e.g., sensory-motor functioning and cognition)' (NRC, 2000: 52). Lindenberger and Ghisletta (Chapter 10 in this volume) clearly provide a noteworthy example of the utility of such approaches for these purposes.

In accord with the NRC recommendations for improving our understanding of the structure of the aging mind, the NIA will place increasing importance on furthering the progress of theory-based measurement, model development, and the explanatory power of future empirical research efforts in cognitive aging.

Cognitive Neuroscience of Aging

For many decades, there was little to no interaction between the fields of human cognitive aging and neuroscience. In part, the union was ill fated because the best approach to connecting human mental behavior with brain activity came from observational studies of head trauma and brain surgery patients. Electroencephalography and evoked response potentials provided exciting findings about electrophysiological activity in the brain related to behavior but still did not open the window for actually 'seeing' the brain at work.

The advent and application of dynamic functional imaging techniques such as PET and fMRI have brought new opportunities and insights into the relationships between neural activity and behavior. Most importantly for cognitive aging, these techniques have spawned the production of new hypotheses and new theories about how the aging brain functions and its capacity, or lack thereof, for adaptation. One example is the finding from several independent laboratories that the performance of working memory in young adults is accompanied by a different pattern of neural activation than when older adults perform the task. Specifically, younger adults show unilateral activation of frontal cortical regions whereas older adults show bilateral activation of frontal regions. Is the activation of more brain regions in older adults a compensatory mechanism whereby it is adaptive and advantageous to recruit more brain regions to do the task, or is the reduction in asymmetry indicative of inadequate brain function, a reduction, perhaps, in the specialization of brain regions because of decreased integrity of fiber tracts and neuronal activity (Cabeza Chapter 9 this volume; Park and Minear Chapter 2 this volume; Reuter-Lorenz *et al.*, 2000)? Not only will the resolution of such questions provide enormous insight into the workings of the older brain, but it will also provide a basis for designing interventions and tracking their success with an imaging biomarker.

Neural plasticity and behavioral adaptability

Much of the supported research effort in aging is aimed at the elucidation of age-related diseases, their causes and treatments, and the difference between these diseases and normal aging. This is particularly true in the area of cognitive aging where studies often assess parameters of cognitive deficit, outcomes of dementia, or risk factors for abnormal cognitive function. Recently, there has been a groundswell of support to 'turn the tables' on how we view aging in general and cognitive aging in particular. Rather than posing research questions from the perspective of decline or illness in older age, there has been a shift in emphasis to maintenance of health or gain of health, from avoidance of negatives to pursuit of positives.

Some older, some newer, but all very important, scientific research efforts point to the adaptability of the older individual, both in terms of neural function and behavioral processes. In the past decade, we have witnessed a change from widely accepted dogma regarding the inflexibility of the adult brain to a new vision of greater flexibility. Previously held tenets were that: (1) we steadily lose neurons from our brains with increasing age and that this loss is, at least in part, the basis for age-related cognitive decline; and (2) that the brain is incapable of generating new neurons. Evidence from older rats, monkeys and humans indicates that there is not widespread or significant neuronal loss with age in cortical regions. Furthermore, exciting data from several laboratories have revealed that the adult brain, including the older adult brain, is capable of generating new neurons and that conditions such as access to a complex environment, learning a new task, or physical exercise are capable of inducing neurogenesis in an area of the brain important for learning and memory. A recent paper by Logan *et al.* (2002) of Washington University in St. Louis illustrates the neural flexibility of the older adult brain. After being provided with instructions for an effective encoding strategy, older adults improved their performance and displayed a pattern of brain activity that was similar to that of young adults.

Much is known and publicized about maintaining a 'healthy heart', but relatively little about the much more complex 'healthy brain'. While research into biological mechanisms and environmental and social effects is yielding promising results in both animal and human studies, a good deal remains to be discovered. For example, as we age, the complex behaviors of attention, language, learning, and memory become vulnerable to insults, resulting in performance deficits that can produce frustration and concern for elders and isolate them from loved ones and society. At the same time, there can be positive changes in cognitive function such as wisdom or greater integrative prowess. Advances in understanding these positive and negative changes with age, and what can be done to preserve and enhance positive outcomes, is at the core of the mission of the NIA.

As noted earlier, the NIA, the NINDS, and the NIMH, have embarked on a new initiative (Cognitive and emotional health: The healthy brain) to understand issues related to cognitive and emotional health in U.S. adult populations – particularly how cognitive and emotional health can be maintained and enhanced as people grow older. Part of the initiative will be devoted to an assessment of the state of epidemiological research on demographic, social, and biologic determinants of cognitive and emotional health in aging populations, and the pathways by which cognitive and emotional health may reciprocally influence each other. Overarching questions include: Can individuals optimize their cognitive function and emotional health? What are the predictors for cognitive and emotional health? How do psychosocial variables influence cognitive outcomes? Can new technologies (imaging) be used to identify those with the 'healthiest' brains? In order to advance the field, both basic research and epidemiological approaches need to be exploited in ways that can inform us about the malleability and plasticity of behavior and brain as we age and the factors that are important for adaptability.

Epidemiological and demographic studies of cognition

The traditional cognitive aging literature is replete with studies that have used laboratory-based approaches with comparatively small convenience samples of community-dwelling older adults. Although such studies have yielded tremendous insights and advances in our understanding of the character, mechanisms, and potential interventions for age-related cognitive change, we recognize that the limitations of small samples and artificial settings may preclude the generalizability of both the empirical findings and their explanations to the older adult population at large. However, over the past decade, NIA-funded studies of cognitive aging that use an epidemiological approach have not only increased in number but have begun to reveal important findings that would not have been attainable by the traditional approach. In turn, insights revealed by these population studies can suggest hypotheses regarding causal mechanisms that require going back to the laboratory setting for more controlled examination. As evidenced by the establishment of the trans-NIH initiative, 'Cognitive and emotional health: The healthy brain', the participating Institutes consider epidemiological and longitudinal research approaches to the understanding of cognitive health of paramount importance.

The NIA supports several studies that employ the epidemiological/demographic approach to cognition. As an example, a recently completed study by Huppert, Ayken, and Martin (2000) was designed to establish the age-specific prevalence of prospective memory impairment in the population of older adults in the United Kingdom, and the identification of risk factors for this impairment. Administration of an event-based prospective memory test to 11,956 participants aged 65+ in the screening stage of a population-based study revealed that: (1) only 54 per cent of the sample succeeded in the task; and (2) only 8 per cent of individuals with very mild dementia succeeded. Given the importance of remembering to carry out intended actions for effectively performing numerous daily activities, the investigators concluded that these findings raise concerns about the well-being and safety of many older people.

In another example of the value of the demographic approach, Freedman, Aykan, and Martin (2001, 2002) reported that older individuals, well into their 80s, exhibited better cognitive functioning in the late 1990s than did comparably aged older adults in the early 1990s. These investigators analyzed data drawn from the 1993 Asset and Health Dynamics of the oldest old study ($N = 7,443$) and the 1998 Health and retirement survey ($N = 7,624$), which are comprised of national samples of the U.S. population age 50 and over. Specifically, Freedman *et al.* examined aggregate changes in the proportion of the community-dwelling population aged 70 and older with severe cognitive impairment. A modified version of the Telephone Interview Cognitive Screen was used for assessing impairment in self-respondents, while ratings of memory judgment were used for proxy respondents. The results revealed a significant decline ($p < 0.001$), for self-respondents only, in the percentage of older Americans with severe cognitive impairment, from a level of 6.1 per cent in 1993 to 3.6 per cent in 1998. Furthermore, these results could not be attributed to shifts in demographic or socio-economic factors, or to changes in the prevalence of vision impairments, hearing impairments, or stroke. A follow-up study controlling for cumulative effects of some of the potentially confounding survey design issues showed persistence of the previously reported significant decline, albeit at a reduced level (i.e., the corrected decline was from 8.6 per cent to 7.1 per cent, $p < 0.05$).

Freedman *et al.* and other researchers have attributed much of the decline in cognitive disability to increased education. As evidence from other NIA-supported studies suggests an important role of education in the maintenance of cognitive health, the Insitute is very interested in exploring the mechanisms underlying the correlation between education and healthy cognitive aging. In addition, because of the well-established relationship between level of education and indices of overall health, the NIA co-sponsored an RFA released by the NIH entitled 'Pathways linking education to health' (http://grants1.nih.gov/grants/guide/rfa-files/RFA-OB-03-001.html).

The NIA supported the first population-based study of cognitive impairment in the U.S., the findings of which suggested that cognitive impairment may affect a significant proportion of older African-American individuals (Unverzagt *et al.*, 2001). The study involved 2,212 African-Americans age 65 and older living in the community and 106 African-Americans age 65 and older living in nursing homes in the Indianapolis area. A total of 457 participants received full clinical diagnostic assessments and were followed for up to 48 months from the start of the study. Applying the findings from the clinically assessed group to the larger community sample, the researchers estimated that 23.4 per cent of the community-dwelling participants and 19.2 per cent of the nursing home residents had Cognitive Impairment No Dementia (CIND). The categorization is similar to that of Mild Cognitive Impairment (MCI) that has been measured in a number of other studies. The prevalence of cognitive impairment grew significantly with age, with rates increasing by about 10 per cent for every 10 years of age after 65. CIND was almost five times more common in the community than dementia. In addition, the researchers found that 26 per cent of those characterized with CIND at the start of the study progressed to a diagnosis of dementia only 18 months later, although 24 per cent of those characterized with CIND at the start appeared normal after 18 months. This study highlights the increasing importance and continued need to learn more about how to measure and characterize the condition of CIND, or MCI, because this category of impairment is emerging as a major risk factor for Alzheimer's disease.

The NIA encourages the exchange of ideas among cognitive psychologists, psychiatrists, neurologists, and epidemiologists about measurement of cognitive function in ways that will not only enhance current survey research in this domain, but also provide a population-based test bed for cognitive measures that have heretofore been administered predominantly under psychological laboratory conditions. The refinement of measurement tools and analytic strategies will aid in the Institute's continued development of research programs in the epidemiology of cognitive aging.

Cognitive Interventions

Given the neural plasticity of the adult brain and the greater degree of behavioral adaptability than was once thought possible, there is every reason to believe that various features of older adults' cognitive performance can be enhanced or at the very least maintained. Coupled with the advent of improved technologies for imparting instructional strategies and other training interventions, the idea that older adults can benefit from accumulated knowledge and understanding about their cognitive abilities has never been more promising. Indeed, numerous studies have already demonstrated that cognitive interventions can improve performance in the laboratory as well as selected everyday activities. Nevertheless, it has been difficult making any generalizations from the findings of this research, as all these studies have differed in the outcome measures examined, in the interventions tested, and in the samples recruited. As a consequence, a clinical trial has been funded by the NIA to address these shortcomings by testing identical interventions at six different sites using common inclusion-exclusion criteria and common outcome measures (Jobe *et al.*, 2001). This cooperative study, known as ACTIVE (Advanced Cognitive Training for Independent and Vital Elderly), was a randomized, controlled, single-blind trial designed to determine whether cognitive training can maintain independence in a sample of 2,832 older adult Caucasians and African-Americans. The primary objective of the trial was to examine whether training interventions for improving memory, reasoning, or speed of information processing can positively affect cognitively demanding measures of daily functioning over the course of two years of follow-up. Participants were randomly assigned to one of three treatment arms or a no-contact control group. Each treatment arm consisted of group training in 10 sessions over a 5- to 6-week period. For the three treatment conditions, four additional sessions of booster training were provided for approximately half of the participants 11 months after initial training. The primary outcome measures included: cognitive tests that were strongly related to the abilities being trained, measures representative of instrumental activities of daily living (e.g., food preparation, medication use, financial management), and assessments of driving. Several important questions addressed by this study were:

1 Can cognitive interventions be effective for a sample of older adults that is geographically, economically, and racially diverse?

2 Will training effects on proximal measures, if obtained, generalize to daily functioning outcomes?

3 Is such basic cognitive ability training a useful pathway to the improvement of everyday function?

Publication of the initial results of this trial (Ball *et al.*, 2002) revealed that each intervention improved performance on its targeted proximal measure as compared with baseline, durable to two years. Thus, these findings provide strong support for the effectiveness and durability of the cognitive training interventions insofar as improving performance on assessments of memory, reasoning, and speed of information processing. Furthermore, the training effects were of a magnitude equivalent to the amount of decline that would be expected in older adults (age 67–81) without dementia over a 7- to 14-year interval, suggesting that these interventions have the potential to reverse age-related decline. Booster training enhanced training gains for speed and reasoning interventions, which were maintained at two-year follow-up.

Despite strong effects of training interventions on the proximal measures, no training effects on everyday functioning were detected at the two-year follow-up. Although the apparent lack of transfer to everyday cognitive function measures may have been attributable in part to minimal functional decline across all groups, including the control condition, it is clear that there remains a crucial need for new research that can explain why generalization of training effects from the laboratory to everyday function is so difficult to achieve. Understanding the basis for this should increase the likelihood of designing more globally effective cognitive interventions.

Translational Research

Translational research is typically viewed as an effort to build on what has been learned from basic research in order to enhance the application of results, procedures, and/or explanatory mechanisms to the everyday functioning of individuals. Consistent with this perspective, the NIA has funded the Edward R. Roybal Centers for Research on Applied Gerontology. These centers were established to conduct applied research aimed at keeping older persons independent, active, and productive in later life and to encourage the application of existing basic knowledge about cognitive (and psychosocial) aging to a wide range of important practical problems facing older adults. This type of approach to translational research has historically served as the foundation for maintaining a strong relationship between government and the scientific community, although the factors that motivate basic versus applied research historically have been characterized as opposite points on a continuum (Stokes, 1997). That is, while government agencies are primarily interested in the application, development, and potential utility of basic research, the scientific community is typically driven by a desire for fundamental understanding.

A recent treatise on science policy by Stokes (1997) proposes a contrasting perspective to the one-dimensional, linear view of translational research. Namely, Stokes suggests that a dynamic two-dimensional model provides a more accurate depiction of the way advances in research and development actually take place. This model purports that research can be motivated by 'considerations of use' and/or a 'quest for fundamental understanding', with these objectives best viewed as falling along different axes in a two-dimensional space (i.e., where each objective is categorized as 'yes' or 'no'). The cell identified as 'Pasteur's quadrant' represents what Stokes refers to as 'use-inspired basic research'. The paradigmatic case of this type of research is that of Louis Pasteur, who, as Stokes points out, sought a fundamental understanding of the process of disease while simultaneously wanting to contend with problems of anthrax in sheep and cattle, spoilage in milk, wine and vinegar, and rabies. In other words, driven in part by practical considerations, Pasteur's studies laid the foundations for the field of microbiology. Thus, although extant knowledge can be increased by pure, basic research and existing technologies can be advanced by purely applied research and development, Stokes perceives richer opportunities through use-inspired, basic research which can enhance understanding of fundamental principals *and* improve technology (Childress, 1999).

How would this perspective apply to the area of older adults' cognitive functioning? One such example is the development of adaptive technologies for maintaining or enhancing cognitive function and performance. While the classic one-dimensional view underlies the recommendation from the NRC's *Aging mind* report that the NIA fund research to develop '. . . the knowledge needed to design effective technologies to support adaptivity in older adults' (NRC, 2000: 35), the two-dimensional view of Stokes would lead one to expect that in the process of conducting research on the development and use of new adaptive technologies, one may simultaneously be able to advance our understanding of both the behavioral and neural plasticity of the aging mind. To this end, the NIA has begun to encourage use-inspired research in adaptive technologies with respect to cognitive aging, as well as in other domains of social and behavioral science research with older adults, in addition to supporting more purely applied research that builds on basic research deemed ripe for translation. Examples of both approaches can be found in the RFA for the second grants competition of the Edward R. Roybal Centers (http://grants1.nih.gov/grants/guide/rfa-files/RFA-AG-03-002.html).

Summary and conclusions

The NIA continues to support cognitive, neuropsychological, and cognitive neuroscience approaches to the study of the aging mind. Developments in theory-based conceptions of cognitive aging are encouraged, as are innovative applications of mathematical modeling techniques. Epidemiological approaches continue to be endorsed, and, as in the past, longitudinal studies will be especially promoted. Future efforts by the NIA to advance the study of cognitive aging include:

1 Collaborating with other Institutes at the NIH on an initiative to uncover predictors of cognitive and emotional health in adults;

2 Supporting investigations in the domains of neural health, cognition in its sociocultural context, and the structure of the aging mind;

3 Funding innovative approaches to clarifying the interface between normal and abnormal cognitive decline;

4 Facilitating the application of extant and emerging neuroimaging technologies to issues of cognitive aging;

5 Encouraging intervention research designed to test the viability of training regimens for improving the daily cognitive functioning of elderly individuals; and

6 Supporting both use-inspired basic research and purely applied approaches designed to provide assistance to older adults with respect to the practical difficulties they encounter in attempting to function independently yet effectively in everyday life.

Acknowledgments

We are indebted to Richard Suzman and Marcelle Morrison-Bogorad for their numerous thoughtful suggestions that greatly improved the final version of this paper. We are also appreciative of the helpful comments provided by Andrew Monjan and Neil Buckholtz.

References

Ball, K., Berch, D. B., Helmers, K. F., Jobe, J. B., Leveck, M. D., Marsiske, M., *et al.* (2002). Effects of cognitive training interventions with older adults: A randomized controlled trial. *Journal of the American Medical Association,* **288**, 2271–2281.

Berkman, L. F. and Syme, S. L. (1979). Social networks, host resistance and mortality: A nine-year follow-up study of Alameda County residents. *American Journal of Epidemiology,* **109**, 186–204.

Burke, D. M. (1997). Language, aging, and inhibitory deficits: Evaluation of a theory. *Journal of Gerontology: Psychological Sciences,* **52B**, 254–264.

Childress, D. S. (1999). Working in Pasteur's Quadrant. *Journal of Rehabilitation Research and Development,* **36**, xi.

Fratiglioni, L, Wang, H. K., Ericsson, K., Mayan, M., and Winblad, B. (2000). Influence of social network on occurrence of dementia: A community-based longitudinal study. *The Lancet*, **355**, 1315–1319.

Freedman, V. A., Aykan, J., and Martin, L. G. (2001). Aggregate changes in severe cognitive impairment among older Americans: 1993 and 1998. *Journal of Gerontology: Social Sciences*, **56B**, S100–S111.

Freedman, V. A., Aykan, J., and Martin, L. G. (2002). Another look at aggregate changes in severe cognitive impairment: Further investigation into the cumulative effects of three survey design issues. *Journal of Gerontology: Social Sciences*, **57B**, S126–S131.

Galvin, R. (1998). Science roadmaps. *Science*, **280**, 803.

House, J. S., Landis, K. R., and Umberson, D. (1988). Social relationships and health. *Science*, **241**, 540–545.

Huppert, F. A., Johnson, T., and Nickson, J. (2000). High prevalence of prospective memory impairment in the elderly and in early-stage dementia: Findings from a population-based study. *Applied Cognitive Psychology*, **14**, 63–81.

Jobe, J. B., Smith, D. M., Ball, K., Tennstedt, S. L., Marsiske, M., Willis, S. L., Rebok, G. W., Morris, J. M., Helmers, K., Leveck, M. D., and Kleinman, K. (2001). ACTIVE: A cognitive intervention trial to promote independence in older adults. *Controlled Clinical Trials*, **4**, 53–79.

Logan, J. M., Sanders, A. L., Snyder, A. Z., Morris, J. C., and Buckner, R. L. (2002). Under-recruitment and nonselective recruitment: Dissociable neural mechanisms associated with aging. *Neuron*, **33**, 827–840.

MacKay, D. G., and James, L. E. (2001). Is cognitive aging all downhill? Current theory versus reality [Review of the book *The Handbook of Aging and Cognition (2nd ed.)*]. *Human Development*, **44**, 288–295.

National Research Council (2000). *The Aging Mind: Opportunities in cognitive research.* Committee on Future Directions for Cognitive Research on Aging. P. C. Stern and L. L. Carstensen (eds). Washington, DC: National Academy Press.

Reuter-Lorenz, P. A., Jonides, J., Smith, E. E., Hartley, A., Miller, A., Marshuetz, C., and Keoppe, R. A. (2000). Age differences in the frontal lateralization of verbal and spatial working memory revealed by PET. *Journal of Cognitive Neuroscience*, **12**, 174–187.

Sanfey, A. G. and Hastie, R. (2000). Judgment and decision making across the adult life span: A tutorial review of psychological research. In D. C. Park and N. Schwarz (eds), *Cognitive Aging: A primer* (pp. 253–273). Philadelphia, PA: Psychology Press/Taylor and Francis.

Seeman, T. E. (1996). Social ties and health: The benefits of social integration. *Annals of Epidemiology*, **6**, 442–451.

Steen, L. A. (1990). Numeracy. *Daedalus*, **119**, 211–231.

Steen, L. A. (1997). (ed.) *Why Numbers Count: Quantitative literacy for tomorrow's America.* New York: College Entrance Examination Board.

Stokes, D.E. (1997). *Pasteur's Quadrant: Basic science and technological innovation.* Washington, DC: Brookings Institution Press.

Unverzagt, F.W., Gao, S., Baiyewu, O., Ogunniyi, A.O., Gureje, O., Perkins, A., Emsley, C.L., Dickens, J., Evans, R., Musick, B., Hall, K.S., Hui, S.L., and Hendrie, H.C. (2001). Prevalence of cognitive impairment: Data from the Indianapolis Study of Health and Aging. *Neurology*, **57**, 1655–1662.

Index